THE BATTLE FOR CHINA'S PAST

D1559169

The Battle for China's Past

Mao and the
Cultural Revolution

Mobo Gao

Pluto Press
London • Ann Arbor, MI

First published 2008 by Pluto Press
345 Archway Road, London N6 5AA
and 839 Greene Street, Ann Arbor, MI 48106

www.plutobooks.com

Copyright © Mobo Gao 2008

The right of Mobo Gao to be identified as the author of this work has been asserted by him in accordance with the Copyright, Designs and Patents Act 1988.

British Library Cataloguing in Publication Data
A catalogue record for this book is available from the British Library

ISBN 978 0 7453 2781 5 hardback
ISBN 978 0 7453 2780 8 paperback

Library of Congress Cataloging in Publication Data applied for

This book is printed on paper suitable for recycling and made from fully managed and sustained forest sources. Logging, pulping and manufacturing processes are expected to conform to the environmental regulations of the country of origin.

10 9 8 7 6 5 4 3 2 1

Designed and produced for Pluto Press by
Curran Publishing Services, Norwich
Printed and bound in the European Union by
CPI Antony Rowe, Chippenham and Eastbourne

To my father Gao Renfa and mother Jiang Yuanrong, whose whole lives were devoted to the well-being of their children.

To those who sacrificed their lives for the improvement of living conditions of the poor and the disadvantaged.

Contents

Acknowledgements

This book has been in process for several years and has been the result of discussions with and feedback from many friends and colleagues. I take this opportunity to thank all of those who cannot be named here.

I would also like to thank Martin Hart-Landsberg, who made detailed comments and extensive suggestions after reading the whole draft, and Greg Benton, who has also read the whole draft and gave valuable suggestions and advice. Their help has had an essential impact on the final product, though of course they are not responsible for the errors and mistakes.

I would also like to thank Yan Hairong, who never fails to give her support, either scholarly, or personally, and Kaz Ross, who went through the draft at one go and made valuable comments and suggestions.

I would also like to express my appreciation of the anonymous reviewers for their support of this book and for their suggestions for improvement.

I of course must thank David Castle, the commissioning editor of Pluto Press. David is not only quick, decisive, and most professional, but also extremely supportive, always ready to accept any author's suggestions that may be beneficial in bringing the publication to fruition. The team at Pluto Press has to be acknowledged to be thoroughly professional as well as highly sympathetic.

Introduction

In 2004 at a friend's party I met a Mr Chen, an energetic recent migrant from the People's Republic of China (PRC) in his late fifties. Chen works for a profitable company in Australia and his main task is selling timber products to China; he mentioned to me that he was in the process of signing a large deal. Chen was confident that in 20 years time China would overtake Japan economically and he talked about how China has been developing fast and so on. In order to quell what I thought was an unbalanced enthusiasm, I mentioned that China was not a high-tech producer, but just a place for foreign companies to exploit cheap labour – the assembling factory of the world. I pointed out to him the fast-emerging social inequalities: that a rural migrant worker may have to work 16 or more hours a day for seven days a week to earn about US$80 a month, and that perhaps this is not something that can be called 'development'. Chen replied: '$80 is good enough for a peasant.'

I could not help but ask: 'Would you accept that kind of payment and life?'

'That is not the same. *Tamen suzhi di* [they are low quality people],' he said.

Then the topic turned to what I was going to do in China for my research. I said I would like to go back to Gao Village area to find out what the rural people think of the Cultural Revolution. He was genuinely surprised:

'To study the Cultural Revolution? Why do you want to find out what the rural people think? Rural China was not much affected [by the Cultural Revolution].'

I replied that: 'The majority of Chinese are in rural China. If rural China was not much affected by the Cultural Revolution, why do you, the CCP and many of the elite intelligentsia keep repeating that the Cultural Revolution was a ten-year calamity for China?' To which Chen said, 'You have very strange concepts.'

This book is about such 'strange concepts', so strange that they challenge the mainstream orthodox narrative; it questions many 'truths' told in memoirs, biographies and autobiographies, both in Chinese and English. It endeavours to find out whether these perspectives, which are officially considered to be unorthodox and 'strange', may be widely shared by most ordinary people in China, the farmers and workers. If they are, the book aims to analyse the reasons behind this gap between the official and unofficial, and between the mainstream positions of the elite intelligentsia in orthodox historiography and opposing views expressed in the e-media.

To many outside China, especially those who have grown up with European cultural traditions, China is an enigma, a place so different that a first visit is most often a culture shock. On the other hand, and somewhat paradoxically, China's increasing similarity to the developed world is seen as a threat. For many inside China however, despite the Maoist revolutions, the West has for over a century-and-a-half been the yardstick of material progress and development, and also of spiritual and personal development. Yet, notwithstanding this view within China, there is a Western perception that the Chinese were or are anti-Western, China-centred and xenophobic. On the other hand, almost every time a politician or head of a state visiting China does not take a tough stand against China – as is perceived to be necessary on, for example, the issue of human rights – the mainstream Western media accuses that government or that politician of kowtowing to China. The apparently huge gap between these conflicting images and perceptions of China requires interpretation and understanding. This book engages with that task.

The possibility, and I still think it is only a possibility, that China may rise to a leading position on the international stage makes China a hot contemporary topic. The notable economic development in China is being hailed not only as a result of post-Mao reform but also as a proof that the era of Mao was a communist-inspired disaster. This book shows that that position is dangerously misleading in four ways. First, it deprives a probable majority of the Chinese of the right to speak up. Second, it hides the ugly fact that there are millions of people who are actually worse off since the post-Mao reform years. Third, it denies the enormous achievements made during the Mao era that paved the way for later development. Finally, it is misleading and it distracts from and precludes imaginings of alternative models of development and other possible forms of human organization.

Many issues surrounding the Mao era need to be re-examined and new interpretations provided. For example, where in the scale of historical achievement and worth does Mao stand? Are the ideas and practices carried out under his leadership relevant and significant to today's China? To judge from much of the writings in memoirs, biographies and autobiographies such as Li Zhisui's *Private Life of Mao*, Jung Chang and Jon Halliday's *Mao: The Unknown Story*, and others written in Chinese, Mao was a callous, calculating, inhumane, power-hungry monster. However, in contrast to those depictions, Mao's bodyguards, nurses and some others who worked with him, like Chen Boda and Wang Li, show Mao very differently and in a more positive light. These disparate views exemplify the contradictory perceptions and evaluations between various 'memories' on this and related issues.

Another example of these polarized views occurred in December 2006, when Deng Xiaoping's son Deng Pufang, who was crippled at the beginning of the Cultural Revolution, told a group of journalists that the Cultural Revolution was not only a disaster for himself but for the whole of the Chinese state and the Chinese people. This almost routine response triggered hundreds of thousands of responses from bloggers and chatrooms. According to an estimate on one website, *Xin lang wang*, only two weeks after Deng's remark there had been more than 20,000 feedback entries covering a staggering 1,166 pages (Blinders 2006). One e-media participant who claims to have witnessed the incident states that Deng Pufang was not crippled because he was thrown out of the window by Red Guards, as it is often claimed or assumed, nor because he had jumped. Deng was trying to escape from the room where he was confined by climbing down a sewage pipe. When the old pipe broke, Deng fell onto the concrete below and crippled himself (Ma Ming 2006). One seasoned e-media activist, Li Xuanyuan, suggests that Deng Pufang should look into the official statistics and consider how many migrant workers have been crippled each year by mining accidents, or have had their fingers and arms cut off in sweatshops all over China, especially in the developed areas of the southeast coast. An overwhelming majority disagreed with Deng's viewpoint, indicating perhaps a more positive view of the Mao era than was generally expected.

Considering that Roderick MacFarquhar of Harvard University, a prominent scholar of the Cultural Revolution, fails to recognize that there is a vast majority of people in China who not only remember the era of Mao as 'the good old days', but who also like and admire the man (Wu Yiching 2006), there is an urgent need to make available much that is unknown to many. It is important to hear the voice that may resonate among the vast majority of the Chinese, who cannot simply be dismissed as ignorant and brainwashed. We need to remind ourselves that in China, as in any other society, there was and there is a social hierarchy, and that different perceptions by different sectors of Chinese society should be considered equally legitimate. Many Chinese expatriates such as Jung Chang dislike Mao because they or their families were the victims of Mao's theory and practice of class struggle. On the other hand, people such as rural farmers and urban workers might not have a reason to dislike Mao. For many of them there may be reasons to think positively of him.

History is not simply a picture or reconstruction of what happened: it is our present construction of the past. The way we construct the past depends on how we conceptualize our world and ourselves in the present. Therefore how one sees the worth of the Mao era depends not only on what one's present circumstances are but also on one's present values and beliefs. In other words, the way we conceptualize ourselves in the present frames our perception of the past. This book analyses the present values and beliefs of those remembering and retelling the past, and examines the way that these values and beliefs frame our understanding of the past.

Of course there are always a variety of values and beliefs at any given time in any society. But there is always one set that is actually dominant. Regarding the Mao era there is currently a two-faceted dominant conceptualization, with one facet that is external to China and one that is internal to it, each interacting with the other. The external facet is the rise to predominance of neoliberalism immediately before and after the collapse of the alternative existing 'communist' model of human development. The triumph of the capitalist market economy is the broad conceptualization that frames our understanding and interpretation of our world and ourselves. The internal facet is the farewell to revolution, and therefore the necessity of denouncing the Cultural Revolution totally and thoroughly. The dominant discursive hegemony of neoliberalism (Wang Hui 2004) and the worldwide conversion to capitalism led to the total denigration of the Cultural Revolution, Mao the man and the times he so directly influenced, and finally, of the whole idea of populist revolution.

This book presents a different conceptualization from that of the neoliberal hegemony, and from its total denigration of the Maoist legacy. Obviously, the book does not attempt to argue that there was nothing wrong with the era of Mao. Nor does it attempt to argue that Mao was not responsible for any of the problems and disasters in China under his leadership. It does not attempt to deny that there was violence and brutality inflicted upon millions of people in the name of revolution. Instead, this work attempts to demonstrate that there are other possible interpretations, other evidence and other arguments than the dominant ones.

Take the case of the Great Leap Forward as an example. There has been a continuous debate about the death toll of the resulting famine, with scholarly estimates ranging from 18 million to about 30 million deaths, but with recent estimates by an e-media participant as low as 200,000. So the claim by Chang and Halliday (2005) that Mao murdered 38 million people, and other claims that he was only partially responsible and that the death tolls were much smaller, need to be reconsidered. There are now so many different interpretations of the Great Leap Forward and Mao's part in it that they need to be re-evaluated.

Clearly, one's values and beliefs orientate one's direction of understanding and even one's selection of evidence for an argument or premise. The Cultural Revolution discourse is a prime example. For many Chinese government officials and members of the intelligentsia who were dismissed from their posts and were ordered to live and work in what was called *Wu qi gan xiao* (the May Seventh Cadre School), the experience is now narrated as 'detention in a labour camp', and a violation of fundamental human rights. But for Mao and others at that time, and for many even now, it was intended to create new subjectivity. It was intended that the urban and social elite would experience physical labour so that they would be able to understand and empathize with the reality of life of the majority of the people. It was meant to be an approach to a new way of governing and governance.

The Chinese Communist Party's (CCP) official view of the Cultural Revolution, corresponding to the mainstream Chinese intelligentsia understanding and interpretation, is well received and supported by the Western media and most of the scholarly community. For example, in Thurston's view the Cultural Revolution led to 'loss of culture, and of spiritual values; loss of hope and ideals; loss of time, truth, and of life; loss, in short, of nearly everything that gives meaning to life' (Thurston 1984–85: 605–6). What Thurston says here more or less summarizes the general evaluation of the Cultural Revolution held by the mainstream Western political, cultural and scholarly elite. This quote, for instance, is cited by Lucian Pye (1986), a prominent US scholar of Chinese political culture, and by Lee (2003), another US scholar on the very subject of the Cultural Revolution.

Many others would argue, however, that while the first two years of chaos and destruction have been highlighted by the 'cold war warriors' and neoliberals alike, the positive and constructive years from 1969 to the early 1970s have been forgotten or obscured (Wang Shaoguang 2006). These positive legacies include a massive infrastructure programme, radical education reforms, innovative experimentation in literature and the arts, expansion of healthcare and education in rural areas, and rapid development of rural enterprises. The Cultural Revolution involved many millions of people who willingly participated in what they saw as a movement to better Chinese society and humanity in general. A whole range of ideas and issues from politics to education and healthcare, from literature and the arts to industrial and agricultural policies were examined, tried and tested.

Some of these experiments succeeded, some failed and some did not have time to come to fruition before they were prematurely terminated. In the sphere of science for instance, if one takes seriously the stated goals of 'mass science', then it is clear that there was, contrary to the mainstream claims, a valuable development of science during the Cultural Revolution (Schmalzer 2006). The archaeological discoveries at Mawangdui led to the discovery of a Chinese medical remedy for malaria, while the delivery of primary healthcare, the development of integrated techniques for controlling insect pests, and the advance of earthquake predictions are examples of scientific progress at this time. Particularly notable for popular scientific education is the science of paleoanthropology. Guided by the theory that labour creates and defines humanity, and that labour is the driving force behind human development, and that therefore the labouring masses are the bearers of the torch of science, popular science such as is exemplified by the magazine *Fossils* emerged in spite of resistance from the elite intelligentsia (Schmalzer 2006).

Mao's political experiment, the Cultural Revolution, like all other social revolutions before it, claimed many victims. It did however, again like other social revolutions, have some positive outcomes. It encouraged grassroots participation in management and it also inspired the idea of popular democracy. The mass criticism practised in the era of Mao in general and during the Cultural Revolution in particular, though ritualized and mobilized from the top, did provide a rich repertoire of protest techniques (Perry 2003). 'Members of the Red Guards were not just passive followers of a charismatic leader, but agents actively involved in a variety of ideological disputes and contests for power' (Calhoun and Wasserstrom 2003: 251). The Chinese were not the brainless masses manipulated by a ruthless dictator so often portrayed in the Western media. They must be seen as agents of history and subjects of their own lives like any other people. Anyone who seriously believes in the inherent value of individualism, in the self-evident truth of the human pursuit of happiness, or the universal value of human rights and democracy should be sympathetic with this position.

In the area of industrial development, Mao took a strongly socialist view, concerning himself with eradicating the usual divide between the rural and urban. Under his leadership a strategy was developed and implemented to trial a decentralized non-Soviet form of industry programme. It was proposed that the rural population could become industrialized without a need to build cities or urban ghettos, a strategy initiated during the Great Leap Forward, shelved because of the famine disaster, but picked up again during the Cultural Revolution. As Wong (2003: 203) shows, by the end of the decade of the Cultural Revolution in 1979, there were nearly 800,000 industrial enterprises scattered in villages and small towns, plus almost 90,000 small hydroelectric stations. These enterprises employed nearly 25 million workers and produced an estimated 15 per cent of the national industrial output. This development provided the critical preconditions for the rapid growth of township and village enterprises in the post-Mao reform period.

In much of the literature that is reviewed and discussed in this book, the Cultural Revolution is conceptualized as a personal power struggle by Mao, who manipulated the party, the army, the students and the Chinese people. However, what was proclaimed and recognized during the Cultural Revolution was that a continuous revolution was required for China to remain a socialist country and to achieve its socialist goals. It was recognized that some CCP leaders were nationalist revolutionaries who joined the CCP to fight imperialism and 'feudalism'. Although these leaders tolerated land reform and nationalization of capitalist industry with foreign connections, they did not like the programme of rural collectivization and the confiscation of properties owned by the Chinese nationalist capitalists. Liu Shaoqi, for instance, did not even like the idea of agricultural co-operatives in 1951 (Tao 2003). There was, therefore, a danger that China would return to capitalism unless there were a revolution ostensibly concerned with changing cultural values and beliefs. And that was why it was called the Cultural Revolution.

Within the conceptual framework of human rights and neoliberalism, the revolutionary goals and strategy of the Cultural Revolution are seen as pointless victimization of all the political and cultural elite. It is either forgotten or ignored that at the time Mao stressed that those who really wanted to restore capitalism were a tiny minority, about 1 to 2 per cent within the party; among this small percentage of 'capitalist roaders', most could be educated to correct themselves and only a few could not be changed. Among the small group of die-hard capitalist roaders, Mao (1967a, 1968) stressed that their sons and daughters should not be stigmatized as being the same as their parents. It was clear at that time that the Cultural Revolution was aimed at educating and was not meant to victimize a whole class of people. However, today this kind of revolutionary conceptualization of tempering new subjectivity is totally forgotten or has become an alien concept.

Just as there are alternative views to the official and dominant judgements of the Mao era, there are also alternative views concerning the 'reform' period. Take the case of rural migrant workers as an example of how different conceptual paradigms can frame different interpretations and understandings. Since the late 1980s, every year approximately 100 to 200 million people from rural China have been either looking for jobs or working in the cities. For many neoliberals, such as Professor Qin Hui, this rural exodus has been the second liberation for the peasants, because he says they now have the freedom to move from rural villages to urban areas to work. For many rural Chinese, however, this liberation is deceptive. It provides a sense of freedom to the rural young, who really have no other choice. Teenagers working for an average 14 to 16 hours a day, seven days a week to earn about 600 RMB a month (a rate unchanged for more than a decade until very recently) under dangerous and hazardous conditions – is this really liberation? Mr Chen would certainly think so. Perhaps we should consider whether those teenagers would feel more 'liberated' by going to school and college like their urban counterparts.

Throughout the book I argue that our conceptualizations may frame our research methodology and our selection of evidence; however I am not saying that there should not be methodological conventions or that one method may not be more rigorous than another. Nor am I suggesting that there are not undisputed facts. It is an undisputed fact that the Great Leap Forward contributed towards a famine. Nor is there any dispute that the Cultural Revolution victimized many in terms of personal humiliation, physical assaults, arbitrary detention, loss of property and even death. But I do argue that there are other facts that should not be ignored and need to be included in any balanced account of China's history.

Parallel to the understanding of the Cultural Revolution as a total disaster is the belief that the post-Mao reforms, supposedly designed by the paramount leader Deng Xiaoping, have achieved economic miracles in China. This claim has been repeated in so many different versions that it has become a cliché. However, a counter-narrative is available from some who know Chinese society well. Lau's (2004: 230) comments are an example of this: 'Now, what can they offer their children? If they make enough money, they hope to send their children abroad so that they have a better life in the United States and never come back to China, because China is going to be hell.'

Through in-depth analysis of memoirs, autobiographies and biographies, by presenting the debate over the Cultural Revolution between liberals and the New Left, and with information gained from fieldwork in rural China and the e-media, the book provides the following:

- a critique of the contemporary discourse concerning the Mao era, with an emphasis on the Cultural Revolution and a re-evaluation of the man and his legacy
- documentation of the various narratives, and debates, especially in the increasingly important e-media, concerning this period
- analysis and evaluation of these narratives and debates
- a general evaluation of the post-Mao reforms in relation to the legacy of the Mao era
- a conceptual framework which shows that our present values and beliefs frame our memories of the past.

The book is therefore not just about memories of the past, but also about what is happening in the present. It is not just about the Cultural Revolution, Mao the man and the Mao era. It is also about contemporary China. On a deep level it is about liberalism versus revolution and about continuity versus change. It is about alternative models of development, and in a word, it is about our quest for betterment and our understanding of human existence.

Chapter 1 opens with a debate on the Cultural Revolution and asks whether it was ten years of catastrophe *(shi nian haojie)*, who were 'the Chinese' who were adversely affected by it, what were the causes of the violence, and what was the extent of violence, whether there were constructive achievements during the Cultural Revolution and if so what were they, and what was the impact on Chinese culture and tradition. This chapter argues that the Cultural Revolution, while very violent, was not a ten-year calamity for China; that the party and elite intelligentsia cannot speak on behalf of all Chinese; that the causes of violence were many and the extent of violence has been exaggerated; that there were many constructive and creative developments during the Cultural Revolution that have been ignored or denigrated by the post-Cultural Revolution narrative; and that the destruction of culture and tradition has been exaggerated. Much of the discussion focuses on the debate over the question of cultural and religious destruction in Tibet. A major argument is that this was not a result of ethnic strife or Chinese chauvinism or imperialism, but due to the theory of class struggle and was justified by a Marxist interpretation of historical progression. In this regard, this chapter will render support to scholars such as Sautman (2006) who argues that the Western world in particular has been hugely misled by claims of the Tibetan exiles that ethnic or cultural genocide has been committed there, and that the same conception that should inform our opinions about China generally applies with regard to Tibet. That conception is that the oppression of the old society was much more widely experienced by its majority over many centuries than any of the mistakes made during the course of transforming Tibetan society.

Chapter 2 develops the argument that memories are not only about events, but also constitute a form of knowledge. The narrative of atrocity of the Cultural Revolution is not just a retelling of past experience but also an act of identification with certain political and cultural values. From the literature of the wounded (or 'scar literature') to the 'calamities' discourse of the Cultural Revolution, the retelling of the past can be seen as an act of political identification with certain hegemonic Western political and cultural values. It was a neo-Enlightenment act to retrieve what was seen as being abandoned by the May Fourth Movement: the striving for a Western vision of humanism and democracy. Since the late 1990s the denunciation of the Cultural Revolution and the era of Mao has gone hand in hand with the discursive hegemony of neoliberalism. By analysing the phenomenon of the 'Two whatevers' (whatever China does is wrong and whatever the United States does is right) among Chinese neoliberal dissidents, the chapter advances the argument for a correlation between the condemnation of socialist revolution and the elite desire for political and cultural value identification with the West.

Chapter 3 is an analytical review of memoirs, autobiographies and biographies on the Mao era published in Chinese language. The literature is vast and this is the first study that seeks to treat it as a whole. The chapter first draws a sketch of the literature. It then analyses several themes in light of traditional Chinese historiography and shows that the literature focuses on personal struggles and court intrigues, while ignoring contentious political and socioeconomic issues in society at that time. The resulting 'history' justifies those writers' present views and opinions but neglects many inconvenient historical facts. In this history, remembered personalities are often portrayed in a Peking opera style, analogous to pure good confronting evil incarnate, and many legitimate memories which might have a different voice and different views are silenced.

Chapter 4 focuses on a critique of Jung Chang and Jon Halliday's book *Mao: The Unknown Story*. It first summarizes how their book is promoted by hype in the media. It then examines the book in detail and reveals how it misinterprets evidence, ignores the existing literature, and makes sensationalist claims without proper evidence. It is argued that it is intellectually scandalous that the Chang and Halliday book has received so many positive reviews given the fact that its scholarship is obviously questionable.

By presenting arguments and discussion in the e-media that are neither available in print and broadcast media nor accessible to those who do not read Chinese, and by in-depth analysis of claims made in the Chang and Halliday book, the chapter reveals how the co-authors have constructed a deeply misleading version of history. The chapter concludes with a discussion of why such intellectual scandal matters to the academic community.

As a counter-narrative to Chang and Halliday's 'constructed story', Chapter 5 argues that there is a known and readily available story that Chang and Halliday chose to ignore. This is the story that gives primacy to the Chinese people and to their part in the revolution led by the CCP under Mao's leadership, a revolution in which Chang's parents participated, a revolution from which Chang herself benefited. It is a story that that does not deny or forget that it was due to this revolution that the average life expectancy of the majority Chinese increased from 35 in 1949 to 63 by 1975, that it was a revolution that brought unity and stability to a nation tortured for so long by disunity and instability, and a revolution that laid the foundation for China to become the equal of the world's great powers. It is a story about a revolution 'of the people' that enabled land reform, that promoted women's status, that improved popular literacy and healthcare, and that eventually transformed Chinese society beyond recognition from its parlous state prior to the Revolution. In this connection the chapter dissects the comparison of Mao with Hitler, since Mao has been compared to Hitler on many occasions. The chapter concludes by analysing why Chang and Halliday are so universally popular in the mainstream media in spite of scathing scholarly criticisms. It is argued that there are strong connections with the discourse of anti-revolution, including the French Revolution, which gained pre-eminence amidst the triumph of market capitalism and liberal democracy.

Chapter 6 confronts the issue of the involvement by US academics in the production of the memoirs of Li Zhisui, and questions the reliability and credibility of his book. The discrepancies between the Chinese and English versions and the reasons behind these discrepancies are discussed in detail. By presenting evidence from publications that repudiate the claims about and representations of Mao and the Mao era, as presented by Li Zhisui, the chapter aims to show how many of the claims Li makes are fraudulent. It is argued that the constructed history in Li is history that is analogous with that which is seen and presented in Peking operas.

Chapters 7 and 8 present a ground-breaking study on Chinese language e-media debates about Mao, the Mao era and post-Mao reforms. Important events and issues such as the Cultural Revolution, the Great Leap Forward, the ideological dispute between Mao and Liu Shaoqi, the Red Guard violence, the differences between the Red Guards and Rebels, Jiang Qing the person, and the state of the economy are debated by e-media participants. While Chapter 7 focuses on Mao the man and the Cultural Revolution, Chapter 8 is devoted to the state of the economy and other related issues. Chapter 8 presents the way farmers and urban workers feel and think about the Mao era in contrast to the post-Mao reform period. Also discussed in Chapter 8 are case studies of how the anti-Maoist and anti-revolution discourse is constructed.

The two chapters basically argue that although the conventional and mainstream media exercise a discursive hegemony by denouncing and condemning the Cultural Revolution in particular and the Mao era in general, there is growing evidence of a counter-response to this hegemony. There is clear evidence that the New Left critique of the neoliberal discursive hegemony is gaining ground rapidly as the effects and consequences of the post-Mao reforms are more visibly and keenly seen and felt within Chinese society.

Chapter 9 evaluates the rural situation from the mid-1980s up to 2003. It focuses on the central Chinese rural heartland, as opposed to the coastal provinces of Shandong, Jiangsu, Zhejiang, Guangdong and Fujian and the northwest poverty-stricken area of Shaanxi, Ningxia, Gansu, Qinghai, Xinjiang and Tibet. This central area includes Shanxi, Hunan, Hubei, Anhui, Jiangxi, Henan, Hebei, Yunnan and Sichuan. Three main sources of information are used: Chen and Chun (2004) on

Anhui; Yu Jianrong (2003) on Hunan; and Gao (2005) on Jiangxi and Shanxi. The study focuses on these provinces not only because this area is the rural heartland that contains a large portion of China's population, but also because, from the perspective of income and development, it can be considered 'middle ground' between the more developed southeast coast and the less developed northwest.

It is argued that even though many are better off in material terms such as food and clothing in the post-Mao era, social problems abound and the social fabric has been eroded by corruption, oppressive taxes and levies, crime and the unaffordable cost of education and healthcare. For millions of Chinese from this rural heartland poverty is still a problem, and the freedom of choice to work as a migrant is not necessarily an improvement in terms of quality of life and long-term well-being. During the Mao era life was basic and austere, material goods were scarce, and there was hunger, but this was compensated for by a considerable measure of social equality, personal safety, and a better education and healthcare system. The chapter discusses the form and content of resistance from rural China, and the way Maoist radicalism has been an inspiration for rural resistance, thus providing a critical account of reaction to change in rural China since the reforms. This chapter advances the idea that the urban–rural divide and related discriminatory policies against Chinese farmers are based on a developmental discourse which induces a kind of development that is detrimental to the environment and cannot be sustained.

Chapter 10 presents an overall evaluation of the post-Mao reforms in relation to the legacy of the Mao era. This evaluation addresses the issue of how different parts of Chinese society experience life differently today. Its findings present a cautionary picture of mixed results, less rosy than that portrayed in the media. It also enters the discourse which asks whether China is a capitalist country or a socialist country with Chinese characteristics. In discussing these issues it first questions the premise of such a dichotomy, and second, it asks whether and in what way these issues matter to the life of the ordinary Chinese. In this chapter, the ways transnational companies exploit Chinese cheap labour and the effects this exploitation has on the global economy and life of the ordinary Chinese are discussed. In this connection the concept of comprador is employed to explain the rise of the few rich who act as middlemen in this chain of capitalist globalization. The chapter furthers questions the sustainability of the current economic development model.

In the conclusion, legacies of the Mao era are further discussed and analysed, however briefly, so as to highlight the conceptual framework that binds various chapters of the book together: the way the past (the era of Mao) is understood depends on one's values and beliefs in the present.

1 Debating the Cultural Revolution

Introduction: who is writing history and who are the Chinese?

Total denegation of the Cultural Revolution has been China's official policy since the death of Mao, and the Cultural Revolution has been condemned as a ten-year calamity for the Chinese people. But who are the Chinese that the history of the Cultural Revolution is written about and who is writing this history? As I discuss in other chapters in this book, most memoirs, autobiographies and biographies about the period are written by a section of the political and/or elite intelligentsia who were the political targets of the Cultural Revolution. This section of the political and intelligentsia elite often claims to be 'the Chinese' and is usually referred to as 'the Chinese'. How about the ordinary Chinese, the urban workers and rural farmers who make up the majority of the people in China? How do they remember the Cultural Revolution? This chapter aims to look into some of these questions.

Let me start with an account by Sun Ge of the Chinese Academy of Social Sciences to illustrate the issue. A couple of years back Sun (2007) gave a talk on the Cultural Revolution in South Korea. She thought she did a good job by presenting a balanced and fair view of how it unfolded. When she finished a student from China in the audience asked Sun a very pointed question: 'What is your family background?' Sun admitted that both her parents were intellectuals who were victimized during the Cultural Revolution. Then the student said: 'So no wonder. My father used to be the production team leader in my village. He still recalls the Cultural Revolution with fond memories because that was his most brilliant (*canlan* 灿烂) years. Those were years when the farmers felt proud and elated (*yangmei tuqi* 扬眉吐气).' Sun was shocked by the encounter and by the realization that there could be views of the Cultural Revolution that were so different from hers.

Let me explain the difference by recalling an exhibition about the Cultural Revolution organized by Stevan Harrell and David Davies at the Burke Museum of Washington University (Seattle) in 2002, because it is very relevant to the question of who the Chinese are that we refer to when we talk of the Cultural Revolution. The title of the Seattle exhibition, 'Ordinary Life in Extraordinary Times', is an apt description of the items on display and of the theoretical orientation of the exhibition itself: the life of China's ordinary people during a period of intense ideological ferment. Items such as cloth buttons, stamps, dresser drawers, and rice, oil, and meat coupons were indeed artefacts of daily life; and yet the way these ordinary objects were made expressed extraordinary ideological content. The resulting combination of the ordinary and the extraordinary is clearly illustrated by, for instance, the message 'the masses of people have unlimited creative powers' that appeared on a bus ticket, an envelope that had the slogan 'increase vigilance to defend the Motherland' written on it, a mirror table that carried the reminder 'never forget class struggle', and cigarette packages that instructed smokers to 'support agriculture on a great scale'.

The Seattle exhibition deliberately avoided any interpretation or evaluation of the items on display or of the Cultural Revolution itself. Thus the display items were accompanied by little in the way of commentary; the objects themselves were expected to speak to the audience. As if to further distance itself from evaluation, the exhibition presented the recollections of two people who voiced opposing positions on the Cultural Revolution. The first recalled the Cultural Revolution with nostalgia, saying that Mao's ideals were good for 'us average people', while the other indignantly condemned the Cultural Revolution as 'barbaric' and a period of 'red terror'. That the exhibition did not take a conspicuous stand *against* the Cultural Revolution clearly annoyed many visitors, if comments left in the guest book are any indication. Some accused the exhibit of trying to be 'politically correct'; others were frustrated that they left without any clear understanding about whether the Cultural Revolution was good or bad; some registered their complaints that the exhibition was too positive about the Cultural Revolution. One unhappy visitor wrote two sentences in Chinese characters in the guest book, the first of which declared that: 'The ten years of the Cultural Revolution were a disaster for the Chinese people.'

Along similar lines a couple of visitors, who identified themselves as 'American physicians', wrote that when they visited China they heard people describe their experiences of the Cultural Revolution as 'terrible'. Those American physicians suggested other visitors to read Jung Chang's *Wild Swans* and Nien Cheng's *Life and Death in Shanghai*. This is interesting and instructive because it indicates that Jung Chang and Nien Cheng are standard references when the Mao era and the Cultural Revolution are under consideration. It probably did not occur to those visitors that the exhibition was not meant to show that the claims of people like Jung Chang and Nien Cheng had any legitimacy. The Chinese hosts of visiting American physicians might not view the Cultural Revolution in the same way that an urban worker or a rural farmer would; nor would anyone classify Jung Chang and Nien Cheng as ordinary. Visitors to the exhibition who came to Washington from

DEBATING THE CULTURAL REVOLUTION

China, either as tourists, students or migrants, and who complained (in Chinese) that the exhibition was biased cannot be ordinary Chinese either. These visitors used the general term *Zhongguo renmin* (the Chinese people) as if their views represented those of everyone else in China. They wrote that they themselves or family members or friends of theirs had suffered an injustice because they were 'sent down to the countryside' during the Cultural Revolution. As the majority of Chinese live and work in the countryside – and did so before and during the Cultural Revolution – should not these critics pause and reflect before they declare that life in the countryside was inhumane?

The *haojie* discourse and the Cultural Revolution

It is therefore not surprising that some visitors questioned the moral legitimacy of a Cultural Revolution exhibition. One visitor asked whether one could imagine an exhibition like this for Hitler, Stalin, or Pol Pot. The assumption, of course, is that the Cultural Revolution was a type of holocaust and that Mao was a monster like Hitler. This is an important question – one that has to be faced by Western and Chinese academics alike. The label *Shi nian haojie* is frequently used to refer to the Cultural Revolution in the Chinese media, in conversations and even in official Chinese documents. *Shi nian* means ten years, referring to the standard official Chinese periodization that the Cultural Revolution lasted ten years. *Haojie* is ambiguous because it can be a modern term for 'holocaust' or a traditional term to mean 'great calamity' or 'catastrophe'. Though 'holocaust' is not usually explicitly used in the West to refer to the Cultural Revolution, the sections of the Chinese intelligentsia and political elite who go out of their way to denounce the Cultural Revolution seem to be inclined to exploit the ambiguity of *haojie* to denigrate the Cultural Revolution. The CCP, under the direction of Deng Xiaoping, adopted a resolution in 1981 on the history of the Mao era. In the resolution the Cultural Revolution is not referred to as a ten-year *haojie*; but, by judicially declaring that the ten years of the Cultural Revolution were the period when Mao deviated from Mao Zedong Thought, the resolution opened a door for total denigration.[1]

In her writings, Vera Schwarcz (1996 and 1998) specifically draws our attention to the meaning of 'holocaust' in *haojie* when she talks about the burden of the memory of the Cultural Revolution. Schwarcz herself does not think a comparison of the Holocaust with the Cultural Revolution is appropriate. In this connection it is worth noting that an edited volume by Law (2003) is titled *The Chinese Cultural Revolution Reconsidered: Beyond Purge and Holocaust*. The book does not set to prove the thesis that the Cultural Revolution was a holocaust, but contains criticism that make implicit assumptions in that direction.

More recently, in one of the most popular electronic publications produced by Chinese dissidents, Cai Yingshen states that Mao *was* China's Hitler and that the Cultural Revolution *was* the same as Nazi fascism (Cai 2002). In *Wild Swans,* Jung Chang puts the Red Guards on a par with Hitler's Storm Troopers.

The post-Mao Chinese authorities have been telling the Chinese and people all over the world that the Cultural Revolution was ten years of calamities and that China's economy was brought to the brink of collapse during that period. However, when they first started their journey to abandon the Chinese revolution they could not afford to be seen as throwing away the whole package of China's revolutionary legacy. Their way of getting around this dilemma was to claim that the period of the Cultural Revolution, when most of them were out of favour, was an aberration and that the ideology of the Cultural Revolution, if there is any for them, was misguided. Along similar lines, most of the Chinese elite intelligentsia, who possess a dignified a sense of owning Chinese history, keep repeating that the Cultural Revolution was the darkest age of Chinese history (Ji Xianlin 1998).

The story propagated by the Chinese authorities and elite intelligentsia spreads fast and wide among the non-academic community in the West. This of course has much to do with the legacy of the cold war, and the relentless push of democracy and a human rights agenda after it. It was evident at the symposium sessions that took place during the Seattle exhibition that once the 'holocaust' meaning of *haojie* was accepted, anyone trying to say anything different about the Cultural Revolution ran the risk of being accused of holocaust denial. At least two visitors accused the Burke Museum exhibition of being 'politically correct' though the 'political correct' line both in and outside China is actually to condemn the Cultural Revolution.

There's no doubt that many suffered and died during the ten-year period. Some committed suicide, others died in factional fighting or after being tortured. Some died because of the harshness of their circumstances, and the lives of others were shortened as a result of their experiences during the Cultural Revolution. I myself was put under house arrest when I was only a teenager and had to face struggle sessions every night for two weeks for what now seem ridiculous reasons. My whole family was affected as a result (Gao 1999a). Denunciation and condemnation of the Cultural Revolution by those who suffered in one way or another is understandable and can be an individual's way to cope and heal the emotional trauma. However, to participate in the official project of reducing every thing to the label of 'ten years of calamities' is another matter.

Here I give just one example. One recent piece on the widely read Chinese-language electronic journal *Huaxia wenzhai* (Chinese Digest), which regularly publishes documents and writings on the Cultural Revolution, featured a partial list of well-known people who died during the so-called Cultural Revolutionary period of 1966–76. The author asserts that all of the people on his list died as a result of persecution during the Cultural Revolution (Dai Huang 2002). Along with such names as Liu Shaoqi, there were also Zhu De, the legendary Red Army commander, and Xu Guangping, widow of Lu Xun, who had been hailed as a cultural icon by Mao and his followers. There is no evidence that either Zhu De or Xu Guangping was persecuted at that time. But the widely accepted assumption is that because the Cultural Revolution was a ten-year catastrophe any well-known personality who died during the period must have died from persecution.

Violence, brutality and causes

Certainly there was violence, cruelty and destruction, but how should we interpret what happened during that period? Were all the acts of violence organized and intended by official policies, as was the case during the Nazi Holocaust? Was there a plan to physically exterminate a group of people, as in Hitler's gas chambers? The violence, cruelty, suffering and deaths that occurred during the initial years of the Cultural Revolution were caused by different groups of people, for different reasons. Some conflicts were of a class nature, others were social in character; some of the violence involved personal grudges, in other cases the violence was due to blindness, ignorance and stupidity.

The fact that there was no planned policy for violence can be seen in the sequence of events in those years. Recognizing the terrible consequences of the 'Red Terror' in 1966 – when in Beijing homes were raided, people judged to be class enemies were beaten up, and detention centres were set up – and determined to stop further terror of this kind, the central committee of the CCP approved a decree drafted by the CCP of the Beijing Municipality and issued it to the whole of China on 20 November 1966. The *zhongyao tonggao* (important notification) decreed that no factory, mine, school, administration or any other unit should be allowed to establish a detention house or makeshift court to persecute anyone. Any violation of the decree would be a violation of the law of the state and of disciplines of the CCP and would be punished accordingly (Xiao Xidong 2002). It is true that documents like this did not stop the violence completely; it is also true that verbal provocations, gestures and instructions by Mao and other leaders incited a new type of violence in early 1967 and at later times. Yet the official policy was clear: *yao wendou bu yao wudou* (engage in the struggle with words but not with physical attack). This policy was recorded in an official

Cultural Revolution document, the *'Shiliu tiao'* (the 16 Articles) and was stressed in speeches from time to time by various leaders. Neither the so-called 1967 January Storm (*yiyue fengbao*) that originated in Shanghai and encouraged the Rebels to take over power from the CCP apparatus, nor the suppression of the so-called 1967 February Anti-Cultural Revolution Current (*eyue niliu*) were meant to include physical fighting and certainly not physical elimination, though both did lead to violence of various kinds.

Much of the violence, brutality and destruction that happened during the ten-year period was indeed intended, such as the persecution of people with a bad class background at the beginning, and later action against the Rebels, but the actions did not stem from a single locus of power. To use 'Storm Troopers' in reference to the Red Guards, for instance, is conveniently misleading. There was no such singular entity as the 'Red Guards' or the 'Red Guard'. First, we must differentiate between university students and school students. It was the latter who invented the term 'Red Guards' and who engaged in acts of senseless violence in 1966. We should also note the difference between schoolchildren in Beijing, where many high-ranking CCP officials and army officers were located, and those in other places such as Shanghai, the home town of three of the so-called 'Gang of Four' radicals. It was not in Shanghai, the supposed birthplace of the Cultural Revolution radicals, but in Beijing that schoolchildren beat up their teachers most violently. It was also in Beijing (in 1966) that the children of high-ranking CCP members and army officials formed the notorious *Lian dong* (Coordinated Action) and carried out the so-called 'Red Terror' in an effort to defend their parents. What they were doing was exactly the opposite of what Mao wanted, to 'bombard the capitalist roaders inside the Party', that is, parents of the *Lian dong* Red Guards. *Lian dong* activists behaved like those of the Storm Troopers, but these were not Mao's Storm Troopers. Mao supported those Rebels who criticized CCP officials including the parents of the *Lian dong* Red Guards. These facts can easily be confirmed by documentary evidence; yet the post-Mao Chinese political and elite intelligentsia either pretend not to see them or choose to ignore them.

Violence such as the *Qingli jieji duiwu* (Cleaning up the Class Ranks) movement in 1968 was premeditated, but this movement was not meant to result in the physical elimination of 'class enemies', though this clearly happened in some places. In any case, much of the violence that took place during the later 1960s was not initiated by either the Red Guards or the Rebels. In fact many of the Rebels became victims themselves, in campaigns such against the May the Sixteenth Elements (Yang and McFadden 1997).

Constructive policies

All the documentary evidence (more details in later chapters) suggests that the initial intention of the Cultural Revolution by Mao, the Chairman of the CCP, was to teach an ideological lesson to the officials within the CCP. Emotional humiliation was intended, but physical violence was not. While the Cultural Revolution radicals wanted to stir up more movements for change, the pre-Cultural Revolution establishment wanted to maintain the status quo. As Mao's plan of regenerating the CCP unfolded, new developments emerged and unforeseen violence of one kind led to another. If anything the CCP under the leadership of Mao, and chiefly managed by Zhou Enlai, tried hard to control violence. Eventually the army had to be brought in to maintain order. By 1969, a little more than two years after the start of the Cultural Revolution the political situation was brought under control and China's economic growth was back on track.

From then on, new socioeconomic policies were gradually introduced and these had a positive impact on a large number of people; these policies *were* intentionally designed. These included the creation of a cheap and fairly effective healthcare system, the expansion of elementary education in rural China, and affirmative-action policies that promoted gender equality. Having grown up in rural China, I witnessed the important benefits that these policies had for the rural people. When the post-Mao regime under Deng Xiaoping reversed the Cultural Revolution policies on these issues, the systems and practices that had benefited the vast majority of China's rural people were allowed (and, in some cases, pushed) to disintegrate. In terms of health and education many of the rural poor became worse off than they had been during the Cultural Revolution. Similarly, many of the gains made in achieving gender equality have been lost.

The 'positives' should also include developments in China's military defence, industry and agriculture. The politically correct line announces that the Chinese economy was brought to the brink of collapse during the Cultural Revolution. However, documentary evidence and special studies of the period (Meisner 1986, Lardy 1978, Rawski 1980 and 1993, Endicott 1989, Bramall 1993, Chow 1985, Perkins 1985, Field 1986, Hinton 1983, and Gao 1999a) all demonstrate that this was not the case. True, China's economy was disrupted in 1967 and 1968, but throughout the rest of the late 1960s and through all of the 1970s China's economy showed consistent growth. Even US official estimates had to acknowledge this state of affairs. In one official report a Joint Economic Committee of the US Congress (1978) states that in the era of Mao China's economy had a 'record of positive growth in both agriculture and industry', that Mao and his fellow leaders 'had already created a significant economic base for the new [post-Mao] leadership to build on', and that the economic impact of the Cultural Revolution overall was not huge. It is also worth pointing out that the development of *she dui qiye* (commune and production brigade enterprises) during the Cultural Revolution were the forerunners of the *xiangzhen qiye* (township and village enterprises) developed in post-Mao China.

When someone kills someone else we usually judge the case to be murder if the action was intentional; otherwise it is a case of manslaughter. Therefore, determining what is designed and what is intended is important in evaluating the responsibility for actions. A good test case would be to compare China, the largest communist country, with India, the largest democracy, using labels for convenience. The Nobel Prize-winning economist Amartya Sen makes the point that, although India never suffered a 'politically induced famine' like the Great Leap Forward in China:

> [India] had, in terms of morbidity, mortality and longevity, suffered an excess in mortality over China of close to 4 [million] a year during the same period. ... Thus, in this one geographical area alone, more deaths resulted from 'this failed capitalist experiment' (more than 100 million by 1980) than can be attributed to the 'failed communist experiment' all over the world since 1917.
>
> (Black 2000)

This interpretation may be disturbing to some and uncomfortable to others, but Sen's argument does show that it is important to distinguish between what was intended and what was not intended during the Cultural Revolution.

Destruction of Chinese culture and tradition

Another issue to consider is the extent of destruction of Chinese culture and tradition during the Cultural Revolution. It is commonly thought that the Cultural Revolution was not only iconoclastic but also barbaric in its destruction of Chinese culture. The Cultural Revolution slogan *po si jiu* (break the four olds – old ideas, old customs, old culture and old habits) certainly adds conceptual weight to this perception. The perception in the West, especially in the non-academic community, that everything traditional in China was destroyed is often reinforced by the grotesque pictures and photos of Red Guards burning books and destroying religious temples and historical relics.

There is no dispute that there were many instances of destruction of this kind. However it is important to determine, first, whether the destruction was universal and, second, whether it was the official policy of the Cultural Revolution to destroy physical objects. Despite every effort by the Chinese authorities to denounce the Cultural Revolution, no evidence has ever been put forward to support charges that physical destruction was officially organized or sanctioned. On the contrary, the official policy at the time was to protect cultural relics from wanton destruction. For instance, on 14 May 1967 the CCP central committee issued a document entitled *Guanyu zai wuchanjieji wenhua da geming zhong baohu wenwu tushu de jidian yijian* (Several suggestions for the protection of cultural relics and books during the Cultural Revolution) to protect traditional cultural institutions and relics. It is noteworthy, as well, that archaeological discoveries of historical significance such as the Terracotta Army and Mawangdui tombs in Hunan province made during this period have been well-preserved. In fact the number of archaeological discoveries (including the Terracotta Army discovered in 1974) was very high and their preservation was swift and effective during the period.

It has to be pointed out that tension between maintenance and destruction of tradition has existed in China for thousands of years; it is not just the so-called communist regime that had to face this problem. Two examples will be sufficient to illustrate this point. First, many aspects of Chinese tradition were abandoned or destroyed by the Chinese themselves but preserved in a modified way by the Japanese instead. Second, since the May Fourth Movement at the beginning of the twentieth century, anti-tradition has been held up as a beacon for modernization for 'progressive' Chinese of all political persuasions. This is generally understood to be the 'Enlightenment'.

It is true that the leaders of the PRC, in general, and of the Cultural Revolution, in particular, did encourage a more radical ideology of anti-Chinese tradition. However, they tried at the same time to preserve some aspects of it. It was Mao who said the Chinese traditional medicine was a treasure house that needed to be exploited (Mao 1958). It was during the Cultural Revolution period that Chinese medicine was intensively supported by official policies. The use of acupuncture-induced anaesthesia was promoted during the Cultural Revolution and many foreign visitors were invited to observe the use of surgical operations at that time.

It was among the Mawangdui discoveries that the earliest known account of the medical properties of the plant *qinghao* was unearthed, along with other cultural relics. The Chinese worked from 1967 onwards to screen 'a broad range of compounds drawn from traditional medicine', but it was in 1971 that they developed an unusual extraction method that isolated what is called *qinghaosu* (artemisinin), the drug that 'is now recognized as the world's best hope for a malaria cure' (Lange 2002). It is worth pointing out here that David Lange, who trumpeted this scientific breakthrough – quoting Hong Kong University's Richard Haynes as saying that 'there has got to be a Nobel Prize here somewhere' – subtitled his report: 'A Little-known Tale of Scientific Intrigue: Post-Cultural Revolution Researchers Using Rudimentary Equipment Unearthed What Is Now Recognized as the World's Best Hope for a Malaria Cure.' Contrary to the headline, the content of Lange's report shows clearly that this discovery was made during the Cultural Revolution and the poster that accompanies his report confirms this as well: the caption in Chinese below a large figure of a female scientist (an example of China's affirmative policy to promote gender equality during the Cultural Revolution) reads *'kexue you xianzu ku zhan neng guo guan'* (there are dangerous obstacles in sciences; but with a bitter fight we can surpass them), a typical Cultural Revolution poster. It is clear that Lange either consciously or unconsciously made the decision not to report the Cultural Revolution in a positive light.

There's no doubt that artists and cultural professionals were persecuted and stopped from working – especially during the early period of the Cultural Revolution. However, efforts were also made to restore cultural activities. Radicals at the time were trying to find a new approach toward literature and art. Take the case of the Peking opera. Thanks largely to the efforts of artists such as Yu Huiyong (who committed suicide after he was arrested by the post-Mao regime) the model Peking operas had some amazing achievements in those years. The artistic technique and skills in music, acting and language developed at that time were the highest of their kind and have not been surpassed since. According to Zhang Guangtian (2002), a playwright and director who has made a huge impact on the stage in recent years, model Peking operas created during the Cultural Revolution were not only revolutionary in content but also in artistic form, a revolution equivalent to the Anhui Troup's performance in Peking two centuries ago (Guo Jingrui 2002). Zhang argues that the characteristics of the performing art of Peking opera, that is, the formalism and style of simplification and concision, were raised to their highest level during the Cultural Revolution. Zhang further argues that by making use of Western wind and string instruments and by combining them with traditional Chinese musical instruments, and by wedding the art of Western ballet with that of the Peking opera, the model Peking operas not only developed a theoretical framework for managing change and continuity in the Chinese theatre, but also demonstrated a successful effort to counter the seemingly unstoppable tide of Western cultural imperialism.

I witnessed an unprecedented surge of cultural and sports activities in my own home town, Gao Village. The villagers, for the first time in the village's history, organized a theatre troupe and put on performances that incorporated the contents and structure of the model Peking operas with local language and music. The villagers not only entertained themselves but also learned how to read and write by getting into the texts and plays. And they organized sports meets and held matches with other villages. All these activities gave the villagers an opportunity to meet, communicate and even fall in love. These activities during the Cultural Revolution years gave them a sense of discipline and organization and created a public sphere where meetings and communications went beyond the traditional household and village clans. This had never happened before and it has never happened since (Gao 1999a).

Another aspect of the Cultural Revolution that has so far been largely neglected by Western academics is the multiplication of semi-official, unofficial and underground cultural activities during these *da minzhu* (great democracy) years. According to one estimate, for instance, more than 10,000 different newspapers and pamphlets were published during the Cultural Revolution (Chen Donglin and Du Pu 1994). There were more than 900 publications in Beijing alone. According to Chen, even Mao paid attention to these publications and the official *People's Daily* reprinted articles from some of the publications. Western academics have made and still do make use of the so-called Red Guard publications to assess China, the CCP, and the Cultural Revolution. There was unprecedented freedom of association and freedom of expression, though in non-institutionalized ways.

Religion and minority cultures: with a special focus on Tibet

As indicated above, modernity and the Enlightenment project have been attacking Chinese tradition for more than a century. As in any country, religious beliefs are an important part of tradition that has been under attack by modernity. On top of and as part of modernity, an important part of the Enlightenment project has been the Marxist ideology, which is known to have been hostile to religion. The extent and degree of religious destruction in the PRC in general and during the Cultural Revolution in particular is undoubtedly serious.

Tibetan culture bore the full blunt of this ideological onslaught because its culture is so closely intertwined with religion. It is understandable therefore that there has been outrage against this kind of destruction. However, how to write and read history in this case is, again, another matter. Reflections by Wang Lixiong, a Chinese expert on Tibet, are worthy of some discussion here. In one of his publications in English, Wang disputes the claim that 1) the destruction of Tibetan temples during the Cultural Revolution was by Chinese Red Guards, and 2) that it was part of the CCP's 'systematic, methodical, calculated, planned and comprehensive destruction' (Donnet 1994: 81). Instead, Wang argues that 'only a limited number of Han [ethnic Chinese] Red Guards actually reached Tibet. Even if some did participate in destroying temples, their actions could only have been symbolic' (Wang Lixiong 2002: 97) for, as Wang argues, most of the destruction was done by Rebels of Tibetan ethnic origin. The destruction of Tibetan culture, just like the destruction of Chinese traditional culture, has to be discussed in relation to the complicated and painful process of modernization and China's official ideology of Marxism.

Furthermore, Wang argues that the Chinese authorities were trying to rein in the wanton destruction in Tibet:

> The authorities in Tibet often tried to restrain radical actions, with the PLA [People's Liberation Army], for example, consistently supporting the more conservative factions against the rebels. Temples and monasteries survived best in the central cities and areas where the authorities could still exercise some control. In contrast, the Gandan Monastery, some 60 kilometres outside Lhasa and one of the three major centres of the Yellow Hat sect, was reduced to ruins.
>
> (Wang 2002: 97)

This description fits well with the general picture all over China: there was factional fighting between radical and conservative forces, the authorities tried to reduce the destructive consequences of the ideological ferment, and the PLA tended to support the authorities.

Of course not everyone agrees with Wang, as can be seen in Tsering Shakya's response (Shakya 2002), which is a spirited defence of Tibetan cultural and religious tradition and a passionate cry for Tibetan nationalism. Shakya's criticism of Wang's speculation about Tibetan psychology is, to me, entirely justifiable and convincing. Wang basically argues that because of the harsh conditions and the overwhelming power of nature on the Tibetan high plateau, the people residing there are more inclined to beliefs in supernatural forces and darkness of nature. In a most charitable interpretation this is a kind of geographical determinism, like Wittfogel's argument that the nature and scale of rice agriculture induced bureaucratic despotism in China, that lacks solid evidence, and is un-falsifiable. Wang's argument, like Wittfogel's, does smell of an orientalist who peeps into the mind of the 'other'.

However I don't think Shakya is fair in some other criticisms of Wang, such as that Wang has a colonial attitude towards the Tibetans.

Wang in fact is very critical of the Chinese regime and actually argues that the present Chinese religious policy is destroying Tibetan Buddhism (Wang 2003) and that the Chinese presence in Tibet and the way Tibet is run by the Chinese is a kind of imperialism (Wang 2004). Wang is one of the few mainland Chinese scholars who actually tries to argue that the Chinese claim that Tibet is historically part of China is at least open to dispute.

Shakya has reasonable grounds to claim that the Chinese presence in Tibet is a form of imperialism or colonialism. However, we have to make a crucial difference between what we may term Chinese imperialism and Western imperialism elsewhere, or the British imperialism in India and Tibet, for a number of reasons. The first reason is that China and Tibet have had a long historical relationship because of geographical proximity. You can call it suzerainty or tributary or whatever relationship, but there is a long historical relationship and therefore there are areas that were already part of Chinese provinces before the Communist takeover where both Tibetans and non-Tibetans, including Han Chinese, have been living together for generations. The second reason is that:

> No major state recognized 'de facto independent' Tibet because China had a claim to sovereignty. A United States State Department spokesman noted in 1999 that since 1942 the United States has regarded Tibet as part of China, and during the 1940s United States actions repeatedly affirmed that view.
>
> (Sautman 2001: 278)

Let us remember that this US acknowledgement was not made in the seventeenth or eighteenth century when colonialism was rife but in the 1940s when nationhood, national liberation and national independence were the main features of the day and when the CCP had yet to take over power in China. Therefore, it is hard to sustain an argument that the Communist regime was a colonialist that invaded an independent state.

The second reason why the PRC was not colonialist in the traditional sense is that as an ethnic group the Tibetan population has increased under the current Chinese control. While the Chinese government has implemented a family planning policy to control China's population, it has much more lenient policies towards ethnic minorities, including Tibetans. This is in contrast to what Western colonialists have done. As Sautman points out, under Western colonialism the colonized perished in droves through famine, disease and repression while colonial settlers gained demographically. This happened in America, where native Americans lost up to 95 per cent of their population, and in Australia, where the aboriginal Australians have almost been wiped out. In Tibet, however, ethnic Tibetans 'have proliferated on a scale never before experienced by that ethnic group' (Sautman 2001: 281).

Our main concern here is not about historical claims of sovereignty but about destruction of Tibetan religious life during the Cultural Revolution. While Wang admits the seriousness of the destruction and condemns it, Shakya also admits to Wang's argument that the destruction was largely done by people of Tibetan ethnic origin. What Shakya argues, and is therefore critical of Wang for failing to realize, is that the destruction of religious institutions in Tibet during the Cultural Revolution was a logical consequence of Chinese colonialism and that Tibetans participated in the destruction because they were either coerced or brainwashed. On the other hand, Wang explains Tibetan participation in the destruction of their own religious institutions by arguing that these Tibetans believed in Mao and his ideas and even took Mao as their god. What underlies Wang's argument is the theory of class and class struggle: lower-class Tibetans responded in the way they did during the Cultural Revolution because Mao was perceived to have changed their lives by a revolution of land reform and emancipation of slaves.

In the context of the two explanations it is worth spending some time to discuss the contents of a book recently published in Taiwan. The book is an edited version of interviews with people living in Tibet, mostly Tibetans, about the Cultural Revolution. The author Wei Se[2] is a PRC citizen of Tibetan ethnic origin who has been banned and censored by the Chinese authorities. The book is a result of several years' work and consists of a selection of 23 interviews out of more than 70 that she had conducted. It is also worth noting that the author is aware of both Wang's and Shakya's arguments, and the Chinese versions of both their articles are included as appendix in the book.

One of the chief aims of Wei Se was to find out why Tibetans participated in the destruction of their own religion. As Wei Se (2006) states in her preface to the book, both Wang's and Shakya's views and arguments are confirmed by these interviewees. However, from my reading, the evidence and arguments coming out of this book as a whole are tipped more towards Wang's interpretation and understanding. According to the interview with her mother, Wei Se's father was very enthusiastic at the beginning of the Cultural Revolution and he loved Mao (2006: 85). Another interviewee states that at that time 'belief in the CCP was like belief in religion' (2006: 95, 97, 98). Another interviewee says that he really believed Mao was right and many others did as well (2006: 167). Another Tibetan who used to be a servant of one of the religious teachers of the Dalai Lama also states that he likes Mao because Mao respects the Dalai Lama, and because Mao supports the poor. He reaffirms that at that time medical services were good for the poor people, and the first thing he said when he recovered from a hospital operation was 'long live Chairman Mao' (2006: 225). Another Tibetan says that at that time people believed that Mao was a living Buddha (2006: 268), and thinks that there are still many Tibetans who, having been liberated by Mao's revolution, have the same feelings for Mao (2006: 271). A former serf declares that without the CCP there would not have been a life for serfs like him (2006: 292). Another interviewee, the son of a well-known living Buddha and the most outstanding Tibetan photographer, states he really believed in Mao and thought everything said by Mao was the universal truth. In the 1980s when he was received by His Holiness the Dalai Lama (outside China) he told his Holiness that it was the truth that the majority of the Tibetans supported the CCP because the CCP really liberated the serfs (2006: 329). The first interviewee, an ordinary Tibetan woman in Lhasa, states that Mao helped a lot of people, that the world cannot do without people like Mao, that Tibet used to be unfair when some were rich while some did not have enough to eat and that Mao's revolution changed everything (2006: 21).

Many of the interviewees hold that there was not much ethnic conflict in the era of Mao. One interviewee of Hui ethnic background states that the Hans and the Tibetans were the same in making revolution (Wei Se 2006: 181). Other interviewees affirm the idea that the dominant discourse was class struggle and the words on every one's lips were *qin bu qin jieji fen*: whether one feels close to another depends on class (2006: 166, 190). A Tibetan interviewee who used to be a neighbourhood committee leader is very upset by the current Chinese policy of giving so much privilege to Tibetans who belonged to the former ruling class (2006: 229). Finally the majority of the interviewees, when questioned, affirm that it was the Tibetan activists of the neighbourhood committees, not the Red Guards, who did most of the damage in religious destruction. These activists were mostly from poor social backgrounds and some of them were considered by some interviewees to be rascals, thieves and thugs.

The interview findings by Wei Se give support to scholars like Sautman who refutes the claims of cultural genocide in Tibet (Sautman 2001, 2006) that was supposedly carried out by the Chinese. It is on record that on 15 October 1966 the Chinese Premier Zhou tried to persuade a group of eleven Tibetan students to go slow in destroying the four olds because, he said, the wiping out of superstition requires a long-term transformation; he suggested that temples and monasteries should not be destroyed because they can be converted to schools or store houses (Ho 2006). One example illustrates the very delicate and yet complex situation at that time: when activists went to destroy the Juela Temple in the autumn of 1966, the resident lama

Mimaciren refused to open the gates, but his own son Lobu climbed onto the wall and opened the main door from inside. (Ho 2006: 80)

Cultural Revolution and cultural creativity

The accusation of destruction of culture and tradition has overshadowed the achievements of cultural creativity during the Cultural Revolution. Take the example of the fine arts. During the Cultural Revolution years of 1972 to 1975 China held four national fine arts exhibitions, with more than 2,000 pieces of art selected from 12,800 works recommended from all over China. The exhibits in Beijing attracted an audience of 7.8 million, a scale never reached before the Cultural Revolution (Lu Hong 2002). According to Lu, the four exhibitions showed three characteristics: new ideological content, new subject matters and the rise of amateur artists (65 per cent of exhibited works were created by amateurs). These artworks included oil paintings, Chinese traditional paintings, print paintings, sculpture, Spring Festival paintings (*nian hua*), picture storybook paintings (*lianhuan hua*), charcoal drawings, watercolours and paper cuts. Among the educated youth sent down to the countryside were several accomplished artists who found inspiration in their lives and work in rural China. These include Liu Borong, Xu Qunzong, He Shaojiao, Shen Jiawei, Zhao Xiaomo, Li Jianguo, You Jingdong, Zhao Yanchao, Chen Xinmin, He Boyi and Xu Kuang. In addition to the much-publicized *Rent Collection Courtyard* (*Shouzu yuan*) – which was conceived before 1966 but finalized during the Cultural Revolution – large-scale group sculptures of revolutionary subject matter also reached its peak of artistic form during this period (Wang Mingxian and Yan Shechun 2001). Works of this type include *Hongweibing zan* (Song of praise of the Red Guard), *Kongjun zhanshi jiashi* (Family history of an Air Force soldier), *Mao zhuxi wuchan jieji geming luxian shengli wansui* (Long live the victory of Chairman Mao's proletarian revolutionary line), and *Nongnu fen* (Anger of the slaves). One might hate the content of this kind of art, one might even hate its form: but to say that there was no artistic creativity during the Cultural Revolution is to create a myth.

Another myth created and accepted, at least by the non-academic community, in the West is that during the Cultural Revolution people were forbidden to read anything except Mao's little Red Book. This portrayal of China as a cultural wasteland is absolutely false. By 1976 there were 542 official magazines and journals and 182 newspapers in circulation throughout China; the number of cinemas or film units had increased from 20,363 in 1965 to 86,088 in 1976; cultural clubs had increased from 2,598 to 2,609; public libraries, from 577 to 768; and museums, from 214 to 263 (Qiu Desheng et al. 1993). Only theatre troupes saw a drop in their numbers during the Cultural Revolution, from 3,458 in 1965 to 2,906 in 1976. But these figures do not include the unregistered unofficial theatre troupes that were created and active in rural China, like the one I experienced in Gao Village.

More importantly, educated youth and many other Chinese read many literary works that they were not supposed to read, such as works by Russian writers, revolutionary or otherwise (Wang Jianzhao 2002). They not only read extensively but they also created their own literature. Artists like Mang Ke and Duo Duo, both now known in the West, wrote and worked creatively during the Cultural Revolution. Others include Bei Dao, Yan Li, Yan Xiaoqing, Peng Gang, Shi Baojia and Yue Zhong. Another example of collective creativity is the *Han Ying cidian* (Chinese–English Dictionary) compiled by a group of academics who worked collectively at the Beijing Foreign Language Institute for ten years. First published in 1978, the dictionary, in my opinion, remains the best of its kind inside or outside China, past or present.

The objects on display at the exhibition in Seattle are evidence that there was an upsurge of creativity among the popular masses during the Cultural Revolution. The chopsticks holder, for instance, is a beautiful piece of art. It is itself made of chopsticks and reflects the tremendous resourcefulness of the labouring Chinese. It is cheap to make and it is practical. Moreover, it cleverly combines the content (chopsticks holder) with the form (chopsticks). If we treasure art and artefacts that have been inspired by religions – institutions with brutal and murderous records – and if we value modern artefacts that are driven by commercialism, then I do not see why we should denigrate the value of art from the Chinese Cultural Revolution just because it came out of a political movement. Culture is not an abstract entity. It is lived experience and creative activities. By living their ordinary lives the ordinary Chinese may continue practising what has been passed on, but they may also cut ties with their past. They may want to set up new practices for their future. In the midst of all the change and continuity, culture was destroyed and culture was created, as the displays in the Burke Museum exhibition show.

If we accept the truth that the Cultural Revolution was ten years of catastrophe, then there is no room for voices that differ from those of the Chinese authorities and the Chinese elite intelligentsia who condemn the Cultural Revolution and who exploit the holocaust discourse (Sahlins 1985) to construct the Cultural Revolution history. The best example of how the Cultural Revolution history is constructed can be seen how the Cultural Revolution is 'remembered'. As it is true in the case of other histories, the history of the Cultural Revolution is 'in its telling' (Taussig 1989). But who is doing the telling? Who remembers what? Who is allowed to voice her/his memory? Who is able to tell her/his memories either orally or in print? What channels and space of memories are provided by whom, for whom? Answers to these questions will be provided in later chapters.

What is the Enlightenment?

In contrast to early Western anthropologists, who took their theories to exotic places in order to interpret exotic societies, the Chinese expatriates, who are financially supported and academically or politically mentored by the West, do not 'tend to situate themselves more on the ship of (capitalist) history than on the shore'(Ortner 1984: 143), but rather depart the airport lounge of China on a plane to the West to receive instruction about the history of the Cultural Revolution as, for instance, Dr Li Zhisui did in recounting the private life of Chairman Mao (as discussed in a later chapter).

When talking about the Cultural Revolution and about their own experiences of being victimized, and then comparing how the US government treats its own people so humanely, for instance in its careful and persistent efforts in recovering and honouring its MIAs in Vietnam, some Chinese elite intelligentsia laud the American practice of human rights. The element missing in this humanitarian discourse is any consideration of the fact that millions of Vietnamese, Cambodians and Laotians who were killed or bombed to dust were also human beings. While we should support the right of US Vietnam veterans to demand compensation for their suffering as a consequence of their participation in Agent Orange warfare, we should not forget what happened to the real targets of this warfare, the millions of Vietnamese who suffered and are still suffering from the effects of Agent Orange.

Those who condemn the Cultural Revolution are still framing their denunciations in the ideological paradigm of Western Enlightenment. As Wang Hui argues, if we use this Enlightenment discourse as a basis of evaluation, then not only does the Chinese tradition stand to be condemned, but all contemporary social practice in the PRC should be denied any moral legitimacy (Wang Hui 2000). According to this yardstick, anything happens in China, past or contemporary, is only transitional until and unless China becomes part of the West in political system and cultural values (Sun Ge 2007). We will continue this discussion in the next chapter.

2 Constructing history: memories, values and identity

Introduction: speech act of identification

Ever since the late 1980s, memoirs, autobiographies and biographies have overwhelmingly stigmatized at the Cultural Revolution as ten years of chaos, calamities or even holocaust. In this influx of remembering, in contemporary China the Chinese appear to have awoken from a nightmare after which justice is sought, wounds are to be healed, the bad and evil are condemned, and the good and reasonable are endued with power and glory. In this enterprise of remembering, the past memories have a moral as well as a truth claim. But can ten years' lived experience during the Cultural Revolution years be reduced to a bad dream? What were so many millions of intelligent and reasonable Chinese thinking and doing in these years?

An answer that is constantly on offer is that the Chinese were either brutally suppressed and/or brainwashed by a Communist regime led by a power-hungry dictator. In contrast to this cold war interpretation, and based on the assumption that the Chinese were no less reasonable then and no less brainwashed now, this chapter argues that the moral and truth claims of this remembering of the Cultural Revolution are necessarily constructions. Inspired by Ricoeur's ideas of memories, forgetfulness and identity, I propose that memory is not a thing that is recalled, but an act of identity. According to what Ricoeur calls 'narrative identity', to tell a story of one's life is to make sense of it (Popkin 2005). But one needs a conceptual framework to organize the story so that sense can be made of. It is argued in this chapter that the conceptual framework in post-Mao China that organizes Chinese memories is dominantly the contemporary version of *qimeng* (Enlightenment), that is, liberal democracy and market capitalism. According to this conceptual framework, anything that happens in China, past or present, is only transitional until and unless China becomes part of the West in its political system and cultural values.

Memories are not only about the past, but also constitute a form of knowledge. The narrative of atrocity of the Cultural Revolution is not just a retelling of past experience but also a speech act of political identity. In the early stage of the development of this narrative, to retell Cultural Revolution atrocities was to rehearse the political speech act of the May Fourth Movement of Enlightenment. Later, since the 1990s, as the cold war appeared to come to an end and as market capitalism took root in China, the narrative developed further towards the political act of identification with the neo-Enlightenment of liberal democracy and market capitalism. It is this act of identifying with dominant political and cultural values in the West that orientates the remembering of the Cultural Revolution.

What is the departure point of those who want to identify with the globally dominant political and cultural values? While the Japanese who wanted to identify with the West (out of Asia and into Europe) took their departure from the ugly Asia, Michel de Certeau's conceptualization of 'place', the Chinese who want to identify with liberal democracy and the values of market capitalism take their departure from 'time', their ugly past, including the very recent past. To the Japanese then, 'to kill the Chinese is throwing off Asia in every conceivable way' because China was the anti-West and anti-modern (Dower 2006). To the Chinese now, condemning the Cultural Revolution is throwing off the ugly past in every conceivable way.

The 'making of history', as Certeau gives it as a title of a chapter in *The Writing of History*, deals with the present as much as with the past. What is required of the present is the framework to construct the past. The writing and debates about the Cultural Revolution are political speech acts of identification. This chapter aims to demonstrate how the identification with the dominant values of liberal democracy and market capitalism (the present) and the remembering of the Cultural Revolution (the past) are connected.

From the wounded to the mentalité: the re-rehearsal of May Fourth

Shanghen wenxue, the scar literature or literature of the wounded, emerged almost immediately after the Cultural Revolution as a series of first-person accounts in the form of short accounts, usually authored by *zhiqing* (educated youth) sent to the countryside or state farms in border regions. Prominent writers include Liu Xinhua, Zhang Xianliang and Liu Xinwu.[1] The so-called scar literature was initially encouraged by the Chinese leadership to place blame at the door of the Gang of Four for whatever was considered wrong or bad in China at that time so as to legitimize the destruction of Maoist policies. It was the emergence of the scar literature that symbolized the beginning of the condemnation of the Cultural Revolution both in and outside China. Subsequently another literary genre, known as reportage (Link 1983a, 1983b), also helped the progression of denunciation of the Cultural Revolution and denegation of the era of Mao.

When the Chinese elite intelligentsia further reflected, they became critical not only of the Cultural Revolution but also of a whole package of CCP policies and practices which were condemned as 'feudalistic' (*fengjian*). Condemnation of the past thus developed from the personal to the state and from the body to the discourse. The theoretical framework that organized such a condemnation was largely the May Fourth (1919) legacy of Enlightenment which blamed Chinese traditional cultural values, that is, the Chinese mentality, for China's impotence when assaulted by the Western powers and by Japan, a brilliant student of the West. The May Fourth Movement discourse was picked up again and, for those members of the neo-Enlightenment Chinese intelligentsia such as Li Zehou, Jin Guantao, Liu Xiaobo, Bao Zunxin, Wang Yuanhua and Gan Yang, the Chinese revolution crystallized in 1949 was a result of nationalism (*jiuwang* – to save the country from dying) that derailed the proper course of Enlightenment (*qimeng* – remove the curtain of igno-rance) of Western liberal values such as individualism, self-autonomy and democracy.

It is ironic that while some of the potent slogans at the beginning of the Cultural Revolution were those that were meant to break down Chinese tradition, such as the *po si jiu* (break away from the four olds), the Cultural Revolution is narrated by the neo-Enlightenment intelligentsia as the manifestation and logical consequence of a Chinese feudalist tradition that values 'despotism', 'servile obedi-ence' and 'blind loyalty to authorities'. It is doubly ironic when one considers the documented evidence that it was Mao who called the Chinese youth to rebel against the authorities, who provoked them not be obedient and not to follow their leaders blindly. 'Throw the emperor off his horse' was one of the most inspiring slogans used by the Cultural Revolution rebels. Indeed, every figure of the CCP hier-archy – including the Cultural Revolution radicals themselves such as Jiang Qing, Zhang Chunqiao and even Mao – was attacked during the Cultural Revolution (Lao Tian 2004). At the beginning of the Cultural Revolution, when the newly promoted Tao Zhu was accused of protecting Liu Shaoqi, Tao immediately issued a statement declar-ing that anybody, including himself, could be criticized except Mao and his deputy Lin Biao (Wang Li 2001: 675). For the neo-Enlighten-ment warriors, however, it was the idea that Mao's authority could not be questioned that was the manifestation of feudalism in the form of blind loyalty and servile obedience. Mao somehow had to have unquestionable authority to call the Rebels to question the authority of the party chiefs at every level. It is a permanent and universal human paradox that one cannot question the authority of somebody or something without having the authority to do so: the questioning of one authority requires another for legitimacy.

There are, of course, also Western scholars who seek to find explanations from Chinese tradition for what has happened during the Cultural Revolution. Barend ter Haar argues that violent struggle was no innovation of the Mao era but had important roots in traditional Chinese culture, which has a 'demonological paradigm and its messianic correlate' (Haar 2002: 27) that contribute to cultural expressions of mass political campaigns of a violent nature. There are similarities between those that happened in historical times and those that happened post-1949 in general and during the Cultural Revolution in particular. The CCP might have tried to root out the Chinese traditional religious infrastructure, but it still used the basic demonological categories and it filled the categories with new contents. Equally, Stefan Landsberger (2002) argues that the unifying symbol of Mao's messianic leadership is rooted in Chinese culture and popular religion.

Some other influential Western academics, however, argue that it was the May Fourth radicalism that was to blame for the violence and inhumanity of the communist revolution (Lin 1979, Leys 1988). For Leys, China was subjected to the tyranny of Marxism-Leninism gone mad. For Lin, it was the totalistic anti-traditionalism of the May Fourth Movement that led to subsequent developments in China. In Leys' understanding and interpreting of contemporary China there is an 'academic Great Wall of China' of 1949 that divides the traditional China and contemporary China (Cohen 1988, Fitzgerald 1999). For the neo-Enlightenment intelligentsia, however, the wall never existed and Mao was a peasant turned emperor-dictator. All the ideas and practices in the Mao era, though they might have been in the name of Marxism-Leninism, can be traced back to Chinese tradition of feudalism. How else can the intelligentsia reignite the Western Enlightenment fire if they want to jettison revolution (*gaobie geming*) by denouncing Marxism, which in fact is one of the prominent descendants of that very Western Enlightenment?

The May Fourth Movement (Schwarcz 1986, Lin 1979) was about abandoning Chinese tradition and embracing Western values because Chinese tradition was considered not only backward and uncivilized but also inhumane and even 'man-eating'. Aspiring members of the Chinese elite intelligentsia either physically went to the West (Japan was already being considered sufficiently Western) to seek the truth, or were devouring Western ideas from an ever growing canon of important textual translations. The overwhelming desire was a wholesale Westernization and a total destruction of the Chinese *mentalité*, that is, everything culturally Chinese. Lu Xun declared not only that one should never read Chinese books but also that *fang kuai zi* (the Chinese script) was a cancer in Chinese culture.

For the Chinese intelligentsia in the 1980s, the Communist victory was a peasant revolution in which nationalism hijacked Enlightenment. China completed to a full circle after more than half a century: Enlightenment had been interrupted by a revolution and a post-revolution make-up lesson was required before China could join the human race. Thus there was Li Zehou's re-Enlightenment thesis and his embracing of Christian individualism, Liu Xiaobo's rejection of collective progress and his advocacy of the Nietzschean hero (Woei 2002). Furthermore, such writers all trace the root of the Cultural Revolution to the faults of Chinese tradition, as their predecessors such as Lu Xun and Hu Shi traced the weakness of China to Chinese tradition.

This neo-Enlightenment teleology either assumes or argues that Chinese backwardness is largely due to the peasantry, and Chinese peasants are thus objectified as being detrimental to modernization (Kipnis 1995). Those who adopt the neo-Enlightenment position interpret Chinese politics in terms of what they call *nongmin yishi* or 'peasant consciousness' (Feng 1989). Feng argues that without considering the peasant consciousness, it is impossible adequately to explain not only what happened in China but also the revolutionary histories of the countries of the former Soviet Union and all the socialist countries, the development of Fascism in France, Japan and Italy, and what currently happens in all Third World countries. According to Feng, China's close-mindedness, power worship, moralism, benightedness, the Taiping uprising, the Boxer movement, and above all the communist revolution all have much to do with *nongmin yishi* (Feng 2003). The CCP bureaucrat and modernist writer Li Shenzhi was hailed as the liberal leader because he condemned the CCP as remnant of despotic Chinese tradition (www.sinoliberal.com/lishenzhi/lisz2003062101.htm).[2]

Clearly, the literature of the wounded by the *zhiqing* started the *suku*: telling of bitterness (Anagnost, 1997) of the Cultural Revolution. The narrative then developed from personal grievances to a theoretical reflection on the Mao era, on Mao himself, and on the very idea and practice of the Chinese Communist revolution. The theoretical framework disposable at that time was the legacy of the May Fourth Movement. As the popular television documentary *He shang* (The River Elegy) tried to show, not only the Chinese political system but also the Chinese civilization was backward and actually uncivilized. The way forward to join the civilized world was to leave behind the Yellow River (peasant) mentality and the close-mindedness of the Great Wall and look towards the open blue-ocean civilization (*haiyang wenming*) of the West.

By the standard of the currently dominant discourse of liberal democracy, *shangshan xiaxiang* (sending the educated youth to the mountain and the countryside) was violation of human rights. This identification with the globally dominant value means that it is

THE BATTLE FOR CHINA'S PAST

irrelevant that most, if not all, educated youth, at least at the initial stage, volunteered to take part in the movement (Leung 1994). It is also irrelevant that for all intents and purposes educated youth 'suffered' only from an urban perspective and to large extent only from hindsight. From the perspectives of the rural residents, the educated youth had a good life. They did not have to work as hard as the local farmers and they had state and family subsidies. They would frequently go back to visit their parents in the cities (Leung 1994), and they had money to spend and wore fashionable clothes. They would bring food in cans and tins that the rural people had never seen (Seybolt 1996). They had the privilege of being allowed to violate local rules and customs, and sometimes behaved waywardly by stealing fruit and vegetables and killing chickens raised by villagers for their own benefit. For most of the rural people, the educated youth were the envy of their life and were respected (Davies 2002). Finally, those educated youths whose family backgrounds were of 'class enemies' actually enjoyed a period of relief because the rural people respected them all without bothering about the class line.

Ever since the 1980s the urban Chinese intelligentsia elite who had dominated the public space have not thought of their experience from this perspective. They compare their life with, and identify with, the affluent West. Their common complaint is that they missed the best formal education that they deserved even though they witnessed the fact that the majority of their compatriots could not even dream of such an opportunity. As Sausmikat (2002) argues, the structure of their account is 'shaped by their current social situation as well as the dominant public discourse'. The dominant public discourse in China since the late 1980s is no longer that of narrowing the gap between the urban and rural, between industry and agriculture and between mental and manual labour, but of narrowing the gap between the West and China.

As Davies (2002) argues in his doctoral thesis on the educated youth, the dominant narrative is not about the historical Cultural Revolution, but about the way it exists and persists in contemporary China. In other words it is not about what happened (historical). Rather it is about what is happening (anthropological). History refers to both the totality of past events and reporting of these events. The problem is, however, that these events are only known through reporting. 'They become events because they were reported' (Davies 2002: 8). Reporting, however, is framed in narrative and 'we perceive the past in the present through the construction of narrative' (Davies 2002: 9). What is reported and the way it is reported is not only selective but also subjective to discursive context. History then can be talked back and is a meaningful terrain for articulating the present.

Be American citizens in thinking

Just as our ways of talking depend upon the world, the world depends our way of talking about it (Shotter 1990: 125). Therefore our way of speaking becomes central because 'We speak in order to create, maintain, reproduce and transform certain modes of social and societal relationships' (1990:121). Remembering is an 'Accounting practice ... within the context of how people render what is otherwise a puzzling, senseless or indeterminate activity visible as familiar, sensible, determinate and *justified* commonplace occurrence' (1990:123). 'An *account* is not a description, which by the provision of evidence could be proved true or false, but it works as an aid to perception, literally instructing one both in how to see something as a commonplace event, and, in so seeing it, appreciating the opportunities it offers for one's own further action' (1990:123). There is no 'ghost in the machine', there is no private 'inner' subjectivity, radically separated from an 'outer, public world', and 'memory, like attention and perception, is selective' (1990:128). When one remembers one's experience of the Cultural Revolution, there is no such thing as 'retrieving' in recall. Instead, recall constructs the memory. 'If any single theme informs of Foucault's [1976] seminar, it is not a quest for political theory, but an appreciation of historiography as a political force, of history writing as a political act' (Stoler 1995: 62).

Those who write memoirs and autobiographies of the Mao era in general, and of the Cultural Revolution in particular, tend to recall their memories with bitterness, condemnation and even horror as if what happened was a nightmare from which they had just woken up. This is because they are using the current discourse to identify with certain values, doing that to construct the past. In this enterprise of constructing the past through the discourse of the present, remembering the Cultural Revolution as a nightmare identifies with the West, its values and its way of life, especially these of the United States. This is not surprising due to the hegemonic position of the West headed by the United States. The political, economic and military superiority can easily be translated as superiority in cultural and life value. These globally dominant values are therefore taken as universally and transcendentally true.

The case of Li Yunlong, a Guizhou journalist working for the *Bi Jie ribao* (*Bi Jie* daily), illustrates the point. Under the pen name of *Ye lang* (night wolf) Li wrote an e-media chat piece in which he called on the Chinese to become an American citizen in thinking (*zai sixiang shang jiaru Meiguo guoji*). Li declared that he could not help but raise his head to pay respect to the United States, a country that has a beautiful environment, a developed economy, and freedom of speech and religion, and that practises political democracy. The United States is a *real Meiguo* (*Meiguo* is the Chinese translation of the United States which literally means 'beautiful country'). 'I wish to migrate to that country but could not,' he laments. 'What should I do? I have decided to become its citizen in my thoughts' (Ye lang 2005).

Sinological orientalism

Professor Jiao Guobiao of Beijing University bemoans how unfortunate it is that the United States had not, during the Korean War, marched straight to Beijing to take over China. He swears that if he had the power he would turn China into the 51st State of the Union. When the United States invaded Iraq in 2003, Jiao posted a poem on the e-media in which he declared that if he was called he would serve in the US army without the slightest hesitation. But he could only wish to be a US soldier in his next life (Xiao Ling 2005). Not surprisingly in 2005 Professor Jiao was invited to visit the United States for six months by the US National Endowment for Democracy to research the subject of 'The Chinese News Industry: Past and Present' (http://www.zonaeuropa.com/ 20050328_3.htm).[3]

This identification with Western values confirms the Sinological orientalist (Vukovich 2005) view of oriental despotism (Wittfogel 1957). Leon Trotsky called Stalin an 'Asiatic' who, like other Asiatic leaders, was cunning, brutal and peasant (Trotsky 1967). Marx's proposition of the 'Asiatic mode of production', a convenient way of avoiding the discussion of evidence that might be messy for the grand history of teleological human development, differed very little from the views of Hegel, Montesquieu, Smith and many other thinkers (Anderson 1974) in relation to China. Oriental despotism reached its logical conclusion when Wittfogel, a communist defector turned cold warrior, preceding Feng, applied the concept of despotism to 'China, Tsarist Russia, Persia, Mesopotamia, Egypt, the Incas, even the Hopi Indians of Arizona' (Cumings 2005). However, the veteran theme of the Oriental other takes on some variations when applied to the Cultural Revolution.

> In contemporary Western images of China, the Cultural Revolution is a potent symbol of the ugly face of Chinese society, as the Nazi era is a symbol of the ugly face of German society. The Cultural Revolution has been a lucrative tool for the West in its critique of the Chinese government; it has given the West the moral high ground in this debate
>
> (Brady 2002: 95)

Two whateverism[4]

Chinese in and outside China who want to identify with the globally dominant values are not only encouraged but constantly promoted by

Western governments and some academics alike. The cultivated image of America as the paradise for freedom and as the avenger against the brutal Chinese political system is so strong that some members of the Chinese elite would go as far as to support whatever the US government says or does, and to oppose whatever the Chinese government says or does. Their speech acts coordinate well with Western political agenda that in China they are often referred to as *fanshi pai* (whateverists). This crude adversarialism is nicknamed on the Chinese e-media *liangge fanshi* (Two whateverism): whatever China does is wrong and whatever the United States does is right. The logic is that since the United States is the number one liberal and democratic country it cannot do anything wrong, and since the PRC is ruled by a dictatorial CCP it cannot do anything right.

A website contributor lists more than 40 'whatevers', contrasting attitudes towards the United States and China (Sumo3, 2004). These include: whatever the US does is democratic and whatever China does is dictatorial; every popular protest against the US government is an exercise of democratic rights, and every Chinese protest against the United States is parallel to the Boxer Rebels or Angry Young Men (*fen qing*); whenever the United States increases military expenditure it is for peace, and whenever China does so it constitutes a military threat; whenever the United States does anything against China it is to protect American interest, and whenever China does anything that it is not in the interest of the United States it is xenophobia; whenever US civilians are attacked it is terrorism, and whenever Chinese citizens are attacked by separatists it is activity for self-determination; whenever the US uses forces abroad it is to overthrow dictatorship and rid the world of evil, and whenever China defends its own territory it is changing the status quo.

After the US bombing of the Chinese embassy in Belgrade in 1999, which killed three Chinese and injured a dozen more, there were angry and ugly demonstrations in the streets of some cities in China. Some of the Chinese elite intelligentsia in and outside China responded to these demonstrations by making two points which are very telling. The first point is that the Chinese government should apologize and compensate the millions of victims of the regime first before they had the audacity to ask Washington for an apology. The second is that those anti-US demonstrations were repeating the behaviour of the Boxer Rebels (Cao 1999), irrational and anti-modern.

Some of the Chinese intelligentsia openly declare that they worship America (An Qi 1998). One well-known Chinese dissident in exile declared that he would rather be an animal in a foreign country than a China person (Zheng 2004). When the invasion of Iraq started, one dissident academic in Hong Kong said that he envied the Iraqis because people all over the world protested against the US invasion and against the death of innocent people. Why was there nobody protesting against the death of people in China, as a result of accidents and SARS for instance (Wu 2003)?

Yu Jie, the initiator of the letter 'A Declaration by Chinese Intellectuals Supporting the US Government's Destruction of Saddam's Dictatorial Regime', says that Mao is the predecessor of Saddam, that human rights takes priority over national sovereignty and that the United States behaved multilaterally because US values were universal values of democracy and human rights (Yu Jie 2003b). President Bush arranged a special occasion to meet Yu Jie and a couple of other Chinese Christian converts in the White House in 2006 (Buckley 2006), a privilege that is usually given to personalities like His Holiness the Dalai Lama.

Liu Xiaobo, another prominent Chinese intellectual, who once declared that China could only be saved by being colonized for two or three hundred years (Chengdan 2003), argued that even if the US invasion were motivated by self-interest the war was good for humanity, as were all other wars that the United States participated in with the sole exception of the Vietnam War (Liu 2003). A BBC correspondent, commenting on the e-media debate by the Chinese on the Iraqi war, admits that these Chinese love America and are more pro-Bush than the Americans themselves (Wei 2003).[5]

The politics of joining the civilized world

The desire to identify with the currently dominant values and worldview is not only strong among the intelligentsia, but can also be seen implicitly within official Chinese government policy and personal statements. The television programme *He shang*, which denigrates Chinese tradition, was supported by the then CCP General Secretary Zhao Ziyang. In a recent book published in Hong Kong that details Zhao's ideas as conveyed in his conversations during the years of house arrest after his downfall during the Tian'anmen crackdown in 1989, Zhao argued that China should follow the United States because the interest of the United States corresponded to the interest of humanity (Zhao 2007). Another veteran CCP leader, Ren Zhongyi, argues that the democratic model of *san quan fen li* (the separation of the three constitutional powers: the executive, the judiciary and legislative) is an achievement of human civilization that has to be embraced (Zhang Deqin 2006).

The Chinese official line is most clearly evident in its pursuit of economic development by adopting the neoliberal rationalism. For example, though a developing country, China under the leadership of

Jiang Zemin and Zhu Rongji agreed to enter the WTO on condition that its market should be more open to the West than the mature capitalist economy of Japan. The former deputy foreign trade minister and chief negotiator of China's entry into the WTO, Long Yingtu, declared that the day when the world's major car manufacturers all settled their production in China would be the day China's motor industry won (http://www.fhy.net 2006). The development of special economic zones and the huge state investment in cities like Shanghai and Beijing are considered by some as designed to Europeanize China's south coast cities at the expense of what is referred to as 'Africanization' of the rural heartland (Zhang Peiyuan 2006).

Media agenda and identification with the West

That the Chinese political and intellectual elite are willing to identify with what they perceive to be advanced Western values can also be seen by how very often the Western, especially the US, media set the agenda of what is news and what is important for the Chinese.

> Twenty-four hours, day and night, for 20 days a billion Chinese viewers sat glued to their television sets as soldiers fought in Iraq. They watched live coverage of government leaders' speeches one after another, government press conferences one after another, official slogans and national flags one after another. They were watching government and military-approved journalists travelling, eating, sleeping, chatting and laughing with soldiers. These journalists were broadcasting live with 'their' troops. You might have thought it was just the classic propaganda of the communists and the communist-controlled media. In actuality, the Chinese were watching CNN and Rupert Murdoch's channels. From the first day of the war, the Chinese government handed over the country's five most popular TV channels to CNN and Murdoch. All the images and messages the Chinese audience got from their TV sets were filtered by CNN and Murdoch's people.
>
> (Li Xiguang 2005).

The Chinese official media has done an excellent job in promoting positive images of the United States. For instance according to one study (Sarabia-Panol 2006), the tone of coverage of the 9/11 attack on the United States by the Chinese daily newspaper the *China Daily* was 25 per cent positively pro-America, 75 per cent neutral and 0 per cent negative whereas the percentages were 9 per cent positive, 41 per cent neutral and 50 per cent negative in the India press and 19.6 per cent positive, 5.6 per cent neutral and 14.8 per cent negative in the Japanese press. More revealingly, 62.5 per cent of the sources of this complete lack of criticism of the United States were from Chinese national officials. According to another study, university students in China get their image and impression of how good the West and the United States are from the official Chinese media. 'The Chinese media talk about how good the United States is every day and sometimes too good to be true', the website commented.

When the Chinese central bureaucrats are impelled to be critical of the United States, the effect of the criticism is usually minimal. In recent years the Chinese government would respond to US criticism of its human rights record by issuing condemnations and even a White Paper on human rights abuses in America. My impression is that very few in China take the Chinese position seriously. Having been immunized by the BBC, VOA and Free Asia, with their constant publicity and promotion of the media agenda to expose the Chinese government as one of the worst political regimes on earth, why would the educated elite believe the conventional Chinese media whose function is openly declared to be propaganda? When Beijing temporarily halted publication of *Zero* magazine for its publication of an essay by Professor Yuan Weishi ,who argued that the impotent and corrupt political system and backward Chinese cultural values were ultimately responsible for China's humiliation at the hands of Western powers during the eighteen and nineteenth centuries, the decision aroused widespread derision and contempt.

Memoirs, values and identification

One of the earliest memoirs in English that had a huge impact on the Western is that by Nien Cheng (1987). Before the Cultural Revolution, Nien lived with her daughter in a big house in the middle of supposedly-communist Shanghai. They had three servants plus a part-time gardener to serve them. Nien's husband was the director of the Shanghai branch of the Ministry of Foreign Affairs of the Nationalist Government and later became the general manager of the Shanghai Office of Shell International Petrol Company. After her husband died Nien became an assistant to a British Shell manager with the title of advisor. But the Cultural Revolution radicalism meant that all the privilege disappeared overnight. Worse still, Nien Cheng tragically lost her only daughter. For Nien identification with Western values was almost automatic and natural, because she was part of the West before she became the 'enemy' of the revolution.

The interesting cases, and the ones that prove the thesis of this chapter, are those of the children of the revolution. Yang Xiaokai was once a teenage rebel and wrote one of the most radical revolutionary pamphlets, *Whither China,* at the age of 17, in his then name Yang Xiguang. Yang then went to the United States and did his PhD in economics at Princeton. He was later converted to Christianity and had a successful career as an economics professor at an Australian university. Before his unfortunate death in 2005 Yang tirelessly advocated neoliberal economic policies for China.

The most successful, that is the most popular and influential, memoir is surely that by expatriate Chinese Jung Chang. Chang naturally assumes that students of peasant background are 'semi-literate' and had 'little aptitude', while she was clever and deserved the best, including a generous Chinese government scholarship to study in Britain. Chang claims that she was the victim of a brutal regime but, In fact, as well as being a Red Guard, Jung Chang was the privileged daughter of China's Communist elite. It is a peculiarity of the reception of *Wild Swans* that it was told and read as a story of great personal suffering, when its author grew up with a wet-nurse, nanny, maid, gardener and chauffeur provided by the party, protected in a walled compound, educated in a special school for officials' children. As a Grade 10 official, her father was among the 20,000 most senior people in a country of 1.25 billion, and it was in this period that children of 'high officials' became almost a class of their own. Still, the enthusiastic Western audience of *Wild Swans* found something to identify in Jung Chang's perennial fear of being reduced to the level of the rest of the population, shuddering with her at the prospect that 'Mao intended me to live the rest of my life as a peasant' (Heartfield 2005).

It was during the supposedly most difficult times of her family that Chang managed to leave the countryside a few weeks after she was sent down, become a barefoot doctor, an electrician and then a university student, and finally receive a generous scholarship to study in the UK, the kind of career moves that were dreams for millions of young Chinese, all accomplished during the Cultural Revolution years before her father was officially rehabilitated.

For anyone to consider that such a personal account of contemporary China is less political is an illusion. There is no personal account outside the political context, and 'the personal can be political in a very literal sense' (Fitzgerald, 1999: 6). This is worth pointing out because few actually realize that 'all histories of China are partly autobiographical' (Fitzgerald 1999: 8). They are 'autobiographical' not only in the sense that writers such as Jung Chang and Nien Cheng write about their lives from which histories emerge, but also in the sense that their memoirs are artefacts which are the results of cultural exchange between China and the West in such a way that foreign readers and writers participate in making Chinese history.

It is certainly not an accidental attribute that Jung Chang felt more at home in the West (Chang 1991) and that Chai Ling and Li Lu, two well-known Tian'anmen student protest leaders, are now respectively a company executive and a stockbroker.[6] Those who became Christians also include one of the writers of the *He shang* script, Yuan Zhiming, who apparently has become a full-time preacher, and the active e-media dissident Ren Bumei. For these Chinese expatriates their identification with Western political and cultural values goes hand in hand with their criticism of China's past or present.

Many in the West are concerned that the CCP is too rigorous in oppressing freedom in China and that China is still an enclosed society. In other words, they are worried that China does not identify with the West enough and believe that is why China cannot be modern (Hutton 2007). In fact they need not worry. It is not just the expatriate Chinese in the West who want to identify with the West in their constructing of contemporary Chinese history. The mainstream Chinese intellectuals and professionals inside China have been trying to fulfil the same historical task. Some of these engineers of intellectual discourse, such as the whateverists examined above, may be considered to be on the fringe of Chinese bureaucratic establishment, but there are also many influential public figures who may be considered Americans in thoughts. Below are just a number of examples.

The issue of whether the collapse of communism in Russia initiated by Gorbachev and pushed through by Yeltsin was a success or failure is controversial in China because either way it has implications for interpreting China's reform and for its future direction. It is in this context that Ma Licheng and Lin Zhijun (1998) argued in their influential book *Jiaofeng* (Frontal Engagement) that whoever argues against the Russian reform is against the reform agenda in China.

Along similar line, Li Shenzhi, who served as Vice-President of the Chinese Academy of Social Sciences and the first President of the Chinese Association of American Studies, and who is considered the godfather of liberalism by many in China, asserted that Lenin was responsible for discontinuing Russia's process of modernization (Yiming 2003), that Mao was a bandit, warlord and tyrant and that China had to change, either through peaceful evolution or violent revolution. Li also declared that if China wanted to modernize it had to follow the United States and had to be prepared to be the grandson of the United States (Zhang Deqin 2006). In case any reader fails to appreciate what Li meant, it is worth pointing out that in the Chinese cultural context, to be someone grandson is to submit to an authority for wisdom and control.

Zhang Xianliang, a prominent novelist, argues that market capitalism is the best and 10,000 years (not just three cheers) to private ownership. Yu Guangyuan, an eminent political economist, argues that China needs market economy and that if there is a dispute on this it is not a dispute between socialism and capitalism but a dispute between the advanced and the backward (Zhang Hengzhi 2006). Li Yining, another influential economist, argues not only that to aim an equal end result for everyone in human society is wrong, but also that to create an equal starting point for every one is not possible. Instead, China should make use of the value of division of labour in a family: the elder brother goes to college while the second brother works to support him. Once you have this rationality then there is no sense of unfairness (Zhang Deqin 2006). Mao Yushi and Xu Liangying argue that modernization is Americanization, and globalization has to be on the basis of Western civilization (Yiming 2003).

The intellectual–business–political complex in contemporary China

Clearly, identification with liberal democracy and market capitalist values is not just about an intellectual debate. Some of these intellectual elite such as Li Yining have vast business and commercial interests. Others such as Yu Guangyuan are think tank heavyweights who give lectures to high-ranking party officials and draft policy papers. Moreover, descendants of most of the top CCP officials from Deng Xiaoping to Zhao Ziyang, and from Zhu Rongji to Jiang Zemin, have US connections (more on these connections in later chapters).

It is therefore not surprising that publication outlets that are critical of the Chinese government from the point of view of the left such as 中流 (*Mainstay*) and 真理的追求 (*Pursuit of Truth*) were banned. A website 中国工人网 (Chinese workers net) set up in 2005 that published the views and opinions of workers was banned in early 2006; the excuse for shutting down this workers' net set up by some poor workers was that they failed to pay the registration fee of 10 million RMB![7]

Conclusion: memories, identity, knowledge and truth

By arguing that memoirs and *suku* (telling of bitterness) of the Cultural Revolution are constructing history I do not intend to argue that there was no bitterness to tell. I only want to show how the telling is constructed. My thesis that the narrative of the Cultural Revolution has been closely connected with a speech act of political identity with liberal democracy and market capitalist values may be criticized on the basis that it is disproved by the fact that the majority of the Chinese bureaucrats of the CCP, which is anti-Western and dictatorial (the very antithesis of Western values of democracy and freedom, they would argue), also denounce the Cultural Revolution. Deng Xiaoping, for instance, confessed that it is difficult to say anything good about the Cultural Revolution because he suffered too much (Zhai 2006). I would argue that these Chinese officials endorse the attack on the Cultural Revolution not just because they were personally attacked during the period, but because they actually identify with a set of values that were different from those of the Cultural Revolution.

It is true that the CCP power holders of Deng's generation were also proponents and practitioners of the theory of class struggle. They came to denounce the Cultural Revolution only after they became the victims of that theory. However, that does not mean they are anti-Western. They are certainly not against market capitalism. Deng Xiaoping and many like him were not really Marxists but basically revolutionary nationalists who wanted to see China standing on equal terms with the great global powers. They were primarily nationalists and they participated in the Communist revolution because that was the only viable route they could find to Chinese nationalism. The two themes of nationalism and class struggle worked together well before 1949 (Dong 2006). But after 1949, the two themes could not fit together so well. For Liu Shaoqi and Deng Xiaoping class struggle was more a means to an end of achieving national unity and dignity. Once that goal had been accomplished the class struggle theme of the Marxist paradigm became irrelevant and the class struggle of the Maoist para-digm was seen as disastrously erroneous. The theme of national unity meant that political control had to remain tight, or democratic reform would lead to national disintegration. The theme of national dignity meant that China's economy needed to catch up with that of the West. Therefore, to embrace market capitalism was a natural course of action for them. What happened after the death of Mao proved this beyond dispute.

To conclude this chapter let us reiterate that, as Ricoeur majestically argues, there are not only repressed memories (more discussion on this in a later chapter), but also manipulated memories and forced memo-ries. Both memory and forgetfulness are subject to an intense manipulation by power. The power that manipulates memories can be that which suppresses certain kind of memories while promoting certain others. It is certainly in the interest of those in power within the CCP to promote the telling of bitterness and to ban memories that show the positive side of the Cultural Revolution.

What happened in 1985 in Xianyang of Shaanxi province is a telling example of this interest. A poster was put up on a wall on Northwest Cotton Factory No 1 in a very busy district. The title of the poster is *Wenhua da geming hao* (The Cultural Revolution was Good). In the poster the authors listed merits of the Cultural Revolution such as the building of the Nanjing Bridge, the creation of hybrid rice crops and the rise of people's consciousness. The poster alarmed not only the city, provincial authorities but also the central CCP. Beijing sent an investigative team to find out what the 'active reactionaries' were up to. The person found guilty was a young worker at a shoe factory. He was sentenced to ten years' jail and died in jail soon after arrest without any apparent cause (Wu Zhenrong and Deng Wenbi 2004).

Memories can also be manipulated by recourse to financial and intellectual assistance and rewards. This is especially so when memories are constructed in the West to suit Sinological orientalism.

> For the liberals of the West's *pensée unique*, Maoism, like all forms of socialism, is an aberration in itself. This a priori approach is completely ideological, reactionary, ahistorical and without scientific foundation, and it is of course taken up by the Chinese right. The right relies on invectives against the 'crimes of the Cultural Revolution' to refrain from analysing the realities of the Maoist phase.
>
> (Amin 2005: 132).

Finally the power that manipulates memories can be a form of knowledge that has truth and moral claims. This is the most effective power of all. It can abuse memories because it orientates memories to certain narrative and 'it is through the narrative function that memory is incorporated in the making of identity' (Ricoeur 2000:103). The kind of narrative is made of memories and forgetfulness that consist of a configuration of protagonists with identities that define action. This kind of knowledge, by manipulating memories, in turn legitimizes orders of power. To take a Foucauldian line, the power that is really persuasive is the one that is based on knowledge, knowing of history and the world. The prevalent knowledge held to be true globally is liberal democracy and market capitalism. The narrative of the Cultural Revolution that is true has to be premised on this knowledge.

3 Constructing history: memoirs, autobiographies and biographies in Chinese

Introduction: scope and rationale

Many memoirs, autobiographies and biographies have been written by authors who have a PRC national background. One category that has dominated the field comprises those written in Western languages, mainly in English, and published in the West; another has included those written in Chinese and published in mainland China, Hong Kong or Taiwan. While memoirs, autobiographies and biographies published elsewhere appear to be more 'objectively' critical of Mao than those published in mainland China, both English and Chinese language publications, ever since the 1980s, have tended to join the chorus of total condemnation of the Cultural Revolution whenever the subject is mentioned. These two categories of writings appear to have increasing importance in formulating specific political discourses and historical narratives and in influencing public perception and opinion of Mao and the Cultural Revolution.

Since the late 1990s, however, voices that challenge the dominant official or semi-official political discourse and historical narratives have also started to appear. Because no challenge to the mainstream discourse of total condemnation is officially allowed in mainland China, particularly in the conventional media, dissenting voices are mostly heard only from unofficial sources such as private conversations as well as the increasingly flourishing but technologically difficult to control e-media. This third category of 'unofficial' literature consists of piecemeal memories and personal testimonials as well as essays or even blogs about Mao and the Cultural Revolution. An evaluation and comparison of these three categories of literature is not only useful but also necessary.

Very little has done in this respect. Joshua A. Fogel (1997) is one of the few who have written about memoirs by Chinese writers. Fogel's work, however, is only a short study of what has been written about the Chinese communist 'philosopher' Ai Siqi. Zarrow (1999) and Kong (1999) have made some very thoughtful and insightful comments, but only on memoirs and biographies in English. Teiwes (1997) also touches on the subject but only talks about the benefits and pitfalls of interviewing CCP party historians and historical participants.

In this chapter I will not talk about the first and third categories, that is, memoirs, autobiographies and biographies in English, and e-media challenges to the mainstream historical narratives; these are discussed elsewhere in this study. Instead I will focus on the second category, that is, memoirs, autobiographies and biographies in Chinese.

Memoirs, autobiographies and biographies in Chinese: a literature survey

Since the late 1980s memoirs, biographies or autobiographies of some sort or another have become a publication phenomenon in China. Volumes and volumes turn out every year and almost every known public figure of the older generations, be it in the field of military, politics, or literature and art, has been written about.[1] After going through more than a couple of hundred of them I find that many writers of this group are cautious and tend to write impersonally without naming names when sensitive personalities are involved. Being sanctioned and encouraged by the Chinese authorities, they tend to fervidly denounce the fallen Gang of Four and Lin Biao while praising other rehabilitated CCP leaders. Their narratives are very often shrouded in the standard official rhetoric, full of statements and propositions but short of supporting evidence. When referring to sensitive political events or figures they usually toe the official line.

Two of the most influential biography writers are Quan Yanchi and Ye Yonglie.[2] Quan's biography of Mao, based on interviews with Mao's bodyguard of 15 years, Li Yinqiao, was a runaway success, so much so that some Hong Kong publishers published a couple of his later books (Quan 1991, 1992). Ye Yonglie (1988, 1990, 1991, 1992a, 1992b, 1993a, 1993b, 1993c, 1993d, 1993e, 1994a, 1994b, 1995 and 2002), a professional writer from Shanghai, has published biographies of Mao Zedong, Zhou Enlai, Jiang Qing, Chen Boda, Zhang Chunqiao, Wang Hongwen, Yao Wenyuan and many other well-known figures such as Ma Sicong and Fu Lei. Ye has managed to tread very cautiously between what is allowed by the Chinese authorities and what can attract a readership. Because he never steps out of the official line politically, he was also allowed to interview and write about sensitive personalities such as Wang Li and Guan Feng, the famous radical leaders during the Cultural Revolution. Sometimes, Ye would simply admit that there are things that cannot be revealed.

Biographical series

Apart from individual efforts there are a number of coordinated efforts in writing about a group of personalities as series. These include *Dangdai Zhongguo renwu zhuanji* (Biographies of Contemporary

Chinese Personalities), under the editorship of Deng Liqun, Ma Hong and Wu Heng (1991), the biographies of the ten marshals edited by Li Yong (1993), and *Anecdotes of and Meaningful Remarks by Well-Known Cultural Figures: A Series* (Yu Qing, 1994). Another series started since 1987 is the memoirs of the generals of the PLA, organized and published by the official army publisher in Beijing. These party and army officials usually have a special writing team with special funding from the government. When Peng Zhen wrote his memoirs he had a team of 40 to work for him (Xing Xiaoqun 2006). According to He Fang (2005), who has researched the memoirs of CCP personalities for his two-volume history of the CCP, very few memoirs can stand up to documentary examination, and many of those who write do so not only to glorify themselves but also to settle scores.

The 'Grand Historian' Sima Qian was supposed to have set up a paradigm for Chinese historiography which depicts personality vividly and provides realistic biographical accounts. However, modern Chinese historiography is full of examples of depicting personalities as caricatures, like Peking opera characters. Even Yan Jiaqi (Gao and Yan 1988), who considers himself a serious political scientist, now in exile, could not avoid this tendency in his portrayal, for instance, of Jiang Qing.[3]

Memoirs by veteran party leaders

Not surprisingly, most of the memoirs and biographies include something about the Cultural Revolution. However, while writers like Ye and Quan concentrate on personal lives to avoid political topics, social themes or taboo areas of the Cultural Revolution, some sensitive personalities themselves may avoid the subject of the Cultural Revolution altogether when writing memoirs. Thus, Bo Yibo (1989, 1991 and 1993), Hu Qiaomu (1994), Shi Zhe (1991) and Li Weihan (1986) all stop short of writing about the Cultural Revolution. Hu Qiaomu, who was often referred to as 'the pen of the Party', confessed that events beyond the 1950s were 'too complex' to write about.[4] Bo Yibo, on the other hand, only promised follow-up volumes. Wu Lengxi (1995), the chief editor of the *People's Daily* from 1957 to 1966, on the other hand, only talks in general terms in three pages about his dismissal during the Cultural Revolution and the conspiracy by Lin Biao and Jiang Qing. Deng Xiaoping's daughter Deng Maomao, in her two volumes remembering her father that were published with a great fanfare in the West, does indeed devote the second volume to the Cultural Revolution years (Deng 2000). However, a lot about the Cultural Revolution was brushed aside, and in these memoirs she hardly says anything about her father's role in casting hundred of thousands innocent Chinese into the enemy class of rightists or about his role in the disastrous Great Leap Forward, both events that helped shaped the way the Cultural Revolution developed (Xu Zidong 2006).

Autobiographical 'fiction'

There is a group of writers who write in Chinese and publish in China, apparently without too much constraint. Examples of this group are Lao Gui (1987), Zhou Changmin (1993), and Liang Xiaosheng (1988).[5] There are a number of reasons for the publication of these works without apparent censorship. First, the books fall in line with the official policy of condemning the Cultural Revolution. Second, they were published in the form of novels, which, according to the authorities, do not present a record of history. Third, they were published by minor publishers in remote provinces and thus initially escaped the central authorities' control. Fourth, they do not name real personalities. Finally, in general, these books are about ordinary people's ordinary lives and therefore sensitive and high-ranking CCP officials are not involved.

These so-called fictional books are actually autobiographical. Zhou Changmin's address is printed in his book, and thus I was able to contact him. He told me that every story in the book was a retelling of true events and only the names of the characters were not real. Xu Zidong (2006) has done a content analysis of about 50 novels of this kind and finds that they can be summarized into four categories: 1) victim stories, that is tales of good people being victimized by bad people; 2) tales with a moral, showing how the writers overcame the bad events in their lives; 3) stories of absurdity (as seen from today's point of view); and 4) stories of misunderstanding and mistakes. Zhou Changmin's memoirs have all these elements.

Family memories

Many others, like Deng Maomao, have written about relatives who were prominent CCP personalities. These include Zhu Min (1996), Dong Bian et al. (1992), Dian Dian (1987), Zhang Hanzhi (1994a and 1994b), Liu Siqi and Wang Hebing (1993), Wang Guangmei and Liu Yuan (2000), Wang Guangying and Liu Pingping et al. (1992).[6] A brief examination of these memoirs shows that most writers and their parents were portrayed as the victims of the Cultural Revolution radicalism but were restored to positions of power and glory or vindicated later.[7]

Understandably, memoirs by the victims or relatives of victims of the Cultural Revolution radicalism often tell stories of brutality and experiences of suffering. Generally, they do not blame Mao directly and personally, but only indirectly by pointing their fingers at the Gang of Four and

Lin Biao. Recently, however, Liu Yuan (Cai Yongmei 2000) and Dian Dian (Dan Shilian 2000) named names and held Mao responsible for their fathers' suffering. Liu Yuan and Wang Guangmei (2000), in a very subtle way of condemning Mao, argue that whatever was successful in the People's Republic of China was the result of joint efforts of Mao and Liu and whatever went wrong was when Mao and Liu Shaoqi went their separate ways.

In her memoirs, Zhang Hanzhi, however, could not blame anyone explicitly for the downfall of her husband Qiao Guanhua, because Qiao was supposed to be a follower of the Gang of Four.[8] Zhang's brief account of the events that led to her husband's demise is so full of innuendo and insinuation that a reader who does not know the intricacies of the inner party struggle would not have a clue as to what she is talking about. Several times, she points the finger of accusation at Wang Hairong and Tang Wensheng, two women who had high profiles during the later years of the Cultural Revolution. The two, working in the Ministry of Foreign Affairs and as Mao's interpreters, were among the few who were able to have access to him in the last couple of years of his life. Zhang does not name the two women but refers to them as *tongtian renwu* (personalities who had access to the Mandate of Heaven).

Not allowed to remember

It is important to point out that those who fell after the downfall of Lin Biao and the arrest of the Gang of Four are not permitted to write memoirs or autobiographies. Or if they are allowed to write, which occurs rarely, they have to conceal a lot, as Zhang Hanzhi does. Those people, who may be called post-Cultural Revolution victims, may indeed have something quite different to say.[9] They are allowed neither to write nor to give interviews, or if they are it is under strict guidelines or constraint. Though active participants of the Cultural Revolution, like Zhang Chengxian (2002), Guo Yingqiu with Wang Junyi (2002), Nie Yuanzi (2005b), She Ruhui (2004) and Wang Li (2001) wrote memoirs, theirs are explicitly 'self-censored'. Nie Yuanzi , Kuai Dafu and Han Aijing, three of the most prominent Cultural Revolution student radicals, all face pressure of many kinds not to say anything that is 'sensitive' (Ding Dong 2006).

The personalities in this category, that is, those who are not allowed to talk *freely* but may have something to say that is very different from the now accepted truth, are many. Here I will just list some of those who rose during the Cultural Revolution and fell immediately afterwards, excluding the Gang of Four, Lin Biao and his lieutenants. Apart from the well-known personalities such as Hua Guofeng, Wang Dongxing, Chen Xilian, Mao Yuanxin (Mao's nephew), Li Na and Li Min (Mao's daughters) and Chen Yonggui, there are many less well-known ones who might have a lot to say about the Cultural Revolution.[10] These include Sun Jian (once a vice-premier), Sun Yuguo (once Deputy Commander of the Shenyang Military Region), Guo Fenglian (a female leader from Dazhai, a commune village that was promoted as a model by Mao), Zhuang Zedong (three times consecutively World Table Tennis Champion and once head of China's Ministry of Sports), Wu Guixian (a female textile worker promoted to the vice-premiership), Lü Yulan a female peasant who was once Party Secretary of Henan province), Wei Fengying (a female worker promoted to be a member of CCP Central Committee), Xing Yanzi (a female educated youth who was once Party Secretary of Tianjin), Li Suwen (a saleswoman promoted to be the Deputy Chairman of the National People's Congress (NPC)), Gu Atao (a peasant woman promoted to be a member of CCP Central Committee), Zhang Tiesheng (an educated youth promoted to be a member of the Standing Committee of the NPC), Mao Diqiu (a peasant in Chairman Mao's home town promoted to be a member of the Standing Committee of the NPC), Wang Xiuzhen (a female textile worker promoted to be Party Secretary of Shanghai), Chen Ada (a worker and once a member of the Standing Committee of the NPC), Yu Huiyong (a musical teacher who was Minister of Culture before his arrest), Hao Liang (Peking opera actor who was Vice-Minister of Culture), Liu Qingtang (a ballet dancer promoted be a Vice-Minister of Culture), Tong Xiangling (Peking opera actor and a deputy to the NPC), Li Qinglin (a school teacher who in 1972 wrote to Mao complaining about his son's difficulties as a result of *Shangshan xiaxiang* and subsequently became a member of the Standing Committee of the NPC).[11]

It is worth pointing out that the people mentioned above were mostly promoted to top positions during the Cultural Revolution from very low social status and many of them were women. This is a clear indication of the Cultural Revolution's radical affirmative policy of promoting women's status and of an attempt to break down the established CCP bureaucratic hierarchy. These people were swept out of the CCP officialdom as soon as Deng Xiaoping and his followers came back to power and have been silenced since. Recently, there has been some relaxation of control, and memoirs of such personalities appeared in Hong Kong as in the case of Chen Boda (Chen Xiaonong 2006) and Nie Yuanzi (2005b). All the same, the trace of strong censorship or self-censorship is obvious in these accounts.

The truth, the whole truth, and nothing but the truth

In any case there is no reason to believe that all those who are allowed to talk are telling us 'the truth, the whole truth, and nothing but the truth', even if they actually want to. Yu Erxin (2006b) provides a good example to illustrate the point. In the memoirs General Mo Wenhua wrote in 1961, he stated that Deng Xiaoping, then Political Commissar of the Seventh Army, left the army in the middle of a fierce battle and went to Shanghai via Vietnam, ostensibly to report the situation to the CCP leadership. Soon after the publication of his memoirs Mo was dismissed from his army post, for no apparent reason. Then in August 1966, when Deng was stripped of his official positions because he was accused of being the number two capitalist roader, Mo was informed that the 1961 disciplinary action against him had been wrong. In his revised memoirs, which appeared in the 1990s, however, Mo says nothing of his assertion that Deng ran away in the middle of a battle. And he blames Lin Biao for his own dismissal in 1961.

Another example of how the Chinese authorities work to make sure publications follow what is allowed officially is the inclusion or exclusion in selected volumes of important CCP leaders' speeches. During the 1980s, speeches of Liu Shaoqi were collected into volumes for publication.[12] None of Liu's speeches made between June 1958 and the summer of 1960, a gap of two years, were included in this official publication compiled by the CCP Central Office of Documentary Research (Lao Tian 2006b). The reason why those speeches are not collected seems to be that some of Liu's speeches during this period were clearly advocating reckless policies and practices of the Great Leap Forward. The post-Mao official line is that the Great Leap Forward famine was all Mao's fault.

Some common themes on Mao and the Cultural Revolution

Most writers of these memoirs, autobiographies and biographies in Chinese assume or argue that the Cultural Revolution was a ten-year disaster and that China's economy was on the brink of collapse by 1976. On the other hand, few writers writing within China openly denounce Mao completely. Mao was blamed for being the initiator of the Cultural Revolution, but many accusations were made against 'the evil people', such as the Gang of Four, Lin Biao and Kang Sheng, who had usurped power and abused their positions to persecute the loyal, upright, honest and intelligent people. Most of these writers in China do not dwell on the subject of Mao's intention to launch the Cultural Revolution. Among those who do, few are inclined to argue that Mao was ideologically motivated, even though the ideological interpretation was officially presented by the CCP 1981 Resolution.[13]

Mao the person and absence of ideas

These writers tend to accept that Mao was a supreme military strategist, a brilliant peasant leader, an unbeatable politician, the only person who could lead the CCP to final victory, the father of national unity and founder of the PRC. Many writers indicate that Mao was not interested in reading original works by Marx and Engels, that he always wanted to read classic Chinese books and that his huge bed was surrounded with *xianzhuang shu* (thread-bound traditional Chinese books). Meng Jingyun, one of the two women who stayed with Mao in his later years, witnessed that the classic *Zizhi tongjian* (Comprehensive Record as a Mirror for Rulers) was with Mao all the time and he read it again and again (Guo 1990).

As for Mao's ideas and policies after 1957, few writers bother to contemplate them. They are assumed either to be excuses for power struggle or as belonging to a romantic or poetic irrational utopia that does not deserve serious consideration. Every positive contribution Mao made in his life had occurred before 1957. After 1957 Mao did nothing right and contributed nothing positive to China and the Chinese people. The emperor would sacrifice the well-being of the Chinese people for his personal power or to satisfy his personal whims such as the Great Leap Forward and the Cultural Revolution. This is the late-Mao thesis that I will come back later. This type of narrative of PRC history presents1962 to 1965 as the 'golden period', the years after the disastrous Great Leap Forward and before the calamitous Cultural Revolution, the period when Liu and Deng were fully in charge of the daily business of governing China. This is in sharp contrast to Mao's own assessment (1967a) that work was not done properly between 1961 and 1965 because a proper form by which the dark side of China could be exposed 'comprehensively and from the bottom up' had not been found. For Mao the proper form was the Cultural Revolution.

According to the post-Mao narratives of contemporary Chinese history, just about every time loyal officials such as Liu Shaoqi, Zhou Enlai, Chen Yun and Deng Xiaoping, had rescued the Chinese economy from the brink of a disaster, Mao the emperor would bring out his personal pet – 'class struggle' – to wreck the economy. Thus, the Socialist Education Movement, the Cultural Revolution, the Movement to Criticize Lin Biao and Confucius in 1974, the Movement of Anti-Rightist Reverse of Verdict in 1975 and the Movement to Criticize Deng Xiaoping in 1976 were either wrongly initiated by Mao himself or misled by the Gang of Four, for no reason other than manipulation of power struggle, all of which damaged the development of the Chinese economy.

The Movement to Criticize Lin Biao and Confucius is accused of being a scheme to victimize Zhou Enlai by innuendo and insinuation. In the late 1980s, Chinese writers on this subject either assumed or argued that it was Jiang Qing and Zhang Chunqiao who distorted Mao's edict so as to usurp power from Zhou. However, since the 1990s the standard line has been that it was Mao who wanted to criticize

Zhou Enlai. For the Chinese writers inside China, a rational explanation of why Mao wanted to turn against his seemingly most loyal
lieutenant is simply not an issue, because to seek an answer would
lead to questioning the very discourse of personal power struggle at
the emperor's court.

Apart from personal intrigues and court conspiracies, Mao's sexual
life is also of great interest. Wang Nianyi, one of the foremost Chinese
historians on the Cultural Revolution, though not putting much in writing, is very serious about the sex story.[14] It is not just that Chinese readers, like those in the West, like to know about the personal lives of the
famous. For the Chinese, to have many women at the court for sexual
pleasure is one of the primary indicators of being an emperor. In traditional China, an emperor could have as many concubines as he chose.
How many women Mao possessed for sexual pleasure is something the
Chinese talk about a lot privately.[15]

With extensive experience of interviewing Chinese party historians
and political participants, Teiwes thinks that Chinese 'scholars of party
history are thoroughly empiricist in the best traditions of Chinese
historiography' but notes that unless one is a member of the inner
circle even a high-ranking participant can be vulnerable prey to 'the
notoriously unreliable hearsay of "small lane news"'(Teiwes 1997: 341).
As Fogel's case study of Ai Siqi shows, if a personality is considered a
positive figure by the current Chinese authorities, memoirs, biographies and autobiographies can be valuable; they may offer more
personal details and the character can be three-dimensional (Fogel
1997). Even in these cases, however, much of the literature is organized
to settle the old score, to enhance and advocate certain positions and to
discredit other positions or personalities.

Despite the fact that those writers of memoirs, autobiographies and
biographies come from diversified backgrounds, have had different
experiences in their lives and write with a variety of motives, the
uniformity in their approach and technique is striking. This uniformity
cannot be explained away by only referring to official censorship in
China. There must be something deeper and more fundamental,
perhaps some traditional legacy of historiography.

Personal power struggles at Mao's court

The theme of the power struggles and conspiracies of the inner court is
the first common denominator of these writings. Although the CCP
official version of the Cultural Revolution dictates that Mao launched
the Cultural Revolution because of his misperception and misunderstanding of the issue of class and class struggle, writers like Ye Yonglie
do not bother to refer to the issue, let alone take it into consideration.

The popular story line of power struggle goes like this: Mao first wanted to get rid of Liu Shaoqi, then he wanted to finish with Lin Biao, and then he wanted to topple Zhou Enlai. In other words, whoever held the most powerful position after himself, and was therefore most threatening to his personal power, was Mao's target.

Many of these writers accept the late-Mao thesis of two different Maos, the early and later Mao. The later Mao became an emperor, like any other emperor in Chinese history, only more talented and more brutal. Mao was the only CCP leader who was thoroughly read in ancient Chinese history and imperial conspiracy, and was therefore an extremely skilful power player. His supreme strategy was to make use of one faction in the CCP to defeat his designated enemy, and then use another faction to defeat his former supporters.

In fact, as Teiwes' research has demonstrated, Mao's supreme position in the CCP after the establishment of the PRC was never and could never be seriously challenged. However, most of these Chinese writers do not attempt to come to terms with this fact. It is true that more and more writings begin to draw our attention to the fact that Lin Biao hated formality and he himself (if not his wife Ye Chun and son Lin Liguo) might never have wanted to be the chairman of the state, a position supposedly threatening to Mao (Teiwes and Sun 1996). However, the question of whether Mao and Lin had disagreement on the issue of policies has never been properly addressed. Only recently in his memoirs published in Hong Kong does Wu Faxian (2006) reveal that as early as in 1968 Lin Biao and Mao openly disagreed over the direction of the Cultural Revolution. The question of why Mao, a dying man himself, wanted to criticize another dying man, Zhou Enlai, is not asked. It is simply assumed to be a personal power struggle. But struggle for what?

What were the roles of the ordinary Chinese men and women during the era of Mao? They are depicted as simply misled, deceived and cheated. The Red Guards were fanatic mobs and the workers and peasants were uneducated idiots who only knew how to follow their emperor blindly like ants.[16] All that mattered was the elite power struggle. Thus, Jiang Qing's ultimate ambition was to ascend to a position like that of Empress Wu Zetian.[17] According to these writers, Jiang Qing deserved to be despised and held in contempt by the old revolutionaries because this 'third-rate' actress in the decadent Shanghai should not have seduced the Chairman of the CCP.

Another radical, Jiang Qing's close associate Zhang Chunqiao, was also depicted as a Peking opera villain. All Zhang Chunqiao wanted was to climb up to higher positions. He had no beliefs of his own and all he did in Shanghai during the Cultural Revolution was to usurp power. Kang Sheng was a *goutou junshi* (dog-headed adviser) whose only ambition and pleasure was to frame the good and the honest. For a long time and with the exception of few writers such as Guan Weixun, Wen Feng and Zhang Zhenglong, Lin Biao was depicted as a *liangmianpai* (double-faced cheat). Lin Biao said all the good words that could have been said in public and did all the wicked deeds that could have been done behind the scenes (*haohua shuojing, huaishi zuo jue*).[18]

It is true that Lin praised Mao with extreme flattery but not subservient language (Teiwes and Sun 1996), but Lin was also one of the very few people who dared to confront Mao and did so on several occasions. For instance, during the Long March soon after the Zunyi Conference, Lin Biao wrote a letter demanding that Mao give the command of the army to Peng Dehuai because Lin thought Mao had made the Red Army soldiers move forwards and backwards without any apparent strategy. On the May Day parade in 1971, Lin broke away from the usual protocol of arriving earlier at the Tian'anmen Rostrum to meet Mao. Instead he kept Mao waiting by arriving late. Then he left earlier, deliberately without saying anything to Mao. On the other hand, Lin Biao was never reported to have attacked Mao behind Mao's back.

In these Chinese writings, the politics was played out as court intrigue. The narrative is a copy of the classic Chinese novel of *Romance of the Three Kingdoms*, only the three kingdoms are not states but three CCP leadership compounds: Zhongnanhai (where Mao and Zhou lived and worked), Maojiawan (where Lin Biao lived) and Diaoyutai (where Jiang Qing and the Cultural Revolution Small Group worked). By the same token, the question of policies and ideas is irrelevant. The 19 years of PRC history from 1957 to 1976 are seen simply as a succession of Mao's consistent errors, stupidity and fantasies, which were made use of by the evil people surrounding him, but luckily resisted and corrected by the wise, the educated – the best people in Chinese society – who were later vindicated.

The big picture of China in the international environment of the cold war is ignored. The issue of alternative models for modernizing China is never considered. A whole range of social and political issues in such a complex society is irrelevant. The affirmative policy towards women in society is now forgotten.[19] The attempt to reform the educational system (Pepper 1996) was interpreted as simply intended to destroy China's education. The policies to narrow the gap between mental and manual labour, between the urban and the rural, and between industry and agriculture were anti-intellectual and anti-human. The experiment to reform literature and art, notably in the Peking opera (Dao 1994), so as to reverse a thousand years of practice of writing about and writing for the elite is seen simply as a plot to make everyone ignorant, and is depicted in black and white terms as cultural obscurantism.

According to this version of history, in the space of 19 years, no economic progress was made.[20] Had there not been the Great Leap Forward and the Cultural Revolution, China would have developed its economy in the same way as Hong Kong, Taiwan, Singapore and South Korea. The question of size, the tortuous path dependence and issues of international politics are cast aside for the sake of emotional speculation. In economic development, writers see no connection, no cause and effect, between what happened in the Mao era and what happened in the post-Mao period. It is as if the China's economy sprang suddenly from a desert after the death of Mao.

Though the above generalization of characteristics does not apply to every author – Bo Yibo for example is far more sophisticated than what is sketched here – I believe the sketch is an accurate description of the general picture: the power struggle narrative manufactured by the post-Mao elite.

Narrative style: jishi wenxue

A common characteristic employed by most biographers in China, though not so much by memoir and autobiography writers, is the *jishi wenxue* style of writing, literally meaning 'literature of recording the actual events'. In the name of being *shengdong bizhen* (vivid, and lively), said to be the heritage of China's ancient historian Sima Qian, anecdotes are turned into a story of real characters, with their dialogues presented in quotation marks. It is fiction in form, but claims to consist of historical facts. Thus, facts are mixed with imagination and arguments are replaced by fantasies. Few writers bother to give any footnotes and there are never any citations of sources.

In the extreme version of this *jishi wenxue*, positive characters have dignified postures and movements. They speak the right language and think the right thoughts. They look good and they walk straight. Negative characters are ugly and stupid. Whatever they do or say is despicable and to be condemned. Positive characters are models to be copied and their behaviour is to be imitated, whereas negative characters are to be despised and hated. There is no ambiguity or ambivalence and the characters involved are either clear-cut goodies or straightforward baddies. The goodies possess no vices and are thoroughly good, even before they are born. The baddies are bad from beginning to the end.

The case of Chen Yi, the Minister of Foreign Affairs when the Cultural Revolution started in 1966, is a good example of this version of history. Chen is portrayed as an upright and outspoken goodie who was against the Cultural Revolution from the very beginning and was critical of the baddie Lin Biao from the start. But in fact Chen was very active in following the Cultural Revolution ideas initially. He named three of his senior officals as *niugui sheshen* (cow ghosts and snake demons – a term referring to bad elements, from which the term 'cowshed' was later taken to refer to the Cultural Revolution victims) at the beginning of the Cultural Revolution. Chen openly called his audience to support Mao's struggle against the capitalist reactionary line (meaning against Liu and Deng) and he said he had to learn from Lin Biao because Lin Biao was Mao's best student (Wang Li 2001: 686). Like Chen Yi, Zhou Enlai also tried very hard to follow Mao during the Cultural Revolution (Wang Li 2001: 924). The Chinese official version of history tries to avoid these inconvenient facts.

Another example can be seen in the way Ye Yonglie portrays Chen Boda as a traitor of the Communist Party. In the history of the CCP revolution the issue of renegade or traitor to the revolutionary cause has been treated very seriously (Dutton 1992 and 2005). This is understandable in a sense because the CCP started as an underground movement and had enormous damage done to its organization by insiders who changed their coat. Liu Shaoqi was expelled from the party during the Cultural Revolution because he was supposedly proved to be a traitor. The accusations against Liu and others such Bo Yibo have been judged groundless since the Cultural Revolution, but the post-Mao authorities still continue the practice from which they themselves had suffered. Chen Boda had been accused of being a traitor and Ye Yonglie, in his biography of Chen, still writes as if it was a fact that Chen was a traitor (Wang Li 2001: 752).

Chinese tradition of historiography

Writers such as Ye Yonglie are not only very much immersed in these techniques but also seem to be aware of their role of constructing history along the Chinese historiographic tradition. Traditional Chinese historiography concentrates on four techniques: *ji zhu, zhuanxiu, kaozhu* and *hengping* (record/archives, compiling, examination/verification and evaluation/commentary). The last is the most powerful and most practised: the task of historiography is to make judgements of who is good and bad so that later generations can follow and copy them as examples and counter-examples.

In this tradition there was very little practice of evaluating the methodology of historiography, very little criticism of historiography itself. The idea of historical methodology started in Tang Dynasty, very late in Chinese history, when Liu Zhiji wrote *shi tong* (understanding history). But Liu was ignored by later establishment historiography. Even *Yongle dadian* (the Yongle Encyclopaedia), which was meant to include everything known by humans at that time, did not include *shi tong*. This is not surprising as Chinese historiography was designed to write history that serves the present (Unger 2002). As early as the Spring and Autumn Period historians were determined to make 'the disloyal treacherous officials fear'. Qing historians were ordered to use the same technique and ideology to evaluate Ming history so that examples could be set for Qing officials. The function of historians was to establish examples for officials by condemning the bad and by praising the good. According to Chen Shengyong (1994), this is the case with the important classical history books *Zuo zhuan* (The Commentary of Zuo), *Shi ji* (The Historical Record), *Han shu* (The Book of Han), *San guo zhi* (The Record of the Three Kingdoms) and *Zizhi tongjian* (The Comprehensive Record as a Mirror for Rulers).

Memories as history

Despite the limitations of this category of literature, occasional exceptions can provide insights and valuable information if one ploughs through them with a critical attitude. In one book, for instance, Quan provides some personal insight into Peng Dehuai's downfall. Quan reveals that at the 1959 Lushan Conference, Mao, who was intending to cool down the Great Leap Forward, initially did not find Peng's letter criticizing the Great Leap Forward too offensive. Mao thought that Peng had *'zichanjieji dongyaoxing* (bourgeois vacillation) and only commented that Peng always gave him negative material. Mao still intended to conclude the conference as had been scheduled. However, when Mao gave his final speech, Peng chose not to sit with other members of the Standing Committee of the Politburo, who, according to the customary hierarchical arrangement, were to sit on a (raised) platform facing the less prominent party officials. Instead, Peng took a seat at a back row among the lesser mortals, with his head recently shaven bald, a clear sign of challenge. Mao remarked that if the army did not want to follow him he could lead another guerrilla war. According to Quan this remark was directed at Peng, who was the Minister of Defence, a typical dry humour of Mao.

After the speech, Mao and Peng bumped into each other when they came out of the conference hall. Mao smiled at Peng, and took the initiative in greeting him and invited him to have a talk, to which Peng replied in a loud voice, 'There is nothing to talk about!' and walked off. This encounter took place in front of many senior CCP leaders. Later when Mao went back to his residence several 'CCP leaders' came to offer critical remarks about Peng and suggested to Mao that the conference should be prolonged to solve the problem of 'the struggle between the two lines'. Quan's account offers an angle that is absent from the version offered by Li Rui, which is widely accepted in the

West. Quan's account is insightful because it reveals the role of other players. Moreover, it reveals, from a bodyguard's point of view, the consequences of breaching the accepted norms and values of maintaining unity at least on the surface, and of respecting hierarchy in Chinese political culture.

There are other valuable insights and information found in these memoirs and biographies. For instance, Wu Lengxi's memoirs clearly show that the theory of revisionism and continuous revolution articulated in the *Nine Commentaries on the Soviet Union's Revisionism of Marxism-Leninism* was not an excuse for power struggle but a result of serious ideological consideration in the context of what was happening in Eastern Europe and the Soviet Union. Wu De's oral history account (2004) shows that for Mao at that time there was a genuine fear of a revisionist coup, though clearly from hindsight there was not even an attempt at one. According to Wu De, General Ye Jianying had shuffled the Beijing garrison, ordered two divisions of the field army to Beijing under instructions from Mao and Lin Biao. It was only after the general had taken control of the public security in the capital in May 1966 that Mao felt it was safe for him to return to it.

Wu De (2004) also reveals that Mao actually advised Li Xuefeng, the new boss of Beijing after the downfall of the former Mayor Peng Zhen, to go to Inner Mongolia or Tianjin to escape the heat of the mass movement as the Cultural Revolution unfolded. Clearly, Mao wanted to protect the party officials, or at least some of them, but at the same time he wanted them exposed and criticized by the masses. This is also shown by Mao's talk about Jian Bozan, the well-known historian of Beijing University. Mao said that Jian wrote so many books that we could not criticize him since we had not read them. We had better let the students who read him do the criticism, Mao said. Mao applied the same mass line with the issue of education reform. He said that as we did not know the profession we had to rely on the masses, that is, the students and teachers to carry out the reforms; hence the rationale for closing down schools before the students had a say on education reform.

Some of the memoirs, biographies and autobiographies by army officers reveal that though they never wanted to question their loyalty to Mao they passively resisted and actively undermined some of the Cultural Revolution efforts. For instance, some army officers recalled how they did not like Jiang Qing or Yao Wenyuan's instruction to criticize Deng Xiaoping (Xiao Ke 1997, Wang Ping 1992, Li Zhimin 1993 and Yang Qian and Zhang Zuoguang 1987). According to Xu Hailiang's recent interview study, in the Wuhan Incident of 1967 the army officers of the local garrison not only kidnapped the Cultural Revolution radicals Wang Li and Xie Fuzhi but also directly challenged Zhou

Enlai when he went to Wuhan to deal with the Wuhan situation. In fact the Incident, which took place under Mao's nose, was intended to give him a warning, as the army officers knew he was in Wuhan at that time (Xu 2005). Mao indeed took notice of the warning and the Cultural Revolution radicals Wang Li and Guan Feng were dismissed not long after the Incident.

Conclusion: discourse, narratives and memories

Just as there is reason to question the historiography approach taken by the Confucian scholars, so there is no reason not to question contemporary memoirs, biographies and autobiographies whose approach is similar. Even in the Western context, where there is a higher degree of scholarly scrutiny, memoirs, biographies and autobiographies cannot be taken at face value. As the distinguished English biographer Richard Holms says, 'biography is essentially and by its very origin disputable' (Hacking 1995:238). That this is the case can be demonstrated by a book in this genre that is widely known in the West, *Wild Swans* by Jung Chang. In a fine study of Chang's *Wild Swans* and Yang's *Spider Eaters*, Kong argues that Chang's memoirs are 'self-invention', 'idealized self-justification' (Kong Shuyu 1999:241), and 'full of imaginative reconstruction of events, using hindsight to alter her recollections' (1999:246). Chang 'has altered her story to suit the wishes of hindsight and her market audience, and ... her memory has changed past events to make her behaviour seem more decisive and less shameful' (1999:247).

Throughout this book, I have consistently argued that how one understands the Cultural Revolution depends on what theoretical framework or approach one adopts. The discourse that was taken for granted at the time of the Cultural Revolution can be judged very differently when different approaches are employed. By this I mean the logic, the rationale and language at the time when history was taking place can either be judged on its own terms or on different terms. On its own terms of the Cultural Revolution discourse, the Chinese people and the Chinese leadership were rational beings like any other and had a set of beliefs and perceptions to regulate their behaviour.

Now the dominant beliefs and perceptions are different and therefore it is to be expected that writers of biographies, memoirs and autobiographies use contemporary beliefs and perceptions to write about past history. The term theoretical framework can be replaced by another term, 'interpretive category', used by Hacking when he talks about memory restructuring. Hacking argues that we have a tendency to specify the past through actions that fall under a new interpretive category, and to think of actions or incidents as 'semantic contagion'. If

I begin to think of my past as one of 'wasted opportunity'; I will start to formulate actions and incidents that admit to this description.

If the writer of a biography, memoirs or autobiography begins to use the interpretive category of power struggle and economic disaster to look at Mao and the Cultural Revolution, then he or she will find evidence to prove that thesis. The category of memoirs, biographies and autobiographies in Chinese has done exactly that.

4 *Mao, The Unknown Story*: an intellectual scandal

Introduction: hyper-promotion of a book

Mao: The Unknown Story by Jung Chang and Jon Halliday became a best seller soon after it was released in the UK, Australia and New Zealand in 2005. The book was promoted by such media frenzy that one of the reviews by the British *Guardian* is titled 'The book that will shake the world'. The BBC programme *Off the Shelf* – more commonly devoted to fiction – gave a 'dramatic' reading of excerpts of the book in a 'voice dripping with cynicism and irony' (Weil 2006). One of the reviewers calls the book 'a work of unanswerable authority. ... Mao is comprehensively discredited from beginning to end in small ways and large; a murderer, a torturer, an untalented orator, a lecher, a destroyer of culture, an opium profiteer, a liar' (Hensher 2005).

The Australian newspaper, a broadsheet paper, collected various trend-setting writers and journalists in Australia and asked them to choose a 2005 Book of the Year. One of the choices by a senior journalist, Nicolas Rothwell is *Mao: The Unknown Story*. This is what he said: reading the book about 'the 20th century's most bloodstained dictator was a litmus event. ... I cannot recall finishing a book that inspired in me such sharp feelings of nausea, horror and despair' (Rothwell 2005: R5)

Jonathan Mirsky (2005a, 2005b), a seasoned journalist who writes for papers such as the British *Observer* and *New York Times* states that the book proves that Mao 'was as evil as Hitler or Stalin, and did as much damage to mankind as they did'. Montefiore (2005) declares, 'Mao is the greatest monster of them all – the Red Emperor of China'. 'China's Monster, Second to None' is the title of another review in the *New York Times* (Kakutani 2005), whose author declares that the book makes 'an impassioned case for Mao as the most monstrous tyrant of all times'. In the *New York Times Book Review* Nicholas D. Kristof (2005) declares the book is 'magnificent biography' and a 'magisterial' work. The last Governor of Hong Kong, Chris Pattern, and the influential German *Spiegel* declared their endorsement of the book. Andrew Nathan could not bring himself to endorse the blatant violation of scholarly norms in the book but still thinks the book contains jade (Nathan 2005). For Willliam Hutton (2005), an influential British political commentator:

Whether it's the news that Mao never actually marched in long stretches of the Long March but was, instead, carried in a bamboo litter he designed himself, or of the scale of his purges and executions, this is a catalogue of disclosures that overturns almost all our received wisdom. The impact will be substantial. It's an impressive achievement.

(Hutton 2005)

'Chang's new book is actually a vast work of scholarship rather than an emotionally-charged personal attack,' asserts Thorpe (2005). Chang and Halliday cast new and revealing light on nearly every episode in Mao's tumultuous life, claims Yahuda (2005), a veteran scholar of the London School of Economics.

Scholarship, what scholarship?

Of course, anyone can make any claims about anything. What is special about *Mao: The Unknown Story* is that the claims are supposed to have been backed up by scholarship and painstaking research. What has impressed journalists, political commentators and some academics alike is that Jung Chang and Jon Halliday claim to have consulted something like 1,200 written sources, the majority of them in Chinese, and to have interviewed 400 people. The book has an impressive display of 68 pages of notes. It took the husband and wife co-authors more than a decade to finish the book, we are told.

The interviewee list

Let us first start with the impressive list of people whom the authors claim to have interviewed. These include dignitaries such as András Hegedüs, a prime minister of Hungary, Prince Mikasa, brother of the Japanese Emperor Hirohito, Eugenio Anguiano, a certain Mexican ambassador to Beijing, Frank Corner, a foreign minister of New Zealand, and Lech Walesa, former President of Poland. Of course His Holiness the Dalai Lama must be included in the list. With enormous financial resource and prestige from the success of *Wild Swans*, Chang could interview anyone she wished. But the question is: what does Lech Walesa or a prime minister of Hungary know about Mao or China?

The list of course also includes many who do or could claim to know about Mao or China, such as Joseph Needham, Steven Fitzgerald (first Australian ambassador to PRC China), Mao's daughter Li Na, Mao's grandson Mao Xinyu, or Liu Shaoqi's widow Wang Guangmei. At first sight such an extensive list might make the book appear authoritative. However, it begs a number of questions. First, one would like to see whether the interviewees have said anything that is relevant to the content or arguments of the book about Mao.

Second, we would like to know how Chang and Halliday dealt with interview information that was contrary to what they set out to prove. Professor Frederick Teiwes is a well-known scholar on CCP elite politics and he is listed in the book's acknowledgements. According to Teiwes, he had met Jung Chang a couple of times but could not say anything substantial about the subject on Mao because Chang would not listen unless what he had to say suited her predetermined ideas. An indication of what Teiwes thinks of the book is that he declined to participate in the special issue to review the book organized by *The China Journal*.

Yes, we are told that Chang interviewed Mao's daughter and a grandson, but do we know what Li Na said about her father and what Mao Xinyu said about his grandfather? It is a standard practice in scholarly writing that you list a source only if it is referred to or cited in the text. If you do not want to tell the reader what an interviewee has said, you cannot include that interviewee as your source of evidence.

How evidence is selected: the example of Gong Chu

In a sense every piece of writing or book aims to argue for or against something and therefore has to select its own evidence, but the selection must be seen as reasonable and justifiable in the context of existing knowledge or known evidence. Scholarship of any acceptable sense has to engage with the existing literature and address opposing views and evidence. Throughout the book Chang and Halliday often write as if there is no scholarship on the subject. If they do cite something from some publication it is to serve the purpose of their agenda to demonize Mao.

Here is one of many examples. Gong Chu, a former senior Red Army officer, who worked with Mao during the early period of the CCP revolution but gave up and ran away to live in Hong Kong before he could see the day of communist victory, published his memoirs in Hong Kong. Chang and Halliday cite Gong as an insider, but only to provide out of context evidence that Mao was a cunning power-hungry manipulator who was cruel but good at nothing. When I read Gong's memoirs I found that the image of Mao that emerges in Gong's book is entirely different from the one presented in Chang and Halliday. Gong's book published in 1978 shows that Mao had ups and downs during the early period of the CCP revolution and was as vulnerable and emotional as any other normal person. When he talked to Gong about how he was oppressed and dismissed by Zhou Enlai,

Mao even shed tears (Gong 1978: 550). Gong states clearly that the first and the clearest understanding of the rural nature of the Chinese revolution came from Mao, and therefore the fact that Mao became the leader of CCP was not due to any luck or accident (Gong 1978: 493). Gong also testifies that land reform in the Jiangxi Revolutionary base area under Mao was mild and did not victimize rich peasants. However when the CCP central leadership from Shanghai, headed by Zhou Enlai, arrived in 1931 they struggled against Mao's *funong luxian* (rich peasant line) and Zhou Enlai wanted to *xiaomie dizhu, zancao chugen* (liquidate the landlord like uprooting the grass). When Gong Chu made plain his opposition by saying that the policy was too radical and that many so-called landed estates were just households with very little land it was Zhou, not Mao, who expelled Gong from the party for a year.

Referencing: a clever deception

The 68 pages of notes in Chang and Halliday have been used as an embellishment designed to impress some readers and to intimidate others intellectually. Instead of using either in-text referencing or numbered footnotes (or endnotes) as is the accepted convention in a scholarly work, a very unusual reference format is adopted in the book, as we shall see below. If the book was fiction and was meant to be such then there would not have been any discussion concerning the notes. But since *The Unknown Story* is meant to tell factual and documentary truth about Mao and about what happened in such a large country for so long, it is expected that the claims made are backed up by evidence. The book gives the appearance of having done that, but has it actually?

The appearance is powerfully deceptive. Let us examine how this is the case. In the text, except for occasional footnotes indicated by a star sign, there is no indication of referencing. The reader who cares about referencing needs to go to the Notes section at the end of the book in which references are arranged like this: in each chapter book pages are listed, then following the page number is a phrase in bold that is either a direct quote from the book or key words about what is discussed. Here are the first few lines of the 'Notes' section on page 677, with references to the text in Chapter 1.

Chapter 1 On the Cusp from Ancient to Modern
Page
3   **Found out emperor's death:** Snow 1973, p. 138.
3-4   **Parents:** Snow 1973, pp. 130–4: *Mao Clan Chronicle*: Mao's father-in-law Yang Chang-chi's diary, 5 Apr. 1915, in *Mao 1990,

p. 636 (E:MRTP Vol. 2, p. 60): Li Xiangwen, pp. 25–51: *Zhao Zhichao, pp. 273–4: visit to Shaoshan and conversations with locals.

As readers we want to be assured that what we are told is an honest presentation of what the author has found. We want to be assured that evidence is presented as accurately as possible and other people's research and arguments are treated fairly and reasonably. References are offered so that the assumption of honesty, integrity, fairness and reasonableness can be checked and confirmed. However, in the kind of references arranged in the Chang and Halliday book we encounter a problem straightway. For instances on page 3 and 4 of the book there are quite a few things said about Mao's parents, but in the references shown above it is not clear how to check the information because there is no indication as to which reference is the source of which bit of information about Mao's parents.

There can be many references listed in the Notes section for one page of text. This gives an appearance of scholarship and painstaking research. No wonder so many journalists take the claimed findings seriously. However, the referencing actually suffers from some serious problems. The following is one of many examples. The text on page 97 is:

> Once he had tightened his grip on the army, Mao turned his attention to the Jiangxi Communists. On 3 December he sent Lie with a list of his foes to the town of Futian, where the Jiangxi leaders were living. Mao condemned the meeting in August which had expelled his ally Lieu as an 'AB meeting' which 'opposed Mao Tse-tung'. 'Put them all down', he ordered, and then 'slaughter en masse in all counties and all districts'. 'Any place that does not arrest and slaughter members of the Party and government of that area must be AB, and you can simply seize and deal with them [*xun-ban*, implying torture and/or liquidation].'

The references for the above paragraph are

Mao Order, 3 Dec. 1930: in Dai & Luo, pp. 94–6, see a follow-up letter on 5 Dec., in Vladmirov, 10 Nov. 1943 (mis-dated 15th). **'AB meeting'**: Mao to Shanghai, 20 Dec. 1930, *ZDJC vol. 14, p. 636 (E: MRTP vol. 3, pp. 704–5); *Liou Di, letter to Shanghai, 11 Jan. 1931, RGASPI, *cit.*; *Provincial Action Committee, Emergency Announcement no. 9, 15 Dec. 1930 RGASPI, 514/1/1008. **Lie torture:** ibid.

The text is meant to say that Mao ordered the slaughter of his opponents in large numbers. But how do we know whether this is not just

Chang and Halliday's claim that is not supported by evidence? First of all, the first note entry '**Mao order, 3 Dec. 1930**' is not exactly the wording in the text. We therefore cannot be sure what Mao ordered. Second, the text aims to show Mao ordered the mass slaughter of his opponents, but which reference is it that is cited for this claim? Is it the citation of Dai & Luo and Vladmirov? According to the order of appearance these two references are cited only to refer to the text before '**AB meeting**', but the 'slaughter' sentence appears only after '**AB meeting**' in the text. Are we to understand then that it is the citation of 'Mao to Shanghai, 20 Dec. 1930, *ZDJC vol. 14, p. 636 (E: MRTP vol. 3, pp. 704–5); *Liou Di, letter to Shanghai, 11 Jan. 1931, RGASPI, *cit*.; *Provincial Action Committee, Emergency Announcement no. 9, 15 Dec. 1930 RGASPI, 514/1/1008' that supports the 'slaughter' statement? Or are these references actually citations for the '**AB meeting**'? Third, the sentence 'Put them all down', he ordered, and then 'slaughter en masse in all counties and all districts' does not make sense. Does it mean that Mao ordered his opponents to be put down and then slaughtered? One would think that the sentence in quotation marks is a translation from Chinese or Russian by the co-authors. One would understand the first part of the sentence 'put them all down' means 'to get rid of them by killing them' which is the same as the second part of the sentence 'slaughter en masse' What is the word 'then' in the sentence for? What is possible, or what the co-authors possibly mean to say, is that Mao gave the order by saying 'put them all down' then someone else carried out the order and 'slaughtered' them. If that is the case why don't the co-authors do that?

Appearance and instant satisfaction

What is clear is that the authors cannot support their claims as well as might first appear. There are many examples in the text. A common move employed by the authors is to cite a reference or even references to a trivial statement or a piece of insignificant information, which is then followed immediately by a substantial or serious claim without reference. There is a source cited for the statement that 'On 29 May he had to return to Red Jiangxi' (p. 118). But immediately after this Chang and Halliday claim that Mao led 'the tens of thousands of troops' into 'an isolated cul-de-sac' and 'a large number fell ill and died' (p. 118), a claim made without any supporting source. However, because there is a reference to the first sentence the appearance is that the substantial claim is also backed by a reference.

The reader who is not a professional in the field would not take the trouble to check whether the claims made in the book have really been made on solid evidence. This is clever showmanship: it is difficult to distinguish between what is authentic and what is a fake. One Chinese writer Zhang Xianliang commented, after his first visit to Singapore and some other modern cities in the West, that in these developed places real flowers look fake and plastic fake flowers look real.

Chang and Halliday have deployed the technique skilfully. With the façade of scholarship established they can then insert crucial claims here and there even though these claims are not properly backed up. How do we find out what is real and what is fake? In our popular culture of instant satisfaction: we do not care so long as it looks right.

Misleading claims and absurd explanations

In trying to explain why Mao turned out to be a decisive leader of the Jiangxi Revolutionary base areas during the late 1920s and early 1930s, contrary to what Gong Chu testifies, Chang tries very hard to sell the message that Mao was good for nothing in military affairs and that it was his personal ruthlessness and Stalin's support that helped Mao to the top. Why did Stalin support Mao instead of someone else? One reason was that 'Mao's drive assumed urgent importance' to Moscow because Russia wanted to invade Manchuria (p. 75). What was this 'Mao's drive' that was so appreciated by Moscow? The book claims that another reason for Stalin's support of Mao was that the first General Secretary of the CCP Chen Duxiu was then turning Trotskyist, and Stalin was afraid that Mao might side with Chen since Chen was his mentor (p. 75). But there is no evidence to back up such a claim.

There are more extraordinary claims: 'The Party had handed him [Mao] the biggest Red Army outside the Soviet bloc after he had broken all the rules. Moscow and Shanghai were palpably bribing him, which meant they needed him.' Why would Moscow and CCP in Shanghai want to bribe him if Mao not only 'broke all rules' but was also such a hopeless good for nothing? Why would the Party and Moscow need Mao? The whole matter is made so mysterious simply because *The Unknown Story* does not want the reader even to contemplate the possibility that it was Mao's military and organizations skills that made him successful.

In order to denigrate the character of Mao, *The Unknown Story* has good fun in telling a story that Mao was a selfish and greedy bastard, 'consuming plenty of milk (a rarity for the Chinese), as well as a kilo of beef stewed into soup every day, with a whole chicken on top' (p. 75). Regardless of whether there was beef in Jiangxi on a daily basis at that time (there could not have been cattle in Jiangxi and water buffaloes were precious farming animals), was it humanly possible to digest a kilo of beef in addition to a whole chicken every day?

A good example of how *The Unknown Story* treats documentary

[71]

sources is its comment on a report of the death of Mao's first wife, Yang Kaihui. According to the co-authors, the day after Yang was executed the local Hunan *Republican Daily* ran a headline 'Wife of Mao Tse-tung executed yesterday – everyone claps and shouts with satisfaction'. To some credulous Western reader, this is an example of how the authors worked hard to research Chinese sources, as local newspapers in the 1930s were consulted. After citing these words, Chang and Halliday's comment: 'This undoubtedly reflected more loathing of Mao than of Kai-hui' (p. 83). The authors do not even contemplate the possibility that one cannot simply take what the local papers said at that time as a given fact, when communist activists were hunted down as 'bandits' by the then Nationalist government.

Regarding Mao's relation with Yang Kaihui, *The Unknown Story* charges:

> During his [Mao's] assault on Changsha, Mao made no effort to extricate her and their sons, or even to warn her. And he could easily have saved her: her house was on his route to the city; and Mao was there for three weeks. Yet he did not lift a finger (p. 91).

There is no evidence to back up such an extraordinary charge. There are numerous claims of this nature made in the book without supporting evidence. For example here is the first sentence in the book: 'Mao Tse-tung, who for decades held absolute power over the lives of one-quarter of the world's population, was responsible for well over 70 million deaths in peacetime, more than any other twentieth-century leader' (incidentally China's population had for decades been not 'one-quarter' but a fifth of the world's). And there are more: 'In late September [Mao] started his slaughter' (p. 91), and 'Moscow also appointed Mao head of the state' (p. 104). 'Given that escapes were few, this means that altogether some 700,000 people died in the Ruijin base. More than half of these were murdered as "class enemies", or were worked to death, or committed suicide, or died other premature deaths attributable to the regime' (p. 113–4).

The book is filled with accusations like these without any evidence or sources to back up. How did Chang and Halliday come up with a figure of 700,000 deaths in Ruijin, for instance? *The Unknown Story* cites two sources referring to the population drop of 20 per cent in Red Jiangxi (p. 113). Even if these figures of population drop were true, they do not give any evidence to the claim that all these people actually died – they could have migrated to other areas because of the civil war – or the claim that more than half of them died as 'class enemies' of the revolution; some of them could have been killed by the Nationalists who would not allow the existence of a revolutionary state within a state.

After claiming that Shao Li-tzu – a prominent KMT official, who, on Chiang Kai-shek's instructions, took the latter's son to Moscow to study – was a CCP mole, *The Unknown Story* declares that 'Ultimately, the agents played a gigantic role in helping deliver China to Mao'(p. 139). As if China could just be delivered to Mao with the help of a few KMT agents. Anyone who believes this kind of stuff is like those who believe that the Bible is literally the history of humanity.

Further evidence of 'scholarship'

Jung Chang is said to be the first person from the PRC to have obtained a PhD degree in linguistics at a UK university. One would expect her to be familiar with the spelling of Chinese names in English. As an indication of what kind of scholarship is involved in *The Unknown Story*, it is worth devoting a few sentences to the way Chinese names are spelt in the book. One should not be surprised that 'Peking' is still used in the book instead of 'Beijing', since Chang would hate to use a term that is initiated by a regime that she now hates so much. However, violation of other conventions that are common knowledge to even a first-year undergraduate student of Chinese is really puzzling. Chang, if not Halliday, should know that in Chinese, surnames comes first and given names come second. However, Chang chooses to refer to a Chinese person by the given name. Thus Li Li-shan, a party notable, is referred to as 'Li-shan' and Mao's wife Yang Kai-hui is referred to as 'Kai-hui'. This is the equivalent of referring to Marx as 'Karl' in scholarly writing.

In spelling Chinese names there are two main systems used all over the world. One is the old Wade-Giles system invented by the missionaries and one is the new Pinyin system stipulated by the PRC government. For cataloguing Chinese resources the Wade-Giles system used to be the standard. Increasingly the Pinyin system has been introduced into library cataloguing. In order to cater for both the older and younger generation of users, some libraries have both systems available. In academic writing one can either adopt one system or another. The norm is to adopt one consistent approach, except for names of well-known figures that have been used for a long time. However, *The Unknown Story* is not consistent in using one system or the other. The authors mix the two systems any way they want.

That is fine, except when their spelling implies erroneous phonetics. For example in the Wade-Giles system in order to make a difference between the aspirated versus non-aspirated sound, an apostrophe is used to indicate aspiration. Thus 'chi' has a very different sound quality to 'ch'i'. In the Pinyin system this difference of sound quality is made by spelling 'chi' as 'ji' and 'ch'i' as 'qi'. However, our linguistics-doctorate author Chang does not make any difference at all. Mao's father-in-law's name Yang Changji (Pinyin) or Yang Ch'ang-chi (Wade-Giles) is spelt as 'Yang Chang-chi' (part Pinyin and part Wade-Giles), and Liu Shaoqi (Pinyin) or Liu Shao-ch'i (Wade Giles) is spelt as 'Liu Shao-chi'. The last names of Mr Yang and Mr Liu do not sound the same, but Chang spells them as if they do.

Further evidence of flaws and misleading claims

It is true that *The Unknown Story* is not without its critics. James Heartfield (2005) is one of the very few who makes a well-researched effort to expose the distortions contained in it. Kakutani also points out the lack of reference in the book to Mao's 'mature writings that might shed light on his politics or values', and the absence of historical context, calling the work 'tendentious and one-dimensional'. Even Steve Tsang of Oxford University, a historian who has no love for Mao and the CCP, has to admit that 'the authors had been 'appallingly dishonest' in the use of sources they claimed to have accessed. Of course Tsang readily agrees that 'Mao was a monster,' but regrets that 'their distortion of history to make their case will in the end make it more difficult to reveal how horrible Mao and the Chinese Communist Party system were, and how much damage they really did to the Chinese people' (quoted in Heartfield 2005).

To approach the subject of Mao, or anybody really, it is perfectly legitimate to have an attitude. 'You don't feel cold analysis in this book, you feel hatred, which helps make it a wonderful read. But history should not work this way', Francesco Sisci of *La Stampa* in Italy states with regret (McDonald 2005). Teiwes also regrets:

> When someone [Mao] is responsible, and I believe he was, for upwards of 30 million deaths, it's hard to defend him. ... But on the other hand to paint him as a totally monstrous personality who just goes out to kill people and protect his power at all cost is not only over the top but a bit crazy in terms of what actually went on.

In order to do that, 'She [Chang] just had her views so set, and was unwilling to entertain other opinions or inconvenient evidence' (McDonald 2005).

Jung Chang claims to have interviewed the last surviving eyewitness at Luding Bridge who was said to have confirmed that there was no battle at the bridge during the Long March. When McDonald went to Luding he did not find a trace of Jung Chang's witness. Instead, he found another eyewitness confirming that a battle indeed took place

(McDonald 2005). Davin points out in the *Times Literary Supplement* a number of historical errors and speculative assumptions. One concerns the death of Wang Shiwei. *The Unknown Story* asserts that Wang's execution was used by Mao to terrify the young intellectuals at Yan'an during the 'rectification' campaign of 1942. However the execution of Wang did not actually take place until 1947 (Williems 2005); it was done without Mao's knowledge and Mao was reportedly furious about it.

'There are numerous such accusations in the book. Unfortunately it is not always so evident to expose them as mere fantasy' (Williems 2005). 'Let me make it clear that I fully share the authors' view that Mao was a monster, as were Hitler and Stalin,' McLynn (2005) declares, but the book has 'too much hate too little understanding'. Even Nathan, whose published political stand is clearly in line with that of Chang, has to admit 'that many of Chang and Halliday's claims are based on distorted, misleading or far-fetched use of evidence' (Nathan 2005).

Another good example of how Chang and Halliday distort and misquote to make misleading statements is provided by Ball (2007). When discussing the Great Leap Forward, Chang and Halliday claim that Mao did not care that people were dying from starvation. Chang and Halliday quote Mao's words at the Wuchang Conference that 'working like this, with all these projects, half of China may well have to die' as evidence to support their charge that Mao 'was ready to dispense with' half of China's population for the sake of Mao's industrialization plan. But as Ball points out, the quote is taken out of the context of the whole speech. If one cares to examine the context what Mao actually meant to say was exactly the opposite of the Chang and Halliday claim: to warn his audience of the dangers of overwork and over enthusiasm in the Great Leap Forward.

When questioned about the sensational claim that the Chinese Nationalist leader, Chiang Kai-shek, intentionally let the Red Army escape on the historic Long March of 1934–1935, the authors, in their defence, point to their seemingly impressive references, the 26 sources for the claim about the Long March. Nathan was compelled to ask 'Of these 26 items, which one, two or three unequivocally support the improbable claim that Chiang let the Reds escape intentionally?' (Fenby 2005) The answer, my friend, is none.

Logical inconsistency within the text

Jin, not a scholar of any known standing in the field, demonstrates that one does not have to bring in any documentary evidence to repudiate 17 of Chang and Halliday's major claims. All one has to do is find logical contradictions in the book itself. Here rephrased are a couple of examples pointed out by Jin.

Red Army let go by Chiang

Chang and Halliday claim that Chiang Kai-shek let Mao's Red Army escape during the Long March. This claim is important for Chang and Halliday's thesis that Mao was good for nothing. Why was Chiang, a staunch anti-communist who considered a communist victory more dangerous to China than Japanese invasion and occupation, willing to let Mao escape? Because he did not want to risk the life of his son, who was in the Soviet Union at that time, so Chang and Halliday say. However elsewhere in the book the authors also state that when Song Qinling – Madam Sun Yat-sen of whom Chang and Halliday wrote a praiseworthy biography back in 1988 but now allege was another Soviet agent – appealed to Chiang to release two Chinese (a man called Niu Lan and his wife) who were arrested as Soviet agents in return for the homecoming of his son, Chiang refused. Jin asks, rightly, was the imprisonment of two little known Chinese more important than the defeat of Mao's Red Army to Chiang?

Mao didn't walk during the Long March

Another claim in the book is that Mao was carried for long stretches of the Long March. One piece of evidence cited to support this claim is the similar claim made by Zhang Guotao in his memoirs. But Zhang's memoirs were written after he fell out with Mao and had defected to the Nationalists. In any case, even Zhang does not claim that Mao was carried all the time. Another piece of evidence is from Mao's reported confession to his bodyguards when Mao said that during the Long March he was carried and therefore read a lot. Again Mao's own words do not lead to the conclusion that he was always carried around. Jin asks, rightly, if the Zhang and Halliday claim were true it would not have been 'unknown' since the claim was already made by Zhang Guotao and what Mao said was published in his bodyguard Ye Zilong's memoirs in 2000.

Murder of 70 million Chinese people

The first sentence of Chang and Halliday states that Mao was the murderer of 70 million Chinese. Of the 70 million one set of figures that Chang and Halliday produce in the text is the 27 million who were supposed to have died in prisons or labour camps during the Mao era. How do the authors come up with these figures? Chang and Halliday claim that there were approximately 10 million prisoners in prisons and labour camps in China every year during the 27 years of Mao's rule, and that the death rate was possibly as high as 10 per cent. Therefore, the death toll would be 10,000,000 x 10 per cent x 27 = 27,000,000. How did the figure of 10,000,000 come about? What was the source of the 10 per cent death rate? In any case, Jin asks, again rightly, on what ground could one draw a conclusion that every death in prison should have been the responsibility of Mao?

As for the 38 million deaths attributed to the Great Leap Forward famine, Chang and Halliday do not get into any of the controversies and different estimates that exist in the literature (Banister 1987, Coale 1984, Jin Hui 1993, Jiang Zhenghua and Li Na 1989, Li Chengrui 1987, Kane 1988) but pick the highest death toll. Chang conveniently omits the fact that her home-town province of Sichuan was one of the worst-hit provinces during the difficult years. Chang does not in her *Wild Swans* or *The Unknown Story* mention any eyewitness account of death by starvation in her home province. Second, the Party Secretaries of other worst-hit provinces like Wu Zhipu of Henan, Zeng Xisheng of Anhui, Shu Tong of Shandong and Zhang Zhongliang of Gansu were all sacked after the Great Leap Forward disaster except Li Jingquan, the Party Secretary of Sichuan, Chang's home province. One wonders why. If it was because Sichuan managed to cover up the disaster so well, then it is reasonable to assume that Chang's father must have done a good job since he was the Deputy Minster of the Propaganda Department of Sichuan province during the height of his career. What motivates Chang to rename her father's Propaganda Department as Public Affairs Department in her writings, Jin asks.

Mao, China's Hitler and Stalin

Almost all Western commentators tend to agree with Chang and Halliday that Mao was like Hitler and Stalin. However it was public knowledge that Mao, unlike Stalin and Hitler, did not execute any of his political rivals. Before Mao came to dominant positions in the CCP he was sidelined and demoted by Bo Gu, Zhang Wentian and Zhou Enlai. Bo Gu and Zhang Wentian suffered in their careers and Zhang even underwent humiliation later in life, but they were not executed by Mao. Zhou Enlai served as the Premier of PRC until the last day of his life. When Zhang Guotao, another of Mao's rivals, defected to the Nationalists Mao agreed to let his wife and children join him. During the Sixth Congress of the CCP Mao worked hard to keep Wang Ming, another of Mao's political opponents, as a member of the CCP Central Committee and Wang later migrated to the Soviet Union and died there. Peng Dehuai was demoted in 1959 and sidelined and humiliated and even brutally beaten up by some Red Guards during the Cultural Revolution. But Peng died of bowel cancer in 1974. Liu Shaoqi was persecuted and humiliated; but he died of a natural death (though he might have lived longer had he not suffered the strain of persecution).

Chang and Halliday have to admit that it was Mao who rejected a report recommending the execution of Liu Shaoqi's wife. In order to twist this fact in their favour Chang and Halliday make a claim that would be comic if it were not for the fact that it was about life and death: that Mao wanted Liu and his wife Wang Guangmei's slow death by torture. So slow that Wang was still alive in the twenty-first century. In 2004 Wang even celebrated Mao's birthday with the latter's relatives (Kong Dongmei 2006). The meeting was called by Wang herself and organized by one of Liu's sons Liu Yuan. Photos were taken with Wang Guangmei sitting between Mao's two daughters Li Na and Li Min.

There are numerous other cases that show that Mao was not like Stalin or Hitler. When Mao was told of Lin Biao's fleeing in a plane, he is reported to have ordered that the plane should not be shot, saying *tian yao xiayu, niang yao jiaren, rang ta qu ba* (you cannot stop it if it rains, you cannot stop it if your mother wants to remarry; let him go). The story of Deng Xiaoping is well known: though humiliated and criticized Deng was never physically harmed. During the most turbulent days of the Cultural Revolution in the second half of 1966, when everyone of the CCP hierarchy was under attack except Mao and Lin Biao, Mao was determined to protect Zhu De and Chen Yi (Wang Li 2001: 714), the two people who were very critical of Mao in the 1930s and, with Zhou Enlai, Zhu and Chen, were in fact responsible for removing Mao from the command of the Red Army.

There is another example that shows that Mao judged people on their ideas. During the Great Leap Forward year of 1958, the Mayor of Shanghai, Ke Qingshi, was known to follow Mao's ideas closely and Mao therefore wanted to promote him to the powerful Politburo. But Liu Shaoqi opposed Ke's promotion, on the basis that Ke had objected to Liu's push in the 1940s for everyone to take Mao as the central leader of the CCP. Mao then asked Ke to talk to Liu and persuade him to forget about that incident (Wang Li 2001: 755).

Fairy tale and how scholarship changes

It is incredible how unreflecting and how shameless modern show business can be. As Heartfield (2005) points out, it was Chang, in *Wild Swans*, the best-ever-selling family memoirs, who tells us that Chiang Kai-shek had adopted a policy of non-resistance in the face of the Japanese seizure of Manchuria and Japan's increasing encroachments on China proper. Chang also claims that it was Chiang who, instead of mobilizing forces to fight the Japanese invasion, had concentrated on trying to annihilate the Communists. But in many instances, *The*

Unknown Story flatly contradicts *Wild Swans*. In *The Unknown Story*, Mao is claimed to have engineered Chiang's abduction by his own general Zhang Xueliang in 1936. But if you read *Wild Swans* Chiang was 'partly saved by the Communists'. If *The Unknown Story* is intended to correct the claims made in *Wild Swans* for the sake of its 10 million readers then Chang should have indicated these corrections either in text or footnotes, Heartfield rightly points out.

Chang's co-author Halliday says that being married to Chang is like a fairy tale (Thorpe 2005). In his non-fairy tale days Halliday condemned the Japanese invasion of Manchuria and China (Halliday 1973). But now he agrees with his fairy tale princess that the Japanese war in China was more or less the result of a Mao/Stalin conspiracy. How does Halliday compare Chang's and his interpretation of the Korean War now with that in his own book *Korea: The Unknown War*, or his understanding of the Cultural Revolution now with his previous interpretation that the riots in 1967 in Hong Kong were 'anti-colonial' and were against an administration where there 'is no democracy' (Halliday 1974)? In those days he wrote about the British colonial oppression in China and Hong Kong; now Halliday goes along with his princess and blames the bloody repression in Hong Kong in 1967 on provocation by Mao. The Korean War (1950–53) is largely blamed on Mao, whereas in his earlier book he stressed the role of Truman as warmonger (Williems 2005).

How times change. So does scholarship.

Does it matter?

What is surprising, or not surprising, is that very few take the trouble to question the methodological flaws in the book. An exception is Phillip Short, whose own biography of Mao was published in 1999. Short says that Chang and Halliday have reduced Mao from a complex historical character to a one-dimensional 'cardboard cut out of Satan', and yet almost no reviewers really think that this is a problem. The case of Kristof is a good example. On the one hand, Kristof tells us that:

> One of those listed as a source is Zhang Hanzhi, Mao's English teacher and close associate; she's also one of my oldest Chinese friends, so I checked with her. Zhang Hanzhi said that she had indeed met informally with Chang two or three times but had declined to be interviewed and never said anything substantial.

Moreover, Kristof complains that in the book, 'Mao comes across as such a villain that he never really becomes three-dimensional,' and that he is 'presented as such a bumbling psychopath that it's hard to comprehend how he bested all his rivals to lead China and emerge as one of the most worshipped figures in history'. Nevertheless, Kristof still declares 'this is a magisterial work' (Kristof 2005). Professor Perry Link of Princeton and one of the editors of the *Tiananmen Papers*, while feeling compelled to say something about the book's methodology, has a largely positive review of it (Link 2005b).

The academic community in general seems critical of the book, as seen in a special issue of the *China Journal* (2006), whereas the media seems to be generally positive. The function of the media is discussed further in later chapters, but it suffices to say here that it will take years, if ever, to deconstruct the Chang and Halliday 'truth' promoted by the media. I totally agree with Thomas Bernstein (2005) who thinks that 'the book is a major disaster for the contemporary China field.' 'Because of its stupendous research apparatus, its claims will be accepted widely.'

It does not matter so long as the politics is right

To demonize Mao is the right politics of course. When someone pasted some criticism of the Chang and Halliday book on the Amazon sales website, it was immediately attacked as 'ugly Chinese propaganda' (Jin Xiaoding 2005). On the other hand, Jin's critique of the book was met with absolute silence by the Western media (no Western media outlet was ready to publish the 17 questions raised by Jin). When the Chinese version of Jin's critique appeared on the Chinese language website *duowei* (http://blog.chinesenewsnet.com), there was a lively debate. Jung Chang had to admit, when asked, that Jin's 17 questions are good questions but refused to provide convincing replies to them. For the Western media it does not matter as long as the politics is right, and the right politics is that Mao must be discredited. In the next chapter I will consider why.

5 Mao: the known story and the logic of denial

Introduction: Mao the known story, a general outline

In the previous chapter I showed in detail how *Mao: The Unknown Story* by Jung Chang and Jon Halliday cannot be taken as an authoritative, scholarly work. The fact that the book has been taken as serious scholarship by the popular media is an intellectual scandal. I have indicated that it should be read as a politically motivated piece of show business aimed at discrediting Chinese revolutionary ideas and practices. In this chapter I will focus on what we *do* know about the Mao era to show that there is already a known story that cannot be untold by clever tricks.

The Unknown Story is supposed to be a biography of Mao, a leader of a party that transformed the landscape of China and beyond, whose ideas and sayings still have an impact around much of the world. However, apart from devoting a few pages to an article that Mao wrote when he was in his early twenties Chang and Halliday in general do not talk about his ideas and policies in relation to his written work or speeches.

There is a known story, a story that cannot be wiped out even if Mao's body was thrown out of the mausoleum on the Tian'anmen Square and his portrait was stripped from the Heavenly Gate of the Tian'anmen rostrum. The story is this: the Chinese people made a revolution led by the CCP, the most important leader of which was Mao, a revolution in which Chang's parents participated, a revolution from which Chang herself benefited. It was due to this revolution that the average life expectancy of the majority Chinese rose from 35 in 1949 to 63 by 1975 (Bergaglio 2006) in a space of less than 30 years. It was a revolution that brought unity and stability to a country that had been plagued by civil wars and foreign invasions, and a revolution that laid the foundation for China to become the equal of the great global powers. It was a revolution that carried out land reform, promoted women's status, improved popular literacy, and eventually transformed Chinese society beyond recognition (Selden et al 1991, Selden, 1971, Selden and Eggleston 1979, Selden 1988).

The known story of Mao who led a revolution that transformed human life of such significance and magnitude cannot be dismissed by a few sensational claims. What were the historical circumstances that were the context of such a transformation? Could social change on such a scale take place simply as a result of a few power-struggle conspiracies and personal plots and schemes? What were the guiding ideas and social and economic practices involved? What were the policies? What did millions and millions of Chinese do and think? What were the values and beliefs during these years? What institutional changes were carried out and why? The known story is full of answers and explanations, as well as unanswered ones. Any attempt to remove the known story from history should involve engagement with the existing literature, so as to dispute or confirm what is already known or can be known. But the co-authors of *The Unknown Story* do not do this. As shown in Chapter 4 they do not even engage with their own writings that have been published.

Evidence of the known story

In order to tell their unknown story Chang and Halliday have to ignore the known story. For instance, Mao is accused of callousness and of not caring about starving peasants during the hard years after the Great Leap Forward. But the known story supported by documentary evidence is that Mao did care. Apart from his personal decision not to eat pork – a favourite food item for the Chinese and for Mao himself (Quan Yanchi 1989) – Mao tried very hard to make policy changes to rectify the situation. What I present below is the kind of evidence in the known story that *The Unknown Story* ignores.

A letter

On 31 October 1960 Zhou Enlai sent a policy letter addressing the issue of the collective system for Mao to approve. The policy letter titled *Dui zhongyang guanyu renmin gongshe dangqian zhengce wenti de jinji zhishi xin* (An urgent letter of instruction by the CCP Central Committee concerning the current policy problems of rural people's communes) was aimed at correcting some policies and practices that had been proved to be detrimental to production and livelihoods during the Great Leap Forward. Mao not only approved the letter but also made extensive comments and corrections to make the letter more effective and more 'right wing'. I will give a brief analysis of these comments in comparison with the original wording.

The original letter had twelve points to which Mao made six comments. The first comment is that the letter should be sent to the villages by telegram instead of ordinary post so that it would reach the grassroots quicker. In the first point the original letter stated that the system of using the production team as the basic accounting unit was fundamental and therefore should be maintained. This was to counter the practice of big communes involving several villages in which absolute equality was the norm and in which labour supervision could not be adequately implemented. By making smaller-scale production teams the accounting unit, involving only a dozen households, the system would allow diversity and differentiated distribution among different villages and would make supervision of labour easier. To this point Mao added that the system of production teams as the basic accounting unit should not be changed for at least seven years (in fact the system lasted until the early 1980s). This change by Mao was intended to give the grassroots a sense of stability and certainty.

In point seven the original letter stipulated that 70 per cent of the produce should be distributed as salary and only 30 per cent in the form of equal supply. Mao commented that the collective system should not be state owned but collectively owned, and therefore 'salary' was not the right word and that distribution should be 'to each according to one's labour', not 'to each according to one's needs'. Mao also inserted, as his fourth comment, that the principle of 'to each according to one's labour' should not be changed for at least 20 years. Mao further stressed that the CCP should be whole-heartedly (*yi xin yi yi*) devoted to production and that this letter should be read by party officials at every level three times. Mao also changed the sentence 'Commune members should be allowed to raise pigs themselves' in the original document into 'Commune members should be *encouraged* to raise pigs for themselves' (my emphasis).

Referring to the percentage of income to be kept in the commune coffers for public goods and services rather than distributed directly to the commune members, the original letter stipulated a level of 10 per cent. However, Mao wanted more to be distributed and less to be reserved and therefore changed this to 5 per cent. In the original letter it was stated that in poor communes or areas that had suffered a decline of production the percentage to be reserved can be even lower or none at all; Mao changed 'can be' into 'ought to be'.

The letter, revised according to Mao's comments, was sent out on that very day. This is only one example to show that if one cares to examine documentary records there is evidence for a known but different story, a story shows that Mao, did care about production and the livelihood of the farmers and was more 'right wing' than some of his comrades

Other documentary evidence

In fact as early as 29 April 1959, Mao (1959) wrote a letter to address six crucial issues about food, grain production and the truthful reporting of production outputs, all stressing moderation and calling for cooling down the Great Leap hype. By doing this Mao confessed that he was a conservative (*baoshou zhuyizhe*). In order to make sure that his letter reached the grassroots Mao took an unprecedented step by addressing it to six levels of government officials: from provincial leaders to district, county, commune and production brigade, right down to production team leaders in villages. Mao was obviously afraid the party bureaucracies at higher level might not pass on the instruction to the grassroots. In this letter he stressed to his audience that the responsibility system (*bao chan*), which by the way was similar to the so-called reform by the post-Mao authorities, must definitely be implemented regardless of any other instructions from higher authorities. Mao also pointed out that for the next ten years at least caution had to be taken so as not to boast about grain production, and that any boastful unrealistic rhetoric (*dahua, gaodiao*) would be dangerous (*weixian*) because for such a big country food is the number one priority (*chifan shi diyi jian dashi*) as shortage of food was no small matter.

Again during early April 1959, Mao at a Shanghai Politburo meeting criticized the zealots at the Central Planning Commission and praised Chen Yun for his cool headedness. Mao wanted the steel and iron production quotas to go down, as suggested by Chen Yun (Yang Bo 2006). In fact as early as 1958 Mao warned the CCP leaders not to report false achievements (Wu Lengxi 1995). According to evidence published on 7 September 2007 in *Luoyang ribao* (The Luoyang Daily), it was Mao who during the Zhengzhou Conference in March 1959 decided to cool down the Great Leap hype, against the prevailing trend at that time, after he met a village leader Li Changwu on 8 March 1959 and listened to what he had to say (Long Pan 2007).

So what was the problem?

The two letters and other documentary evidence clearly show that there were other CCP leaders at various levels that were so irrational that Mao had to restrain them or to bypass them. They also show that the Great Leap Forward was a genuine policy mistake and that Mao was not the only person who was responsible. However, ever since the post-Mao reforms Chinese historiography has been attempting to place the blame on Mao alone. It became inconvenient to expose those who acted more recklessly than Mao but were rehabilitated after his death. Li Jie, one of the main writers of the four volume *Mao Zedong zhuan 1949–1976* (A Biography of Mao 1949–1976) published in 2004, said that it was difficult to write the Mao biography, but not because there were things about Mao that could not be published. Rather, it was mainly because there were things about other leaders, especially those who were in the good book of official history, that were not allowed to be said (Nong Nuji 2006a).

Mao of course should bear the primary responsibility for the Great Leap famine; but other Chinese leaders such as Deng Xiaoping (as I have discussed elsewhere in this book) were also responsible, and Liu Shaoqi was one of them. Liu at least on one occasion in 1958 even talked about forming a commune as big as a county, and about revolutionizing families by having husbands and wives living in different dormitories (Qiong 2007). On 19 September 1958, when told by a local leader in Jiangsu that one mu of land could produce ten thousand jin of rice, Liu wondered whether more was possible and suggested ploughing the soil deeper to produce more (Qiong 2007).[1] In his memoirs, Wu Lengxi, the then editor of the *People's Daily*, remembered that Mao time and again urged him to be cautious in reporting so as not to mislead the party and the public. Wu (1995) confesses that he made mistakes by not having really understood what Mao meant and what the consequences were. Wu says that at the height of the Great Leap hype Mao was in the minority who warned caution whereas he himself followed the majority, which included Liu Shaoqi (Wu Lengxi 1995).

The famine death toll

The Great Leap Forward has to be the most disastrous period of the Mao era for rural Chinese. However, for Chang and Halliday to pick the highest number of estimates of famine death and to state that Mao had murdered these people is sensationalism beyond the common sense of decency. There are a number of points here in relation to the famine death toll. Scholars have made different estimates, ranging from 10 to 30 million deaths. These are estimates for many reasons. One is that there were no reliable demographic censuses to make possible an accurate figure. Second, it is hard to know whether some casualties during the Great Leap Forward were deaths by hunger or premature deaths due to hardship. Third, some estimates try to assess the 'missing' population on the basis of normal death and birth rates and therefore may have included millions of those who might not have been born. In the words of Patnaik:

Some scholars have used a very dubious method of arriving at grossly unrealistic and inflated 'famine deaths' during this period (1959–61) by taking account not only of the higher crude death rate (which is a legitimate measure) but also counting the 'missing millions' as a result of the lower birth rate, as part of the toll. There is a great deal of difference between people who are already there, dying prematurely due to a sharp decline in nutritional status, and people not being born at all. The former

[85]

can enter the statistics of famine deaths according to any sensible definition of famine, but people who are not born at all are obviously in no position to die whether prematurely or otherwise.

(Patnaik 2004)

Fourth, nowadays natural disasters such as floods and droughts are not considered a factor for the famine during the period. But in Barmé (2007) an eyewitness account testifies that in 1960 there was the worst flood disaster in century in his area and 'The water came right up to our kang. … The hunger was too great. It was hell. The natural disasters added to the effect, and that's the truth.'

If Chang and Halliday's 38 million toll is correct that means one in twenty Chinese died of starvation during the Great Leap Forward, something that could not be hidden away no matter how hard the authorities tried. It is also worth noting that in the village case studies that I know of, no death toll due to famine during the Great Leap Forward is reported. These studies include Gao 1999a, Seybolt 1996, Endicott (1989) and Hinton (1983). The two villages studied by Seybolt and Endicott were in two of the worst-hit provinces, Sichuan and Henan.

The final point related to the famine issue is the nature of responsibility. Mao should certainly be held primarily responsible for the consequences of the Great Leap Forward. First he should be held responsible for initiating the movement by criticizing Zhou Enlai, Deng Zihui and other more cautious leaders before the Great Leap Forward started. Second Mao was mainly responsible for the quick and dramatic collectivization around the winter of 1957 and spring of 1958. The sudden change of organization from co-ops to big collective communes meant that no adequate supervision and monitoring system could be implemented to manage grain production. This organizational failure undoubtedly had detrimental consequences in grain production. Eventually there was a food shortage everywhere in China and disastrous famine in some areas. But to identify Mao as the person responsible for a policy disaster is not the same as to say Mao was the murderer of so many people. Who is supposed to be the murderer of the millions of Russians whose life expectancy has been shortened by ten years after the collapse of the Soviet Union?

From this perspective, it can be convincingly argued that the Great Leap Forward was a disastrously failed trial of a different model of development that embraced local enterprise and decentralized industry, a work force that could be both industrial and agricultural, and a community that was not solely urban or rural. In fact, some of these ideas were followed up during the late 1960s and early 1970s when township and village enterprises that had started during the

Great Leap Forward were encouraged to consolidate and develop further. The issue of how to make the rural population part of an integrated development still faces China today. According to Wen (2005), even with the present rapid rate of industrialization and urbanization there will still be 800 million people living in rural China by 2050. Therefore, I would like to argue that the Great Leap Forward idea was not some kind of madness, but theoretically guided rationality.

The economy in the Mao era

There is plenty of evidence that supports the known story in which hundreds of millions of people were affected positively. The increase of life expectancy in the era of Mao alone, in the words of Williems (2005), has given an estimated 35 billion extra collective years of life to the Chinese people. Though living standards remained low, and were for many at subsistence level, it is plain truth that except for the Great Leap Forward Years of 1959 and 1960 and the Cultural Revolution years of 1967 and 1968, Chinese economic growth was not only steady but also outpaced most developing countries. By 1976 China had laid down a sound industrial and agricultural base for an economic take off. These facts are proven and accepted by both Chinese and Western scholars in their macro studies (Meisner 1986, Lardy 1978, Rawski 1993, Chow 1985, Perkins 1985, and Field 1986) as well as micro case studies (Forster 2003, Bramall 1993 and Endicott 1989). Even the Chinese official statistics released by the post-Mao authorities who shout loud anti-Mao rhetoric of economic calamities cannot deny these facts.

One should be cautious in quoting claims by the post-Mao Chinese authorities that intend to denigrate the Mao era, so as not to fall into the trap that 'it must be true since the Chinese themselves say so'. The instinct that 'the Chinese would not say things bad about themselves unless they were true' does not work all the time. Foster's case study of Zhejiang is a good example to illustrate this point. The post-Mao authorities and elite intelligentsia in Zhejiang province condemn the Cultural Revolution by stating in the literature that the it caused 'grave losses to economic construction' and that: 'the leftist policies caused the gross output of agriculture over four successive years (1968–71) to be lower than the that of 1967.' But if one looks into the details one finds that 'Zhejiang experienced double-digit rise over the following five years from 1969 to 1973. These were of the impressive magnitude of 19.2 per cent, 16.2 per cent, 15.4 per cent, 10.2 per cent and 11.5 per cent' (Forster 2003: 147). The Cultural Revolution did not 'cause the disaster to the provincial economy' and there was 'a rapid growth of rural industry' (Forster 2003: 148).

In 1966 the proportion of industrial output value from collective
and commune/brigade run industrial enterprises to state enterprises was 17:83; in 1976 it was 37:63, with the output value of
collective industry growing at the annual average rate of 15.8
per cent over the 10 years.

(Forster 2003: 148)

Forster's research shows that during the period, the tea industry in
Zhejiang province grew rapidly.

The yardstick of Hitler: a favourite European comparison

Instead of discussing Mao, a political figure of such consequence, in
the context of political, social and economic importance, Chang and
Halliday focus on character assassination. Of course one can write a
biography that focuses on personality, on private life and private
thoughts. Such a biography may indeed bring insights and understanding that cannot be found in biographies of a non-personal nature.
However, this cannot be achieved with the single-minded intention of
personality attack. One needs to reveal the personality's inner tension
and conflicts. We need to see the complexities, paradoxes, ironies and
tragedies, in other words, the unintended consequences of human life,
individually or collectively.

The development of a complex character is applicable to all good
biographies. In the particular case of Mao there is another dimension
to his character. That is, the personality of Mao has to be examined in
the context of Chinese history, tradition and culture. Any decontextu-
alized comparison of Mao with a European figure is intellectually
infantile if not politically motivated. In *The Unknown Story* and elsewhere, such as in the media reviews of the book, we are constantly
urged to compare Mao with Hitler.[2] However, in my understanding,
Hitler and Mao belonged to completely different worlds. Mao became
a leader in the long process of a popular revolution that transformed
the political, social and economic landscape of a large country whereas
Hitler was the leader of a regime that invaded other countries for no
understandable reasons other than the desire for conquest. Hitler was
the leader of a regime that designed scientific means and methods to
physically wipe out other ethnic groups. Hitler and Mao worked for
very different causes and were utterly different personalities.

If they read what Hitler said, saw the way he made speeches, knew
what he did, most, if not all, Chinese – this is an educated guess since
there is, to the best of my knowledge, no scientifically designed survey
on this – could not help but come to the straightforward conclusion
that this person must be clinically insane. Quite simply, a personality

[88]

like Hitler would never have risen to prominence in politics in Chinese society. He would have been a laughing stock and treated with utter contempt and disdain. On the other hand, Mao was viewed then and still today by many in China (here 'many' really means many) as a philosopher, a thinker, a military strategist, a revolutionary statesman. The idea that Hitler had charisma never stops baffling and puzzling me. In fact there is no proper term in Chinese to translate 'charisma', but Weberian charismatic leadership features prominently in the political theory of Western tradition (Wang Shaoquang 1995). This only shows how dangerously misleading it can be to use the lens of Western theoretical concepts to approach Chinese phenomena.

Of course Chang, and others, would say that the Chinese people are still under thought control, are still brainwashed and therefore cannot see what she sees, as she keeps on telling journalists who run to her like a flock of sheep. Despite a lot of anti-communist cold war rhetoric in the literature I have not seen any well-researched evidence to support the judgement that so many Chinese still refuse to hate Mao simply because they are brainwashed. Incidentally, the fact that this contemptuous elitist attitude towards the masses of Chinese people is conceptually contradictory to the very value of democracy and of human rights is hardly noticed.

If these supposedly benighted Chinese were to be given many years of education including several years' studies in countries like the UK and then allowed to settle down in one of those Western countries –better still if they were to marry an Englishman, as Chang did and can afford a middle-class modern Western life style – then it is very plausible that they too will be 'de-brainwashed', and awaken to hate Mao. Imagine how Marx (and possibly Mao) would laugh in his grave: it is after all, material circumstances that condition the human consciousness.

Mao's personality: the known story

In the simple, black and white caricature in *The Unknown Story*, Mao is portrayed as a callous monster with no feelings even for his own family. However, what is known in the literature tells a different story and Chang and Halliday have not taken the trouble to look at that, though they are supposed to have interviewed this and that person and consulted so many documents in Chinese. In his memoirs Mao's bodyguard Li Yinqiao described how during the famine year of 1960 one of Mao's daughters, Li Na, came home from boarding school to have dinner after three weeks' absence. The cook and her mother Jiang Qing made some arrangements so that the dinner for the whole family was special. When the meal started, Li Na was so hungry and ate so fast that both Mao and Jiang Qing stopped eating. Eventually Li Na finished all and everything on the dinner table. Both the cook and Jiang Qing were sobbing and Mao was so moved by the whole matter that he stood up and walked first into his bedroom and then back out to the courtyard, totally lost, not knowing what to do.

Chang and Halliday, like many in the West, would argue that we should not trust accounts like this since this was officially published in China. One should not forget that though the Chinese authorities do not allow any personal attack against past CCP leaders – a very decent attitude one would think – most of the information we know about China, including information condemning Mao, is found in Chinese official publications. In any case what motive would Li Yinqiao have to tell lies about such details of daily life? We know that Liu Shaoqi is officially rehabilitated as a victim of Mao's wrongdoing. It is therefore officially politically correct and rewarding to say good things about Liu. However any observant researcher of the literature in Chinese cannot fail to notice that hardly any personal memoirs by Liu's former bodyguards or those who had served him or worked with him have much to say about Liu that is personally warm.

The logic of denial of the known story

The Taiwanese publisher Yuanliu had contracted to publish the Chinese version of *The Unknown Story*, but abandoned the project after it became clear that the authors could not factually back up at least some of their claims. Especially controversial for the Taiwanese publisher is the claim that one of the KMT's most prominent generals, Hu Zongnan, was a CCP agent. Descendants of Hu demanded that the publisher delete such a claim or they would face a lawsuit. For Chang and Halliday, it is important for such claims to be kept in the book. The book sets to prove that two known stories are not true. One known story is that the CCP triumphed over the KMT because, among other factors, the CCP leader Mao was an excellent military strategist. But the book wants to prove that Mao was a monstrous murderer as well as a useless military leader. The second known story is that the KMT was defeated because it was led by a corrupted dynasty of the four powerful families (Seagrave 1986) and because it had no socioeconomic programmes that could win over the majority of the Chinese in rural China. But Chang and Halliday do not want anything to do with social and societal forces in the story. How can you explain the success of the CCP led by Mao when a largely peasant army fought at huge odds against the modern KMT army, supported by the most advanced and powerful force in the world, the United States? To overturn the two known stories, Chang and Halliday have to say that China was delivered to Mao by agents such as Hu Zongnan.

The Chinese version of *The Unknown Story* appeared eventually, thanks to the *Kaifang* magazine in Hong Kong, one of those anti-communist popular publications that constantly spread rumours about mainland China. The book of course has to be published for its usefulness in sustaining anti-communism.

Let me give one example of many of how Chang and Halliday can be rather loose with the truth. In order to inform the reader about the evil of the Chinese communist regime Chang (2006a) claims that when she was sent by the Chinese government to study in the UK she had to be accompanied by another student whenever she went out or else she would be sent back to China. She also claims that she was probably the first student from mainland China to enter a public bar and the first to go out alone.

In fact that the Chinese government sent students to study in the UK as early as 1972. I myself went to the UK as student before Chang in 1977, along with 17 others. The Chinese embassy did advise us that we should go out at least in pairs for reasons of safety. But we were never told that if we ventured out alone we would be sent back to China. In the beginning we went in groups to classes and out to parties or shopping. But after a while when we got used to our new environment, we would go out alone whenever we wanted. We visited bars and sometimes went alone to the red light district in Soho. I even dated a local girl. Two of us even took a tour trip from the UK to the United States. None of us was sent back to China.

Academic reception

One would assume that by the commonly accepted standard of scholarship *The Unknown Story* should be dismissed immediately. We all know that if the methods are not sound the resulting conclusions should be treated with suspicion. It is true that even in natural science researchers tend to start with presumptions and assumptions. We all tend to seek evidence to prove our conceptualizations or model of explanation. However, we also know that if a scientist or a scholar or a writer distorts evidence deliberately or knowingly the work should be condemned as a fraud.

The academic community did launch a serious effort to review the book in the *China Journal*. Benton and Tsang in their review criticized Chang and Halliday's 'flawed assertions', for the fact that they 'misread sources', 'use them selectively' and 'out of context' (Benton and Tsang 2005: 95). Benton and Tsang have repudiated ten major claims made in the book one by one. Timothy Cheek thinks the book is 'a great waste of effort', and the book's 'TV soap opera-"Dallas" (with Mao as "JR")', offers 'very little that is new'. To Cheek, 'It is propaganda' (Cheek 2005: 110). As Barmé rightly points out, Chang and Halliday's telling of history has a 'callousness' and 'evokes the image of Oriental obliquity' (Barmé 2005: 138). Chan (2006), in his *coup d'œil* review, shows unequivocally that Chang and Halliday's so-called 'New information is manufactured out of a manipulation of facts to such an extreme that they can no longer be sustained by empirical evidence,' and that the co-authors 'prioritize entertainment, sensationalism and titillation over historical accuracy'.

On one occasion, responding to the scholarly criticism, Chang claims, correctly, that 90 per cent of the reviews of their book are positive and that the reason why some academics are critical is that they have to be critical in order to save face, or they would have to admit that they have got it all wrong (Chang 2006b). Right or wrong, by the end of 2006, *The Unknown Story* has already been translated into twelve languages and 13 more language versions are being translated. The book is on the bestseller list in every language version that has been translated so far (Chang 2006b).

One has to wonder why *The Unknown Story* is so highly acclaimed. Even the supposedly left-wing or progressive (whatever that means these days) British flagship paper the *Guardian* takes the book tremendously seriously. Perhaps a self-proclaimed serious paper also has to fashion some market. 'Together, however, they [Chang and Halliday] make a formidable literary partnership, a yin and yang of exotic glamour and scholarly erudition' declares the *Guardian* (2005). A Western yang and a Chinese yin together are really exotic, a fairy tale of glamour. But scholarly erudition? You must be joking.

It is obvious that in writing her biography of Mao, Chang starts with an attitude, an attitude of hatred and therefore the desire to bring down Mao's personality in the scale of history. This can be achieved and all indications are that Chang already has. People, educated or otherwise (and who would want to be told that they are not educated), like ready-made and easily consumable commodities. Here is one.

Revolution: from farewell to burial

As we saw in Chapter 2, the 'forward-looking' neo-Enlightenment Chinese intelligentsia bid their farewell to revolution only a few years after its foremost leader, Mao, died in 1976. By the early 1990s the intellectual climate internationally was such that a farewell was seen as not intellectually rigorous enough. Revolutionary ideas and practices not only had to be dead but also nailed into the coffin under our feet. There was the fall of the Berlin Wall and the collapse of the Soviet Union. The communist party in Russia was dismantled under Yeltsin. Even symbols of revolution had to be dismantled. In the Soviet Union the 7 and 8 of November were public holidays to celebrate the October Revolution in 1917. In 1992 after the collapse of the Soviet Union, the holiday was shortened from two days to one. Then in 1996, the name of the holiday was changed to the 'day of harmony and understanding' (a rough translation). In 2004 under Putin the holiday was again changed by shifting its date to 4 November and it is called something like 'People Unity Day' (Zhang Jie 2007).

Time magazine confidently declares that if they (the brainwashed public?) ever get to read Chang's 'atom bomb of a book', it will cure them of Mao admiration. 'Chang and Halliday have plunged a dagger deep into the heart of the Mao legend, so deep it is hard to imagine anything like a full recovery', declares another reviewer (French 2005). That explains why an intellectual scandal is not treated as such. Yes, Mao has to be brought down. To have the portrait of Mao on the Tian'anmen rostrum is offensive to all the cold-war knights, later converted or not. Without a complete uprooting of the CCP in China it is not yet the End of History. That is why, in spite of some acknowledgements that Jung Chang's historiography is faulty, almost all mainstream reviewers nevertheless feel compelled to kowtow to the theory that Mao indeed was a mass murderer (Williems 2005)

In this global climate of liberal democracy and neoconservative market capitalism triumph, the fall of the Berlin Wall is not enough to draw the final curtain. The Chinese still stubbornly remain 'communist' by refusing to dig Mao's grave. Therefore, the Great Wall of China is still to be brought down so as to bury revolution permanently. It is here that we can see the significance of and connection with the way the French Revolution is evaluated.

Furet and the French Revolution

Inspired by Furet's work, Simon Schama (1989) suggests that the terrorist zeal of the French Revolution created the political and ideological precedents of the twentieth century totalitarian regimes and even of the Holocaust. Furet's basic argument is that there was not much socioeconomic basis for the French Revolution, as the Marxist tradition would have argued. Instead, the French Revolution took place largely because of a political discourse, a popular Rousseauianism that was prevalent on the eve of 1789, which, according to Furet, was dangerously illiberal and therefore the cause of the Terror and violence following the French Revolution. Furet's criticism of absolutism, and especially his battle cry for individualism, could not have come at a better time than during the 1980s when Margaret Thatcher claimed that there was no society but families and when Soviet Union was about to collapse.

In the Furet and Ozouf's *Critical Dictionary of the French Revolution* (1989), which was a publication phenomenon, 'missing are virtually all the major social groups that contributed to ... its felt effects; the nobility, clergy, bourgeoisie, peasants, artisans, and women' (Berenson 1995: 96). This was 'not history from the bottom up, no concern with everyday life and popular culture, and nothing about the production of grain, subsistence crisis, or the economy in general, save for some brief entries on taxes, assignats, and nationalized land.' 'In the effort to break with the Marxist social interpretation, Furet and others have created a history with the society, economy, and popular culture left out' (Berenson 1995: 96).

But all these do not matter. Furet and others like him were in line with the intellectual trend and they therefore drew unusual media attention. The French media crowned Furet in 1989 'the King of the Bicentennial' (Berenson 1995: 96) and American publishers brought out his books immediately after they appeared in French.

In this global intellectual climate, the Chinese revolution cannot be tolerated. The foremost leader of this revolution Mao is a symbol, a metaphor, a battle cry of an alternative set of values that is still threatening, or at least offensive, to the capitalist domination of the globe. Now we are inundated with arguments and comments by China's 'neoliberal dynasty' (Kwong 2006) that the spread of liberal market capitalism is not only good for the Chinese but also for humanity; burial of revolution is the watchword.

In any case, one can afford to bury the revolution after it has done its job.

Is revolution inevitable?

Revolution in human history is not the manifestation of a design by someone, Deity or human, but a process in which some events, though not necessary, become inevitable at a certain point whether one likes it or not. Collective actions take place under certain circumstances in spite of any particular person's wish. In an insightful socioeconomic ecological study of Huaibei peasant rebellions Perry argues that peasant insurrection is a 'sustained, structured, and sensible form of collective action' (Perry 1980: 2) and that 'under conditions of scarcity, violence against fellow competitors is often a rational strategy' and 'Denial of essentials to others is seen as contributing directly to one's own chances for survival' (Perry 1980: 3). In other words, persistent worsening of socioeconomic conditions will lead to violent collective actions. The difference between rebellion and revolution is whether these actions are guided by a politico-socioeconomic programme.

At least two revolutions in modern China are events of such inevitability, the Republic Revolution of 1911 and the Communist Revolution of 1949. The process that fermented the Chinese Communist Revolution ran for a long time. According to the London-educated anthropologist and sociologist Fei Xiaotong (1987 and 1992), traditional

China had a well-developed industry, which was not concentrated in urban cities but dispersed in rural areas. It was this rural industry combined with agriculture that structured Chinese society in which the landlord class and urban commercialization were supported. It was this structure that enabled a rental class to collect a high rate of land tax from the peasantry because incomes from rural industry helped sustain their livelihoods. However, when Western industrial goods penetrated the Chinese market, the consequences were disastrous because the collapse of rural industry meant it became impossible for the peasantry to make a living. Fei here only talks about normal capitalist trade penetration into China's interior. He was not even talking about colonial plunder and the opium trade, for the defence of which the British launched a war. Therefore, Fei argues, conditions were ripe for a peasant revolution. The solution was not only land reform but also income from sources other than land, for land was not enough to support the Chinese population. Both solutions required the re-structuring of the Chinese society.

Today, with hindsight when the job of re-structuring Chinese society has been accomplished, amid the triumph of liberal democracy and market capitalism, revolutionary solutions are seen not only as excessive but as senseless destruction. Regarding the issue of land reform in China, He Zhiguang (2007), in a publication that appeared in the Chinese Communist Party official historical journal *Yanhuang chunqiu*, asserts that during the 1950 land reform Mao overturned Liu Shaoqi's peaceful reform and declares that Mao's intervention was the first step to push back the wheel of history in new China, because the land reform carried out the barbaric violence of class struggle. Mao's policy of land reform was the first step in developing an anti-democracy, anti-humanity and anti-science ultra-leftism, He asserts.

An alternative model of development

Ultimately the issue of evaluating contemporary China comes to the model for modernity. According to mainstream economic history and the history of ideas, large-scale industrialization and urbanization not only embody the best model but an inevitable and a progressive one. Underlying this teleological view there is an assumption of a binary dichotomy: tradition versus modernity, rural versus urban, agriculture versus industry, handicraft versus large-scale industry, organic versus mechanical, status versus contracts, rule versus bureaucracy, water-mill versus steam, advanced versus backward and so on. Taking this assumption for granted and given the empirical and daily-life evidence of the superiority of the Western model of liberal democracy and market capitalism the preferred development model seems obvious.

But is it? Could there be other models that not only make the planet earth sustainable but also create new subjectivity? Do the ideas of Mao give us some direction for that? Badiou certainly thinks so. Badiou (2006) thinks that the Cultural Revolution was an attempt, albeit a failed one, to create new subjectivity. Why is it then that the Cultural Revolution has been seen as only violent and destructive? The logic of burying the revolution requires a narrative that highlights the violent and destructive aspects of popular revolutions. As pointed out by Wang Shaoguang (2006), the current literature focuses on the destructive part of the Cultural Revolution but pays little attention to its constructive part. The destruction mainly occurred at the beginning of the Cultural Revolution, in the years 1966 and 1967, and to some extent even in 1968, but the constructive period lasted from 1967 onwards until 1976. The logic of burying the revolution requires a narrative that denies the constructive aspects of populist revolutions.

6 How a medical doctor doctors history: a case study of Li Zhisui

Introduction: expatriate Chinese memories – a literary phenomenon

As a source for the interpretation and understanding of China's contemporary politics and society in general and of the Chinese Cultural Revolution in particular, memoirs and biographies written by the Chinese themselves have drawn increasing attention from Western academics.[1] The impact that Nien Cheng (1987) Yuan Ming (1994), Li Zhisui (1994) and Jung Chang (1991) have had in the West clearly demonstrates the importance of this genre. One of the most comprehensive monographs on the Cultural Revolution in English, by Barbara Barnouin and Yu Changgen (1993), relies heavily on the memoir and biography literature and claims to have corrected a few Western misperceptions of the Cultural Revolution.

Doctor Li Zhisui's memoirs have created a stir in the West. Even the respectable academic journal, *The China Journal* (formerly called *The Australian Journal of Chinese Affairs*) invited Anne Thurston, David Bachman, Lucian Pye and Geremie Barmé for a special discussion of Li's book in its No. 35 (January) 1996 issue. As for Jung Chang's *Wild Swans*, its popularity is phenomenal. It sold more than 5 million copies worldwide in more than two dozen languages and became the 'biggest grossing non-fiction paperback in publication history' (Kong Shuyu 1997). Many schools and universities use the book as a textbook of modern China. But greater impact does not necessarily mean better understanding. As one personal friend, Cathy Farnworth, who learned Chinese and worked in China commented, someone who did not know anything about China would hate the country after reading Chang's book.

Writings by those Chinese outside China who were participants in contemporary Chinese history are understandably valued by Western scholars. Having settled in the West, these so-called expatriates can write about events that they had participated in without obvious political censorship. The underlying assumption is that they could tell the truth without external pressure. These writers can therefore provide an 'insider' knowledge that a Western writer does not have. The main aim of this chapter is, by a case study, to demonstrate that we are well advised not to take at face value the accounts by former Chinese who now reside in the West. We have to be aware of their backgrounds, their personal interests and prejudices in the production of our knowledge of history.

Memories and the politics of knowledge production

As an indication of personal interest in constructing history we may first take Yuan Ming as an example. The fact that Yuan (1994) idealizes Hu Yaobang, the General Secretary of the CCP during the first years of post-Mao reform, should not be surprising since the latter was his patron and protector at the height of their careers.

That one's personal past is at stake is only one aspect of the production of knowledge. There is also another aspect of knowledge production: what is expected to be well received. We have to be aware of the politics of the market. Writers such as Jung Chang may turn 'their experience into recognizable stories that satisfy the expectations of a Western public', and a 'literature of suffering' that 'moulded through outraged victimization and a broad generational consensus, and simultaneously as an affirmation of a superior Western way of life' (Zarrow 1999: 166–67). Like the film *Raise the Red Lantern* directed By Zhang Yimou, which invented scenes of Chinese tradition to suit the West's curiosity – the kind of scenes that would puzzle the Chinese themselves – the tendency of the post-Mao literature and arts professionals to commercialize Western voyeurism of the Orient is too obvious to ignore.

Though Li's memoirs have been widely reviewed (Mirsky 1994, Young 1994, Bernstein 1994, Link 1994, Wills 1994, Elegant 1994, Buruma 1995 and Teiwes 1996), Li deserves a case study for two reasons. The first is that the image of Mao propagated in the book needs to be corrected. The second is that we need to look at the production process to reveal at least some aspects of how knowledge of contemporary China is manufactured in the West.

Let us start with the academics. Two of the Western scholars involved in the production of the book are not just obscure academics working at some obscure topic in isolation but influential public intellectuals propagating ways to change China. One of them is Andrew Nathan who has served:

> on the Advisory Committee of Human Rights Watch, Asia, and on the board of Human Rights in China. He is frequently interviewed about East Asian issues in print and electronic media, and he has served as an advisor to several film documentaries

on China and as a consultant for businesses and government agencies.

(Columbia Education Resources Online
http://cero.columbia. edu/help/authors.html)

The other, Anne Thurston, a self-claimed 'independent scholar', is a consultant to the National Endowment for Democracy and host of *Views and Perspectives* on Voice of America (Johns Hopkins University http://apps.sais-jhu.edu/faculty_bios/faculty_bio1. php?ID=56).

The book

The Private Life of Chairman Mao is supposedly written by Mao's personal physician of 22 years and close confidant. Simultaneously published by Random House in English and the Chinese Times Publishing Company of Taipei in Chinese, the book purports to reveal Mao's private life, and to denounce the Mao era as an unmitigated disaster under the dictatorship of an evil monster. That the publication of this book has such a purpose is confirmed by the review headlines 'The tyrant Mao as told by his doctor (Bernstein 1994), 'Unmasking the monster' (Mirsky 1994), 'Mao the monster (Elegant 1994) and 'The emperor has no clothes: Mao's doctor reveals the naked truth' (Wills 1994). The book was highly acclaimed by prominent academics like Lucian Pye, who thinks 'this work has tremendous value' (DeBorja and Dong 1996: 2), and Andrew Nathan, who in his Foreword praises the book's 'unique' and 'most revealing' value.

For those who are familiar with the literature in Chinese, there was in fact very little that was really new in the book when it hit the Western market. For the significant figures and events described in Li's book, memoirs and biographies published previously in China and Hong Kong have revealed as much, if not more. For instance, it was widely claimed in published volumes that Mao behaved like an emperor and almost every word of his was taken as an imperial edict. Decisions were made by personal whim and those around him were expected to pick up the pieces afterwards. Jiang Qing was hysterical, paranoid, unpredictable and vicious. Because she was Mao's wife, even top-ranking CCP leaders tried not to offend her. Lin Biao was presented as being chronically sick and having used every opportunity to praise Mao so that he could gain more power. Zhou Enlai was depicted as acting subserviently to Mao so as to save his own skin. The 'Hundred Flowers' campaign was Mao's plot to lure the intellectuals out so that he could strike them as 'rightists'. The Great Leap Forward was Mao's personal fantasy, which led to the death of millions as result of starvation. The Cultural Revolution was a power struggle that ultimately aimed at finishing Liu Shaoqi. And so on. Broadly speaking, there was not much that was new in Li's memoirs.

The memoirs purport to show inside knowledge of personal power struggle at Mao's inner court, an area where Teiwes has expertise, having in fact worked on this topic throughout his career (Teiwes 1967, 1974, 1978, 1979, 1983, 1984, 1990, 1996, 1998; Teiwes and Sun 1999). According to Teiwes (1996), Li uses 'Cultural Revolution style analysis'; Li was 'on the fringe of these events', but claims to be Mao's political confidant; his interpretation was 'anti-Mao', 'reflecting conventional views', 'uncritical' and 'dependent on official sources' (Teiwes 1996: 179–80) and Li 'simply got key aspects of the story wrong' (Teiwes 1996: 182). Teiwes testifies that a substantial part of Li's memoirs are 'recycling widely available information and interpretations' and that with regard to elite politics there is only one piece of information which provides something new; 'The rest contains no surprise' (Teiwes, 1996:179).

Knowledge gap

Li's memoirs were not based on original records or personal diaries. All his original diaries were burned by himself during the Cultural Revolution. Instead, the book is based on restructured memories, which might 'be wrong' and 'fallible' as Li's collaborator, Anne F. Thurston, later had to admit (Thurston 1996). One inevitable question then is why the book is considered to be so valuably revealing. When a colleague of mine, who has long been in a professorial position in Chinese politics working in Australia, said to me that the book revealed so much that he had not known, I replied that in fact for those who were familiar with what has been written in the Chinese literature there was not much that was new. This colleague of mine did not seem to register my remarks. This makes one wonder: is it possible that many a scholar in the field of Chinese studies does not actually read widely what is written in Chinese? I suspect that this is true, for probably two reasons. One is that for one who has learned Chinese as a second language the non-alphabetic script is not exactly easy to read widely and profusely. Second, some scholars may believe, and there is a reason for it, that Chinese materials, including volumes of books, are not worth reading until and unless they are closely related to one's specific target of research. There is therefore an inevitable knowledge gap between what is already available in Chinese and what is accessible to the non-Chinese speaking world.

The knowledge gap provides a partial answer to the question of why the book is so highly acclaimed: what appears new is valuable. However, there is more to it. New information per se may not be interesting or even relevant. New information has to be structured and made relevant to an argument or a theory. It is therefore worth stressing a truism that scholarship is not independent from politics.

Knowledge production and the market

At any given time of human history, scholarly research has been orientated or even dictated by a particular ideology, or by strategic national interest. This is not only a question of the intention of individual scholars but also a question of resources that are available (Dirlik 1996). Furthermore, seemingly non-political values and beliefs influence research agendas and approaches. More of this is discussed in other chapters. Finally there is commercialism. Publishers like Random House want to make profits and therefore there is a motive for Random House to 'sex up' Li's memoirs for the market.

Put in these contexts it is more understandable why high profile scholars like Andrew Nathan would, in his Foreword to Li's memoirs, show a more hostile attitude towards Mao than Li himself whose basic theme is anti-Mao (Teiwes 1996). These contexts explain not only why such books are highly acclaimed but also why two US scholars are willing to be involved in such projects.

With perhaps a few exceptions, all authors need assistance and help in their work. US scholars' involvement in Li's book is nothing unusual. However, the nature of assistance can vary and hence have different influences on the end product. It is inevitable that personal views of Chinese history by those involved could and would influence Li's approach, selection of materials and interpretation of historical events. One is particularly struck by the peculiar fact that both the Chinese and English versions of Li's book are products of translation. The English version is acknowledged to be translated by Professor Tai Hung-chao while the Chinese version is acknowledged to be translated by Li himself. One wonders what the original manuscript was. According to Tai, it was Random House the publisher who wanted to add more 'juicy bits' such as Mao's sex life to the book, to attract a larger readership. Li was in disagreement with this line of approach but eventually overruled by Random House (Tai Hung-chao 2000).

The logic of the differences in two versions

In fact the production process of the book has far more serious implications than just commercial considerations. Li Zhisui (1996), in a letter that appeared posthumously, admitted that the Chinese edition was not his original Chinese version but a translation from English and that substantial parts of the original Chinese manuscript were cut by Thurston. One wonders to what extent the English version of the book was written by Li himself. In an Open Letter (for the English text of the Open Letter, see DeBorja and Dong 1996) published in the *Asian American Times* in New York, *Wen hui bao* in Hong Kong and the *Straits Review* in Taiwan in February 1995, the signatories of the letter denounced the book and pointed out the discrepancies between the English and Chinese versions. In the Chinese version, claims such as that the memoirs were based on Li's diaries, that Li was the best doctor in China, and that Li could recall Mao's words verbatim are absent. Absent in the Chinese version are also claims about Mao's womanizing behaviour spreading venereal disease, statements like 'I [Mao] wash myself inside the bodies of my women' or Mao was 'devoid of human feelings'. Absent also were some of Thurston's notes.

Some of the omissions in the Chinese version indicate the awareness by the production team that such outrageous claims may be 'sexy' to the English readers but cannot be included in the Chinese version since they are too obviously false to the Chinese insiders. Other omissions are due to political reasons. For instance in the English version, when talking about Deng's absence from the 1959 Lushan Conference, it asserts that when in hospital for foot trouble Deng Xiaoping made a nurse pregnant and the nurse was forced to have an abortion. That was taken out in the Chinese version. Deng had not only 'reversed the verdict' of the Cultural Revolution but also made China part of the capitalist world. The Taiwan publisher might feel that such a capitalist roader, though the real butcher of the 1989 Tian'anmen Massacre, was not to be offended. Or more likely the publisher knew that the Chinese readers could not be fooled so easily by such an unsubstantiated claim.

Who is to be fooled and why?

Other discrepancies pointed out in DeBorja and Dong (1996) are also revealing, for they again indicate an understanding by those who were involved in the production of this book that a Western reader is easily and willingly deceived, or has to be fooled. For example in the English version there is this statement: 'As Mao's doctor, I was allowed unimpeded access.' Compare this with the Chinese version: 'As Mao's doctor, only I, when performing a medical examination, have some opportunities to see Mao and have a few words with him' (DeBorja and Dong 1996: 48). And there are more. In English it is, 'When Mao returned from Beidaihe [in the summer of 1955], I began seeing him every day, the excuse we often used was his study of English' whereas in Chinese the second part of the sentence starting with 'excuse' is absent. 'The study of English' bit is absent in the Chinese version because among the readers of the Chinese version there would be Chinese insiders who would know that Li was not Mao's teacher of

English. The Chinese version of 'Mao stated in his speech at the Chengdu meeting' becomes 'During our talk in Chengdu' in English. Different wording is required here because a Chinese insider would know that what follows the opening of the sentence is actually from Mao's officially published words, not words conveyed to Li in a personal chat. This kind of truth cannot be shown to the English reader because the selling point in the English-speaking market that claims to show why the value of Li's book is that Mao revealed Chinese politics to Li personally, the kind of information that is not available officially.

Protests from the insiders

Apart from the Open Letter, a statement of protest signed by Wang Dongxing, Li Yinqiao, Ye Zilong and others, altogether 150 people who worked with Mao or for Mao, was issued (DeBorja and Dong 1996: 4). A great deal of fuss was made when Li, supposedly Mao's personal doctor, claimed that Mao was sexually promiscuous. The statement protests strongly against this claim. The Chinese authorities, predictably, also denounced both Li's book and a BBC documentary that echoed his account. Both the protest statement and the Chinese authorities' apparent indignation were dismissed by the Western media, of course. However, another response cannot be dismissed so offhandedly. Lin Ke, Xu Tao and Wu Xujun (Lin Ke et al 1995), who worked as Mao's secretary, personal doctor and chief nurse respectively, have presented a scathing critique of Li.

The very fact that these people are either speaking or writing inside China means that many Western scholars may not take their views seriously. This is a legitimate concern since there is heavy censorship by the Chinese authorities and all kinds of political risks in speaking against the Chinese government. But to be critical of Li's anti-Mao book is not exactly supporting the then Chinese government either since there was a powerful faction inside the CCP that had been very critical of Mao. In any case, like all other writings, including that by Li Zhisui and Andrew Nathan, we have to assess Lin Ke et al's account against known documentation, its internal consistency and its compatibility with well-researched knowledge. This is what I am going to do next.

Was Li Mao's personal physician?

Lin Ke et al claim that Li's memoirs contain many errors and false-hoods; one of the most obvious is the claim that Li was Mao's personal physician as early as 1954. It is logical to assume that Li's claims are more trustworthy than Lin Ke et al because Li was writing outside

China. However, Lin Ke et al do present original documentation as evidence. There is an entry in Mao's medical record signed by Li which shows that Li took over the responsibility for looking after Mao's health on 3 June 1957. On the other hand, there is no original documentation in Li's book that unambiguously shows that Li was Mao's doctor before 1957. In the book there are only two pictures of Li dated before 1957. One is of him standing alone at the Zhongnanhai compound (where some CCP leaders lived) and the other shows him swimming with two people. The caption of the swimming picture claims that Li is swimming with Mao, but Mao is not in the picture.

Wu Xujun, who was Mao's chief nurse (*hushi zhang*), argues the other photo also makes a false claim. The caption of that photo claims that it was taken at Mao's residence. In fact, as is shown by the background wall in the photo, the photo was taken at a clinic where Li worked, which was far from Mao's residence (Lin Ke et al 1995: 146–7). Wu points out that more than 180 pages of Li's memoirs are devoted to Li's so-called eyewitness account of China and Mao during the years between 1954 and 1957, but during those years Li was not even Mao's general practitioner (Lin Ke et el 1995: 150).

How much did the doctor know?

Lin Ke et al also point out Li's mistaken claim that he had found Mao to be infertile. To affirm that Li was wrong about Mao's infertility Li Ke et al interviewed Professor Wu Jieping, a medial authority who looked after Mao (Wu was alive when Li Ke et al was published). Yet Li was a doctor; how could he make such a mistake? The reason, according to Lin Ke et al, is that the book has to say somehow that Mao was infertile. Otherwise the book has to answer the inevitable question of where Mao's illegitimate children are since the book claims that Mao had slept with so many women.

In order to get Li to 'reveal' all the important political events about which Li knew nothing or could not care less, the English version added incidents in which Li was present at many exclusive party meetings including even the CCP Politburo Standing Committee meetings. It is claimed that Li was present when the Cultural Revolution Small Group meeting took place in Wuhan on 8 February 1967. But Lin Ke et al (1995) argue that it was impossible for Li to have been present at all these meetings because that was against CCP party discipline and regulations. Lin Ke himself, who was much closer to Mao in political and policy issues, was not able to attend meetings at this level.

Lin Ke et al point out that personnel such as nurses, bodyguards or secretaries who worked with Mao and had Mao's trust all have some personal memento from Mao, like his notes, instructions, letters or calligraphy. But Li could not produce even one such personal item. Lin Ke et al point out, as Li himself admits, Mao did not like doctors interfering with his life habits and therefore would not like to have a doctor around him unless absolutely necessary. Moreover, Li did not seem to be someone whom Mao could trust personally. Therefore it is logically inconceivable that Mao would confide to Li his important thoughts that he would not confide in with others who were closer and more trusted, like Lin Ke or Wu Xujun who was Mao's trusted chief nurse. Li Zhisui was only Mao's general practitioner (*baojian yisheng*) and Lin Ke et al find it laughable that in the memoirs Li is portrayed as omnipresent and omniscient person, as if in 20 years Li had been with Mao every day wherever he went for a meeting whether in or outside Beijing.

Li not only pretends to have attended the CCP Eighth Congress with Mao, but also claims to have witnessed the clashes between Mao and Liu/Deng. Specifically Li claims that it was Deng, against Mao's own wishes, who proposed statements that opposed personality cults and who proposed deleting a stipulation in the Party Constitution that Mao thought should be the guiding thought in every line of work. In fact, it was Mao who in April 1956, when he made comments on the document evaluating the historical lesson of the Soviet Union, suggested that China should guard against personality cult (Lin Ke et al 1995: 48). It was Mao who suggested that Liu Shaoqi, Zhu De, Zhou Enlai and Chen Yun be elected as additional deputy chairmen of the CCP and that Deng Xiaoping be promoted to be the CCP General Secretary (Lin Ke et al 1995). It was also Mao, as early as 1954, who made the suggestion of avoiding the term 'Mao Zedong Thought', as it was too arrogant. The CCP, following Mao's suggestion, issued a guideline to refer to 'Mao Zedong's instructions' and 'Work by Mao Zedong' instead (Lin Ke et al 1995: 50). All these facts can be confirmed by official documents such as those in Mao's collected volumes of speeches.

Li's memoirs make a claim of Mao sleeping with women under a big quilt. Lin Ke et al ridicule such a claim because it was a well-known fact that Mao never used quilts after he moved to Beijing but always used towelling coverlets (*maojin bei*). How could some one who claims to know Mao intimately get such a simple fact wrong? The answer is simple: because the story is fabricated. That is why, when questioned by a Chinese audience face to face, Li admitted that he had never seen Mao in bed with a woman (Li Zhisui 1994).

What did the medical doctor know about politics?

Another critique of Li's memoirs is also worth considering here. It is an account by Qi Benyu (1996 and 2004), a prominent member of the

Cultural Revolution radicals in Beijing. Qi was arrested at Mao's instruction in January 1968 when Mao saw the danger of a backlash within the army against the Cultural Revolution. Qi was subsequently imprisoned for 18 years. Therefore it is reasonable to assume that he would not have any personal interest in defending Mao. Qi first of all dismissed the notion of a 'private doctor' or 'personal physician' by saying that Mao did not have a private doctor. Every one was 'public' in those days and Li Zhisui was one of a team of medical staff who looked after all the personnel at the Zhongnanhai compound until 1957. Later Li was recommended by Wang Dongxing to be Mao's health-maintenance doctor, a Chinese version of a general practitioner. Second, Qi thinks Li was a good doctor professionally but politically naïve and ignorant, and therefore had no knowledge or expertise to comment on Chinese politics.

Qi gives some examples. Regarding the Great Leap Forward Li did not know or does not say that it was in fact Mao who first made suggestions to cool down the CCP elite and to make corrections to rectify the exacerbated situation. Regarding the Cultural Revolution:

> aside from his account of the support-the-left activities (*zhi zuo*) in which he [Li] personally participated, most of the Cultural Revolution part of his memoirs consists of stuff gleaned from newspapers, journals and other people's writings. To make Western readers believe that he had access to core secrets, Li fabricated scenarios, resulting in countless errors in the memoirs.
>
> (Qi 1996: 187)

Qi thinks 'It's really preposterous' (1996: 189) that Li claims that he was present at so many meetings because even Mao's most trusted Red Army veteran doctor Fu Lianzhang, who had been on the Long March and later was promoted to be Deputy Health Minister, was not allowed such access. Nor were Mao's personal secretaries and bodyguards. Up to the beginning of the Cultural Revolution even Wang Dongxing, the chief of Mao's personal guards, was not allowed such access.

The politics of sex

Qi lived 'in the vicinity of Mao Zedong for many years' (Qi 1996: 192) and had frequent contacts with all the people who worked for Mao. Therefore he should have known if Mao had been fooling around with women. Qi does think that Mao should not have married He Zizhen when his first wife Yang Kaihui was arrested by the local KMT warlord but still alive. At the beginning of the Cultural Revolution in 1976 Qi even asked Zhou Enlai about Mao's extramarital affairs. But Qi declares that in all those years he had never heard even a rumour of Mao sleeping with any women outside his marriage and that Li's accusations about Mao's philandering were lies and fabrications. Qi states that Mao's bedroom had no locks and was never locked. The duty office of the guards, secretaries, nurses and attendants was just outside the door. The office operated on a round-the-clock basis, and was staffed 24 hours a day; 'all activities were entered into records' (Qi 1996: 195). Qi states that Mao was very respectful to 'female comrades' and he had never heard of any complaint of sexual harassment against Mao. He did hear such complaints against other powerful people on the compound. Qi (2004) continued to hold these views in another interview that took place in 2004.

History as doctored by the doctor and his US mentors: a critical analysis

Compared with memoirs and biographies written in China, Li gives a more sympathetic and more believable portrayal of Jiang Qing, who was isolated, lonely, depressed and desperately wanted attention. However, Li's assertion that Jiang Qing wanted to be a modern Wu Zetian, a powerful empress, was blatantly parroting the Chinese official propaganda and Chinese intelligentsia's accustomed Confucian approach to history.

The most surprising aspect of Li's book is his portrayal of Wang Dongxing as understanding, intelligent, skilful but not at all fearful. Wang was one of the few most powerful men in the Mao era and carried out routine duties to implement Mao's personal instructions. It is very hard to reconcile Li's two portraits: on the one hand his description of a vengeful and power paranoid emperor Mao and on the other of a benign Wang Dongxing who was Director of the Central Office of the CCP and head of Mao's bodyguards. Li claims that Wang Dongxing is his friend, but Wang nonetheless joined the protest against Li's book.

Li's account of events such as Mao's meeting with his former wife He Zizhen, his quarrel with Peng Dehuai at Lushan and the dismissal of his bodyguard Han Qingyu, are claimed by Lin Ke et al (1995) to have contained errors of detail that were exactly the same as those told by Ye Yonglie. The fact that dancing parties were organized for the top leaders and that Mao had many young women around him in his later years was no secret before Li's book was published.

For someone who claims to have had Mao's confidence even in political matters, Li fails to offer any insight on many significant figures and events. For instance he gives no explanation as to why Lin

Biao, who hated ceremonies, and hated meeting foreigners (Jiang Bo and Li Qing 1993, Jiao Ye 1993, Wen Feng 1993, Guan Weixun 1993, Teiwes and Sun 1996), and who was designated as Mao's successor in the State Constitution in 1969, wanted the position of Chairman of the State, the primary function of which would be to meet foreigners. According to Quan Yanchi, far from being a good-for-nothing coward who acted subserviently to Mao in order to gain power, Lin Biao was arrogant and was one of the very few who dared to confront Mao personally if he disagreed with him. The only thing Lin Biao would not do was to criticize Mao publicly or behind his back. That Lin Biao wanted to take power from Mao was a conventional view touted by the Chinese government official line. According to Wang Nianyi and He Shou (2000) there was very little evidence that Lin Biao wanted to pursue a power struggle with Mao at the fatal Lushan Conference in 1970. Mao was angry with Lin Biao not because the latter wanted to take power from him, but because Mao was afraid that there was a Lin Biao faction against his Cultural Revolution line.

The Chinese intelligentsia like to use Mao's own words of 'luring snakes out of holes' to argue that Mao had conspired to 'strike' down intellectuals by inviting their criticisms of the CCP leadership prior the Anti-Rightist Movement in 1957. Li not only believes this but also goes further by claiming that Mao's real aim was to incite attack against the political foes who had challenged him during the Eighth Party Congress in 1956. However, Mao's own words should not always be taken at face value to interpret his intention and action. It is not only possible but likely that Mao used the phrase 'to lure snakes out of holes to strike' to justify his backfired plan of the Hundred Flowers (which was designed to invite criticisms of the CCP) to those of his comrades who were against the idea at the very beginning. In a book based on his doctorate thesis, Zhu Di (1995) argues convincingly that Mao's Hundred Flowers policy to rectify the Party was intended to reduce the tensions and conflicts made manifest by protests and strikes in Chinese society in 1956 after Khrushchev's 'Secret Report' denounced Stalin and the political events in Poland and Hungary. There were a whole range of complicated theoretical and practical issues, which cannot be discussed here, that worked together to lead to a nasty Anti-Rightist Movement.

Zhu Di's arguments may well be just one interpretation, and the book was published in China, a fact that reduces its credibility for many in the West. However, the fact remains that Zhu Di's book is well researched with footnotes and is based on documentary evidence that can be checked and examined. In contrast, even if Li was Mao's personal physician since 1954 as claimed by Li himself, what Mao actually said to Li in private cannot be confirmed by supporting evidence.

There are other questionable claims made by Li about Mao that cannot be backed up by documentary evidence.[2] To support the theme that all Mao's moves after 1956 were aimed at toppling Liu Shaoqi, Li claims that Mao wanted to close down the special clinics for top-ranking CCP leaders because he heard that Li Shaoqi had suffered lung disease. However, according to Lin Ke et al (1995), Mao ordered the closure of the special clinics in 1964 whereas Liu Shaoqi's lung disease was already cured in 1963.

Mao's accusation in 1965 that the Ministry of Health was the 'Ministry of the Urban Lord' not only had nothing to do with any power struggle, but had much to do with policy direction. Towards the end of the 1950s Mao retreated to the second line of leadership and let Liu Shaoqi, Deng Xiaoping, Zhou Enlai, Chen Yun and Peng Zhen run the day-to-day affairs of China until 1965. It was during these years that China's healthcare became more routinized, bureaucratized and professionalized. In this process of professionalization, healthcare became a system that catered for the urban sector, especially the CCP, PLA and professional elite. Mao was not happy with this state of affairs and therefore wanted to change policy directions. To do so he had to upset the establishment, and therefore particular individuals in the establishment were affected. It was not an issue of personal ego but a policy issue, though policy change inevitably involved personal power struggle. What happened during the late 1960s and early 1970s, like sending many urban doctors to rural areas, setting up the 'barefoot doctor' system and the policies and practices that improved healthcare for tens of millions of rural people, clearly confirms that the change in the health system was not a power struggle issue but a policy issue.

Li also claims that whenever Mao disliked anyone, or suspected anyone's loyalty or wanted to punish anyone, he would send that person into exile to a labour camp. This interpretation, again, runs against documentary evidence. Mao regularly sent his bodyguards and his personnel to grassroots unit to work and to live with the ordinary people for the purpose of getting to know what life was like at grassroots and of improving their personal qualities. He sent his most valued son Mao Anying to work with peasants as soon as the latter came back from Moscow to Yan'an. During the Cultural Revolution, Mao sent his daughter Li Na to an farm in Jiangxi. It was the CCP's declared policy that its party officials should live and work with the ordinary people. As a person from a rural background, Mao's decision to send his staff and children to the countryside might have been inspired by the rural Chinese cultural value that one had to *chi ku* (eat bitterness): that is, to undergo hardship, to appreciate life and to be a worthy person. It is reasonable enough that people like Li from wealthy and Western-trained backgrounds could not understand such a philosophy. However, to ignore documented evidence so as to twist

Mao's stated intention to suit the theme of personal power struggle is a different matter.

Once the theme of personal power struggle is set up as a theoretical framework, there is a tendency to argue that every move by Mao was designed to underpin his personal power. In his Foreword to Li's book, Nathan states that 'After the famine began, Mao retreated to a secondary position of power' (Li Zhisui 1994: xii). What is not said but implied in this statement is that Mao had lost power and had to launch the Cultural Revolution to re-gain it. In fact by giving up the Chairmanship of the State and by retreating to the second line of government, Mao did not retreat to a 'secondary position of power'. The Chinese term *er xian* (second line), a term used, again, by Mao himself to refer to his resignation of the post the chairmanship of the State, does not mean a second line of power. Anyone who knows the real nature of Chinese politics should know that the real power lay in the hands of the Chairman of the CCP. Liu Shaoqi as Chairman of the State and Zhou Enlai as Premier of the State Council were at the forefront of day-to-day affairs. But the Chairman of the CCP was meant to be pulling the strings behind the curtain (Teiwes 1988).

The statement by Nathan quoted above also implies that Mao retreated because of the failure of the Great Leap Forward. However, it was Mao himself who raised the issue of *er xian* and volunteered to give up the State Chairmanship as early as 1956. In April 1959, when Liu Shaoqi was publicly declared to have taken over the post of Chairman of the State, Mao's prestige both in name and in reality remained intact. A serious crack in his prestige began to appear only after the Lushan Conference later in 1959 when Peng Dehuai mounted a challenge to him. Even that challenge was not serious because the full effect of the disastrous Great Leap Foreword was not manifest until a year or so later.

Here are another couple of damming statements by Nathan: 'He [Mao] thought there was more to learn about leadership from the pages of Chinese history than from textbooks of modern engineering. While people starved, he imagined that they had more than they could eat' (Li Zhisui 1994: xi). The first sentence again implies more than it states. Even today no Chinese leader, or Western leader for that matter, would think textbooks of modern engineering can teach them how to lead their country. The point Nathan wants to make is that Mao was to blame for the boasting and falsification of agricultural productivity and the backyard furnaces making iron and steel during the Great Leap Forward that led to disastrous consequences. However, the reality was more complex than this criticism implies. To start with, backyard furnaces were not Mao's invention. Nor did they come about because of Mao's order. In fact, as even Li has to admit, Mao was very sceptical and kept on asking: if backyard furnaces were so good, why do foreign countries have big iron and steel plants instead? As for the credibility of reports of agricultural outputs in astronomical figures, there is documentary evidence that Mao did not believe them and, as testified by Wu Lengxi (1995), Mao warned caution all the time, though he was assured by the distinguished scientist Qian Xuesheng (Li Rui 1994, Cai Yongmei 1992) that it was possible to produce tens of thousands of kilograms of rice on one mu of land if the crop had enough ventilation and light.[3] Qian probably meant that it was theoretically possible if planting was close enough and if the problems of ventilation and light could be solved.

Liu Shaoqi, known to be pragmatic and level-headed, not only supported of the Great Lead Forward ideas that proved to be disastrous but also initiated them. It was he who, with Zhou Enlai and Lu Dingyi, the Minister of Propaganda, on a train in April 1958, discussed the idea of factories running schools and schools running factories. Liu wanted Wu Zhipu, the Party Secretary of Henan Province to experiment with these ideas, and Henan became one of the worst hit famine provinces. It was Liu who said that China could catch up with the UK in two years and who demanded that the farmers should produce yet more when he was told about already incredible yields. It was Liu who said that the public canteen was good for liberating women from the kitchen and that back-yard steel making was worth experimenting with because even failure would teach a lesson (Bo 1997: 731–33, Chen Xianong 2006: 159).

Bo Yibo (1997: 753) mentions that a 'responsible comrade' (*fuze tongzhi*) in mid-September 1958 even suggested to Mao that every one in China should eat to their full without having to pay, but Mao did not accept this suggestion. Bo does not want to reveal the name of the comrade. According to Chen Xianong (2006: 168–170) the comrade was none other than Liu Shaoqi. It was not just Liu. In May 1959 both Zhu De and Zhou Enlai raised the idea of ceasing the practice of public canteens, but Deng Xiaoping and Peng Zhen wrote to Mao to oppose the idea of abolishing them (Chen Xianong 2006: 198). During the 1961 Guangzhou Conference Chen Boda, after an investigative tour, also submitted a report to Mao suggesting the abolition of public canteens. Mao tabled the report as the number one document for the conference. However, during a discussion on the matter both Tao Zhu and Zhao Ziyang (later Premier and then General Secretary of the CCP during the post-Mao reform until he was purged by Deng for opposing the Tian'anmen crackdown) argued against Chen Boda's suggestion by saying the public canteen practice was good (Chen Xianong 2006: 195).

Even Deng Xiaoping had to admit openly that he and other CCP leaders should be also held responsible for the Great Leap Forward disaster because they supported the ideas and policies. However, Deng did not want to admit that what he did was more than passively support Mao. Deng was the General Secretary of the CCP at that time and was not only responsible for implementing the Great Leap Forward policies but also for acting as the interface between the centre, headed by Mao, and various regional and provincial leaders who put the ideas and policies in practice. It is therefore not surprising that during the Seven Thousand Delegates meeting in Beijing in early 1962, when Mao made a public criticism of himself for the Great Leap Forward disaster, Deng defended Mao by saying that mistakes were made because his office of the General Secretariat did not follow Mao's ideas to the spirit (Zhang Suhua 2006). Deng's defence of Mao was so effusive that even Mao was embarrassed (Wu Lengxi 2000: 317). It is also not surprising that Deng defended his ally and friend, Li Jingquan, who was the CCP boss of the Southwest region and principal leader of Sichuan province where the famine death toll was the worst (Zhang Suhua 2006).

The second sentence by Nathan quoted above is very ambiguous. During the height of the Great Leap Forward in 1958, Mao, like other CCP leaders, did have the illusion that peasants could produce more than they could eat. However, by 1959 he began to be cautious. In fact, it was Mao who put a stop to some of the stupid practices of the Great Leap Forward in late 1958, as pointed out by Lin Ke et al (1995). As early as March 1958 Mao instructed the chief editor of the *People's Daily*, Wu Lengxi, not to publish a report from Henan on its wish list of what could be achieved in three years. Mao said the tone must be adjusted and cold water had to be poured on those who were full of themselves (Wu Lengxi 1995: 63–4). Again and again in April, August and November 1958 Mao told Wu that the media had to be cool-headed and had to tone down publicity about unrealistic production targets, that they should not inspire unrealistic production targets, and that their news and reports had to be realistic, cautious and down to earth. In June 1958 Mao instructed Peng Zhen and Deng Xiaoping to make sure that the media changed their direction from inflated reporting to cool realism. According to Wu (1995) it was not Mao but other leaders who were in charge of the propaganda work who were slow to change.

It is true that Mao might have acted as an emperor and his words were treated as God-given by many. However, anyone who has a rudimentary knowledge of China should know that not everything that happened in China under Mao's rule was his own doing. It is therefore incredible for a scholar of international standing to make simplistic and naïve statements such as 'He [Mao] froze the people's standard of living at subsistence level in order to build a massive wasteful industrial structure' (Nathan in Li Zhisui 1994: x). Mao is taken as a God who had not only the power but the intention of freezing the Chinese people's standard of living.

As it is common knowledge, most of the concrete economic policy measures that were responsible for the people's standard of living were not designed, let alone implemented, by Mao himself. The policies of monopoly sale and purchase of agricultural produce, the rationing of commodities and the grades of salaries, some implemented before the Great Leap Forward and some after, were designed by people like Chen Yun, Li Fuchun and Bo Yibo. The policy of squeezing the peasantry and controlling consumption was based on the Soviet model to accumulate capital for industrial development.

In fact Mao was not happy with China's copying the Soviet Model of economic development in which everything was planned from the centre. The Great Leap Forward was an attempt to find an alternative in which planning was not concentrated in Beijing. An indication of this idea is the fact during the Great Leap Forward all the important conferences about policies were not held in Beijing but locally: Zhengzhou, Wucahn, Hangzhou, Shanghai and Nanning. Clearly Mao wanted a decentralized model of development in which various levels of leadership and the broad masses of workers and farmers participated in the planning process of economic construction. It was largely due to the work along this direction during the Great Leap Forward and later in the Cultural Revolution that China's post-cold war reforms were able to develop differently from those of the former Soviet Union and to succeed (Shirk 1993).

Mao's strategy of a different approach was not only premised on the fact that there were not enough technical and professional experts in China when the Communists took over power. More importantly, as brilliantly analysed by Schumann (1968), Mao did not want the professional and technical elite to monopolize economic planning and management. He wanted the non-expert to lead the expert (*waihang lingdao neihang*) and wanted politics to control economic activities and ensure that 1) a correct political line was upheld and 2) the masses and revolutionaries who were not experts were not marginalized in production and construction.

Of course to do that Mao had to bring the others along, and in trying to bring his colleagues along he was very often bullying and dictatorial. At the end of the day, most, if not all, of Mao's colleagues did go along and some of them even went further than Mao intended. According to Chen Boda (Chen Xiaonong 2006), it was Bo Yibo, Chair of the powerful Economic Commission who was responsible for the backyard furnaces. In fact the three fatal ideas all came from Bo: China could catch up the UK in two years (in this he was supported by Liu Shaoqi), that industry should focus on the production of iron and stee, and that the target output of iron and steel in 1958 should be double the 5.35 million tons produced in 1957 (Chen Xiaonong 2006: 181–4, Bo Yibo 1997: 706–7). Li Rui, the self-proclaimed secretary of Mao (more of him in another chapter) on the other hand, choses not to reveal these suggestions of Bo Yibo's in his influential *A Record of the Lushan Conference* (Li Rui 1994) because that would weaken the anti-Mao thesis of his book.

Mao must be held principally responsible for the Great Leap Forward disaster since he not only was at the centre of the policy-making process (MacFarquhar 1974–1997) but also encouraged the Leap from co-ops to the commune system and even bullied Zhou Enlai and Deng Zihui (Teiwes and Sun 1999) for their initial cautious attitudes. However, documentary evidence (see discussion in other chapters) and recently available testimonials do suggest that the picture is much more complex than what is usually presented as in Li Rui (1994) and Alfred Chan (2001). It is certainly not as simple as Nathan wants us to believe.

Of course, there was a power struggle within the CCP, as there is a power struggle in any political institution, past or present, oriental or occidental. Like any politician, Mao wanted power and control. However, to reduce everything to personal power and control not only lacks insight but is actually naïve and fanciful. To reduce every event or policy change to a personal power struggle is exactly what Li does. For instance, the fact that Mao was critical of Khrushchev's secret report denouncing Stalin is interpreted as Mao's attempt to maintain the need for a personality cult and to avoid the potential danger of his being demoted. This kind of interpretation is infantile. As a leader of the largest communist party in the world, Mao's criticism of Khrushchev was not only not personal but also logical and consistent. Personally, Mao should have felt vindicated by Khrushchev's denunciation of Stalin, who had never really trusted him. From Mao's point of view, Stalin could and should be criticized, but the criticism must be constructive. Mao actually thought that a correct evaluation of Stalin should be 70 per cent positive and 30 per cent negative. For many this judgement did not do enough to condemn Stalin's brutality and reflected Mao's identification with Stalin's murderous ways of dealing with his political rivals. But the matter was far more complex than that.

Pragmatically Mao's defence of Stalin was a tactical defence for the sake of the strategic cause of communism. In Mao's view, Khrushchev's denunciation of Stalin would seriously damage the cause of Communism all over the world. Subsequent events proved that Mao was right. Theoretically, he had serious ideological disagreement with Khrushchev. To start with, he did not agree with Khrushchev's argument that peaceful transition from capitalism to communism was possible. Furthermore, Khrushchev had not the intellectual capacity to entertain the Maoist idea that a capitalist class might develop inside a communist party. It was those principled and principal differences between Mao and the Soviet leaders that finally led to the fallout between China and Soviet Union (Shen 2007).

Within the existing theoretical framework of the communist movement at that time, Mao's worries were entirely logical and non-personal. What Khrushchev initiated was 'revisionism', which was the primary ideological target during the Cultural Revolution launched by Mao. Subsequent developments also proved that Mao was right. 'Capitalist roaders' were inside the CCP and the reversion to capitalism in the former Soviet Union and China were initiated by Communist leaders themselves. If our evaluation of Mao is made within this framework, Mao's criticism of Khrushchev, which anticipated the Cultural Revolution, made political and ideological sense.

Conclusion: history what history?

This chapter has presented some critical analysis of Li Zhisui's memoirs in relation to the process of the production of knowledge, and to many claims about Mao and CCP politics and events. Clearly the value of such books is very limited, much more so considering the production process. Of course, we cannot demand that all writers of memoirs and biographies should address all the social and political issues. To write memoirs especially, every individual writer is bound to write from his or her own experience. Not everyone is a political scientist or sociologist or historian. However, the reader would demand a little more from a book on Mao, especially one that is assisted and managed by scholars on China. In Li's memoirs, however, there is no social history and there are no policy issues. There are only power struggles and personal intrigues.

In a sense the issue comes down to whose history we are talking about. Li and his mentors want to write a history that is not only anti-Mao and anti-communist, but also elitist and sensational. It is ironic – and if not that ironic it is certainly curious – that prominent scholars in the West, who obviously take themselves to be cold warriors and therefore guardians or promoters of democracy, actually take the same approach as elitist Confucian historiography: no social policies and political theories are important enough to be discussed unless they are related to the personal power struggle of Mao, who led one of the most important social revolutions in the twentieth century.

Li's approach to history can be seen by the claimed exchange between him and Mao on the subject of Qin Shihuang, the first emperor of China. Li says 'But the Chinese people hated him because he executed the Confucian scholars and burned the classic books' (Li

Zhisui 1994: 122).[4] The term 'Chinese people' is used here of course to contrast himself with Mao the dictator who is known to be less critical of Qin Shihuang. This is a standard line of the elitist Chinese historiography: the real Chinese people – that is, the majority of the Chinese population – are denied their history, but they are always spoken on behalf of. The peasants rose against the Qin regime not because of the execution of scholars and the burning of classic books but because of the heavy levies and coolie labour. It is doubtful whether the majority of the Chinese, past or present, even know that Qin Shihuang executed scholars and burned classic books. It is no less doubtful whether they care about it.

Li, who was praised and trusted in the West because he was Western trained (Nathan in Li Zhisui 1994: xiii), says of Empress Wu Zetian (AD 627–705) that 'She was too suspicious, had too many informers, and killed too many people' (Li Zhisui 1994: 123). In reality, Wu Zetian might be very different from the caricature of a bitch and a witch portrayed by the Confucian scholars, whose attitudes towards women are well known. In responding to Li's opinion (if the conversation indeed took place), Mao tried to insert some politics and social history into the interpretation of Wu Zetian, telling Li:

> Well, Wu Zetian was a social reformer. She promoted the interests of the medium and small landlords at the expense of the nobility and the big families. If she had not been suspicious, if she had not relied on informers, how could she have discovered the plots the nobles and the big families were hatching to overthrow her? And why shouldn't she execute the people who were plotting to kill her?
>
> (Li Zhisui 1994: 122)

However, to Li, this only shows that Mao wanted to copy the cruellest rulers in Chinese history. He observes that 'Mao's view of history was radically different from that of most Chinese.' 'Morality had no place in Mao's politics' he asserts (Li Zhisui 1994: 122). It was no wonder that Mao had to say to Li that the latter's view of Chinese history was all taken from Peking operas.

7 Challenging the hegemony: contrary narratives in the e-Media (I) – Mao and the Cultural Revolution

Introduction: emerging contrary narratives

Discussions of various biographical and memoir writings in previous chapters clearly show that the dominant narrative is a total denigration of the Cultural Revolution and almost instinctive denunciation of the Mao era, either explicitly or implicitly. I have argued that this hegemonic narrative, in many ways methodologically similar to traditional Chinese historiography, does not only purport to serve the present (in Chapter 3) but is also framed by the present (in Chapter 2). This construction of an anti-Maoist (Chapter 4) and anti-revolutionary (Chapter 5) history went hand in hand with the collapse of existing socialism and ascendance of neoliberalism in China (Wang Hui, 2004).

Hegemony can never be total and there have been dissenting voices from the very beginning when the anti-Maoist and anti-revolutionary were forming alliances in and outside China. The dissenting voices in China have gathered pace since 1997 after the American bombing of the Chinese embassy in Belgrade, as represented in the journals *Dushu* and *Tianya* (Wang Hui, 2004). There have, however, also been dissenting voices from another source, and that is the e-media, both inside and outside China. These dissenting voices have been getting louder and louder as the consequences of post-Mao reform have been more and more visible and more keenly felt.

The issue that draws most attention in the e-media is the evaluation of Mao the man. Very much related to that evaluation but often discussed separately is the issue of assessing the Cultural Revolution. For a long time in China it has been taken for granted that the Cultural Revolution had nothing positive to talk about and 'the ten-year disaster of the Cultural Revolution' had become the accepted wisdom, just as it was once accepted that the sun revolved around the earth. However, the wisdom is increasingly being questioned now in the e-media. In May 2007, a familiar e-media participant with the pen name of Jingan Jushi (2007) proclaimed: 'China should objectively and historically evaluate the merits and demerits of Mao.'

Media effect, public space and e-media

That media set the public agenda and have an effect on what the public thinks is a well-known social phenomenon in contemporary life. McCombs and Shaw (1972) are credited as the first to have researched agenda setting; they found that there was an almost perfect correlation between media agenda and public opinion. Funkhouser (1973) also demonstrated a strong correlation between US media agendas and public concerns, as measured by the ranking of issues in opinion polls. A study in West Germany by Brosius and Kepplinger (1990) demonstrates that while people's own previous knowledge was important, media coverage did indeed raise public awareness. The media might not tell the public what to think but they do tell them what to think about. Brosius and Kepplinger also show that public awareness in turn exercises a significant causal influence on media coverage. Again, Dearing and Rogers (1996) show that among the agenda-setting research studies reviewed in their research, 60 per cent confirm a correlation between media and public agenda. They also find 1) that news organizations tend to hunt in packs, continually monitoring each others' output and following very similar editorial strategies, and 2) that real-world indicators are relatively unimportant in setting the media agenda.

Members of the Glasgow University Media Group also confirmed these findings. People are able to resist dominant messages if they can deploy personal experience in a critical way or have knowledge acquired through alternative sources (Eldridge et al 1997). For example those with direct experience of life in Northern Ireland were more likely to question the dominant news definition of the 'Troubles' (Miller 1994). However the Glasgow Group also finds that personal experience cannot be artificially isolated from 'broad media and cultural factors' (Kitzinger 1999: 8). 'Peoples' experience cannot be regarded as a separate resource uncontaminated by previous media exposure' (Manning 2001: 223). Kitzinger (1993) and Miller et al (1998) show that media 1) supply 'facts and figures', 2) develop vocabulary and 3) generate images that have a powerful impact upon public understanding. In other words, 'the media can be powerful influence on what audiences believe and what is thought to be legitimate or desirable' (Philo 1999: 287)

The Chinese government exerts very strict control over the official media. Precisely for this reason, the e-media as an alternative play a more important role in China than they do in the West, making it possible for unofficial values and attitudes to be expressed and promoted among the Chinese. There have been lively debates on many issues important to China and the world on the e-media despite continuous official attempts of censorship, including arrests of Internet users. By 2003 there were reportedly 70 million registered users of the Internet in China. According to what is still an emerging research (Hughes 2003, Hughes and Wacker 2003, Chase and Mulvenon 2002, Kalathil and Boas 2003), Internet access can be a potent tool for change in attitude, values and even social structures.

The widely publicized case of Sun Zhigang provides evidence that the e-media does indeed play a very influential role. In June 2003 Sun, a rural migrant, was arrested, detained by the police and then beaten to death in Guangzhou for no reason other than the fact that he was not carrying the right papers with him. The news was exposed by *Southern Metropolis Daily* and was spread by the e-media, which were flooded with protests. The Chinese government ordered an investigation of the case and finally enacted a law that abolished the notorious detention centres targeted at migrant workers. Though one cannot say for certain that e-media protests were the direct cause of this very significant change, which affected tens of millions of migrant workers, it certainly played a key role as catalyst.

There has been another example in 2007. Having failed to find any conventional ways to get themselves heard, 400 fathers signed an Internet petition that asks the public to rescue their children working in illegal brick kilns as slaves. The e-media publication led to national outrage, so much so that the central government had to intervene to rectify the slave labour situation in China (Bu Luo 2007).

It is within the context of this great surge of e-media that the hegemony of the public space by the state media and official media has been challenged. It is within this context of challenge that the e-media counter-narratives of Mao, the Mao era and the Cultural Revolution emerged. In this chapter, the first part of a study of the e-media challenge to the mainstream narratives, I examine how attempts are being made in the e-media to re-evaluate Mao and the Cultural Revolution. In the second analysis of the e-media challenge in the next chapter I will outline some of the main arguments for repudiating the mainstream narrative regarding issues of the Chinese economy, the Great Leap Forward, Jiang Qing, healthcare, education and so on. Obviously the issues of the two chapters overlap and the discussion of the state of the economy cannot be separated from the evaluation of Mao. Even so, the issues are divided between two chapters here so that each chapter is not too long and that the discussions can be structured for easy reading. E-media coverage in these two chapters focuses on the Internet, excluding any coverage of media such as SMS (mobile phone short message service), MSN and QQ.[1]

Ma Yinchu, population control and elite attitudes

Mao was a very complex personality, and as a political leader his ideas and work had impacts on the lives of millions of Chinese. Evaluation of a man of such historical importance inevitably requires us to engage with almost every issue of human life in China. One of these involves China's population. There has been a consensus among the public policy makers that there are too many people in China and the population has to be controlled. If, for the sake of argument, we put aside the moral or theological issues of whether human life is intrinsically and inherently sacred, we should note that there can be endless debates on how many people within a national boundary are considered to be too many and whether people are valuable resources or a waste of resources. For a brief period of time, at least during the 1950s, Mao happened to be one who thought that humans might be resources rather than constraints on China's economic development. However, this does not mean Mao did not agree to some control of the population. In fact during the 1950s and 1960s measures were taken to slow population growth, though not as coercively as during the post-Mao reform years.[2]

Nevertheless, one of the crimes that Mao is being accused of is that he made the Chinese population explode because he wrongly criticized a demography professor who advocated population control. Yi (2007) confronts the issue head on by arguing that it was groundless to blame Mao for the great population surge in China and that the accusation was politically motivated. According to Yi, in 1979 Hu Yaobang, then the Minister of Organization and Secretary of the CCP, is reported to have shed a few tears when he read the file of Professor Ma Yinchu of Beijing University and said something like: if the Chairman listened to Ma Yinchu, China would not have had more than 1 billion people now. This wrongful criticism of one person led to a population increase of many millions. On 5 of August 1979 an article with a rhythmical and poetic headline '*Cuo pi yi ren, wu zeng san yi*' (Wrongful criticism of one person led to a damaging population increase of 300 million) appeared in the so-called intellectual paper the *Guangming Daily*.[3] The headline summarizes what has been the accepted wisdom on the issue of population in contemporary Chinese historiography. When Ma was rehabilitated he was hailed as a Marxist. Yi, however, argues not only that Professor Ma was not a Marxist but also that he said nothing original but just repeated a platitude of Marx's adversary Malthus, whose view on population has been proved to be wrong. Yi argues that China's population increased so much not simply because there were too many births but also because there were fewer deaths. This was the result of the social and economic revolution and improvement of living conditions for the majority of the people in China.

But that is precisely the issue: should the state waste money on the uneducated low-quality people? On a social occasion in June 2007 I met a professor from the prestigious Beijing Normal University, Huang Zuoyue, a highly educated member of the Chinese intelligentsia, who looked smooth and urbane. When Huang told me that Chinese government at all levels had so much money these days that officials did not how to spend it, I asked why they did not spend the money on education and healthcare for the poor. Professor Huang's response was something classic: There are too many people in China and if you spent one dollar on each person it would be too costly. This is a professor who, during our conversation, not only thought it acceptable to build *en suite* bathrooms in professors' offices at some leading Chinese universities but even expressed pride in the plan.

Pointing out that the Chinese elite all jump onto the wagon of condemning the Great Leap Forward famine as if it was Mao who had murdered millions of people, Yi then asks: Why don't they condemn the population control policy for murdering so many millions? What about the 1.7 millions girls that are missing according to the normal gender ratio? Shui Han (2007), another e-media participant, argues that the missing girls actually number as many as 40 million. Shui Han presents detailed historical evidence, elaborate charts, figures and statistics to show that Mao was right (and Ma was wrong) in not advocating a coercive population control policy because the very strength of China lies in its population. In order to combat a population control policy that is considered to be disastrous Shui Han has created a population policy website (http://www.shengyu.org/) to encourage debates.

The credibility of Li Rui

One influential argument constructed by memoir, autobiographic and biographic writings about Mao is that after 1956 he did nothing positive for China. This is the so-called later Mao thesis (*wan nian Mao Zedong*). One person who is very influential in promoting the later Mao thesis is Li Rui. Following the veteran tradition of constructing China as an Oriental despotism, Li Rui thinks China under the late Mao was ruled by autocracy. His utterances attract a serious audience and one high-profile US academic with a mainland China's background credits Li for first applying the term 'autocracy' to the Chinese regime and uses it a key word in the title of his recent book (Pei 2006). In a list of the 50 most influential people in China produced by Kerry Brown (2007) for Chatham House and Open Democracy, Li Rui is included ahead of Jiang Zeming, the General Secretary of the CCP for eight years, and His Holiness the Dalai Lama. Li used to be the Deputy Minister of Irrigation and wrote more than a dozen of anti-Mao works, including the very influential *The Tragedy of the Late Mao: Personal Record of Mao's Secretary.*

Li Rui's condemnation of Mao is influential for several reasons. One is that he is one of the high-ranking party officials, a so-called insiders' insider. Another is that he claims to be a Mao expert since he has written a biography of the young Mao that had inspired many Mao admirers. However what seems most compelling is that Li claims to be Mao's secretary and to be recognized as such in the field (Pei 2006: 4). In order to question Li's credentials, one of the e-media participants goes to a great length to show that Li's claim to have been one of Mao's secretaries is misleading (Yue 2006). According to Li himself, he was asked by Mao to be a secretary but declined, pleading the excuse of being too busy. Li then agreed to be Mao's part-time secretary (*jianzhi mishu*), which in fact meant that Li was, in Mao's words, a *tongxun yuan* (correspondent). During this period Li was not stationed in Beijing but worked full time at the Hunan Provincial Propaganda Department in Changsha. How can Li claim to be Mao's secretary when in fact even the role of being a correspondent lasted only 19 months, from January 1958 to August 1959? Mao wanted Li to be one of his correspondents after listening to a debate on the pros and cons of building the Three Gorges Dam. Mao was impressed with Li's argument against such a project and decided to shelve it. As Huang Yunsheng (2007) further points out, Li's role as a correspondent secretary was confined only to matters of irrigation and hydropower because of that encounter.

Li Rui is accused of being economical with the truth in another instance. During the early years of the PRC's history China copied the Soviet Union by conducting the May 1 Labour Day parade during which slogans were chanted to indicate the CCP's policy and ideology. Li Rui claims that for the 1950 May Day parade Mao himself inserted 'Long Live Chairman Mao' as the last one on the list of official slogans.[4] But Huang avers that Li is lying. First of all, Li said that the information was given to him by Zhu De's secretary orally, but Li did not made such a claim until after Zhu's secretary had safely passed away. Second, the official list of slogans published in the *People's Daily* on 27 April 1950 did not contain the slogan 'Long Live Chairman Mao'. The last entry on the list was actually 'Long Live the Great Leader of the Chinese People, Comrade Mao Zedong'. Third, the slogan list was first drafted by the Central Propaganda Ministry, as always, and they did propose 'Long Live Chairman Mao'. It was Liu Shaoqi, not Mao, who crossed it out and changed it to 'Long Live the Great Leader of the Chinese People, Comrade Mao Zedong'. This can be confirmed by the handwriting of Liu Shaoqi as seen in the first volume of *Manuscripts by Liu Shaoqi since the Establishment of the PRC* that was published in April 2005.

Li was once openly challenged when he was an invited speaker at the highly acclaimed Yuexi Seminar Series in Zhengzhou. As he was repeating his usual anti-Maoist stand by claiming that the upright and honest Peng Dehuai had been victimized at the Lushan Conference in 1959 by the dictator Mao, some members of the audience asked why Li and his follow anti-Maoists did not want to mention the fact that it was not Mao but Liu Shaoqi who condemned Peng first in 1959 and then again in 1964, or that the latter wanted to plot with the Russians so that a Chinese coup similar to that in Russia would take place. Li was also asked why he did not want to mention the fact that both General Su Yu and Zhang Qian made the explosive claim that the Russian ambassador to China approached the then Chinese Foreign Minister Chen Yi about such a coup,[5] and that Zhang Wentian and Kang Sheng claimed that Peng actually said that 'Russian soldiers should be invited' to solve China's problem.[6] For once Li was lost for words (He Yuan 2007).

Challenging the late-Mao thesis

Dai Yugong (2006) confronts the late-Mao thesis head on. He argues that the practice and ideas of the later Mao are more valuable to today's China than those of the early Mao. Along these lines a widely circulated e-media piece cleverly titled 'Mao's Commentaries on the Current Affairs in China' (Wuyou zhixiang 2006) uses Mao's words to comment on some of the salient social developments in post-Mao China. In the area of education the blatant disregard for the education opportunities of the majority and single-minded concentration of resources on the privileged few in post-Mao China has attracted most criticism by the e-media participants. There is discussion of the privileges of students in the so-called key schools, who enjoy the latest computers, piano rooms and sports centres in stark contrast to the situation in rural China where the poor cannot afford even a simple textbook in the twenty-first century, and in that context Mao's directive on 14 June 1952 that *guizu xuexiao* (aristocratic schools) should be abolished is cited. The issue of study methods is raised – the way that students at school are fed too much book knowledge, and that the workload demanded from them is too heavy – and Mao's comment on 21 December 1965 is cited, in which he warned that the educational system did not teach much that was useful, that the way so much book knowledge was used and the way discipline was imposed damaged students' health; that is exactly what has been happening since the end of the Cultural Revolution.

The practice of maintaining well-resourced schools for the political and intellectual elite started in the early 1950s. After the disaster of the

Great Leap Forward, with the support of Liu Shaoqi and Deng Xiaoping, the ideology and practice of developing key schools for the children of the elite in the name of training experts for economic construction became even more dominant. In all major urban centres the sons and daughters (princelings) of high-ranking party officials and army officers attended special schools where a few academic high achievers were also enrolled. While the princelings thought they were the natural inheritors of the country and therefore entitled to the privilege, the academic high achievers from the non-politically correct classes felt alienated and resentful. In fact it was in those schools that the precursor of the Cultural Revolution took place: the line was drawn between students of the 'red' family background (the princelings) and those from 'black' family background (families of 'enemy' classes). As a result of the Cultural Revolution policies key schools were abolished and there were experiments with a fairer system and a more practical curriculum. However, as soon as Deng Xiaoping came back to power in the late 1970s the system of key schools was re-established.

Mao's famous criticism on 26 June 1965 of the Ministry of Health is cited to remind readers of the current dismal situation of healthcare in China. In that criticism Mao pointed out that most Chinese lived in rural China but the country's healthcare system was designed to cater for the urban population that comprised only 15 per cent of the total. Mao caustically suggested that the Ministry of Health should be renamed as the Ministry for the Urban Lords. To reverse the situation some medical personnel from the urban centres were either encouraged or forced to move to rural areas, while an affordable but effective 'barefoot doctor' system was established. When Deng Xiaoping came back to power in the later 1970s, the policy was again reversed.

Reminding the reader that television programmes nowadays are mostly about emperors, ghosts, sex or the rich and the famous, Mao's criticism of the direction of literature and arts in 1963 is cited, in which Mao said the many arts and literature departments were ruled by the dead. Along the lines laid down in his talk on the literature and arts at the Yan'an Forum in 1942, Mao wanted literature and arts to change direction so that the work and life of the workers and farmers who were the producers of food and daily necessities and bearers of a lived culture became their main subjects.

Another comment by Mao is particularly relevant to the issue of land seizure and the dismantling of people's homes for development since the 1990s. On 15 November 1956, commenting on the local protest against removing residents for an airport construction in Henan, Mao told the then General Secretary of the CCP Deng Xiaoping, who ran day-to-day affairs, that 'even a bird needs a nest. How can you force people to move without consultation and without proper settlement?' Mao demolished Deng Xiaoping by saying to him that 'you Deng Xiaoping also had a nest and what you would do if your nest was destroyed?' Mao even said: 'I welcome the fact that the masses threw stones and waved their hoes as protest.'

This is one of the strategies that e-media participants employ to counter the demonization of the late-Mao era: expose what has gone wrong in the post-Mao era. Another such effort was made by Ping Gu (2006), who laments the fact that post-Mao China has broken eleven world records for bad governance.[7] Among these eleven are: the worst healthcare in terms of fairness; the most expensive tertiary education in terms of purchasing power parity; the greatest disparity between the rural and urban; the worst environmental sustainability; the most polluted country; the country most prone to mining accidents; the country with the highest number of suicides; the most expensive bureaucracy; the highest number of death penalties; and the highest absolute numbers of illiterate or semi-illiterate adults. Some of these world firsts were of course the same as in the Mao era, such as the high rate of illiteracy in absolute terms, for the simple reason of China's large population base. But fairness in healthcare, affordable of education for the majority, mining and work safety, the cost of bureaucracy and levels of inequality were evidently better during the Mao era, especially during the late-Mao years.

Challenging Jung Chang and Jon Halliday

As soon as *Mao: The Untold Story* appeared in English there was a fierce debate in the e-media in Chinese. Unlike reviews in the West the majority of the e-media participants were critical of Chang and Halliday. One commentator says that the book takes the venerable Chinese historiographic approach to its extremity and the result was a moral tale. It is like the new Romance of Three Kingdom (*Sannong Zhongguo* 2006). Even Zhang Lifan, son of Zhang Naiqi, who was one of the three most prominent victimized Rightists, could not help but join the criticism of the book. Zhang fully supports Chang's political stand, but has to acknowledge that it is a pity that Chang wrote a fiction instead of a history, a mistake that misses the chance of throwing Mao into 'the rubbish dump of history'.

Another widely circulated critique of Chang is by a self-proclaimed science student in the UK, Jin Xiaoding. As discussed in Chapter 4, Jin does not have to examine documentary evidence to point out the logical contractions in the Chang and Halliday book. When Jin's 17 questions were post in the e-media, Chang's brother Zhang Pu participated in the debate on behalf of his sister. However, his defence is seen as a dismal failure by the e-media participants since he did not come up with any convincing response. In another contribution to repudiate the Chang and Halliday claim that the famous Luding Bridge Battle between the Red Army and the Nationalists did not take place during the Long March, an interview with a veteran solider Tang Jinxin (2007), who is 91 years old and who describes how he participated in the fierce battle of Luding, is circulated in the e-media.

Liu Shaoqi, Deng Xiaoping and the Great Leap Forward

One important aspect of evaluating Mao has to do with how Mao handled Peng Dehuai's criticism of the Great Leap Forward at the Lushan Conference in 1959. The version of the event that is most widely accepted is the one offered by Li Rui, according to which Mao not only took action to topple Peng but also used the opportunity to further implant reckless leftist policies that precipitated the famine. However, recently there have been a number of contributions on the *Wuyou zhixiang* (Utopia) website that try to revaluate the event. Wu Lengxi (2007) and Zhang Hengzhi (2007) have presented evidence and arguments that 1) for six months before the Lushan Conference started in 2 July 1959 Mao made continuous efforts to cool down the Great Leap hype, 2) the purpose of the Lushan Conference was to improve the situation, 3) initially Mao did not take too much notice of Peng's letter of criticism and intended to conclude the conference as planned in spite of Peng's letter, and 4) it was some other CCP leaders who argued and persuaded Mao to extend the conference to 'struggle against Peng'.

Yun, quoting Liu Shaoqi's speeches, argues that it was Liu who hunted Peng down by accusing Peng of aiming to usurp power from the party. Liu specifically referred to Peng as a leading member of the Gao Gang and Rao Shushi anti-party clique, an accusation with which Zhou Enlai concurred (the 'anti-party clique' refers to the event in 1955 when the Gao Gang and Rao Shushi launched a campaign to reshuffle the CCP top leadership to replace Liu and his lieutenants). Liu also accused Peng of working with 'foreign influence', referring to Peng's visits to the Soviet Union and Eastern Europe immediately before the Lushan Conference.

Wu confirms that during the Politburo meeting in Beijing on 12 to 13 June 1959, Mao criticized himself for the recklessness of the Great Leap Forward policies and admitted that Chen Yun had been right after all to be cautious. Wu recalls that Mao's personal secretary Tian Jiaying was pleased that Mao made self-criticism and thought that it was then up to the party secretaries of various provinces to make self-criticisms at the planned Lushan Conference. When Peng's letter was circulated, Wu Lengxi, Hu Qiaomu and Tian Jiaying all thought there was nothing particularly controversial about it. Except for one single reference to bourgeois fanaticism, Peng's letter was not even as sharply critical of the Great Leap Forward as the conference resolution that the three of them had been instructed to draft. After a private conversation with Mao, Tian Jiaying was convinced that Mao was forced to agree to criticize Peng by the argument that if nothing was done the revolutionary left might as well be disbanded (*zuopai jiu yao sanhuo le*).

Zhang Hengzhi (2007) goes even further. He argues that it was Liu Shaoqi and his lieutenants who encouraged the Great Leap radicalism and Mao was the cautious one. But Mao was ready to shoulder the responsibility when the mistakes became obvious since Mao he not want to damp the revolutionary spirit of the radicals. Zhang further argues, by quoting Liu Shaoqi, that Peng's letter was directed at Liu. The fight between Liu and Peng left Mao with little choice: Liu had only recently been made Mao's official successor, and if he sided with Peng then the CCP would split. It was Liu who wanted to get rid of Peng and it was Liu who said in 1961 that anyone could be rehabilitated except Peng. It was Liu who said that Peng, like Wei Yan,[8] had a treacherous bone (*fan gu*), that he had the character of Zhukov (the Russian general whose role was crucial in Khrushchev's coup) and the hypocritical style of Feng Yuxiang.[9] Mao was drawn into the Peng affair reluctantly and that was why Mao said on 24 October 1966 that Deng Xiaoping had never come to seek advice from him since 1959, and that he was not happy with the August 1959 Lushan Conference because the outcome was pushed through entirely by Liu and Deng and he was given no choice.

According to Zhong Yanlin (2006), Deng Xiaoping was at least initially very enthusiastic in promoting the Great Leap Forward. For instance when the leadership inside Henan Province was split on the speed of economic development at the beginning of Great Leap Forward, Deng Xiaoping, as the General Secretary of the CCP, supported the radical Wu Zhipu, the party boss of Henan, by saying that Wu was on the side of truth (Xu Ming 1998). Deng also protected Li Jingquan, the party boss of Sichuan province (Zhang Suhua 2006), from any punishment when the Great Leap Forward disaster was revealed. Henan and Sichuan were two of the three provinces worst hit by the famine. As Zhang Suhua (2006) points out, Deng headed the office of the General Secretariat of the CCP that had carried out the day-to-day instructions of the CCP and therefore was directly in charge of putting the Great Leap Forward policies into practice. Therefore what Deng believed and wanted to be done must have made great differences. For instance on 5 September 1958, Deng's office issued a telephone conference decree instructing every level of party authorities to meet the quota targets for iron and steel production. The instruction was so specific and strict that the wording was: '不但一吨不能少，少一斤也不行' (not a ton less of production is allowed, not even a half kilogram less). When Deng toured the northeast in September 1958, he made several passionate and rousing speeches to encourage Great Leap Forward policies and to praise the newly established commune system. Finally, though Deng did not participate in the Lushan Conference to attack Peng he did publish an opinion piece in the CCP mouthpiece *Red Flag* criticizing Peng and singing the praise of the Great Leap Forward policies (Zhong Yanlin 2006).

Debates on issues related to the Cultural Revolution

In previous chapters, I have argued that Chinese memoirs, autobiographies and biographies either assume or argue that Mao's motivation for the Cultural Revolution was a personal power struggle. All developments subsequent to the downfall of Liu Shaoqi were more or less explained by this power struggle thesis. Along these lines, the campaign to criticize Lin Biao and Confucius in the early 1970s, for instance, is said to be Mao's scheme to overthrow Zhou Enlai. However, e-media participants have begun to question the power struggle thesis. In an article published in the e-media, Xiao Yu (2000) quotes Fan Daren, one of the important polemics writers during the above-mentioned campaign, to dispute the claim that the criticism of Lin Biao and Confucius had anything to do with Mao's intention to target Zhou Enlai. Fan, the main writer in the team writing under the pen-name of *liangxiao* (two universities), which consisted of academics from the two top universities of Beijing and Qinghua, testifies that the writers in the team did not intend to criticize Zhou Enlai when they were writing articles to criticize Confucianism, that they were not told to do so, nor was it even hinted that they should.

Disagreement between Mao and Liu Shaoqi: the two-line struggle thesis

Because of the proclaimed 'end of history' and beginning of an new era of clashes of civilizations, the intellectual consensus all over the world seems to be that not only should the Russian and Chinese Revolutions be jettisoned but that even the idea of revolution should be buried. This global intellectual climate change has been so convincingly persuasive that the two-line struggle thesis that was offered as the rationale for the origin of the Cultural Revolution has been considered largely discredited. The dispute between Liu and Mao is seen as largely a personal power struggle. However, e-media participants in China want to bring the issue of the two-line struggle back.

The gist of the two-lines struggle is this: not long after the Chinese economy had recovered from the Great Leap Forward there were rival lines of thought within the CCP on China's future development. One line of thought was advocated by Liu Shaoqi, Chairman of the State, and the other by Mao, the Chairman of the CCP, the ruling communist party.

By the early 1960s Liu did not seem to object to the idea that something had to be done in China or protests and turmoil against the CCP similar to those in Hungary and Czechoslovakia would occur. However, the two chairmen had completely different views on what the problems were and what measures to take. The Liu line of thought saw the problem organizationally as CCP grassroots corruption by elements from outside the party. The Mao line, however, saw the problem as being ideologically inside the party. Liu was of the idea that the communist cadres at grassroots level in rural China were either bribed by the former landlords or corrupted by capitalist thoughts of comfort, pleasure and greed. Therefore measures had to be taken to uncover the embezzling and corrupted cadres. Moreover, those measures should be imposed from top to bottom and from outside forces organizationally to wipe out these elements of corruption. In contrast, the Mao line of thought was that the majority of the grassroots cadres were either innocent or just following policies from above. Corruption and embezzlement were just symptoms of a deeper problem of ideology, the ideology of capitalist values and beliefs. To change the ideology fundamentally, measures had to be taken to correct those inside the party who made the policies. For Mao the organizational measure of dismissal or punishment of this and that cadre at grassroots level would not solve the root problem. The fundamental solution had to come from changes of values and beliefs, and those changes required a cultural revolution. Hence the idea of the Cultural Revolution was developed. The above is only a sketch of the two-line struggle; a more detailed explication and articulation can be seen in Wang Li (2001), one of the chief radicals who interpreted Mao's ideas during the beginning of the Cultural Revolution.[10]

In what follows next I will present a brief case study of how the two-line struggle developed between Mao and Liu during 1964–65. This case is presented here along the lines of Ming Mu (2007), which appeared on *Zhurengong* website. In the e-media debates most of the participants do not sign their real names and I believe Ming Mu is a pseudonym. I cite this source as an example because I find it totally convincing and Ming Mu, unlike other e-media debates participants, cites documentary sources such as Bo Yibo (1997), Feng Xianzhi (1996), Liu's letter to Mao, Liu and Mao's speeches as well as records of the central committee of the CCP work conferences.

In order to prevent what was perceived to have happened in the former Soviet Union, Mao decided to carry out what was called the Socialist Education Movement and Liu was put in charge of this. In November 1963 Liu sent his wife, Wang Guangmei, to the Tao Yuan Brigade of Hebei province to do a pilot project on Socialist Education in rural China. In June 1964 Liu took a work tour in Hebei, Shanghai, Henan, Shandong and Anhui, promoting his wife's work in what was called the Tao Yuan Experiment. Liu asserted that Wang Guangmei's pilot project showed grassroots organization in rural China was completely rotten, either corrupted or changed politically to be on the side of class enemies: the landlords, rich peasants and counter-revolutionaries. Liu ordered all senior party officials to carry out investigations like Wang by staying in one village for a long period of time (the Chinese term is 蹲点 *dun dian*). Liu shocked his attentive audience when he forcefully told them that those who did not *dun dian* would not be qualified to be members of the CCP central committee. He also added that Mao's work should not be taken as dogma, that Mao's investigative method of group interviews was out of date and that a new way of encamping in a village to establish contacts (*zhagen chuanlian*) was required.

Mao's idea was totally different however. He thought that the majority of grassroots cadres should not be the targets of struggle and that parachuting in so many people from the outside to one place to carry out struggle was politically wrong and technically impossible: it was wrong politically because the assumption was that the local people could not be trusted. It was technically impossible because there was no way in which resources could be mobilized to carry out the task for the whole country. When Mao's personal secretary Tian Jiaying, on Mao's instructions, conveyed the two points to Liu, Liu frowned and said nothing. Though he was not very keen on the Tao Yuan Experiment, Mao initially agreed to make the Wang Guangmei Report a CCP document for circulation, as Liu recommended. However, he soon changed his mind and ordered the withdrawal of the Report. According to Wang Li (2001), this was mainly because Jiang Qing had reported Liu's work-tour speech to Mao by saying: 'Liu is already criticizing you when you are still alive, whereas Khrushchev made the secret report denouncing Stalin only when the latter was dead.' However, Wang Li admits that he interpreted Mao's change of mind in that way only because that was what Jiang Qing had told him. He also admits that Mao changed his mind after consulting other provincial leaders such as Li Xuefeng, Wu Lanfu, Tao Lujia and Liu Zihou.

To carry out the struggle against grassroots cadres, Liu sent work teams totalling 15,000 people from outside into the county of Xincheng, which had a population of less than 300,000. Mao asked Liu: how could such vast human resources be mobilized to carry out Socialist Education in the whole country if so many people were required for one county? However, the disagreement about the methods of conducting Socialist Education was not the real issue, as Yang Shangkun realized and noted in his diaries (Yang 2001). The real issue was that Mao and Liu had a completely different attitude towards the so-called masses. Mao's view was that the Socialist Education Movement should not be carried out by outsiders. It should be carried out by the masses themselves locally and the party should rely on the local masses. He said that those who embezzled a couple of hundred Chinese dollars (according to the statistics in the Wang Guangmei Report, most of the accused cadres were accused of misappropriating this amount of money less) should not be taken as class enemies. So long as they admitted their mistakes and repaid the money they should allowed to work again, Mao said. Mao's idea was that only the very few top leaders of any organization should be the target of socialist education and education should be conducted by the members of that organization.

In Mao's opinion, Liu's method would strike against the broad sector at grassroots level in order to protect the small group of leading officials (the Chinese term is 打击一大片保护一小撮). Mao further rebuked Liu by saying that the Socialist Education Movement should not be about money and corruption but about a broad ideology of socialism versus capitalism. Unlike Liu, who still thought that the class struggle in China was between the communists and old class enemies of landlords and capitalists, Mao believed that nature of class struggle had changed after the communist victory, that the old categories of class enemy were toothless and that there was a new class that was putting the revolution in danger. Mao's line of thought was that the danger of China turning into capitalist state did not lie with the broad masses at grassroots but with leaders inside the party who could take China onto a capitalist road, hence the term of 'capitalist roaders' that was used during the Cultural Revolution.

After the disagreement between Mao and Liu over the aims and measures of the Socialist Education Movement surfaced, some senior leaders asked Liu to make a self-criticism to Mao and to others of the central leadership and Liu did. But Liu's humiliating climb-down delayed the final confrontation only for a year. In 1966, Mao launched his attack on the 'wrong' ideological line in cultural and educational spheres, because according to him, a cultural revolution carried out by the broad sector of the masses was the only way to regenerate the Party (Wang Li 2001). On the other hand, events proved that Liu either was incapable of understanding, or refused to understand Mao's line of thought. When the Cultural Revolution started to unfold, Liu, being in charge of the day-to-day work, again sent work teams formed by personnel seconded from various party organs into schools and universities in Beijing. The work teams then started to strike against the broad sector of the masses of old categories of class enemies. As a result hundreds and hundreds of students and teachers in Beijing University alone were targeted as class enemies and counter-revolutionaries. Some were put under house arrest and others were paraded in struggle meetings. Mao was angry and again accused Liu of striking against the broad sector in order to protect the small group of leading officials, and of being the leader of a reactionary line; Liu thus became one of the main targets of the Cultural Revolution.

According to Wang Li, Mao only wanted to get the CCP on the right ideological line and did not want to get at Liu Shaoqi personally. Initially, Mao still wanted to keep Liu within the CCP, but also wanted him and other leaders to go through the process of an ideological struggle so as to regenerate the party. When Liu Shaoqi, Deng Xiaoping and Tao Zhu (and many others) had been officially deposed from office, Mao said 'down with (*da dao*) only for a year, at most two years'. He also stressed that if there was a war (with the Soviet Union, Taiwan or the United States in mind at that time) these people should be restored to their former positions straightaway (Wang Li 2001: 681). Towards the end of 1966, however, Mao realized that those who resisted his ideological line were many and very strong. But he said that he was determined to carry the Cultural Revolution through to the end and said to Wang Li and his Cultural Revolution radical comrades that 'if they shoot you I will go with you' (Wang Li 2001: 710). Wang Li and others present at this conversation were shocked by Mao's remarks and Wang did not realize what Mao meant until many years later.

Other unofficial views of the Cultural Revolution

Also circulated in the e-media (Shui 2006) is the report of a workshop organized and participated in by some high-ranking retired party officials on 13–15 May 2006, which evaluates the Cultural Revolution positively and challenges the post-Mao version of events. This was unprecedented in a number of ways: first because no such workshop had ever been heard of in China before; and second, because it was reported in the e-media for all to read. Important views expressed at this workshop include:

- It is necessary to draw a distinction between Rebels and Red Guards – the former were supported by Mao to target 'capitalist roaders' inside the party while the latter were actually followed the party bureaucrats in ideology and political line.

- In Deng's crusade of denigrating the Cultural Revolution, members of the intellectual elite such as Ji Xianlin, Ba Jin, Ye Yonglie and Yan Jiaqi constructed a 'cultural blockade' against the Rebels and made the Rebels appear to be responsible for the destruction and victimization that was initially done by the Red Guards and then by office holders inside the party.[11]
- The Rebels treated the party officials humanely in their ideological fight.
- Mao did not intend to suppress all of the party officials, but wanted them to go through the experience of learning from the masses before they were allowed back into office (as testified by Wang Li (2001) who avers that Mao said to him personally several times that even Liu should be allowed to be a member of the CCP Central Committee).
- Even at the height of struggle against 'capitalist roaders', there were always instructions that the people who were targets of struggle had to be physically protected and well fed.
- Most of the so-called armed fighting was not factional fighting among Rebels but oppression of Rebels by party officials.
- Most of the important party officials were called to Beijing for protection after a few struggle sessions and many others came back to power within two years.
- In the revolutionary committees that were set up during the Cultural Revolution, the army representatives never took the Rebel representatives seriously.
- Only in Shanghai was the situation a little better for the Rebels because the Rebels had direct support from the centre.
- The army was strongly against the Rebels.
- Mao's Cultural Revolution strategy was forced upon him after all other efforts failed.
- Mao was hesitant during the Cultural Revolution, but thought that the cadres could be made to change their attitude by a mobilization of the masses.
- The enemies of the CCP, like the landlords, capitalists and Nationalist officials and officers, were pardoned, but the Rebels were still treated as enemies of humanity

Sea change of attitudes

These views are contrary to the official verdict as well as the mainstream views and would not be allowed to appear in conventional media in China. These contrary narratives reflect a sea change of attitudes among the broad masses of people. The process of attitude change, as seen for instance in the case of Yang Fan, reflect a lot of what has been happening in terms of understanding the Cultural Revolution unofficially. Yang went to kindergarten, primary school and secondary school with Liu Yuan and Bo Xicheng.[12] The three of them, according to Yang (2006), went through a stage of fierce denunciation of the Cultural Revolution. But now they have reached the stage where they, notably Liu Yuan and Bo Xicheng, do not hate Mao for what happened, but see the Cultural Revolution as failed idealism. Yang thinks that there are positive lessons to be learned from the Cultural Revolution.

Wang Xizhe the dissident

Wang Xizhe was a one of the famous co-authors of the *Li Yizhe Posters* (a pamphlet criticizing the Cultural Revolution and the problems of the Chinese political system that was circulated widely in the early 1970s) and is now a dissident in exile. Wang, however, still holds the view that the Cultural Revolution led to some positive ideas and democratic practices. In this respect he is in disagreement with other Chinese dissidents. In one widely circulated piece, Wang (2006a) asks the dissident Lin Feng, 'Since we dissidents are supposed to oppose whatever is proposed by the CCP and support whatever is opposed by the CCP, why do you support the CCP when it denigrates the Cultural Revolution?' (for the dissidents' Two whateverisms see Chapter 2). Wang (2006b) also rebuts Han Zhu who asserts that the Cultural Revolution was a populist Nazi movement. Wang should know because he was first very active in Cultural Revolution activities and then wrote one of the most articulate critiques of many aspects of the Cultural Revolution's developments.

Kong Qingdong and the cowshed

'Cowshed' is a term used by the Chinese to refer to a practice during the Cultural Revolution when 'the bad elements' or *niu gui she shen* (cow demons and snake ghosts, a traditional Chinese term referring to folk tales about bad spirits that would do harm to the innocent and weak) were sent to a camp to work and study in order to change their mentality. The camp is then termed *niu peng,* a shed for 'the Cow demons'. Kong is an outspoken academic but very critical of the fact that condemnation of *niu peng* (the cowshed) in memoirs has become a fashion, similar to the Mao-era fashion of *yi ku si tian* (to recall the bitterness of the pre-1949 life and to tell of the sweet life of today). Nowadays, *niu peng* is portrayed as more horrifying than prison. However, Kong (2006) argues that much of what happened at that time was just *xuexi ban* (a study class). To rebut the accepted wisdom that everything that took place during the Cultural Revolution was bad, Kong talks about how his father was put into one of these *niu peng* because he was accused of carrying a false CCP membership card. Kong recalls that the *niu peng* was not something that was terrible at all. In fact his father took his six-year-old son with him at Kong's own insistence and there they had a good time, with better food than at home and a lot of collective activities. They did not have to work and it was much like attending a university or school: studying, watching films and sleeping. Or more aptly for Kong, it was like a summer camping holiday.

Memoirs of different narratives

There are also attempts to write memoirs of the Cultural Revolution that present different memories from those prevalent in the conventionally published literature. One that has been circulated widely in the e-media is Lao Tian's oral history of the Cultural Revolution in Chongqing. This oral history raises some important points such as that the Red Guards or Rebel groups that defended the established power holders were not persecuted, even though they might have committed greater violence and destruction, and that the February 1967 suppression of the Rebels, directed by the powerful Marshal Ye Jianying, led to tens of thousands of victims in Sichuan alone. This oral history shows that even with Mao and the Cultural Revolution radicals' support in Beijing the Rebels were constantly suppressed at grassroots level because the army supported the old power holders. Even after the establishment of the revolutionary committee that included Rebel representatives, the management of the day-to-day affairs was still in the hands of the old bureaucrats. Furthermore, the Rebels had no legitimacy in criticizing anyone unless they were either supported from above or locally by the army, and despite Mao's appeal for leniency on behalf of the Rebels, Rebel leaders were time and again detained or jailed or put under house arrest. In one case even Zhou Enlai and Mao's personal intervention did not help one Rebel leader. These are revealing and astonishing details that demand new research and new theoretical approaches towards the history of the Cultural Revolution.

Challenging Wang Youqin

Wang Youqin, a Chinese expatriate now residing in the United States, has become some kind of celebrated expert in archiving assaults on teachers by students during the Cultural Revolution. Wang, for instance, blames the Red Guards for the death of a teacher, Bian Zhongyun, in

Beijing at the very beginning of the Cultural Revolution. Ma Beiming (2006, 2007a and 2007b), a well-known name in the e-media, however, challenges this. Ma argues that the death of Bian Zhongyun (the first casualty of the Cultural Revolution) might not have been caused by Red Guards for political reasons but for personal reasons. On another occasion Ma also points out that as soon as Song Bingbing (one of the chief Red Guards) and six of her classmates saw that Bian's life was in danger they organized rescue activities to save his life, including upbraiding hospital staff for hesitation. Ma further points out that Wang Youqin not only withdrew this piece of information when she wrote about the death of Bian but also accused Song of being principally responsible for Bian's death (Ma 2007a), an accusation that Song denied in *The Morning Sun*, a critically acclaimed documentary on the Cultural Revolution made by Carma Hinton.

Conclusion: the question of truth

With limited evidence and because of the lack of references in Ma's papers I cannot make a judgement of the dispute between Wang and Ma. It is important, of course, that a judgement is made because that ultimately brings us to the question of truth and which version to believe. But the dispute about the case of Bian does indicate that truth is never simply black and white. What is important for the purpose of this book is to show that no claims can be made without being challenged these days, and increasingly these challenges are arguing in favour of the Mao era.

It is also important to realize that what is believed to be true is always based on what is available, factually true or otherwise. Human beings can believe something to be true for many years, generations or even centuries before the so-called truth is debunked. Therefore another aim of this book is to show that the e-media have produced evidence, arguments and views that are different from those represented in the conventional media available to many readers. Quite likely, this readership is bigger than the readership of refereed journal articles and reputable published books, or even the conventional media. In this sense whether a particular claim is factually true becomes less significant. What is significant is that counter-knowledge is being produced and another truth is manufactured.

8 Challenging the hegemony: contrary narratives in the e-media (II) – the Mao era

Introduction: history in socioeconomic context

One of the easily accepted arguments in attacking Mao the man is that he was a person of no original ideas, whose dark political manoeuvring was simply aimed at gaining and maintaining personal power. Looking from a perspective of this power struggle thesis, all the costs and victimizations on the trail of Mao's political action were not only senseless and distasteful but actually evil. In Chapter 7 I have focused on how e-media participants challenge this accepted evaluation of Mao the man and some issues related to the Cultural Revolution. One attempt in challenging the power struggle thesis is to bring the two-line struggle thesis back into the big picture. I find the two-line struggle thesis very convincing and believable because it fits more with documentary evidence and because it has more explanatory power in revealing the behaviour of the actors both at the top and at the lower levels at the time. It is more convincing and believable also because it involves politico-socioeconomic history instead of personal intrigues at Mao's court. In this chapter we will see how e-media participants challenge the mainstream wisdom on the Mao era by relating to the big pictures of political, social and economic issues.

The state of the economy in the Mao era and during the Cultural Revolution

Ever since the arrest of the Cultural Revolution radicals immediately after the death of Mao in 1976 (so immediate that Jiang Qing is reportedly to have protested that Mao was being betrayed when his dead body was still warm), there has been manufacturing of claims to show that Mao did not know and furthermore did not care about China's economy, that the Gang of Four deliberately wanted to destroy China's economy and that towards the end of the Cultural Revolution the Chinese economy was on the brink of collapse.

Deng Xiaoping was the architect of the fabrication of this truth. Deng (2007) claimed that the Cultural Revolution held China up (*danwu*) for ten years and that for 20 years after 1957 China politically was in a chaotic situation (*hunluan zhuangtai*) while its economy remained slow and stagnant (*huanman he tingchi*). Recently, many e-media participants have made strenuous efforts to counter what they consider the groundless demonization of Mao, the Cultural Revolution and the Mao era.

The existing literature

To combat the Deng line of denigrating the Mao era, several strategies have been employed by e-media participants. One strategy is to translate and circulate the existing literature that has either been ignored or made unavailable to the Chinese audience. Two examples stand out in this case. One is the extraction of materials concerning China's economy in Meisner's (1986) defence of the Mao era. Meisner's careful array of statistics and analysis provide a convincing argument that China's economy performance during the Mao era in general and the Cultural Revolution in particular was better than that of the average third-world country. His defence of Mao and the Chinese economy under his leadership appears and reappears on various e-media in its Chinese version.

In this regard it is worth pointing out that Hinton's criticism of the post-Mao reform and his re-reflections of the Cultural Revolution translated by David Pugh, first posted on *Zhongguo gongren wang* (The Chinese Workers Website), is also circulated widely.[1]

As another example of the strategy of pasting and re-pasting existing materials in the e-media, in www.creaders.org forum, Lesson (2006) pastes a ten-page piece detailing the economic achievements during the period of the Cultural Revolution. Here he quotes Han Deqiang's '*zhong wai duibi wushi nian*' (China in comparison with foreign countries in the past 50 years) to show that from 1965 to 1985 the average annual GDP growth rate of the United States was 1.34 per cent, UK 1.6 per cent, West Germany 2.7 per cent, Japan 4.7 per cent, Singapore 7.6 per cent, South Korea 6.6 per cent, Hong Kong 6.1 per cent and India 1.7 per cent (Han Deqiang 2006). During the same period (the collective system was not totally dismantled until the mid-1980s) China's growth rate was 7.49 per cent.

Responses to three responses

There are three common responses to this strategy. One is to claim that the economic growth rate during the Mao era was not that impressive since China's economy was so backward to start with, and it is an accepted wisdom that the growth rate is usually high when an economy starts from a low base. This response actually confirms that

PRC took over a legacy of backward economy and the era of Mao made rapid progress.

The second response is to claim that statistics based on information provided by the Chinese authorities are not reliable. This response however shows a lack of critical reflection in at least two ways. First, it was the post-Mao political and professional elite who had conducted a comprehensive statistical evaluation. Those Chinese political and professional elite who had been the victims of Mao's Cultural Revolution and other political movements had no reason to inflate statistics for the benefit of the Mao era but every motivation to show the Mao era in negative light. Therefore, if anything the officially sanctioned Chinese statistics are most likely to present a more negative picture. Second, those who are critical of Mao and China's economic performance in the Mao era base their criticism on statistics which are also provided by the Chinese authorities. To claim that the statistics from China are unreliable when they could render a positive evaluation on the one hand but use statistics from the same sources to present a negative evaluation on the other is logically inconsistent and hypocritical.

The third response is represented by a respected professor, Qin Hui of Qinghua University, who argues that it is doubtful whether the kind of growth in the Mao era is anything worth talking about. Qin argues that India's economic performance was as good as that of China without much human cost and that the Chinese economy during the late 1920s and early 1930s of the Republic period was as good as and even better than the Mao period (Zhong Lantai 2006). The underlying argument is that there could not have been, or cannot be, better economic performance under a communist regime. This is the reason why there has been so much debate and concern over the comparison between China and India and an increasing trend of positive appraisal of the Republic period under Chiang Kai-shek. Amartya Sen's famous thesis that democracy could prevent large-scale famine – famine usually is not really the result of shortage of food but the result of unaccountable governance – is constantly cited in this debate. However, as Chomsky (2000) points out, Sen's other thesis, that equity and equal rights to public goods are essential for the well-being of people, is always ignored by the anti-Maoists. Sen argued that compared with China's rapid increase of life expectancy in the Mao era, the capitalist experiment in India could be said to have caused an extra 4 million deaths a year since India's independence. That 'India seems to manage to fill its cupboard with more skeletons every eight years than China put there in its years of shame, 1958–1961' (Sen 2000) is an argument that academics like Qin Hui do not want to contemplate.

Debates on comparisons

Ever since the 1980s a favourite argument of the anti-Maoists has been to compare China with the four Asian 'tigers' of Hong Kong, Taiwan, Singapore and South Korea so as to demonstrate the superiority of market capitalism. Han Deqiang (Lesson 2006) argues that the fact that people in Hong Kong, South Korea, Singapore and Taiwan had a higher living standard than the people in China should not be interpreted as an indictment on the Chinese economy in the Mao era. The fact that living standards were lower in China had more to do with the international environment of the cold war and to the necessity for China to develop a basic industrial and national defence infrastructure.[2] Han argues that the post-Mao reforms of 20 years benefited from achievements of the 30-year Mao era. The metaphor Han uses is that the progress in the 30 years of the Mao era was like riding a bike up a hill, and once at the top it is was a faster and easier ride downhill, for the reform of 20 years.

Recently on the website *Wuyou zhixiang* (Utopia), there appeared a piece titled 'Mao Zedong has changed the Chinese nation' (Nong Nuji 2006b). In this piece the author attacks the e-media activist Yu Fei who is nicknamed Yu Minzhu (Yu Democracy) because of his rhetoric. Nong attaches 18 tables and diagrams detailing the economic achievements of the Mao era, including one on the economic achievements during the Great Leap Forward, one on the record of major economic events from 1956 to 1976, one on industrial and one on agricultural outputs, one on investments, one on student numbers in education and one on personal income, together with three attachments on different economic index and growth rates among China, India and the United States of America. The data and statistics show that China's economy during the Mao era not only made great strides but also outperformed India.

The Great Leap Forward famine

That the Great Leap Forward resulted in a large-scale famine and that even basic daily necessities such as soap and rice were rationed present two powerful arguments that the economy in the Mao era was disastrous. The Great Leap Forward has always been controversial and there have been endless debates about the exact death toll of the famine. Many of the e-media debate participants argue that the death toll has been greatly exaggerated by the post-Mao regime. However, even the lowest estimate of several million deaths cannot gloss over the disaster.

One response to this from the contrary narratives has been to say that famine had been frequent in Chinese history. To counter the argument that it was during the Mao era that greatest toll from famine in all of history occurred, Jiang Chuangang (2006) lists how famines occurred frequently in the first half of the twentieth century in China, citing the famines from 1928 to 1930 in Gansu and Shaanxi when more than 10 million are claimed to have died of starvation, or the 1936–37 famine in Sichuan when cannibalism is claimed to have taken place, or the 1942 famine that plagued central China and in which Henan's population is claimed to have halved. Jiang also pointed out that, according to statistics compiled by the Information Service of the Research Centre of China's Population and Development, the population of 1958, 1959, 1960 and 1961 was respectively 653,460,000, 660,120,000, 662,070,000 and 664,570,000, with an increase of 11,100,000 people in three years. Though the population increases of these years were lower than those during the years of 1956 to 1958, the increase was still on average 5.46 per cent, higher than the world average at that time, and much higher than pre-1949 years. Jiang further points out that the death rate of 1959, 1960 and 1961 was 1.459 per cent, 1.791 per cent and 1.424 per cent, an average of 1.558 per cent, which was about the same as the world average death rate at that time, and much lower than the death rates in pre-1949 years. During the three years of famine 30,952,300 people died, and compared with the lower death rate of 11.40 per cent during 1956 to 1958, there were an extra 8.3 million deaths, not as many as the 30 to 40 million claimed by anti-communist literature such as Chang and Halliday (2005).[3]

Li Xuanyuan is a heavyweight e-media participant in challenging the anti-Maoist truth. Here is a brief case study of Liao Bokang by Li that shows how anti-Maoist truth is manufactured. Liao Bokang was promoted to important positions by the post-Mao authorities, serving as CCP party secretary of China's largest city, Chongqing, and Chairman of the Political Consultative Committee of Sichuan province. In 2004 Liao published an article in the *Dangdai shi ziliao* (Documentation of Contemporary History) compiled by the Academy of Social Sciences of Sichuan province. In that article Liao claims that in Sichuan alone the death toll was 10 million (remember this is the province where Jung Chang grew up, where her father served as the deputy propaganda chief of the province and yet Chang does not or cannot provide any direct documentary evidence or witness account of the famine death toll either in *Wild Swans* or *Mao: The Unknown Story*). Liao further claims that he was interviewed in 1962 by the then Secretary of the Communist Youth League Hu Yaobang, as well as by the Director of the CCP Central Office Yang Shangkun, and reported the 10 million famine death toll in Sichuan to them. When questioned by Yang about evidence of the figure of 10 million Liao said that the figure was from a Sichuan provincial document. Yang was surprised that he did not know of such a document since every provincial document had to pass through him. It turned out that what Liao meant was that there was a Sichuan province document that recorded that there were a total 62.36 million people in Sichuan in 1960. Liao then explained that the death toll must be 10 million since the total 1957 population as shown by the annual state statistics was 72.157 million. Li Xuanyuan (2007) then asks three questions: 1) how do the 72.157 million figures come about? 2) Can one arrive at a 10-million famine death toll by just taking away one year's figures from those of another? 3) Why did Liao wait until 2004 when both Hu Yaobang and Yang Shangkun were safely dead to reveal such important meetings?

Li then provides two instances of demographic movement from his personal experience (Li is also from Sichuan province) that may explain some of the demographic change. These instances of demographic movements have hardly been noticed or studied by scholars of the issue. One instance is a personal move that was not accounted for in official statistics. Because of starvation the husband of Li's older sister left his village in 1959 and moved to Tianchi coal mine to work as a miner. Because he left without permission, his village cancelled his household registration. He registered as a rural person when he came back to the village in 1963. This is an example of one person missing during the famine years but one person more on the official records afterwards.

Another instance is that there were officially sanctioned move-ments. When the Great Leap Forward started there was great expansion of local enterprises and industrial decentralization. In the process millions of rural people were enrolled into the industrial sector. When the famine began to take effect the Chinese authorities, at Chen Yun's suggestion, repatriated those workers. This movement created a situation in which some people appeared to have disap-peared from rural areas during the Great Leap Forward but then reappeared as rural residents. Furthermore, this sudden movement and then a sudden repatriation in a matter of three or four years of so many millions of people inevitably created problems for records even if there had been a good statistics collection system. But, as everyone in and outside China agrees, there was no such system. Li, again, provides a personal experience of this demographic change. In Gao Village where the total population was not more than 200 at that time there was an inflow of a family of four repatriated from Jingdezhen (Gao 1999a).

Food shortage and a metaphor

The main argument presented by Lao Tian (2006a) and others about the rationing of food highlights the difference between the strategy of national consumption and that of national accumulation. A metaphorical argument that is widely circulated in the e-media is that there is a difference between *xi panzi* (washing dishes) and *jiao xuefei* (paying tuition fees to study). The author of this argument starts with a well-known phenomenon that many PRC Chinese students, when in an affluent Western country, would rather wash dishes in a restaurant than study because the immediate cash income is too tempting, especially when compared with wages they could earn in China. Those who wash dishes can earn and save enough money to buy a car (a luxury item in China) and even eventually a house. This is consumer culture. However the other approach is to save and borrow to pay tuition fees to pursue a course of study. This would mean many years of hard work and of little consumption. The end result is totally different: those who study will eventually end up with a higher social status. This metaphorical comparison is used to argue that during the Mao era the Chinese had to work hard but to consume little (like someone paying tuition fees) so that eventually China could manage to build up an industrial and economic base to become the equal of the great global powers. The post-Mao strategy is like washing dishes to earn money to consume: China is now an assembly line of the world, or a gigantic low-technology migrant worker.

The four modern inventions

Participants in the e-media debate constantly remind their readers that post-Mao China has hardly made any technological advance, and that all of China's important industries that were built up during the Mao era have either declined or been taken over by foreign companies (for more on this, see Chapter 9). Along these lines, La (2007) presents a 'four new inventions' argument to show that the Mao era performed better technologically. According to one poll survey of more than 50,000 respondents, the four winning entries of modern Chinese inventions, as opposed to the four old inventions of paper, compass, mobile printing and gun powder, are the hybrid rice crop (*zajiao shui*dao 杂交水稻), the laser typesetting and electronic publishing system of Chinese characters (*hanzi jiguang zhaopai* 汉字激光照排), artificial synthetic crystalline insulin (*rengong hecheng yidaosu* 人工合成胰岛素) and the compound Artemether (*fufang gaojiami* 复方篙甲醚), the last being the malaria cure discovered at Mawangdui as discussed in Chapter 1. These technological inventions that have won the title of Modern China's Four Most Important Inventions were all developed during the Mao era (Tian Fu 2007).

In connection with this, the abandonment of the Chinese development of civil aircraft Yun Shi (Transport 10) by the post-Mao authorities has been widely publicized in the e-media. One e-media participant even suggested that Shen Tu, the head of the Chinese Civil Aviation at the time, who later defected to the West, was either a CIA spy or was bribed by the American aviation industry. It was Shen Tu who argued against developing the Chinese civil aviation industry and who favoured buying American aircraft instead.

A chronicle of achievements

To support this line of argument for the success of the Mao era, a chronicle of the important economic events has been widely circulated. This includes many examples that counter the perception that Mao did not care about China's economical development. According to the chronicle, on 19 February 1966 Mao directed that China should work to mechanize agriculture within 25 years. The 1972 entries of the chronicle list the import of equipment for eight large chemical fertilizer and fabric factories. Other entries include the successful annual Guangdong trade fair and China's trading relationship with more than 150 countries. This also shows that Mao did not intend to close China to the outside world economically and that China wanted to modernize its economy. The chronicle lists many scientific and technological achievements from 1966 to 1976, including the first Red Flag car, the invention of total synthetic crystalline bovine insulin, the atom bomb and hydrogen bomb, the first Chinese transistor computer and later the integrated circuit computer, the first Chinese automatic three-dimensional camera, the first 100,000-ton tanker, the invention of Qingda antibiotics, the successful launch and recovery of a satellite, the first electron railway, the development of Dagang and Shengli oilfields and the Beijing Yanshan Oil refinery and so on. It even lists China's first environmental conference and government policy to combat water pollution. Xiang Nanzi (2006) lists the figures for railway construction in China in the Mao era and during the post-Mao reform, and asks the reader to consider the fact that the average annual growth of railways from 1950–78 was 942 kilometres whereas during the period 1978–95 it was only 353 kilometres. Therefore, it is false to claim that it was only when Deng Xiaoping carried out the reform that China's economy began to develop.

Living standards and economic policies

In another contribution to the electronic journal *San nong Zhongguo*, Chu Su (2006) points out that Mao was always careful not to let the Cultural Revolution obstruct economic activity. It was Mao who first raised the formula of *zhua geming chu shengchan* (grasp revolution to promote production) when the Cultural Revolution document of the Sixteen Points was drafted. Mao also inserted this formula in one of Chen Boda's articles 'The two-line struggle in the Great Cultural Revolution' which has been recognized as one of the important documents that launched the Cultural Revolution. Mao also refused to approve Chen Yonggui's (the Party Secretary of Dazhai Brigade who was promoted to be a vice-premier of the State Council) suggestion of making the production brigade, instead of the production team, as the basic accounting unit.[4]

One important evidence for the argument that economy stagnated during the Cultural Revolution was that workers' salaries actually went down over ten years, from an average of 583 yuan a year in 1966 to 573 yuan a year in 1976. However, Chu points out that during the same period the total expenditure on salaries in China went up by 65 per cent. What happened was that while the salaries were kept down, more people became employed. Obviously in a country where there was no inflation and where prices of all the daily life goods were capped by the state, salary increases are not as important as full employment for equality and for ensuring the livelihood of all. In another contribution, Chu (2007) lists detailed figures of how China developed high-tech national defence science, how Chinese petroleum and electronic industries developed and how local industries and irrigation infrastructure expanded during the Cultural Revolution period.

The strategic significance of the third-line industry and the cold war

Apart from listing evidence and statistics that show the economic development and technical achievements during the Cultural Revolution, Chu presents two points directed at the critics of Mao and the Cultural Revolution. One was the development of the third-line industry, which used a lot of capital and resources to build up industrial bases such as the satellite-launching base in China's remote south and northwest. Chu quotes Deng Xiaoping and Jiang Zemin to show that with hindsight, especially since the Iraq war, the third-line policy was far-sighted and strategically significant for China.

Chu's other point concerns the accepted wisdom that the Mao era chose to close itself off from the outside world and that China opened up only after Mao's death. Chu points out that as early as 1964 and 1965 Mao raised the prospect of allowing the Japanese to open up factories in China. It was not Mao or China that refused to open to the West. Instead, it was the West that imposed economic sanctions against China. It was Mao who initiated the re-establishment of relationship with the United States The US government led by Richard Nixon and Henry Kissinger responded to Mao's initiative only because they hoped to play the China card to balance the perceived threat of the Soviet Union and wanted China to help end the Vietnam War. It was the US strategic shift that made it possible for China to be more open to the outside world. Countries that had been following the US cold war strategy, such as Japan and Australia, established diplomatic relations with China soon after Nixon's 1972 historic visit of China. It was during the early 1970s that more than a dozen huge industrial and manufacturing projects were started, along with large-scale imports of equipment.

Infrastructure build-up, accumulation and delayed benefit

E-media participants accuse the post-Mao economic rationalists of manufacturing the belief that in the collective period farmers in the commune system were lazy because of the 'iron ricebowl' mentality (the unbreakable food bowl). More and more e-media participants are ready to accept the argument that the increase in food production during early years of the post-Mao reform was not the result of change of land ownership from the collective to the private, but the result of increased benefits from developments achieved during the Mao era – infrastructure such as irrigation and technology improvements such as chemical fertilizer and improved seedlings. During the 20 years of the collective period, the amount of irrigated land rose to 48 per cent of China's arable land, and this 48 per cent produced more than 70 per cent of China's grain (He Xuefeng 2007). Substantial increases in grain production occurred from 1978 to 1984, when the commune system was still largely in place in China. On the other hand, in 1985 when the dismantling of the collective system was finally accomplished, nation-wide grain production went down dramatically the first time in years (Hu 2004).

Qiong Xiangqin (2007) argues that the increased agricultural production in the early 1980s had nothing to do with dismantling the collective system, but much to do with the increase in prices and the opening of the market. He also points out that the post-Mao reformers ambushed the rural residents by dismantling the collective system by stealth and by coercion. As late as 1982, the then Premier Zhao Ziyang (1982: 1260) declared that the socialist transformation of rural China into a collective system was necessary and absolutely correct. But a year later in 1983 the CCP issued a command to dismantle the collective system, ordered the rural organizations to change the collectivist name of commune to *xiang* (township – a term used in pre-1949 China) and distribute land among households even though many were opposed to this. Some resisted the pressure, and there are still around 2,000 villages that have kept the collective system; these include Liu Village and Nanjie in Henan, Huaxi in Jiangsu, Daqiu in Tianjin, Henhe and Doudian in Beijing, Zhouzhuang, Banbidian in Hebei, Honglin in Hubei, Houshi in Dalian, Yankou and Ronggui in Guangdong, Tengtou and Wanhai in Zhejiang.

When the food rationing of the Mao era is compared with the seeming abundance of food available on the market in today's China, the argument that it is the post-Mao reform of privatization (the dismantling of the collective system by contracting land to individual households) that increased productivity and grain production appears irrefutable. However, e-media participants argue that it was a matter of timing and that even without the dismantling of the collective system grain production would have increased as much. Recently a piece (Ai 2007) circulated on the e-media raises the question of who has solved the problem of feeding the Chinese people. Ai's argument is that grain production in China has less to do with the household responsibility system than with technology. The two technological breakthroughs that boosted grain production in China were hybrid rice seeding developed by Yuan Longping and hybrid wheat seeding developed by Li Zhensheng. Yuan started working on his project in 1964 and succeeded in developing the *Nanyou 2 hao* (Nanyou No 2) in 1973 and Li succeeded in developing his *Xiaoyan 6 hao* (Xiaoyan No 6) in 1979. Both scientists worked during the Mao era and during the Cultural Revolution.

Dou (2007) argues that before the rural reform started, agricultural production had already shown a rapid growth. For instance, grain production in 1979 increased by 16.73 per cent compared with that in 1975. And if one looks at the overall period of the Cultural Revolution the figures were even more impressive: between 1965, one year before the Cultural Revolution started, and 1975, one year before it officially ended, grain production increased by a staggering 46.23 per cent (Dou 2007). With the increase in chemical fertilizer available to Chinese farmers, Dou argues that if the collective system had remained intact, the total grain production in 2000 would have reached 6 million tons, whereas in fact China only produced 4.62.17 million. Dou reaches this conclusion by examining the available official statistics and by working on the assumption of how chemical fertilizer input affects grain output.

E-media participants also skilfully employ postcolonial theory to argue that Western countries built up their industrial bases and economic well-being by colonizing and plundering the vast areas of the world that were endowed with rich land and natural resources and by exploiting the cheap labour of the slave trade. China has had none of these options and therefore had to tighten its belt.

Manufacturing truth

These participants further argue that much of the 'truth' of economic failure in the Mao era has been manufactured by the anti-Maoist and anti-revolutionary Chinese media. Lao Tian (2006b), by analysing the content of newspaper reports of that time, gives a good example of how the anti-Mao and anti-Cultural Revolution truth has been manufactured. It is now widely accepted that during the Cultural Revolution the Gang of Four used the political rhetoric of *ge zibenzhuyi de weiba* (cut off the capitalist [commercialism] tails) and **ningyao** *shehuizhuyi de cao* **buyao** *zibenzhuyi de miao* (we would *rather* have socialist weeds *than* capitalist crops) to sabotage economic activities. But according to research into the content of the *People's Daily* from 1950 to 1976 by one e-media partici-pant, there were 26 news reports dealing with the topic of 'cutting off the capitalist tails'; of these only five showed a positive attitude towards such rhetoric and the rest (21) were actually critical of it. Another e-media participant quoted by Lao Tian uses *ningyao ... buyao* (rather ... than) as a key word to search the *People's Daily* and finds that during the Mao era from 1949 to 1976 there were only 22 news reports or opinion pieces that used the grammatical structure *ningyao ... buyao*. From 1976 onwards, however, there were many more news items that used this grammatical structure as a way of criticizing the Cultural Revolution by inventing slogans that were supposedly used during it. Phrases such as 'we would rather have socialist late trains than capitalist trains on time', 'we would rather have a low socialist growth rate than a high capitalist growth rate' never appeared in the Mao era, but were later invented by the media to criticize it. It is clear that the post-Mao media framed many topics in this grammatical structure and then claimed that they were advocated as Maoist policies.

Signs of a re-evaluation of Jiang Qing

Emerging quietly are a number of voices that attempt to re-evaluate Mao's wife Jiang Qing (Xin Ma 2006). Qi Benyu's rebuttal of the claim that Mao and Jiang did not get one well was widely circulated (Yu Erxin 2006a).[5] It is also claimed in the e-media that during an interview, the famous Rebel leader at Qinghua University Kuai Dafu avers that Jiang was an outstanding Chinese woman in almost every aspect. She was caring and very cultured, as shown by her very good handwriting, her knowledge of Marxism and her talent for organization and publicity. It is also widely reported in the e-media that Jiang had special talents in arts (Tian 2006).

Jiang Qing and He Zhizhen

In a recent interview, Zhu Zhongli admits that her best selling biogra-phies of Jiang Qing, *Nühuang meng* (Dream of being Empress) and *Jiang Qing mi zhuan* (A Secret Biography of Jiang Qing), contained fiction because no account of Jiang Qing could be published unless she was demonized in it (Shi 2007).[6] Zhu also admitted that she had known Mao and Jiang well since the Yan'an days and that it was not Jiang Qing who seduced Mao, as has been popularly portrayed, to advance her career. It was Mao who pursued Jiang. Mao liked Jiang not only because she was pretty and young but also because she was talented and very knowledgeable about Marxist revolutionary ideas. Unlike other senior revolutionary leaders at that time Jiang Qing had actually read some Marxist-Leninist classics. She published writings that showed her understanding of Marxism in the 1930s in Shanghai before she arrived in Yan'an.

It has been an accepted wisdom in the biographical and memoir literature that Jiang lured Mao by hook and by crook, and therefore pushed He Zhizhen (Mao's third wife before Jiang Qing) away from him. Jiang Qing was therefore considered immoral and an evil person, a decadent, third-rate Shanghai actress who conspired to victimize a veteran woman revolutionary. But according to Zhu, He Zhizhen did not have much in common with Mao apart from their revolutionary experience in Jiangxi, whereas Jiang's ideas on literature and arts inspired Mao even in his late years. Zhu gives one incident to show the limitations of He Zhizhen. Once when He saw Mao having a hug with a foreign journalist she went over and smacked the journalist on the face, not knowing that hugging in foreign countries might mean no more than a handshake. Zhu says that it was He's own fault that Mao divorced her. Zhu, a qualified doctor who was responsible for looking after the high-ranking party officials in Yan'an, actually suggests that He was then already clinically crazy. She wanted to leave Yan'an to go to the Soviet Union for treatment, although Mao strongly objected to that. He Zhizhen had several miscarriages and, despite Zhu's efforts to cover up, Mao eventually realized that some of his wife's pregnancies had nothing to do with him (Shi 2007).

In defence of Jiang Qing: a feminist perspective

In an interview circulated in the e-media, Chen Yonggui also speaks very highly of Jiang Qing and considers her a good example of being incorruptible (Tian 2006). Many people gradually come to realize that much of the slander piled on the character of Jiang Qing may have something to do with deep-seated gender discrimination among Mao's revolutionary comrades. It was Mao who had a liberal attitude toward the gender issue. When some CCP cadres around Mao raised objection to his marriage with Jiang on the ground that she was a divorced woman who had a dubious life in Shanghai, Mao is reported to have said that he himself was a divorced man. Lan Yezi (2006) argues that so many accusations against Jiang actually stemmed from Chinese male prejudices against women. One accusation levelled at Jiang was that she lived with men without getting married. However this could also be seen as modern, progressive and revolutionary at that time. A further counter to the accusation is to ask whether men are accused of the same crime. Lan argues that it is not fair to accuse Jiang of marrying Mao to advance herself. A woman cannot marry anyone without having to answer charges of an ulterior motive. Liu Shaoqi married five times and yet that was a non-issue in the official discourse.

Jiang Qing and the arts

Jiang Qing is often accused of not only being a third-rate actress but also of being responsible for wiping out artistic expression and creativity. This again is widely repudiated in the e-media. Yang Chunxia (2006), the main female actor in the opera *The Azalea Mountain*, argues that the model Peking operas, largely initiated by Jiang Qing, are still unsurpassed as monumental productions. Ting Guang (2006) even asserts that the model Peking operas were an unprecedented achievement in the history of Chinese literature and arts. What Jiang was trying to do, with the full support of Mao because the latter found her ideas inspirational, was to create new arts both in contents and forms. The experiment of the Peking opera clearly shows that Jiang and her followers were trying to achieve something new by combing three elements into one organic performance art: revolutionary content (women's liberation and participation in society as in *The White Haired Girl* and *The Red Regiment of the Woman's Army*), traditional Chinese art (Peking opera) and Western techniques of artistic expression (ballet and wind and string music instruments). Of course Jiang Qing could not take all the credit for this unprecedented artistic revolutionary enterprise. Other Chinese artists had been doing this for decades, even before the well-known talk given at an art forum in Yan'an by Mao in 1942. But it was Mao who articulated this effort by popularizing the idea of *Yang wei zhong yong, gu wei jin yong* (to use the foreign to serve the Chinese and the past to serve the present). Jiang Qing was one of the most articulate and most persistent in pursuing this goal. Because of this she made many enemies among the artistic elite.

Resistance to revolutionary arts

There was a powerful conservative establishment in the literary and arts circles that not only wanted to maintain the content and form of the arts that they know and cherish but also hated those who wanted to make changes. It was precisely for this reason that Mao criticized the pre-Cultural Revolution arts establishment in China for their failure to produce literature and arts along the lines that were sketched out in his talk at the Yan'an Forum in 1942, and it was for this reason that the revolution for artistic change was part of the 'Cultural Revolution'. The fact that the diagnosis was right has been proved by what has happened since the post-Mao reform: the performing and visual arts have been dominated by *diwang jiangxiang, caizi jiaren* (emperors, prime ministers, generals, scholars and pretty women – Mao's diagnosis of the pre-Cultural Revolution arts). The majority of the Chinese – the rural people – are bombarded with programmes that have nothing to do with their own lives. For the elite of the artistic establishment, the very idea of art expressing the life of the ordinary people is an anathema. For them, art can only be created by and for the high class.

Mao's ideas of art meant the end of the art world as we know it. The example of Hao Ran, a well-known novelist in the Mao era is a good illustration. Hao recollects that he was criticized soon after the death of Mao and was not allowed to see foreign visitors, who were told by the post-Mao authorities that Hao was a fraud, an illiterate whose books were ghost-written by someone else (Cai 2006).[7] Hao himself, however, has never regretted his work of revolutionary art and is proud of his novels. He claims that his work made a positive contribution to the Chinese people and the fact that a person like him can be writer of significance is a miracle that can occur only in a country under leaders like Mao. All these revisionist views are widely circulated in the e-media.

The issues of health care and education

The provision of healthcare and education to the vast majority of the poor in the Mao era was a historic achievement unprecedented in human history, an achievement that had to be admitted even by those who hated the Chinese revolution. What is remarkable about these achievements is that even the rural Chinese benefited from them.

Inspired by economic rationalism and with a declared aim of making education and healthcare more efficient, the post-Mao Chinese government have carried out reforms that reversed Maoist policies. Guided by the principle of 'entrepreneurizing education' and 'marketizing healthcare' (*jiaoyu chanyehua, yiliao shichanghua*), the post-Mao authorities concentrate their meagrely allocated resources on the elite schools and hospitals in urban centres while the rest were pushed to the market for their own survival. Many of the e-media participants are scathing in their criticism of these reforms.

The deterioration of healthcare and education services, especially for the rural people, is an indictment of the post-Mao reform regimes in Beijing. However, very few of the Chinese political and intellectual elite want the comparison between the two systems to be made. What happened to Professor Chen Meixia is a good example. in 2001 she wrote an essay in English in praise of the healthcare system during the era of Mao. In this paper Chen is very positive about the achievements of healthcare during the Mao era and especially during the Cultural Revolution as the result of four important health strategies. These were: 1) healthcare was primarily directed to serving workers and farmers, 2) the main focus was on preventative medicine, 3) the healthcare system was a combination of Western and Chinese medicine, and 4) the masses were mobilized to tackle health issues. However, the post-Mao regime abandoned all of these strategies for ideological reasons. Chen sent this article to some Chinese scholars and asked them to translate and circulate it, but heard nothing from them. It was not until 2006 that the essay was translated and widely circulated in the e-media.

The three big new mountains

According to Yang Guang (2007), the Chinese per capita expenditure on education in 2005 was only a quarter of the average expenditure in developing countries, and China numbered the eighth from the bottom in UNESCO's ranking in education investment. The central government's share of cost on healthcare decreased by 32 per cent in 1978 to a meagre 15 per cent in 2005 (Yang Guang 2007). Most of this expenditure was on urban centres and heavily orientated towards the care of the government officials. It was not until more than a decade after these changes began that their consequences began to be keenly seen and felt. The net result of these reforms is that the vast majority of the Chinese are either struggling or entirely unable to provide their children with education or medical treatment. With housing increasingly unaffordable for all but a few of the urban residents, the Chinese are now talking about the 'three big new mountains' on their backs, healthcare, education and housing (Yang Guang 2007). The phrase 'three big new mountains' reflects what Mao described as the three big old mountains that oppressed the Chinese people in pre-1949 China: imperialism, feudalism and comprador bureaucratic-capitalism.[8] As Yang's analysis shows, healthcare has not really been marketized and education has not really been entrepreneurial. Both are an excuse for the government to shed its responsibility. Instead, both education and healthcare have become money-making organs for those in management control.

The voice of the workers

Workers do not mince words about what they think about these reforms. The headlines of contributions that published on *Zhongguo gongren wang* (Chinese Workers Net) shows this clearly and here are some headlines related to welfare concerns such as education and healthcare:

'Compared with the present, welfare was great in the pre-reform years', 'My experience of healthcare when I was a child', 'The great reversal: healthcare in the People's Republic of China', 'Who is paying the cost of reforms?' and 'The unfairness of healthcare in China: 80 per cent goes to the privileged in the party, the government and army'.

Recently, *Zhongguo gongren wang* (Chinese workers net 2007) published recorded interviews with workers in Zhengzhou by a group of university students from Beijing. It was eye opening for the students to learn that the privatization of state-owned enterprises led to no evidence of greater efficiency, but to misery for the workers and enrichment of the managers. The students admitted that they were shocked to find that the workers not only have fond memories of Mao but also praised the Cultural Revolution. One worker said that education, health and housing are three big problems whereas in the Mao era the workers did not have worry about them at all. The worker also said that in the Mao era the Four Big Freedoms – speaking out freely, airing views fully, holding big debates and putting up big-character posters, plus the freedom to strike – were written into the Constitution, but now workers dare not go out and demonstrate in the street. 'We want to commemorate Mao every year but the government would not even allow us to do that.' Another worker said that the unfairness in today's society had tilted life in favour of the rich so much that China is like a boat that is about to sink. Another worker complains that when people like him get sick they dare not go to the hospital. Instead, 'we wait to die. In fact many commit suicide to release the family from the financial burden.'

The voice of the farmers

The website *Sannong Zhongguo* (agriculture in China, rural China and farmers in China) regularly publishes contributions on the current rural situation and on how the people in rural China think and feel about the Mao era and the post-Mao reform policies. Many of these contributions are made by those who were born and grew up in the countryside but moved to urban areas later in their life. Consistent with my fieldwork findings in Jiangxi and Shanxi, the overwhelming voice of the rural people is that they recall the Mao era with fondness and complain a lot about the post-Mao reform policies. According to this voice, Mao is their number one admired and respected leader whereas Deng Xiaoping and Jiang Zemin either do not register or are mentioned only in their criticism (Xiao Er 2007). Visiting his home town in Henan, Xiao Er, a university student from Henan University also asked his fellow villagers about the Great Leap Forward famine. The villagers pointed out that there were natural disasters (*tian zai*) and they would add that Mao, Zhou Enlai and other leaders took the lead in bearing the hardship. They would also argue that the increase of grain production had more to do with the improvement of infrastructure such as irrigation, technological breakthrough such as better seeding and availability of chemical inputs such as fertilizer and insecticide.

Education and revolution in the big picture

Analytical discussion of the ideas and practices of education in the Mao era is also circulated in the e-media. For instance, Cheng and Manning (2003) argue that education reform under Mao was in fact not something crazy worked up by a fanatical Mao. It is in fact within the tradition of Marxism and the Western radical criticism of education for its elite and urban orientation, its neglect of practical skills and its separation of school from society and education from work. In China the criticism started with the May Fourth Movement, and Cai Yuanpei, the president of Beijing University, for instance, advocated work–study programmes. Marx of course envisaged 'well-developed men' in communist society, ideas inspired by the French Revolution to create 'new men'. In the early Soviet period the first commissioner of Soviet Education, Anatol Lunacharski, issued a report on education that enunciated seven basic principles with an emphasis on an 'early fusion of productive labour and academic institutions: and school as a productive commune'. V.N. Shul'gin, director of the Institute of School Methods in Moscow, even argued that children should not grow up in schools nor in kindergartens, but in the factory, the mill, the agricultural economy, the class struggle. Mao's idea that labouring people ought to 'be simultaneously intellectuals while the intellectuals should also be labourers' was just a natural progression along these lines. Mao's epistemological assumption can clearly be seen in one of his major works, *On Practice*, which claimed that true knowledge comes only from practice and that productive activity is the fundamental source for learning.

A re-evaluation of Kang Sheng?

There was even a call to rehabilitate Kang Sheng, who has been portrayed as an evil character in the literature in both Chinese and English (Lin Qingshan 1988, Byron 1992), given his role in Yan'an in pursuing suspected spies that victimized many. According to Wang Li (2006), Kang Sheng was not only a very cultured man but also a moderate during the Cultural Revolution. Kang was not a cold-blooded KGB monster as he is popularly portrayed. To illustrate, Wang reveals that Kang Sheng once protected Deng Tuo during the anti-rightist movement. At some stage at the beginning of the Cultural Revolution Kang even acted to cover for Liu Shaoqi. He also briefed Zhou Enlai about Mao's idea of the Cultural Revolution prior to the events unfolding so that Zhou could avoid making the mistake of not following the Mao line. Kang Sheng was also against *po si jiu* (destroy the four olds) and against any destruction of *wenwu* (cultural and religious relics and artefacts). Instead of destroying *wenwu* or collecting them for his own benefit (as he is often accused of doing), according to Wang, Kang made a great contribution to protecting them. He was a knowledgeable connoisseur and a passionate collector of Chinese cultural relics and artefacts, and donated all his collections to the state upon his death.

The Chinese themselves say so

These contrary voices have steadily become louder and louder (that is, more strident and frequent) in the e-media. However, this reversal of attitude toward the Mao era and the Cultural Revolution, if it is going to happen at all, will take a long time to catch the attention of the West. When the Chinese authorities and elite intelligentsia started to condemn and denounce the Cultural Revolution, the West understood the atrocity discourse quickly by applying the logic that 'the Chinese themselves say so'. Those of the political left and of progressive persuasions were quickly persuaded to surrender their belief. Or they have been marginalized. Will 'the Chinese themselves say so' reversal be as effective, so that it will be chatted about over coffee by the elite, and even be placed on the flashy magazines under the coffee tables of the non-elite? It is very hard to imagine so. The denunciation of the Cultural Revolution and Mao fits the anti-communist political agenda and anti-Chinese racist agenda well, but the reversal of that verdict does not.

Manufacturing truth and e-media counter-action

E-media contributors also increasingly dissect how the mainstream media is controlled by the government and made to propagate the success of post-Mao reform. Ma Ming (2006), for instance is scathing about how the media sets the agenda along this direction. Ma points out that a film based on Hao Ran's book *Jin guang dadao* is forbidden because it commits the political crime of re-telling the story about the good old days of the Mao era. 'What are we allowed to watch instead?' Ma asks. We are allowed to watch the dynasties and emperors and to be told how wonderful they were. Yes, these were even better old days.

One instance of this propaganda is worth telling here. There are many media stories and reports about Xiaogang Village, the village that supposedly took the initiative of dismantling the collective system, doing so in secret because this was at odds with the political climate in the 1970s, an initiative that was hailed as another 'liberation'. Even when a television programme provides accounts of China's success in feeding its huge population, it may use pictures of Xiaogang Village as the background. However the media and those who join the chorus fail to mention how much the state has donated to this village to promote it as a model of the household responsibility system. In spite of government's pouring money into the village it is still poor today, so poor that its leaders are reported to have visited the still collectivized Nanjie Village to consider the possibility of re-collectivization (Yuan Wenbiao 2006).

The official history propagated by the media claims that the dismantling of the collective system by Xiaogang Village was so effective that grain output in the village increased from an annual 30,000 jin to 120,000 jin in 1979. What the media do not want to reveal is that 30,000 jin was the yield in 1978 when there was a terrible drought, whereas on average the annual output was 190,000 to 200,000 jin during the collective period. In 1979, the year when the land was divided up, the output actually went down 40 per cent compared the annual average under the collective system. Some years later the media claimed that in 1997 the village yielded an output of 1,200,000 jin, indicating that this was a tremendous success of post-Mao reform. Again what the media did not say is that the figures were the total amount of grain yielded in several villages that had been amalgamated and were jointly renamed Xiaogang Village (Lao Tian 2007b).

Another aspect in manufacturing the truth about this village is also revealed in the e-media. In 1978, due to the drought that year, other villages all started to contract responsibility to small teams while still maintaining the collective system. However, the situation in Xiaogang Village was so divisive and there was so much internal tension, even among members of the same lineage, that they were not able to form teams. It was under these circumstances that the village head Yan Junchang decided that the land was to be carved up among the households. The so-called historical act had nothing to do with the villagers' courageous rebellion against the collective system. It had more to do with the village leaders' inability to get the village organized.

The legacy of Mao and the e-media

Information of this kind can be increasingly seen in the e-media for three main reasons. The first is that the consequences and problems of the reform policies are now being seen and felt by the majority of the people, as discussed in other chapters. There is backlash against at least some of the reform policies.[9] The second reason is that e-media has become more user-friendly and more accessible. As a result the previous monopoly of the media by the political and elite intelligentsia has been broken. The third reason has much to do with the legacy of Maoism. The ideas of Mao and the staging of the Cultural Revolution actually trained and prepared many people, who were young and idealistic at that time, to think and reflect critically about political and social issues. Some of this 'Cultural Revolution-generated thinking generation' have become dissidents and anti-communists. But there are some who do not oppose communism for the sake of opposing and do not embrace capitalism as an ideological crusade. These are the people who have begun to raise their voices by questioning every accepted aspect of the manufactured truth.

Conclusion: voices from the bottom for a battle that has just begun

The e-media have provided a space for voices that cannot be heard through the conventional media. As I have acknowledged, many of the claims by the e-media debate participants may be erroneous and many of their arguments are unsubstantiated. For instance, recently a person using the pen-name Zuo Ke (2006) went as far as to argue that the Mao era was the golden period for China's development of the computer industry. To fully engage in this issue alone would require a book-length study. By presenting their voices I do not intend to argue that only their voices represent the truth. Instead, I wish to show that the hegemony of the official discourse on the Cultural Revolution and the Mao era has been challenged by these voices. If we don't want to listen to these voices, many Chinese will.

Apart from uncoordinated contributions along these lines in various blogs, bulletin board systems, websites and chatrooms, there are a number websites that are specifically designed to counteract the Chinese political and elite intelligentsia's monopoly of the mainstream conventional media and interpretation of history. In the resurrected Chinese Workers Net, for instance, most of the published pieces were positive about the Mao era and critical of the post-Mao reform. Here are few headlines as illustrations:

- Whose is thorough democracy? Of course it was Mao's big democracy.
- Compared with now, the pre-reform welfare was great.
- Forever remembering.
- Regarding workers from rural China and care for work injuries: the collective had the strength to protect us.
- Memory of an old coal miner: we had the best of times in production and coal mining safety.

- Healthcare during my childhood.
- How did we develop collective enterprises: the economic basis for us being masters.
- Re-appearance of the plague: the snail fever disease spreads again.
- Worship of Mao was not a phenomenon of brainwashing.
- What have transnational companies brought to us?
- Are the American media objective and neutral?
- Who is bearing the cost of China's reform?
- Is private ownership necessarily democratic? How does the elite hegemonize the discourse of reform?
- Liberated peasants will never forget Mao: stories by grandma.
- We would elect Mao again.

This challenge to the elitists has not gone unnoticed or unchallenged. Some websites were not allowed to operate for long. The Chinese Workers Net was shut down only a few months after its appearance. The website *Shiji Zhongguo* (Century China) was also shut down in 2006 after a few years of operation. But there are some websites that are still in operation at time of writing such as *Mao Zedong qizhi wang* (the Mao Zedong Flag net), http://www. maoflag.net/, *Wuyou zhixiang* (Utopia), http://www.wyzxwyzx.com, *Sannong Zhongguo* http:// www.snzg.net/default.asp, *Gong nong tian di* (Space for the workers and farmers) https://www.fsurf.com/index. php?q=aHR0cDovL3d 3dy5nb25nbm9uZy5vcmc per cent3D, *Huayue luntan* (Huayue forum) https://w7.spetra.net.ru/dmirror/http/69.41.162.74/HuaShan/ GB2.html. The Gansu site of *Xinlang* launched a migrant worker blog page in 2007. In its first issue, the two pieces of short writing in a simple style by migrant workers gave a very positive evaluation of Mao (http://blog.sina.com.cn/m/hongbie#feeds FEEDS 1261878412 (accessed on 18 January 2007).

In 2005, when there was some indication that the Hu Jintao and Wen Jiabao leadership was re-orientating China's development priority for the first time since the 1980s, and when Wen Jiabao was reported to read the e-media regularly, the neoliberal elite was alarmed. Professor Zhang Weiying, the Oxford-trained economist, appealed to the Chinese leadership not to be pressurized by the populist voices of the e-media. Another neoliberal, Gao Changquan (2006), found it incredible that *Wuyou zhixiang* had the audacity to publish pieces that attack Deng Xiaoping and praise Zhang Chunqiao for his theoretical articulation of the proletarian revolution. These are calls to battle, and the war in China between the capitalist model and an alternative may yet be won by either side.

9 The problem of the rural–urban divide in pursuit of modernity: values and attitudes

Introduction: the year 2003

This chapter deliberately restricts its analysis to the period before 2003. It is clear that since that year the Hu Jintao and Wen Jiabao leadership, which came to power in 2002, has adopted a different stance towards rural China. It has apparently paid heed to the many-faceted social and economic problems in rural China that the previous Jiang Zemin and Zhu Rongji leadership did not address. The most notable change was the 2003 abolition of all agricultural taxes. Boyang County of Jiangxi province, where Gao Village is situated, was one of the counties that benefited from this reform. When I visited Gao Village in early 2005 I immediately noticed the difference. Of many visits of the village, this was the first when I did not hear any complaint against the government policies from any of the villagers. Not only was there no tax of any kind, there was even some subsidies for farming the land. For the villagers it was unbelievably liberating because taxes have had to be paid since history began in the village. However, it is still too early to see whether the reform will succeed and too early to evaluate its long-term effects, though the limitations of the tax-free reform are already apparent (Yep 2004). Nonetheless, 2003 may be a watershed year for the rural Chinese, as it was the year when the 2,500-year practice of taxing rural China to finance the government and support urban consumption came to a close. Therefore, this chapter will only discuss the rural situation up to 2003 in its relation to the era of Mao.

The rise of China, but the risk of collapse

Amid the persistent fears of the rise of China in the Western media there are frequent predictions that the Chinese system is so unsustainable that it will collapse sooner rather than later (Chang 2001). On 8 January 2004, the highly influential *New York Times* published a warning that 'China may be in [a] bubble now' (Chan 2004). Would we be surprised if the Chinese system collapsed (either politically or economically or both)? Obviously this question is too ambitious to address here, and is outside the scope of this chapter where I evaluate the rural situation. But it is clear to me that even if the Chinese system collapses, the direct cause is unlikely to come from rural China. Li Changping specifically addresses this issue by stating that a large-scale peasant rebellion in contemporary China is not likely (Li 2004).

Meanwhile we have become accustomed to media reports that China has been experiencing a major economic boom and is the engine of economic growth in Asia with its huge increase in volumes of trade, and that China is the playground for modern architecture (Thornton 2004, Stucke 2004, Samuelson 2004, Einhorn 2004a). For the urban residents of the booming southeast costal cities, the China they know and care about is the one in which the goal of life is to achieve 'middle class' status – a status that includes family cars, holidays abroad and children studying overseas. But in the other China the picture is completely different (Gao 2003). In some rural areas we can still see 'unimaginable poverty', 'unimaginable helplessness', 'unimaginable silence and unimaginable tragedy' (Chen and Chun 2004).

The urban–rural divide

According to research conducted by the Chinese Academy of Social Sciences, after 20 years of reform urban residents now earn 2.8 times more than rural people (Cheng 2004). If factors such as rising costs of education and health are taken into consideration, the gap is as high as six times, the highest in the world. According to another study, of the average rural dweller's per capita income of 2,618 RMB in 2003, agricultural contributions fell below 60 per cent, while the contribution from migrant workers' earnings rose from 8 percentage points to more than 40 per cent. The average net annual income of migrant workers, after living and travel expenses, came to 3,768 RMB (about US$500) in 2003, according to the survey, which was based on interviews in 20,089 rural households in China's 31 provinces (Kynge 2004). According to the Chinese official media, there was a 5.8 per cent reduction in grain production in 2003 compared with 2002, and 99 million rural residents left their homes as migrant workers in 2003, a 5 million increase compared with 2002 (*Xinhua News* 2004). According to another study, urban residents who make up only 15 per cent of China's total population consume two-thirds of the country's healthcare resources while the other 85 per cent of the population have access to less than a third of the country's healthcare resources (Song Bingwen et al. 2003). Clearly, the rural–urban divide has been widening and the deteriorating rural situation has been ignored by the Chinese leadership for a long time.

Three stories of rural pain

The rural situation discussed here does not include the southeast coastal provinces of Shandong, Jiangsu, Zhejiang, Guangdong and Fujian. Nor does it include the poverty-stricken areas of the northwest provinces of Gansu, Qinghai, Shaanxi and Tibet or Xinjiang. The southeast costal provinces can be categorized into two subgroups. The first consists of the Pearl River Delta and some parts of Fujian, where investment from outside mainland China have created a special kind of development. Zhejiang and Jiangsu belong to the second subgroup where TVEs (township and village enterprises) advanced rapidly during the late 1970s and throughout the 1980s and have developed into private enterprises since the 1990s. In the areas of northwest there is a lack of agricultural resources and very little, if any, local industry. Even the environment is hostile to human existence. The central provinces of Shanxi, Henan, Hebei, Hunan, Hubei, Anhui, Jiangxi, Sichuan Guizhou, Guangxi and Yunnan, plus areas of Fujian and Guangdong, the so-called 'grain belt' areas (Unger 2002), are not only China's agricultural base but also major sources of migrant workers.

Chen and Chun's investigation into rural poverty became a media event when their book on the rural situation in Anhui was published in 2004. The book was soon banned by the Chinese authorities, but an English version appeared in 2006. The following three stories are told by Chen and Chun and may be seen as a metaphor for the agony, hardship and the complex situation faced by most of the rural people in central areas.

The story of Ding

In 1993 a group of farmers wrote a letter of complaint about the problems of corruption and abusive levies. Ding was beaten to death by local township security guards for leading the complaint group. Angry at this brutality several thousand villagers got together to protest, an event that made the death known to the central government through a Xinhua News Agency journalist, Kong Xiangying. However, in order to cover up the abusive levies and taxes under his government, Dai Wenhu, the party secretary of Lixin County, reported to Beijing that Ding's death had been caused by a civil dispute. After an investigation by a team from Beijing into the event, the State Council issued the document *Guanyu jianqing nongmin fudan de jinji tongzhi* (an urgent circular concerning the reduction of the burden on farmers). Followed by a State Council meeting on the issue and another document, a decision was made in Beijing that more than 120 different levies and taxes were to be abolished, reduced or postponed. Some of those who were responsible for Ding's death were executed, imprisoned, or disciplined.

Brutal taxes and levies

The Ding story looks like a story that ends well: justice was done and the central government took measures to reduce the peasants' tax burden. But decisions made in Beijing are one thing; whether they are implemented throughout the country is another. This is illustrated by another story from the same province Anhui where Chen and Chun made their study. Zhang Guiquan, who had been convicted of rape and corruption, was appointed village head before he had even finished his prison term. When the villagers organized a team to investigate amount of levies Zhang collected and his methods of collection, he and his sons killed four members of the investigative team. Again to cover up the grave tax and levy situation the country newspaper and television station reported the news as a village feud and the death of four men as the result of manslaughter.

The three Wangs

The third story started in 1993. The party secretary of a village committee, Gao Jianjun, took away Wang Hongchao's television set because the latter did not pay the 6 RMB demanded for what was claimed to be a school building construction fee. Wang Junbing and Wang Hongchao went to the *xiang* (township) government to complain, but their complaint was ignored. The two Wang's plus Wang Xiangdong then went to the county government demanding a re-appraisal but were rebuked and physically pushed out of the reception office before they could even say what they had come about. After organizing a couple of protest marches involving several hundred villagers to the county town, to no avail, the three Wang's decided to take their complaint to Beijing. Though the authorities in Beijing, after hearing their case, gave instructions to rectify the situation, and though the country authority under pressure from Beijing ordered the village committee to refund to the villagers all the illegal levies, nothing was actually done at the village level. Moreover, Wang Junbing was sacked from his land management job at the township and the other two Wangs were beaten up by *xiang* government personnel.

What followed looked like fiction, but unfortunately was real. One dark night a team of five men consisting of local police and security guards went to arrest the three Wangs. The villagers were quickly alerted to the late night raid. Many of them got up quickly and surrounded the intruders, who would not admit that they were sent by the *xiang* government officially to arrest the three Wangs. The villagers disarmed the five men but later let them go after they admitted that they were actually police. But that was enough for the county government to send a police force of more than a hundred to suppress the 'rebellion'. Before the police reached the village more than a thousand people had fled to Henan province (as the village is on the border between Anhui and Henan). The police nevertheless arrested twelve villagers, mostly the elderly, women and children. Some men were beaten up and were shackled, and they were asked to pay 7 RMB for the cost of the shackles. Wang Hongchao, Wang Xiaodong and Wang Hongxin, who also escaped, set off for Beijing again but were ambushed by the county police, who had been waiting for them.

Meanwhile a villager Li Xiwen, also from the county where the Wangs were suppressed, killed himself by jumping down from the Beijing Letter and Complaint (*Xin fang ban*) reception building in his despair at finding no way of redressing what he considered an injustice. And there is more. On 29 October 1994, a clear Sunday, 74 villagers sneaked into Tian'anmen Square and knelt together before the national flag of the People's Republic of China, asking for justice. Only then did the central government urge Anhui to solve the problem. Wang Xiaodong was released after 19 months imprisonment and Wang Junbing was appointed party secretary of the village committee to replace his corrupt predecessor.

Rural Chinese: beasts of burden on whom modernity is built

Why is it that so many central government documents and decrees could not stop the ever increasing tide of levies and taxes? According to Chen and Chun (2004), more than 90 different levies and taxes that had been imposed on the Chinese peasantry in Anhui province from various departments of the central government, and an additional 269 were imposed by local governments. The central government issued decrees and documents in general terms with instructions to reduce taxes and levies, like the stipulation that total taxes and levies on any household should not be more than 5 per cent of the family's annual income. But in practice financial and fiscal policies and revenue and expenditure regulations designed for and by the central government actually led to an increase in the burden on rural residents.

Taxation reform

One of the reforms designed by Premier Zhu Rongji was to establish a two-tiered tax system, one tier for the central government tax and one for the local government tax, called *guo di shui fenjia* (separation of taxes collected by [the central] state and taxes and levies collected by the local governments). The intention was to make sure that central state government tax revenue would not be infringed upon by local authorities. The central government was to collect value-added tax and consumption tax whereas the local governments were to collect business tax, personal and enterprise income tax.

As a result of this reform, local governments' revenue fell, and to cover their loss of revenue they taxed the rural residents. In 1993, for instance, the financial income of the central government was 95 billion RMB and in 1994 it increased to more than 290 billion. In contrast, the financial income of the local governments over the same period fell from 339 billion RMB to 231 billion. Meanwhile, financial expenditure allocated from the central government to rural China increased by only 44 billion RMB, from 131 billion to a mere 175 billion, whereas the financial responsibilities of local rural governments increased from 332.2 billion RMB to 403 billion. In other words, Premier Zhu wanted local governments to pay more to the centre but at the same time take on responsibilities for greater expenditure (Chen and Chun 2004). Amnesty International, whose criticisms of countries like China usually focus on political and civil rights, published a study condemning the Chinese social and economic policies that push for development at the expense of millions of rural migrants (see Watts 2007).

What was the extra income collected by the central government used for? It was used for more urban development. One indication of this is the high-speed magnetic railway from the city of Shanghai to its airport. The rail track is so short that the train has to stop only a few minutes after it reaches its full speed. It uses Germany technology so expensive that even the Germans have not built a single railway of this type. It was an expensive toy with a billion dollar price tag for the city of Shanghai to boost its image of being modern and advanced.

Let us join the Western world

The creation of an elite class is now considered a sign of modernity and a way to catch up with the West. In almost every urban centre one can encounter advertisements encouraging consumers to become a member of the *guizu* (literally 'expensive clan', but often translated as 'noble' or 'aristocratic' in English). Thus you can see furniture advertised as *guizu* furniture and a piece of sportswear as *guizu xiuxian* (aristocratic leisure wear) and a real estate compound as *guizu cun* (noble or aristocratic village). Another example of development for the benefit of the elite is the fashion for building golf courses. China is well known for its lack of arable land and water resources, yet there is fierce competition to build golf courses. In 2006, the president of Xiamen University, Zhu Congshi, announced that his university had constructed a beautiful golf course to train students to become members of the elite. Zhu declares that training an elite is an example of educating the best for the public interest (*Wuyou zhixiang* 2006).

I don't see it, so it doesn't exist

As for the majority of the rural Chinese, they are assumed to belong properly to another class. The case of Yang Shanlu is typical of those in rural China, and his life is taken for granted as a normal for a Chinese peasant. Yang has 3.3 mu of land to farm and his costs in 2000 came to a total of 997.5 RMB (made up of: seeding 67.5, insecticide 20, fertilizer 190, electricity for irritation 140, rent of a buffalo 500, mechanical harvesting 80). He harvested 1,815 kilo of rice earning a total of 1,488.30 RMB, at the government set price of 0.82 RMB a kilo, plus a canola crop income of 400 RMB. Taking away the capital input and 365.2 RBM state tax, there he was left with only 525.6 RMB. The net per capita annual income of the family of four who worked on the land for a whole year was 131.4 RMB. On top of that the village accountant came to demand 120 RMB for irrigation ditch costs, 68.85 for building an electric irrigation station, 22.95 for irrigation infrastructure repair, 54 for road maintenance, levies that totalled 301.18 RBM (Chen and Chun 2004).

During his briefing to the media at the National People's Congress meeting in 2001, Premier Zhu Rongji declared that the state would change the rural tax system from collecting fees to a unified tax. Zhu said he would only impose a tax of about 50 billion RMB instead of the current 120 billion on rural residents. In order to compensate the local governments for the loss of income, the central government would subsidize the poorer province with a total of 20 to 30 billion RBM. In fact, as Li Changping (2002) convincingly shows, the real financial expenditure of the local governments came to more than 700 billion RBM and about 70 per cent to 80 per cent of that is raised as taxes and levies from the rural residents. Premier Zhu was either blissfully ignorant of the facts or simply pretended that the problem did not exist.

The rural–urban divide: values and attitudes

A journalist named Mang Bisheng was once approached by a rural woman of about 40 who was looking for someone to *gao zhuang* (to lodge a complaint). She knelt down crying in front of Mang (kneeling in front of someone is an age-old symbolic gesture of humiliation and appeal for addressing injustice). Mang asked to see a written account of her complaint. The woman, shaking, first took out from a paper wrap something like sinew. It was some tendon that her village head and gangs had taken out of the woman's feet to stop her from travelling to seek justice. Mang was deeply moved and tried to help her to get justice. However, after several attempts, not only was he unable to do anything but he also lost her written document (Mang 2004).

One reader from the *Renmin wang* e-media chatroom asks a rhetorical question: As we urban residents talk about buying cars and about taking a holiday abroad do we realize that it is the rural residents who support our bid to join the world? (http://www.people. com.cn, accessed 4 February 2004) The Chinese expression of this bid is *yu shijie jiegui* (literally meaning 'join the rail track of the world'). This is a slogan that the Chinese political, business and intelligentsia elite constantly use to indicate their ambition to be part of the Western world in material wealth and life style.

It is quite likely that the urban elite do not realize how much the rural people are made to sacrifice for their modernity, because it is not in the realm of public discourse. Even though some do know the extent of what the rural people contribute to their Europeanization of urban cities, they think it is a necessary sacrifice. The following quote from Huang Ping exemplifies Chinese urban elite thought about the plight of the rural Chinese:

> Our conception of society (including that held by those in the government and the majority of the urban residents) holds that rural China is nothing but a residue of the process of modernization and is bound to be eradicated. It is backward and should not be allowed to exist. The 900 million peasants are China's baggage and burden, a tumour to be removed the earlier the better. Why should we invest in rural China? It is not necessary. This is their view, the view of our government and certain big name scholars. They pay lip service to rural poverty; but what lies deep in their mind is: let rural China die off and until it does the function of rural China is 1) vegetable basket, 2) ricebowl and 3) producing a low-quality population. Rural China is the source of human quality deterioration. Rural construction? No, stop them giving birth and suppress their revolt instead and that will fix it.
>
> (Huang Ping 2004)

The reason that the post-Mao government did not invest in rural education and rural health was not because there was no money. It was because of their ideology and policy orientation. They believe not only that capitalism is the only road to achieve China's dream of being strong and wealthy but also that it is inevitable that the poor and the disadvantaged masses will have to bear the consequences of what they call the primitive stage of capital accumulation. These values and attitudes, reinforced by the mainstream economists, have held a dominant position in public discourse ever since the 1980s.

In order to copy the West, or to learn the magic recipe from the West, the central and local governments, the latter led by the former, allocated enormous amount of resources for government personnel and officials to make study or inspection tours abroad. While two-thirds of

US Congressmen reportedly do not have a passport, it would be hard to find any Chinese officials from the upper middle rank up who have never been abroad. According to one account (Li Ming 2004), expenditure on overseas inspection tours by the Chinese authorities amounts to US$30 billion per year. That would be enough to help 50 million Chinese out of poverty or to pay for the education of 3 million children from primary school to university.

Since the post-Mao reforms, the key function of the local governments in rural China has been to get money out of the rural people and to stop them from having more children. No wonder a phrase widely spread among the farmers in Anhui during the late 1990s was: *San cui san hai* (Three demands and three hazards). This refers to three demands from the government – grain, cash and life, the last of which refers to family planning – while the three hazards are fire, robbery and government officials.

The situation had become so bad that the Hu Jintao and Wen Jiabao leadership felt that something had to be done. This was indicated by the *People's Daily*, which published a commentary calling for an end to the quasi-apartheid system, arguing that income gaps have to be closed. The paper states that:

> nine provinces and autonomous regions, plus the vast rural areas under the jurisdiction of Chongqing Municipality, have remained appallingly poor. This poverty belt, stretching from Yunnan in the south to Xinjiang in the north, makes up more than half of China's land mass and it contains 285 million people – a population bigger than that of the United States.
>
> (*People's Daily* 2004b)

This official acknowledgement refers mainly to the poverty-stricken northwest areas, but not most of the central provinces.

It has been a hard task to persuade the Chinese elite policy makers that it is morally wrong to have designed an economic development plan driven by the aspirations of the urban Chinese citizens for the living standard of the developed countries when the majority of the rural residents in inland China are struggling to survive. Although there are increasing numbers of urban poor, even these urban poor refuse to work for the same wages and in the same conditions as rural migrant workers – a clear indication of apartheid against the rural population.

Post-Mao reforms: myths versus reality

For a long time since the 1980s there has been a consensus among the majority of the Chinese political and intelligentsia elite that the post-Mao destruction of the collective system performed miracles. With this mind set, they either ignored or pretended not to see the reality that could be seen even by a discerning outsider. For instance, Unger (2002) points out that more than 60 per cent of the increase in rural income between 1978 and 1982 was achieved before the commune system was dismantled and that per capita rural income in 1990 (338 RMB) was barely higher than in 1984 (336 RMB), and, quoting Scott Rozelle, another China specialist, 'the 1990s witnessed much the same story' (Unger 2002: 172).

China rural heartland

A sense of rural prosperity during the mid-1980s soon dissipated and the rural Chinese had to become migrant workers to earn a living. Gao Changxian, my brother in Gao Village, is an example of an ordinary farmer in the grain belt area. He used to have a little shop in Gao Village and, with his wife Gao Mingxia and three children of primary school age, they managed well enough and were considered to be well off in the village in the early 1990s. Gradually, as the children grew bigger and more money was needed for education, the situation became progressively worse. Most of the young villagers left and there were not enough customers to keep the shop going. First Gao Changxian's wife left for Xiamen as a migrant worker and then his second teenage daughter. Finally Gao Changxian himself also had to head off for Xiamen. Being in their forties and having no qualifications, it was very difficult for Gao Changxian and Gao Mingxia to leave two children behind and to live as migrant workers in an urban structure that treated rural people as non-citizens of their own country (Gao 2005). For the urban elite, Gao Changxian and his family, and all the other rural migrants, are either quietly ignored or are seen as deserving of their situation because they are lower-quality human beings and are born to be beasts of burden for the benefit of high-quality people.

Migrant workers

The dire circumstances of rural migrant workers have been ignored until recently by the media. A major TV event in China since the 1980s has been the performance for the Spring Festival New Year's Eve titled *Chunjie lianhuan wanhui* (Spring Festival Nationwide Joint Evening Performance). It is watched not only by the whole urban nation but also by millions of ethnic Chinese overseas. It is so popular and so much part of the contemporary Chinese cultural establishment that the annual event is simply referred to as *Chun wan* (Spring Evening). Usually the programme includes dancing, singing and *xiangsheng* (a kind of stand-up cross-talk comedy routine), mostly by the urban and educated. If rural China is mentioned, it is usually the topic of jokes and ridicule. In the 2007 *Chun wan*, for the first time since the post-Mao reform, a group of children from a Beijing migrant school set up by the migrants themselves performed a poetry recital on stage to the national audience. According to one commentator (Fenghua yuan 2007), the poem moved the nation. Here is my translation of the poem:

If you want to ask who I am
I am always unwilling to tell
Because we are the butt of your urban children's jokes.
Our school yard is small
Not big enough for a rocking horse;
Our campus is non-existent and
Every now and then we are hunted to move from one place to another.
Our lights are dim
Our chairs are shaky and creak when we sit on them,
But we do our work well
And our results are good.
We love our mothers
Because they sweep the street of this city for you;
We love our fathers
Because they build the skylines of the new century.
Others like to compare their parents' status;
We can only hope to compare today with tomorrow.
Like you urban people
We are also children of China
And happy New Year to you

In recent years, loss of land has become the main cause of social unrest. The development policies aimed at increasing GDP have led to an increasing loss of agricultural land and a decline in grain production. The gravity of this situation is illustrated by the case of Pei Lianggeng from Hebei. Pei used to be a large-scale grain grower and was named as the 'National Grain Selling Model' in 1989 but now he only farms 12 mu of land (*Xinhua News* 2004b). As there is no hope of earning a living by farming many millions, like Gao Changxian and his family, have to leave their homes to be migrant workers. A migrant worker from rural China has to work in appalling conditions for twelve hours a day or longer (Chan 2003), very often for seven days a week, to earn about US$80 a month. According to McCool (2004), rural migrant 'workers received an average 16.5 cents an hour when the legal minimum in China was 31 cents an hour.[1] The working week was seven days when five days was legal and people toiled for up to 20½ hours per shift.' Still hundreds of millions of rural youth leave their home to be migrant workers.

Shangfang *and resistance*

Shangfang (to appeal for help from higher authorities) has been a phenomenon in Beijing; the reception office that was officially set up to receive complaints provides some hope, however illusionary, for hopeless people that they may find some redress of grievance and injustice. According to Xie (2004) there is in Beijing a so-called *shangfang* village where the *shangfang* rural people stay temporarily. He claims to know more than a hundred peasants who have been imprisoned for their *shangfang* activities. One woman, Hao Wenzhong, has been *shangfang*-ing for 19 years, during which she has been detained 197 times, and was put into psychiatric hospitals 17 times. On 6 January 2004, four *shangfang* people were arrested and detained by the police in Beijing; according to Xinhua News Agency, they were arrested because they committed criminal act of organizing other *shangfang* people to demonstrate on the Tian'anmen Square (Niu and Li 2004).

These *shangfang* activities are very similar to those described in traditional Chinese plays, Peking operas and novels, where they are called *gao zhuang* (lodge a complaint against an official with his superior, Perry 2001). A typical scene portrayed in classical Chinese literature is *lanlu gao zhuang* (a victim of injustice would suddenly appear in the middle of a road, kneel down before the official sedan chair passing by and then submit a written document appealing for redress of an injustice).

There has been increasing resistance, as indicated by Yu Jianrong's report (2003), which is an in-depth investigation of one county and focuses on the form and likely consequences of rural resistance. Rural protests, as noted by China scholars such as Bernstein, Perry, Bianco, Gilley and Unger, actually started as early as the 1980s, the perceived golden age of post-Mao rural reform (O'Brien 2002). According to Yu the rural residents were so desperate that they were organizing themselves. This was such a sobering reminder to the Chinese leadership that Yu was given a million-dollar research grant to study the problem (Ye 2004).

In the county that Yu has investigated there is a core group of 80 people known as the *Jian fu daibiao* or *Jian fu shangfang daibiao* (Representatives on reduction of tax and levy burdens, or Representatives for appeals to the superior authorities). They are middle-aged men who have been educated to junior middle school or above, and most have served in the army or have been migrant workers. They know what they are doing and have some access to social resources, and they are ready to make significant sacrifices, including imprisonment or even death. They are regarded as 'heroes' by the villagers, who would even protect them by fighting with the police or by raiding local government offices. However, the villagers are very careful not to have any overt organization and therefore do not have any written records of their meetings or memberships. At one stage, representatives from different villages even held meetings in the capital city of Hunan, and in a January 2003 the 27 representatives there called for the establishment of a *Nongmin xiehui* (Peasant association).[2]

Whenever the villagers have some grievance they go to these representatives rather than any state-authorized organizations. What is ironic is that the ultimate authority on which this kind of resistance relies is the central government of the CCP. These informal and quasi-unofficial organizations resort to central government documents, published laws and regulations to justify their resistance to taxes and levies, and their actions against corrupted local officials (O'Brien 2002). These representatives have also developed clever ways of organizing their activities. One is to set up a loudspeaker in a market place to broadcast the central government documents that mandate reductions in tax burdens and laws against corruptions.

Theirs is not the passive daily resistance of the weak, but resistance organized along the lines of upholding the laws and regulations of the state and of the party. According to Yu, the state has been losing its control at grassroots level and if appropriate policies are not taken *hei shili* (black forces: local ruffians and scoundrels) will take over by infiltrating the existing local governments, or new organizations would adopt measures such as kidnapping and blackmailing. It appears that the Hu Jintao and Wen Jiabao leadership took Yu's report seriously. One year after the report of 2003 the central government started abolishing all agricultural taxes, as mentioned at the beginning of this chapter.

Conclusion: the state and the countryside

It is unlikely there will be any large-scale *nongmin qiyi* (peasant uprising) in contemporary China. However, Maoist radicalism has left its legacy. One aspect of that legacy, as Yu's study shows, is that the rural people have become politically more conscious and more active. Currently, migration to urban areas is acting as a safety valve. Without it, resistance would have been more intensive and extensive. Another aspect of the Maoist legacy is that some (though not many) of the urban elite who are now in their fifties, having lived and worked in rural China, are ready to speak on behalf of the rural poor. Chen and Chun are actually following in the footsteps of a few educated Chinese in the Mao era who began to look into the life of the most disadvantaged in China. Others I have mentioned include Li Changping, Yu Jianrong and Cao Jingqing. But as early as 1968 an educated youth from Beijing, Zhang Musheng, wrote a manuscript *Zhongguo nongmin wenti xuexi: guanyu Zhongguo zhidu de yanjiu* (A study of Chinese rural problems: a research study of the Chinese system), which questions the Chinese government's exploitation of the peasantry. The manuscript was circulated widely in the form of mimeographs and handwritten copies (Yang Jian 2002).

Finally, let me point out an insight of Wang Xiaotao (2004) to conclude this chapter. Wang rejects Vivienne Shue's (1988) thesis that local rural officials are also rational actors defending the interest of the local residents, Helen Siu's (1989) argument that these officials are loyal to the state, and Jean Oi's (1989) argument that rural local officials act both as agents of the state and as representatives of local interests. Rather he argues that the conflict in rural China is no longer between the state and farmers, but between farmers and local officials. It is the state that has to face the dilemma of choosing between them. In other words, the local officials do not represent farmers, nor are they agents of the state. They have rapidly become a powerful class of their own. Whether the state can mould them into state agents who are institutionally accountable is a crucial question for the stable development of rural China. The so-called grassroots democracy – village elections that have been experimented and have been supported internationally, for example by the Carter Foundation – has so far failed to achieve such an outcome.

10 The battle of China's history: seeing the past from the present

Introduction: a little incident

On 26 June 2005, in Chizhou City of Anhui province, a Honda vehicle bumped into Liu Liang. Following this accident, the driver of the vehicle, a businessman named Mr Wu who runs a private hospital, and Liu Liang started to argue, and the argument quickly developed into a physical fight. One of Mr Wu's companions in the car, a hospital security guard, reportedly beat Liu up. Liu was later taken to a hospital to be treated for his injuries. However, a rumour soon spread around the area that Liu had been beaten to death, and tens of thousands of local residents surrounded the police station where Mr Wu and his companions were being held. The protesters demanded that the police handover the detainees because they believed that the police were protecting Mr Wu, a rich businessman. When the police refused this demand, some of the protesters turned the Honda over and burned it, and then proceeded to do the same to a police car. They then burned the police station and robbed a supermarket because its boss was rumoured to have given soft drinks to the police. According to newspaper reports, the incident developed so fast because: first, Mr Wu declared that it did not matter if Liu was beaten to death – all he had to do was to pay 300,000 RMB (about US$4,000); and second, the police were perceived to be protecting the rich (Reuters 2005).

This kind of incident is commonplace in present-day China, and it sharply highlights a sense of popular antagonism towards the rich and the police. It does not matter what really happened. It does not matter, for example, who was responsible for the car accident, whether Liu really died, whether the boss of the supermarket was colluding with the police, or whether Mr Wu had three bodyguards who beat up a young student (in fact Liu was not young, nor was he a student). It was the perception that the rich were taking over and the police were on their side that mattered. Since 1999, Chizhou City has implemented policies to attract capital by setting investment quotas as a performance indicator for every level of government bureaucracy. Newspaper reports suggest that it was popular opinion that businessmen from Shanghai, Jiangsu and Zhejiang had taken over land in Chizhou for development, with little or no compensation being paid to the local community (Reuters 2005).

In the context of evaluating the Cultural Revolution, this chapter, like the previous one, further appraises the post-Mao reforms. In such an appraisal the issue of whether life is better for the Chinese in general at the beginning of the twenty-first century will be dealt with briefly. The chapter then asks how far and in what way China has 'gone capitalist'. It will also examine whether and how Maoist socialist legacies still matter in China. Finally, the chapter finishes with a brief discussion of how ordinary workers and farmers see the Mao era in comparison to what has been happening since the post-Mao reforms

Three questions about the post-Mao reforms

When talking about the achievements of the post-Mao reforms, it is often taken for granted by the media that life for people in present-day China is better than it has ever been. But there are people such as the unemployed, the sick, the weak and millions and millions of rural people who would argue that by the beginning of the twenty-first century life has deteriorated to its worst point in the history of the PRC. This discrepancy of opinion reflects not only the growing socioeconomic stratification of contemporary Chinese society but also differences in beliefs and values.

Most prominent Chinese CCP leaders, from Zhou Enlai to Deng Xiaoping and from Jiang Zemin to Hu Jintao, are nationalists rather than communists, and their overwhelming aspiration has been to make China strong and wealthy. Like many revolutionaries in developing countries, political radicalism for many Chinese revolutionaries was a means to an end of national unity and a wealthy China. If market capitalism is the way to achieve this end, then by all means go for it.

Mao too was a Chinese nationalist. However, it can be argued that for Mao national unity and national wealth were not just ends in themselves. Mao was a post-Lenin Marxist who wanted to open up a path for new politics (Badiou 2005, Bosteels 2005). Some ideas experimented with during the Cultural Revolution were Maoist attempts to create new subjectivity (Wang Hui 2006). Maoism, including many of the ideas of the Cultural Revolution, contributed to the imagination of modernity without capitalism (Amin 2006). It can be argued that the rationale of the Cultural Revolution is that cultural transformation is crucial to the consolidation of social and political change (Dirlik 2006). Deng, on the other hand, would embrace any way, black cat or white cat, in order to make China strong and wealthy. Thus, there is a crucial difference between Mao's vision and what Deng Xiaoping wanted to see in China. Even in terms of material civilization it is not unequivocally clear that China is stronger and wealthier at the beginning of the twenty-first century. Yes China is wealthier, but not necessarily stronger. For many, China is unstable and is weaker when facing the global capitalist onslaught.

In the context of these issues there are three questions that need to be asked about the post-Mao reforms. The first is to what extent material improvement in the post-Mao reform years should be attributed to the Mao era. The second question is who benefits most from the post-Mao economic development. The third question is what approach and what kind of development is good for the quality of human life in China, and whether this kind of development can be sustained.

Who planted the seeds of the post-Mao era?

One indication of positive development is that millions of Chinese have been lifted out of absolute poverty in the past three decades. It is an undisputable fact that even the rural people at the bottom of the Chinese society, rural people like those who have been described in my book *Gao Village* (Gao 1999a), are better fed and clothed since the 1980s. It is an undisputable fact that even basic daily necessities such as a bar of soap were rationed during the Mao era. So why is there abundance in the reforms years as opposed to scarcity under Mao? The answer to this question is related to the first question raised above, that is, to what extent did the Mao era contribute to subsequent economic developments? This question has already been addressed in various forms in previous chapters.

Who benefits most from the post-Mao reform?

Regarding the second question new evidence suggests that 'China's poorest [have become] worse off after the boom' (McGregor 2006). According to a recent estimate based on official Chinese data and analysed by the UN:

> From 2001 to 2003, as China's economy expanded nearly 10 per cent a year, average income for the poorest 10 per cent of the country's households fell 2.5 per cent. Those roughly 130 million Chinese earn $1 a day or less, the World Bank's global benchmark for poverty.
>
> (Batson and Oster 2006)

What development can be sustained and better for the quality of life?

In relation to the third question raised above, it is worth considering whose economic development it is and for what purposes. China focuses on export-orientated capital accumulation (Hart-Landsberg and Burkett 2007) and has become the world's 'manufacturing shop floor', but what good is that for the Chinese when China is just a sweatshop that produces cheap goods for other countries, especially wealthier Western countries? Most of these 'made in China' commodities are destined for markets outside China and are therefore not available in China. 'China's exports to the United States account for about half of its total exports', an estimate based on direct and indirect measures, that is, including goods re-exported from other countries (Hart-Landsberg and Burkett 2007: 19). 'According to Morgan Stanley, low-cost Chinese imports (mainly textiles, shoes, toys, and household goods) have saved US consumers (mostly middle- and low-income families) about $100 billion dollars since China's reforms began in 1978' (Gilboy 2004).

China does not really own this factory either. Most enterprises and manufacturing facilities are owned by foreign firms, companies or multi-nationals who take the lion's share of the profit. 'In 2005, not only did foreign-invested companies account for 58 per cent of total exports by value from China, they controlled a remarkable 88 per cent of exports in high-tech categories' (Miller 2006). It is therefore obvious that much of the purported development is not really for the direct benefit of most ordinary Chinese such as the rural people. And, although figures such as 100 million Internet users and 300 million mobile phone users in China are impressive, they are not that significant in relative terms in the context of China's nearly 1.4 billion people.

There is certainly a genuine sense that China is on the rise on the international stage, and the country's economic development has led to a fear of China. That fear can be seen by US headline publications such as *The Coming Conflict with China* (Bernstein and Munro 1997), *Unrestricted Warfare: China's Master Plan to Destroy America* (Santoli 2002) and *Seeds of Fire: China and the Story behind the Attack on America* (Thomas 2001). For many Chinese however, as discussed in the e-media debate chapters, China has become demonstrably weaker as the post-Mao reform policies took roots. China always bows to US pressure and the Chinese government is impotent when it is bullied by the United States. To support their view, the critics point out that the United States continues to sell arms to Taiwan despite China's protests; that the United States forced a Chinese cargo ship, *Yinhe*, to be searched in international waters; that the United States deliberately bombed the Chinese embassy in Belgrade; and that a US spy plane could force the destruction of a Chinese fighter jet and the death of its pilot yet still be allowed to land on Chinese territory. If China has any bargaining strength in international relations it is her nuclear power and missile capacities. And these capacities are the legacies of the Mao era.

As for the fact that China had overtaken Japan as the largest holder of foreign currency reserves in the world (US$863 billion as opposed to US$860 billion) by 2006, it not only shows a weakness of China but also the obscenity of the global capitalist system. To earn these so-called foreign currency reserves, China has been trapped by a system that favours the rich against the poor. Millions of China's migrant workers literally shed their blood and sweat to subsidize the wasteful consumption of citizens of the United States and other wealthy Western nations, as shown in *Mardi Gras Made in China*, a film by Redmon (2006). When the US dollar depreciates, as it is doing at the time of this writing, the value of China's dollar reserves vanishes into thin air.

Is China a capitalist country? And does it matter?

Whether China is a capitalist country and whether this matters is related to all the three questions raised above. When Mao launched the Cultural Revolution in 1966 the overriding ideological rationale was to prevent 'capitalist roaders', that is, CCP officials in high positions who had capitalist ideas and tendencies, from 'restoring capitalism'. Deng Xiaoping was criticized and deposed as the CCP's 'number two capitalist roader' (the number one being Liu Shaoqi, a former chairman of the PRC). Deng wrote a couple of self-criticisms, and in one of these he swore that he would never reverse the verdict of the Cultural Revolution (Deng 1972). In 1976, when Deng was made to criticize himself once again, Mao reportedly said: 'Oh yeah, "[Deng said] never reverse the verdict", we cannot rely on his words.'

While many may not agree with Mao's ideas, policies and their associated practices, it is hard not to conclude that Mao was correct in his perception of Deng Xiaoping. For, if China was socialist to any degree after the 1949 Revolution, it has now changed beyond all recognition, and this change is largely due to Deng and his follow capitalist roaders, who, it should be noted, were criticized and humiliated during the Cultural Revolution for the kind of ideas and tendencies found in them (Hart-Landsberg and Burkett 2005a, Hinton 1990). Put another way, if it is possible to argue that China of the Maoist era was a two-way street – that is, it could either move towards real socialism, which is what the Cultural Revolution was designed to do, or move towards full-scale capitalism (Sweezy and Bettelheim 1972) – then, it appears to have been moving irreversibly towards the latter since the late 1980s, due to post-Mao reforms.

Inequality and the social status of the working class

There are three major lines of argument to suggest either that China is already a capitalist country or that it is well on its way to being a significant player in the capitalist world. The first holds that market forces and profit seeking have driven the continuing decline of the social status of the working class and resulted in increasing inequality (Chan 2001, Sato and Li 2005, Wang Shaoguang 2003). As Blecher (2006) explains:

> Karl Marx urged the workers of the world to unite. 'The proletarians have nothing to lose but their chains. They have a world to win.' China's workers, however, have lost their world. In the Maoist period, they were an exalted, pampered, and yet, paradoxically, extremely radical class. Under China's structural reforms of the past two decades, they have fallen fast and hard. Employment security is nonexistent and unemployment is rampant. For those fortunate enough to have dodged the axe, wages have not kept pace with those of other sectors or with inflation, and poverty – particularly 'deep poverty' – is skyrocketing. State-supplied housing, medical care, and education have declined in quality and availability, and increased in cost to workers.

No one really knows how many millions are unemployed in China today. According to one estimate, the current unemployment rate is 14 per cent among urban permanent residents. This figure is based on survey data collected by the Chinese Academy of Social Sciences, and does not include the rural population. Though millions of rural migrant workers are employed in sweatshops, the economic reform measures have meant reduction of employment in the urban sector. According to an International Labour Organization study quoted by Hart-Landsberg and Burkett (2007), between 1990 and 2002, regular formal wage employment in China's urban sector declined at an annual rate of 3 per cent and employment in state and collective enterprises fell by 59.2 million over the 13 year period.

Liu Jian (2005), the Director of the State Council Poverty Aid Office, suggests that the number of people who fell below the official poverty line actually increased by 800,000 in 2004. The official poverty line, according to Liu, was by 2005 an annual income of 637 RMB (less than US$80), which means 53 RMB (about US$6) a month, or 1.8 RMB a day.[1] Based on this criterion, the minimum amount of social security payment to urban residents was set at 56 RMB a month, just above the poverty line. In terms of purchasing power in China, 1.8 RMB is just about enough to buy a bowl of the cheapest noodles – but only in a county town, not in big cities like Shanghai (Liu Jian 2005).

Even for those who are fortunate enough to have a job there is clear evidence that the working people are subjected to the treatment of an 'underclass'. Lee (2007), for instance, reports how workers – be they insurance salespersons or bar hostesses – are manipulated into serving the profit-seeking capitalist economy in post-Mao China. On the other hand, there is opulence for the few. According to Lardy (2006), total worldwide sales of Bentley automobiles in 2003 came to 200, with 70 of them sold in China at 2 million RMB each: 250 times the average urban income.

Polarization between the rich and poor in present-day China is officially admitted to have crossed the danger line of social unrest. China's Gini co-efficient, a standard international measurement of income inequality, reached 0.454 in 2002, far above 0.4, which is the threshold generally considered a cause for concern. A recent study by Wang Xiaolu (2007) suggests that income disparity is in fact much worse. The officially available statistics, on which the World Bank-recognized 0.454 Gini co-efficient was based, did not take into account what Wang calls 'grey income', which is monopolized by the 10 per cent of China's highest income households. According to Wang's study, in urban areas the income of the 10 per cent of the highest income households is not the widely accepted nine times but 31 times higher than that of the poorest 10 per cent. If rural and urban areas are combined in this calculation, the difference is 51 times.

Even though members of the urban working class have been confronting a deteriorating situation (Hart-Landsberg and Burkett 2007), few if any at all are willing to take up the kind of jobs and levels of pay that are associated with migrant rural workers in urban centres (Bian 1994). For migrant workers from rural China the monthly wages of factory workers in 2003 ranged between $62 and $100, only marginally higher than in 1993. To earn this meagre wage, millions of rural Chinese not only have to work under appalling conditions but also have to leave their families; an estimated 20 million children have been left behind in this way (Kwong 2006)

Privatization of the economy

The second perspective from which one can argue that China is a capitalist country is to note that China is in the process of being further privatized: the means of production are increasingly being handed over to private 'business entrepreneurs'. Although major and strategic industry and infrastructure such as banks, telecommunication, railways and the military are still owned by the state, China is preparing for a more radical process of privatization. Indications are that everything but the military, telecommunications and energy industries, along with some parts of the transportation sector, will be opened to private competition (Pomfret 2000). According to a report partly funded by the World Bank, private business already accounted for more than half of China's economy in 2000. Similarly, Ross Garnaut of the Australian National University and Song Ligang of Beijing University estimate that officially registered private firms, foreign enterprises and family farms made up 50 per cent of the Chinese economy as early as 1998, with that share rising to 62 per cent if private firms that were still officially labelled collectives were counted (Garnault and Song 2000). Multinational corporations now account for 34 per cent of Chinese industrial output, which is greater than the 30 per cent share attributed to state-owned enterprises, and the percentage of the former keeps growing (Wang 2003).

Joining the transnational capitalist world

The third perspective from which one can argue that China is either already a capitalist country or rapidly moving towards it is that China increasingly is run by transnational capitalist firms (Hart-Landsberg and Burkett 2007). Take the automobile industry as a case in point. Nowadays, all the important car production plants in China are owned by either foreign companies or joint venture companies. Professor Hu Xingdou (2005) argues that by making China the sweatshop of the world, the developed West not only exploits cheap Chinese labour but also Chinese intellectual and knowledge sources. He asks his audience to think of the example of Guangdong and the Pearl River Delta, where on a car journey from Guangzhou to Shenzhen, from Zhuhai to Foshan, a journey of thousands of miles, one would see nothing but an endless stream of factories. But according to Hu, even with a manufacturing industry of this scale, the total GDP of Guangdong is no greater than the profits of a multinational company like McDonald's.

One commentator calls this kind of development the Dongguan model and increasingly Suzhou and even Wenzhou are moving towards it (Jin Xinyi 2005). Suzhou used to have its own industry and product brands such the Xiangxuehai refrigerator, Kongque television, Chunhua vacuum cleaners and Changcheng electric fans. These local brands have now disappeared. The Xiangxuehai refrigerator disappeared after its manufacturer entered into a joint venture with a Southern Korean company, Sansung; the Kongque television disappeared after its makers entered into a joint venture with the Dutch corporation, Phillips (Han Yanming 2004).

The strategy employed by foreign companies is first to enter into a joint venture with an existing Chinese enterprise and demand the best assets, tax and infrastructure concessions while making use of Chinese labour and expertise. They then use their technological and financial advantages to squeeze the Chinese partners out of the enterprise. This happened to Xibei Bearing Co Ltd with a German company FAG, to Ningxia Machine Co Ltd with a Japanese company, to a petroleum equipment company in a joint venture with an American company, and to the Lanzhou Camera Plant with a Japanese company.[2]

The following examples show how the profits are shared when foreign firms operate in China. A Barbie doll may sell in the US market at a retail price of US$10, but its FOB price from China is only US$2, of which US$1 is for management and transportation costs. Of the other US$1 spent in China, 65 cents are spent on materials. Only 35 cents are left for the Chinese workers to share. Similarly, Han Yanming (2004) notes that a factory in Suzhou produces 20 million computer mouses a year for Logitech International SA to sell to the US market for US$40 apiece. Logitech takes US$8, distributors and retailers take US$15, and a further US$14 is paid for the materials and parts. The Chinese side gets only US$3, which includes the cost of labour, electricity, transportation and so on.

Another example of how the transnational capitalist chain exploits Chinese labour is a case study reported by China Labor Watch. A Puma shoe factory run by a Taiwan businessman employs about 30,000 workers in Guangdong; the retail price of a pair of its shoes in the United States ranges from US$65 to US$110. The average Chinese worker gets paid US$1.09 per pair, while Puma spends US$6.78 per pair on advertising. The retail value of the shoes made by a worker in one week equals all the money paid to him or her for a whole year. The average hourly wage rate paid to a Chinese worker is 31 US cents, while the profit the company makes from each Chinese worker is US$12.24 per hour. The workers regularly have to work from 7.30am to 9.00pm, but sometimes have to work overtime until 12pm with no increase in the hourly rate. Sometimes they do not even get paid at all for overtime. They have a one-hour break for lunch and an hour and a half for dinner. They sleep in the factory compound, with twelve people in one room and one bathroom for 100 people to share. They are not allowed to talk at work and cannot leave the factory compound without permission. The penalty for arriving five minutes late at work is the deduction of three hours' pay. There are no regulations on workplace health and safety conditions in the factory (China Labor Watch 2004).

Joint ventures not only make profits but also shift production relations in China. In an in-depth study of two key model joint ventures, Chin (2003) finds that there has been a significant shift to capitalist social relations of production in China's joint venture sector. The study suggests that China's foreign-invested sectors operate according to the logic of capitalist accumulation, or 'accumulation by dispossession' coined by David Harvey, and that a hegemonic regime of labour control has developed in these ventures. The 1995 Chinese Labour Law has specific stipulations to protect workers' rights and working conditions (Du Guang 2005). But privilege and concessions are allowed to exempt foreign companies from the Labour Law. Such labour concessions were first made in special economic zones, but were later extended throughout the country, and now the Chinese Labour Law does not bind Chinese private enterprises either.

It is frequently argued that China's embrace of transnational companies is a necessary step towards upgrading its industrial and technological sophistication; the growth of China's production and export of electronic and information technology goods is cited as an example (Lange 2005). But as Branstetter and Lardy (2006), cited in Hart-Landsberg and Burkett (2007), argue, these electronic products – produced in huge volumes at low unit costs – are not really high-tech and China does not really produce them. Rather China assembles them from imported parts and components which make up 85 per cent of the value of the exported products. Moreover these products are largely assembled in foreign-invested firms. In 2003, for example, foreign-invested firms accounted for approximately 75 per cent of China's exports of electronic and telecommunication goods and 90 per cent of its exports of computer-related goods.

Return and rise of the comprador

The way foreign firms are allowed to operate without labour or environmental conditions reminds one of pre-1949 Treaty System through which foreign companies and Chinese compradors enriched themselves. The term 'comprador' is sometimes used to describe the way in which China is now part of global capitalism. William Hinton (1993), in a response to Tang Zongli's rhetorical question 'Is China Returning to Semi-Colonial Status?', uses the term *maiban* (comprador or purveyor) to denote what has been happening in post-Mao China. This reference to the term 'comprador' as a means of explaining the nature of Chinese development provides two insights. One is that Chinese compradors in East Asia, including Hong Kong and Taiwan, are coming back to mainland China (Heartfield 2004). The second insight is that China's political, business and intellectual elites are acting on behalf of transnational interests and to benefit themselves in the process.

In the most comprehensive study of the Chinese comprador before the 1940s, Yen-p'ing Hao defines a comprador as the 'Chinese manager of a foreign firm in China, serving as a middleman in the company's dealings with the Chinese' (Hao 1970: 1). The rise of a comprador class, he continues, was a product of the Treaty System, 'which provided places and opportunities for Chinese and foreign merchants to pursue their calling' (Hao 1970: 9). The concessions offered to transnational companies in the special economic zones are in many ways similar to the pre-1949 treaty ports where special privileges were offered to foreign firms.

Chinese compradors, who fled to Hong Kong and Taiwan after the communist victory in 1949, or their descendants, have returned. Businesspeople from Hong Kong or Taiwan, who know how to bribe bureaucrats and how to exploit cheap labour because of their cultural and language advantages, skilfully play this comprador role. The general picture is that a Western company has the soft technology, such as design and marketing, and the comprador manages the production and supplies the products to the company. Companies like Nike, for instance, demonstrate considerable concern about design and selling, but little concern when it comes to how their products are made. The compradors take orders from Nike and are slave drivers in China who supply cheap shoes to Nike.

Apart from the return of pre-1949 compradors there has been a rise of new Chinese compradors who are engaged with trade or who work for foreign firms. Those people either directly control the trade or smooth the greasy operations for foreign firms and reap rewards in the process. The end result is that a few Chinese get rich but the state gets virtually nothing in return. In spite of special treatment of tax concessions such as no tax for the first five years of operation and lower tax rates than required for Chinese firms, foreign enterprises still uses Chinese administrative and legal loopholes to avoid tax. According to a recent study by the Chinese Bureau of Statistics, up to 2005 two-thirds of all the foreign firms claimed losses (*Zhonghua gongshang shibao*, 28 March 2007; see also Fuxi 2007). One of the ways of doing this is 'transfer pricing', that is, inflating the prices of imported goods and deflating the prices of the assembled commodities that are mostly exported. The Chinese compradors are rewarded in the process when they help the transnational companies exploit the tax loopholes. According to Chinese official sources, 'tax evasion by multinationals costs the country 30 billion yuan (US$3.88 billion) in tax revenue each year' (Chung 2007).

The Chinese compradors also use a two-tier system to create their own 'foreign companies' by first transferring funds overseas as investments in 'suitcase' or 'paper' companies, and then repatriating them as foreign investment in China. According to Mei Xinyu, a senior researcher at the Chinese Academy of International Trade and Economic Cooperation under the Ministry of Commerce, 'of China's utilized FDI of $72.4 billion in 2005, a third was Chinese investment overseas that came back disguised as foreign capital take advantage of the tax breaks' (Chung 2007).[3]

Many of the sons and daughters of the CCP office holders, the 'princelings', have joined the comprador class in its rise. According to Gilley (1998), Jiang Mianheng, son of the former General Secretary of the CCP, who gained a doctorate from Drexel University in Philadelphia, become a key player in Shanghai business, starting with the city-owned investment firm Shanghai Alliance Investment, serving on the board of China Netcom, which relied on him to ease its way through government regulatory agencies. Jiang also served as the chief executive officer of Shanghai Simteck Industrials, a telecommunications company. Though Jiang was whisked away to Beijing to become vice-president of the Chinese Academy of Sciences in 1999, he remained active in business and was responsible in 2000 for putting together an alliance between Simteck and Shanghai Alliance Investment and Taiwan's Hung Jun Group to build a semiconductor plant in Shanghai with an initial investment of $US 75 million. Jiang also engineered a deal between Simteck and Shang Chulan groups which make appliances and computer products (Gilley 1998). There is also evidence that Jiang played a comprador role for the media tycoon Rupert Murdoch for the latter's business venture in China (Kahn 2007). Mr Murdoch also had business dealing with Ding Yuchen, the son of Ding Guangen, a long-time Chinese central government propaganda chief (Kahn 2007). Simon Jiang, son of Qiao Shi (another powerful CCP figure), was involved with LyberCity Holdings and the software firm Zi Corporation. He developed plans for a major high-technology business park in Shenzhen. Zhu Rongji's son Zhu Yunlai was connected with the Bank of China group in Hong Kong (Gilley 2001a).

According to a Chinese official report (Yang Tao 2007), in a couple of years a large number of state-owned enterprises have been transferred to private owners. Many of the enterprise owners are actually state employers holding government managerial and professional positions, and the proportion of this group of enterprise owners rose from 33.8 per cent of the total in 2004 to 67.4 per cent in 2006. This huge transfer of wealth from the state to the private sector, unprecedented in human history and carried through quietly and almost unnoticed, has been largely beneficial to those who hold political power and have connections with the establishment. According to one report, which claims to be based on official research done jointly by the Research Office of the State Council, the Research Office of the Central Party School and the Chinese Academy of Social Sciences, 90 per cent of the more than 3,000 billionaires in China are the so-called 'princelings', sons and daughters of high-ranking party officials (Boxun 2006a). These people became rich by charging commissions for FDI, by taking the difference when imported equipment was priced above the level of the international market, by exporting and importing rare commodities, by property speculation, land seizure and banking, by smuggling luxury cars, by contracting for large projects, and by using inside information to manipulate the stock and financial markets.

Like the compradors of pre-revolution China, the current Chinese business elite and the bureaucrats who side with capital are not 'independent merchants' *per se*. Like the pre-1949 compradors, their contemporary counterparts have become the *nouveaux riches* by virtue of their salaries, commissions, and exploitation; only a minority have risen by virtue of their own business abilities. Like many of the famous compradors who purchased official titles such as *daotai* (upper middle rank official) during the Qing China, contemporary compradors are also given titles such as representatives of the National People's Congress at county, city, province and central levels, and many of these business elite actually hold CCP party membership cards. Not unlike their predecessors, contemporary compradors want their children to be educated in Western ways, and hundreds of thousands of young students are being sent to the United States, the UK, Australia and other Western countries to study.

Many of this comprador class hold or seek foreign passports or residency status. Capital flight from China, according to some estimates, has been exceeding the levels of FDI since the late 1990s. According to a release by the Assistant Minister of the Chinese Ministry of Public Security, 4,000 'corrupt' Chinese officials had fled the country with a total capital of $US50 billion by 2005 (Caoyan Jushi 2005). In short, the role of the comprador in the chain of the world capitalist system offers yet another demonstration that China is basically a capitalist country

Capitalism with Chinese characteristics?

Wang Hui (2005), one of the sharpest observers of contemporary Chinese politics and society in China, thinks that China is caught between 'misguided socialism and crony capitalism, and is suffering from the worst of both systems'. While the Chinese authorities like to claim that their path of development is 'socialism with Chinese characteristics', some commentators think 'capitalism with Chinese characteristics' is more appropriate (Chin 2003). Some commentators would refer to China's development since the 1980s as either crony capitalism or gangster capitalism (Holmstrom and Smith 2000). One veteran China watcher has defined it as 'high-tech feudalism with Chinese characteristics' (Kwong 2006).

The Chinese authorities claim the PRC can still be considered socialist because most of the important means of production are still owned by the state. But state ownership *per se* does not necessarily mean socialism. Many of the major means of production in capitalist countries, such as France or the UK (before Margaret Thatcher), were owned by the state. In any case the notion of state capitalism has been frequently used to refer to the former Soviet Union (Chattopadhyay 1994, Fernandez 1997, Haynes 2002, Resnick and Wolff 2002), and the notion can equally apply to China.

Social stratification

Regarding social stratification in the urban sector in the Mao era, it is true that there was no business and economic elite class. But there was a political and professional elite class who had all kinds of entitlements (Yang Jiang 2003) despite Mao's political movements aimed at them. Since the post-Mao reforms, however, the privilege and entitlements of the political and professional elite class have been restored and encouraged to grow. Furthermore, Deng's policy of 'let some get rich first' has resulted in the creation of a business elite class.

Deterioration of working conditions encouraged by the state

Even today, no state-owned enterprises in China would allow the kind of penal labour disciplines and harmful working conditions that prevail in privately owned firms (Chan 2001, Weil 2006). Western companies' hypocrisy and Chinese authorities' complicity can be illustrated by an open letter to President Jiang Zemin, jointly written by the CEOs of Phillips-Van-Heusen, Reebok, and Levi Strauss in 1999, which requested a meeting to discuss the possibility of 'working together' to improve labour rights in China (Emerson 2000). The sincerity of this request is open to question precisely because the letter was 'open'. It is meant to serve the purpose of presenting an image of the companies as 'caring' to their Western customers. The intention of spinning is confirmed by the fact that McDonald's in China tried to prevent workers in its franchises from forming trade unions, the fact that 'fast-food giants McDonald's, Kentucky Fried Chicken (KFC) and Pizza Hut have been caught underpaying their young workforce in China by as much as 40 per cent below the already abysmal legal minimum wage' (Kolo 2007) and the fact that the multinationals lobbied in 2007 to delete or reduce the force of terms in favour of workers when the Chinese government attempted to introduce a labour law so that workers are in some way protected by contact (Shafer 2007).[4]

In any case, the Chinese government showed no interest in talking to the three CEOs (Emerson 2000). In fact, the plight of the migrant workers is not what concerns the Chinese authorities. The Chinese ruling elite at every level has been competing to lure outside capital by giving preferential treatments to capital and would side with capital whenever and wherever there is a labour dispute. Although Chinese labour law stipulates that the maximum working week should not exceed 44 hours, one case study shows that workers in factories that produce shoes for Clarks and Skechers may work as long as 81 hours a week (Zhong Dajun 2005). This, of course, is not an isolated case. Many studies have demonstrated the horrifying working conditions for migrant workers (Solinger 1999, Gao 1999a, Gao 2004, Chan 2003 and Weil 2006). When there is a dispute between a worker and a capitalist the Chinese authorities would be more likely to intervene on behalf of capital. When a party official in Guangdong was asked by a Chinese Central TV journalist why, in a dispute between a foreign-owned enterprise and a Chinese migrant worker, he ordered the judge to rule in favour of the foreign capitalist owner the party official replied: 'We have so many migrant workers but not many capitalists to choose from. Don't we need to speak on behalf of capitalists for development? Development is the core value and that was Deng Xiaoping's instruction' (Zhai 2006).

The urban sector and the urban poor

Another characteristic of contemporary Chinese capitalism is the increasing reduction of social security for urban residents. Urban Chinese used to have very good social security provisions, but now they have to pay contributions towards education and healthcare that used to be free. To all intents and purposes millions of rural migrant workers are part of the urban sector, as they have been living and working there for about three decades. But they are not allowed to send their children to state schools in cities unless they can pay a fee that is beyond any except the very rich. In Shanghai, for instance, because of its negative population growth, the school population has been shrinking. But local authorities chose to merge schools or simply close them down rather than enrol the children of migrant workers. When I put this issue to Professor Xu Mingqi at the Institute of World Economy of the Shanghai Academy of Social Sciences his answer was: 'Well, even in the United States there is the Green Card system'.

Land seizures

Another defining characteristic of contemporary Chinese capitalism is that land has increasingly been confiscated with little or no compensation, often by private firms. Again, this differs from the policies of other developing countries that practise conventional capitalism. It is different because, under the Constitution, land in China is owned by the state and no private individual is allowed to own land. Even for residential housing the ownership entitlement of land covers only the right of use. The Chinese authorities sometimes cite this as an illustration of the superiority of socialism when compared with India where private ownership of land is the norm. The Chinese authorities boast that China can build highways quickly whereas law suits and settlement of land use in India would make development too complex if not virtually impossible. Indeed, some Chinese economists endorse the kind of land confiscation that is currently taking place as China's necessary 'land enclosure', comparable with what occurred in the UK during its early stage of industrialization.

Environmental destruction

Another salient characteristic of Chinese capitalism in the 1980s and 1990s was the almost total disregard, whether intentional or unintentional, for the environment. The following is the testimonial of Pan Yu, Vice-Minister of China's State Environment Protection Administration:

> This spring, the State Environmental Protection Administration produced the country's first official estimate of GDP adjusted downward for environmental losses. According to these calculations, it would cost $84 billion to clean up the pollution produced in 2004, or 3 per cent of GDP for that year. But more realistic estimates put environmental damage at 8–13 per cent of China's GDP growth each year, which means that China has lost almost everything it has gained since the late 1970s due to pollution.
>
> (Pan 2006)

Ordinary citizens in China nowadays cannot be sure of what is in the food they consume every day. It has been suggested that athletes at the 2008 Beijing Olympics may show drug positive in tests simply because of their consumption of antibiotics and hormone-induced food. One Chinese official suggested that all the food to be used for the Olympics should be tested on mice first, and the competitors should be asked not to eat outside the Olympic Villages (Li Yang 2006).

It could be argued that environmental problems are less severe in more developed countries only because these countries have already passed the early stage of modernity. This indeed is a position that the Chinese neoliberals take, as discussed in Gao (2004) and elsewhere in this book. In other words, develop first and clean up later is the answer. Environmental degradation takes place in other developing capitalist countries as well. However, what makes the Chinese case different is that state ownership of rivers, mountains, and land is often treated as equivalent to no ownership and no responsibility. The whim of a bureaucrat in charge, or a successful bribe to the same effect, can set off a project or an event with tremendous environmental consequences. It is little wonder that most of the worst polluted cities in the world are currently located in China. The water in most of China's lakes and rivers is undrinkable because of pollution. 'Environmental ills annually cause 300,000 deaths and cost $200 billion – equivalent to 10 per cent of the gross domestic product – due to loss of work, medical expenses and government outlays' (Kwong 2006).

Some policies result in environmental degradation even when their ostensible goal is the exact opposite. Take the case of Yunnan, where 94 per cent of the land area is mountainous, as an example. In 1981, the CCP and the State Council issued a policy document[5] known as *San ding* or the 'The three fixed': fixed mountain rights, fixed forestry rights and fixed responsibility. The policy was designed to copy the so-called success of the responsibility system in agriculture by producing a kind of forestry responsibility system. It was assumed that giving individual households the right to manage sections of forestry would ensure that the same households would look after the forest in a responsible fashion. What happened instead was that the locals used their rights to chop down the trees and sell them. Within three years, the once thickly forested mountains were chopped bare. Any forest that was left was due to the impossibility of access. Now the locals have nothing to rely on for their livelihood and are dependent on government handouts (Zhang Deyuan 2005).

White cat, black cat: the argument of efficiency versus fairness

From the late 1970s until his death, Deng Xiaoping was adamant that there should be no debate on whether China was a socialist or capitalist country, because he believed the debate would pose an obstacle to development. He proposed a deliberate strategy of ambiguity so that capitalist elements could creep into the system. This pragmatic approach was ideologically legitimized by the philosophy that 'practicum is the sole criterion of truth', which was summarized by the post-Mao Deng-led authorities as one of the essential elements of Mao Zedong Thought.[6]

What was clear to China's political and intellectual elite policy makers was that the Western style of life and material abundance was to be desired, and if a way could be found to achieve that goal, it did not matter what 'ism' it took. It does not matter whether the cat is white or black so long as it catches mice. This strategy of development eventually rendered the debate about the colour of the cat seemingly a non-issue. Since then, even though there has been a split between the so-called New Left and Liberals among the intellectual elite (Gao 2004, Kipnis 2003, Zhang Xudong 2001 and Hu 2004), the dominant voice in China's intellectual discourse has been economic rationalism, which argues that efficiency should take priority over fairness. The underlying assumption is that if and when efficiency leads to greater wealth in the country, everyone will be better off.

Seeing the past from the present: a hole in the discursive hegemony

Since the neoliberal guru Milton Friedman's first visit to China in 1980, there has developed a neoliberal dynasty (Kwong 2006) that has exercised what Wang Hui (2004: 9) called a 'discursive hegemony' over intellectual discourse for over a quarter of a century. According to the idea of development embodied in this discourse, a generation of Chinese has to be sacrificed, and those who are to be sacrificed are the 50 million workers who lost their jobs, plus 800 million peasants (Li Yang 2006). One economist, former Dean of the prestigious Guanghua Management Institute at Beijing University Li Yining, argues that all welfare measures should be abolished so as to maintain work enthusiasm. Another economist thinks that Chinese society can progress only if the gap between the rich and poor is increased (Li Yang 2006). Only recently, since the leadership changed from Jiang Zemin/Zhu Rongji to Hu Jintao/Wen Jiabao, has there been concern that China might be Latin-Americanized (Caoyan Jushi 2005). Dissenting voices have now begun to crack a hole in the hegemonic discourse of 'efficiency first and nothing else matters' (Liu Guoguang 2005 and Wang Hui 2006).

In summary, the intellectual consensus of 'development no matter what' has broken down. Now Mao's legacy has started to be looked at a little more seriously. The past can be viewed positively now because the failure of the present is obvious even to some of the political and intellectual elite, such as Professor Liu Guoguang (2005), who used to be staunch supporters of Deng Xiaoping but now begin to question the capitalist road that Deng has taken.

Conclusion: truth and belief values of socialism and China's future direction

The image we usually have in the West of contemporary China is that it is a highly regimented, regulated and strictly controlled society. China is usually interpreted as a dictatorship (either party dictatorship or personal dictatorship), or a country run by a state of factional politics, or a state of ideological control. Clearly each of these approaches offers some insight into the mechanism of Chinese politics, but what actually happens is often the result of the interactions of many factors that cannot be explained by a single conceptual model. Much of what has happened in post-Mao rural China, for instance, is often the result of unintended policy, and sometimes a result of lack of regulation or management from the state. To interpret what happens at the grass-roots we need to have a much more sophisticated conceptual approach that involves people's truth and belief values.

Truth and belief values of a political discourse

We could advance our understanding of what has been happening in China a step further by suggesting that the power of political discourse at any given time may be too strong for a change at that particular time until and unless the truth and belief values of that discourse are discredited. A brief outline of the so-called rural reform will illustrate the point. The household responsibility system (*baogan zhi*) that eventually led to the collapse of the collective system was not conceptually original, nor politically innovative. Before the system was officially sanctioned all over the country many villagers practised *baogan zhi* in various forms in many places on and off in the Mao era. It was off sometimes when agricultural policy was more radical and on at other times, depending also on inclinations of local leaders. 1978, two years after the death of Mao and after the arrest of the Maoist radicals the Gang of Four, is considered a watershed year of reform as it was then that a resolution on rural China was passed by the central committee of the CCP. But in fact that 1978 resolution explicitly stated that *baogan zhi* was not allowed (*bu xu*). In a 1979 central government document the word *bu xu* (not allowed) was changed to *bu yao* (do not); and only in 1980 did a CCP document state that *baogan zhi* was sanctioned as a kind of socialist responsibility system. It was not until the mid-1980s that the collective system was finally dismantled. The reason for this gradual change is that the Maoist legacy of a socialist discourse of public (or collective) ownership was not something that could be thrown out of the window at the desire of any small group or individual. To establish the belief that privatization of land is legitimate takes a longer time.

Truth and belief value of exploiting the peasantry

After the death of Ding Zuomin, one of the key figures in the three stories outlined in Chapter 9 that highlighted the miserable life of the rural poor, there was a consensus that something had to be done about the tax and levy burden on rural residents. A new agenda of lessening tax burden on farmers was therefore evolved. But the truth and belief value of the discourse that upheld the need for exploiting the peasantry was not easy to phase out, again because in the knowledge system of both Marxism and anti-Marxist liberalism the truth of and belief in industrial and urban development at the expense of the peasantry have been taken for granted.

On 8 November 1993 a cross-departmental provincial conference was held in Hehui, the capital city of Anhui, to discuss the issue of rural tax reform. With the support of other speakers, He Kaiyin, policy adviser to the Anhui provincial government think tank, made a passionate plea for change. But he was unable to answer a hostile question from the head of the Rural Taxation Office of the Provincial Finance Department: 'who is going to pay the salaries of the personnel and government offices all over the province [if local governments were not allowed tax and levy the farmers]?' Only Premier Zhu Rongji had the answer: the costs would have to be paid by taxing the business, the commerce and urban sectors. But this was not what Zhu wanted to do.

The case of He Kaiyin described in Chen and Chun (2004) also demonstrates that policy initiatives in contemporary China come from diversified sources, even from government-employed 'research' or 'investigative' personnel (such as He Kaiyin). Even a journalist who writes an internal report may set an agenda for policy making which may take years to fruition. Clearly there is no single locus of power, and power and knowledge interact. That is why the change of truth and belief value is as important as change of a leadership. And that is what I mean by political discourse.

Do the values of socialism matter?

It is in this sense that the values of socialism still matter in China. The fact that Marxism-Leninism is still used to legitimize political suppression is a double-edged sword for the Chinese authorities. An essential part of Marxist-Leninist ideology is the value of socioeconomic equality and justice. The disadvantaged in China can and do still use this value regime to justify their protests and resistance. Yu Jianrong (2005) points out that the values embedded in state socialism are still useful for resistance. He notes that urban Chinese workers usually appeal to the state for support in their protests against their employers, whereas the targets of rural protests are state agents of the local governments. In other words both rural and urban residents take central government's declared socialist values as justification of their protests, a justification that the Chinese authorities in the name of CCP find difficult to renounce.

Take the case of rural resistance outlined in Chapter 9 as further illustration. A kind of organized and rational resistance has been active, strong and emerging from very early on, and is very hard for the state to handle. A resort to simple brutal force does not always work. There are two reasons for this. First, the CCP, of which Mao was one of the founding fathers and the most dominant leader, is still the ruling party and it has not denounced the value of the political discourse of social and economic justice. Second, the truth and belief values of class struggle, though officially abandoned by the state and by most of the intellectual elite, have not been totally eradicated among the people. One of the primary differences between the Stalinist Soviet Union and the Mao era in China is that, unlike Stalin who employed an efficient and iron state machine to crack down on political opposition, Mao always mobilized the masses and let them consume the truth and belief values of class struggle in practice. One of the consequences of this 'mass line' is that the ideas of class struggle have become part of human value, knowledge and truth. In other words, the discourse of class struggle legacy from the Mao era has made the farmer and other ordinary Chinese 'battlers' aware of their rights and the idea of equality (He Xuefeng 2007).

Learning from past failures

Once upon a time, the discourse that 'only socialism can save China' became the truth and belief value for many of the bright and intelligent Chinese. Having seen the seemingly abundant material wealth in Western capitalist countries, most of China's political and intelligentsia elite have gradually abandoned this socialist truth and belief value. Hence, the truth and belief values of market capitalism discourse have become dominant, as the Chinese political and intelligentsia elite has taken Deng's 'Let some get rich first' and 'Development is the core value' as guiding principles for government decision making. The underlying assumption of this development strategy is that since socialism cannot make China wealthy and powerful, China needs to learn from capitalism (Xu Jiatun 1992). The policies and practice of special economic zones to attract foreign capital and to exploit cheap rural labour have been premised on this idea of a catch-up lesson of capitalism.

The socialist truth and belief value of land ownership

The truth and belief values of using capitalist means to achieve wealth and prosperity have been widely accepted in China now. But the truth and belief values of socialism have not been completely abandoned, as least regarding land ownership. The tension between the two truth and value regimes can be seen in the Chinese Constitution. The 1993 Amendment to the 1982 Chinese Constitution adds a clause stating that 'China is at the primary stage of socialism' and committing the country to 'building socialism with Chinese characteristics'. The 1999 Amendments further add that: 'China will stay at primary stage of socialism for a long period of time.' This is a crucial modification to allow the development of the private sector and to justify China's opening up to Western capitalist influence. In other words, at a primary stage of socialism it is necessary and legitimate to adopt capitalist or non-socialist elements in the system.

However, the truth and belief values of socialist ownership of land are still powerful. This can be seen in the aborted land ownership reform experiment suggested by He Kaiyin. The basic ideas of He's plan had two elements: one was that, though the state should own the land, the villagers should be given permanent ownership of the land use rights. Furthermore, ownership of land use rights can be transferred and can be inherited. The other leg of the reform plan was that the villagers would only have to pay the state one tax a year as rent, and that tax should be fixed for several years. All and any other taxes or levies should be rendered illegal. He's plan aimed not only to solve the tax burden problem but also the land ownership issue once and for all. His ideas were persuasive enough for the authorities to entertain the idea of an experiment.

Though there was informal support from the then Premier Li Peng, actual ground support from the provincial government, and even support from the party secretary and governor of the county where the experiment was to take place, the opposition from the chairman of the county's People's Congress, widely known as a powerless rubber stamp institution in China, was enough to shelve He's plan (Chen and Chun 2004). For the opposition to say that the reform plan violates the law regarding land ownership was enough to silence not only He and his reform team but also the party secretary and the governor of the county. He Kaiyin then tried to persuade the leadership of three other counties to implement his reform plan and the party secretaries of the three counties supported him; but again the plan was aborted in each of the three counties because of opposition from their People's Congresses.

The People's Congress was traditionally just a rubber stamp in the past because it was logically meant to be like that. The CCP was supposed to work for the people and the People's Congress was supposed to support the CCP for that reason. The governing logic is therefore that in a socialist country there should not be major and principled contradictions between the CCP and the People's Congress. However, as the post-Mao reform extended its boundaries, the CCP started to take the lead in advancing capitalist interests that can be contradictory to the interest of the ordinary people. Logically, then, the People's Congresses are no longer obliged to support the CCP all the time and they do not, as the defeat of the He proposal shows. Though development by using capitalist means has been accepted as a strategy, some of the truth and belief values and beliefs of socialism still remain. One key truth in this knowledge system is the public ownership of land in a socialist country. By claiming to uphold this key truth the People's Congress claims the right to block the programme of land privatization, even though the CCP leaders supported the programme.

In any case, the CCP finds the collective ownership of land in rural China works well for its march towards capitalism. To start with, the collective ownership of land gives the CCP some socialist legitimacy in theory. In practice, collective ownership of land provides a dumping ground from which an abundant source of cheap migrant labour for urban manufacturing industry is tapped. And it is cost-free for the state. In cities like Beijing, Shanghai and Shenzhen, there are few ghettos that offend one's sense of decency, as found in many developing countries. Even though there are an estimated 100 million migrant workers all over China at any given time, one does not see children rummaging through rubbish dumps. The key to China's success in avoiding ghettos lies the existing land ownership system. Every rural Chinese migrant worker has a family with some land that they can resort to for basic survival. When migrant workers are unable to find work, or grow too old to work in a sweatshop, they may return to their native villages where a piece of land is nominally theirs to use. It is for this reason that the migrant workers are able to leave their children at home in their native villages. What the People's Congresses of the three counties wanted to preserve was the last refuge for the rural poor.

The socialist truth and belief value of labour law

In the absence of an established legal system to protect individual rights, the socialist legacy of the Mao era matters a lot even now. It is often claimed that trade unions in the Mao era were not only decorative but actually another organ protecting the interest of the state. This line of thinking is based on the assumption that the relationship between trade unions and the state ought to be antagonistic in a communist state. This anti-communist cold war assumption fails to notice that the mode of production in the Mao era was so structured that the social relationship between the workers and the state was not meant to be antagonistic. There might be disputes and grievances in individual cases, in which case trade unions might act on behalf of the workers, but in general workers and management were supposed to work together for the same goal; workers were supposed to be owners and masters of the means of production and therefore supervise and participate in management. It was precisely in order to strengthen this supposed social relationship that the Cultural Revolution was launched. It was for this reason that workers and masses were encouraged to participate in the 'Four Big Freedoms' (*Da ming, da fang, da bianlun, da zibao* – speaking out freely, airing views fully, holding great debates and writing big character posters) during the Cultural Revolution. It was for this reason that the Four Big Freedoms were written into the Chinese Constitution in the Mao era.

When the mode of production is transformed, that is, when the means of production are no longer publicly owned and when workers are no longer supposed to be the owners of these properties, the relationship between the trade unions and the state then become antagonistic. Deng saw clearly what the problems would be. So in 1980 he ordered the abolition of the Four Big Freedoms. In 1982 when the Chinese Constitution was amended, the clause of the Four Big Freedoms, together with the freedom to strike, was stricken out (Hu 2004).

Clearly the post-Mao regime has started to axe the Maoist legacy little by little, but there is still substantial amount that remains intact. As has been discussed, collective ownership of land remains intact. Another part of the Maoist legacy that remains intact is related to labour conditions and regulations in state-owned enterprises. The truth and belief values of socialism mean that workers have the right to rest at least one day a week, the right to legal holidays, the right not to work overtime more than three hours a day or 36 hours a week in total, the right to be paid overtime rates not lower than 150 per cent of the normal rate for a working day or 200 per cent during holidays, the right to be paid on time, the right to maternity leave of no less than 90 days and healthy and safe work equipment. However, in private and foreign owned enterprises, these labour regulations do not apply (Du Guang 2005). Though the freedom to strike has been abolished, the 'capitalist roaders' have yet to wipe out the labour legacy of the Mao era in state-owned enterprises.

Mining accidents offer another example of how socialist values still matter. According to one estimate, there were more than 4,000 deaths from mining accidents in 2004 alone (He Qinglian 2005). Another estimate puts this figure at 6,000 (Armitage 2005). According to one estimate, the coal mining accident death toll is as high as 30,000 a year in China (French 2007). Li Qiang (2005), the head of a labour-watch organization based in New York, maintains that China only produces 35 per cent of the world's coal but suffers 80 per cent of the world's mining accident deaths, with the death rate 30 times higher than that of South Africa and 100 times higher than that of the United States.

But these accidents happen mostly in private mining firms. The situation in private mining is that those with capital can force miners to sign contracts that stipulate that compensation for death should not exceed 20,000 RMB. A miners' life has thus been made so cheap that business contractors are not interested in investing in safety. While media publicity eventually resulted in an increase in the price of a life to 200,000 RMB in some mining areas, local government authorities would prefer to cover up accidents and not to collect death figures. To make life easier for private contractors some local governments simply report a dead person as missing (Chen Bisheng 2005).

Again, thanks to the socialist legacy of the Mao era, this kind of violation not just of human rights but of human life does not prevail in a state-owned coal mine.

The socialist truth and belief values of healthcare and education

State-owned enterprises are among the few institutions that uphold socialist values through their labour regulations. Other important socialist legacies from the era of Mao such as healthcare and education in rural China have been cut back so much by Deng and neoliberal policy makers that it will be difficult for them to recover. In 2003, the new CCP central leadership in Beijing decided to allocate some state expenditure to rural China, something that had not been done since the late 1970s. A document to this effect was sent to various state departments, but these departments refused to endorse it. Consequently, when a meeting was convened to finalize the document, a meeting that was to be attended by all the relevant ministries, no documentation was tabled for the agenda. Hu Jintao, furious at this deliberate sabotage, declared at a Politburo meeting that with or without documentation it was his decision that the policy had to be implemented. Six months later, an inspection team that he sent out revealed that no new funding had been allocated to rural areas (Wen 2005).

During the SARS epidemic the Minister of Health was sacked and a policy of investing more in rural China was declared. To implement this new policy 'the iron lady', Vice-Premier Wu Yi, was assigned to act as health minister. Five billion RMB was allocated to implement preventive health measures in rural China. However, all of that money was eventually used in county and urban centres instead. It turned out that rural health clinics and facilities had all been privatized. The Ministry of Health, under Wu Yi, had no idea of how to allocate funding from the central government to private health businesses in rural China. The CCP central government is one of the few, if not probably the only government, in the world that has money to allocate but does not know how to do it. According to Wen Tiejun (2005), in 2003 the central government had money that was left unused and the state banks had 600 billion RMB that could not be loaned out.

The battle of China's history

The appraisal of post-Mao reforms in this book is not meant to argue that the past is better than the present or that there is nothing good about the post-Mao reforms. For many people in China the present regime is less oppressive and suppressive. Even the label of landlord and rich peasants as a class classification was abolished in 1978, an initiative that I consider the best ever by the post-Mao Hua Guofeng leadership. It is also absolutely indisputable that there is no longer any shortage of consumer goods, and that the people in China as a whole have more material possessions. The Chinese as a whole have more money, they have more to eat, they have more and better clothes to wear, and many of them even travel more for pleasure.

It is therefore very puzzling that through all my travel and work in rural China – including a trip to Long Bow Village, a village that has been extensively documented by Hinton, and especially my in-depth study in the Gao Village area – I have heard expressions of admiration and even love of Mao everywhere, but hardly any enthusiasm for Deng. I have encountered only a couple of people who preferred Deng to Mao and these were descendants of former 'class enemies' such as landlords or rich peasants. They attributed their liberation from class labelling to Deng Xiaoping, although in fact the abolition of class labels was accomplished in 1978 before Deng became the paramount leader. Mao's portraits can still be seen in the average rural household, but one can hardly find a portrait of Deng Xiaoping anywhere. During my interviews I found that even those who did make it by getting rich first in rural China preferred Mao as a leader, and they refer to Deng derogatively as 'Deng aizi' (Deng the dwarf).

That rural people prefer Mao to Deng is not because they are benighted, brainwashed or plain stupid as suggested by some Chinese elite intelligentsia. On the contrary, they are able to compare the era of Mao with that of post-Mao reforms in a broad picture. For them Mao was the foremost leader that led the country to unity and stability. It was during the era of Mao that a basic and fundamental industrial, agricultural and scientific foundation was laid for later development. Yes, everyone had a hard life, but it was no harder than before 1949. More importantly, they understand that they had to tighten their belts not because they were exploited for the benefit of Mao, his families or any Chinese individuals who were in leadership positions. In their understanding everything, including mistakes and disasters like the Great Leap Forward, was meant to build a better society for everyone. They find that they cannot apply the same interpretation to the policies and intentions of the post-Mao reform leadership. They think the post-Mao authorities are simply reaping the fruit of the hard work done in the past, and for their own personal benefit.

My research in the Gao Village area in the past two decades and my recent research in Long Bow Village suggest that many rural people think that even if China had retained its collective system they would have had the same kind of living standard as they have now. Wang Jinhong, who served as the Party Secretary of Long Bow Village from 1966 to 2003, had no doubt this when I interviewed him in February 2005. He had built a huge and comfortable two-story house during the 1980s, but he insisted that he would have done the same if Maoist policies had continued.

According to one research study in Henan province, some rural people actually think they could have done even better, and for everyone. The survey was carried out in a county that had above average living standards at the time of research in 2000. Among the 200 questionnaires returned (out of 208), only 11 per cent agreed that living standards had gone up a lot since the reforms. In contrast, 55 per cent of the respondents thought that their standards of living had not gone up much, 11.5 per cent felt they had not risen at all, and 22.5 per cent stated that they were worse off since the reforms (Zhuo Yi 2003). Similarly, 41.5 per cent of them stated both that their living standard would have been more or less the same and the societal habits and customs (*shehui fenqi*) would have been much better if Maoist policies had continued. About 90 per cent of the respondents thought that in terms of healthcare, agricultural mechanization, irrigation improvement and technical innovation, reform policies have made the situation worse.

The fact that rural Chinese did not possess this or that consumer good in the past was not the fault of Mao, they would argue. The fact that they do have them now is not to Deng's credit either, they would say. Some of these consumer goods were not even invented then. The fact that grain yields are higher now than those during the era of Mao was not because they had no incentive to work hard then, as suggested by economic rationalists. The land yields more now because chemicals are used more extensively and intensively.

China's future direction

How is China likely to develop in the future? No revolution is visible on the horizon. Resistance and isolated insurrections do, and will continue to, take place, but collective actions that will overthrow the current regime are unlikely. The more extensive and intensive use of chemicals is set to continue. China as the world assembly factory will continue to produce cheap commodities for the world's rich. More and more of China's industries and enterprises will be taken over by international capital. While China has become entrenched in the global capitalist system the plunder of natural resources, the thirst for raw materials and environmental abuse will worsen. In this scenario China's future may well be the future of global environmental catastrophe. This is one likely development.

The second scenario is that scientific and technological inventions will come quickly enough to phase out the existing production technology so that environmental deterioration can be halted. Some would argue that the replacement technology is already there. But the problem is how to get human beings all over the world to act together quickly enough when our national and international policies are guided by not only the evolutionary instinct for survival of the fittest, but also the animal desire for instant satisfaction here and now. This second scenario is possible, but its likelihood depends on our efforts.

The dialectics of human competition rationalized by economic rationalism may in fact lead to disastrous military conflicts between China and the rest of the world over limited resources, or spheres of influence and control. This worst scenario is not unlikely, and certainly not impossible, especially if China is not ready to submit to Western dominance.

The fourth scenario is that Mr Democracy comes along to take over China. For many of the Chinese elite intelligentsia of the Enlightenment tradition, once China becomes democratized the Chinese people will live happily ever after. Leaving aside the issue of whether democracy one way or another will provide solutions to the contemporary problems in China that require urgent solutions, it is far from clear how to make democracy come about. The Iraqi situation has demonstrated that imposition from outside does not work to anyone's benefit. The most sensible approach is therefore to induce internal changes in China so that more accountable and more responsible governance and government can take root.

The idea of taking root has a metaphorical implication here. For something to take root it needs to adjust to the environment and to take in whatever nutrients are available. The Chinese 1949 revolution and Maoist legacy have become part of the Chinese environment and cannot simply be discarded. Therefore the most fruitful approach is to absorb what is already there, including China's long tradition as well as its recent socialist heritage. Many lessons can be drawn from these heritages. Negative lessons can be drawn from the Mao era, so that violence should be avoided as much as possible and measures should be taken before violence erupts. Positive lessons – such as popular democracy; grassroots participation in management and production; and cheap and locally adopted and traditionally proved healthcare and education – can also be drawn from the Mao era. The ideas and practices of Chinese socialist democracy should be made use of. It is along these lines that we should imagine an alternative model of development in China. Modernity does not have to be totally Western either in terms of governance or in terms of production organization and technology.

Notes

Chapter 1

This chapter is an extended and revised version of a paper that appeared in *Critical Asian Studies*, 34: 4 (2002), pp. 419–34. Substantial discussion of the debate about the Cultural Revolution in Tibet is added. I take this opportunity to thank *Critical Asian Studies* for the permission to re-work the paper.

1. Khrushchev's total denunciation of Stalin the man not only set back the cause of Communism all over the world but also made him look treacherous and hypocritical, for he had fanatically supported the regime when Stalin was alive. Learning from Khrushchev's historical lesson, the CCP resolution does not denounce Mao utterly, and more importantly, does not denounce Mao the man. Instead, the resolution in fact says that Mao deviated from Mao. This apparent logical absurdity is, by any standard, politically and philosophically a stroke of genius.

2. Pinyin transliteration of the author's name in Chinese characters; her name in English spelling is Woeser.

Chapter 2

This chapter is based on a paper presented at the 'Is a history of the Cultural Revolution possible' workshop with Professor Allan Badiou, Washington University, Seattle, 22 to 26 January 2006. The first version of the paper was presented at the Chinese Studies Association of Australia Biennial Conference, 9–12 July 2003, Sydney. I take the opportunity here to thank Tani Balow and Wang Hui for the invitation to Seattle. I thank Peter Zarrow and John Fitzgerald for the panel in Sydney, and Wang Hui, Feng Chongyi, Anne-Marie Brady and Wu Yiching for comments.

1. For representatives of this genre see *The Wound* (*Shanghen*, 伤痕) by Lu Xinhua, *Mimosa* (*Ling yu rou*, 灵与肉) by Zhang Xianliang, *The Snowstorm Tonight* (*Jinye you baofengxue*, 今夜有暴风雪) by Liang Xiaosheng, *Bloody Dusk* (*Xuese huanghun*, 血色黄昏) by Lao Gui , and *Frozen River of the North* (*Damo binghe*, 大漠冰河) by Zhang Kangkang. For the review of the wounded see Barmé and Lee 1979, Link 1983a, 1983b and 1984.

2. In 2003 the year when Li Shenzhi died a conference in Sydney, '当代中国思潮研究：李慎之与自由主义在中国的命运', was organized by Feng Chongyi from which a collection of papers were published in Chinese as 《中国自由主义论丛》 .

3. The poem can be found, among others, at http://www. epochtimes.com/gb/4/5/11/ n536305.htm.

4. The Chinese term for 'Two whateverism' is *Liang ge fanshi*. It is derived from one of Mao's out of context quotes that 'whatever is opposed by our enemy we should support and whatever is supported by our enemy we should oppose'. In the early 1980s the term *fanshipai* (whateverists) was used by Deng Xiaoping and his followers, who accused the then CCP leader Hua Guofeng of being a Two whateverist: whatever Mao said must be followed and whatever Mao did must be correct. The information on whateverism presented here also appears in my writing on Chinese electronic media and Chinese dissidents elsewhere.

5. Some of the material about the Two whatevers presented here is also used in Mobo Gao (2004–2006).

6. Chai Ling, after finishing a Princeton MPA and a Harvard MBA runs a software company, Jenzabar.com, in Massachusetts (Harrison 2003). On her business web page she uses the claim of being nominated twice for Nobel Prize to advertise *Dongfang ribao*. Chai Ling states that we all want the American dream, the movies of the West and success. Li Lu runs Himalaya Capital Partners L.P hedge fund (Buruma 2003).

7. Thanks for donation from Taiwan and to the Taiwan Labour Net who provides a free service the http://www.zggr.org reopened in 2006.

Chapter 3

1. Nancy Hearst and Tony Saich (1997) in their 'Newly Available Sources on the CCP History of the People's Republic of China', list memoirs by Chen Zaidao, Cheng Zihua, Geng Biao, He Changgong, Kang Keqing, Kong Congzhou, Li Zhimin, Liao Hansheng, Liu Zhen, Lu Zhengcao, Luo Ronghuan, Qin Jiwei, Song Renqiong, Su Yu, Wang Ping, Wang Shoudao, Xiao Jingguang, Xu Shiyou, Yang Chengwu, Yang Dezhi, Ye Fei, Zeng Sheng, Zhang Zongsun, Liu Xiao, Li Rui, BoYibo and Nie Rongzhen. They also list the publication of diaries by Luo Zhanglong, Yun Daiying and Chen Geng.

2. Other memoirs, biographies and autobiographies include those by Tie Zhuwei (1986), Peng Cheng (1989), Lin Qingshan (1988a, 1988b, and 1988c), Mu Xin (1997), Zhang Yunsheng (1988), Yu Gong (1988), Chen Hua (1992), Ren Jian (1989), Ma Luo et al (1993), Qing Ye and Fang Lei (1993), Wen Feng (1993), Shen Danying (1992), Jiao Ye (1993), and Guan Weixun (1993).

3. In fact the first author of this co-authored book was Yan's wife Gao Gao. The revised English version of this book published by Hawaii University Press is much improved in terms of scholarship.

4. Hu Qiaomu died in 1992. The book was written on the basis of more than 20 talks that Hu had with a group of writers sanctioned by the CCP authorities.

5. Lao Gui's book is translated into English by Howard Goldblatt, and published by Viking in 1995 under the name of Ma Bo.

6. Dong Bian was married to Tian Jiaying, Mao's personal secretary, who committed suicide at the beginning of the Cultural Revolution.

Dian Dian is Luo Ruiqing's daughter. Luo was the Minister of Security and Chief of Staff of the PLA before the Cultural Revolution. Luo was one of the first to fall as the Cultural Revolution unfolded, and tried to kill himself by jumping from a building. He survived but was permanently crippled. Luo was released from jail in 1973 and was put in charge of the administrative work of the Central Military Committee of the CCP in 1977. In July 1978 he was admitted to a West German hospital for treatment of his crippled legs. Though the operation was successful, Luo died in the hospital of a heart attack in August of 1978.

Zhang is the second wife of Qiao Guanhua, who was one of the most talented diplomats of the PRC. Appointed personally by Mao, Qiao led the first PRC delegation to the United Nations in 1971. Soon after, he was appointed Minister of Foreign Affairs, a position that proved to be the beginning of his downfall. He was accused of being involved with the Gang of Four and disappeared from the political scene after 1976. Qiao died in 1983. Zhang Hanzhi herself was a personality of note. Her father Zhang Shizhao was Mao's long-term personal friend and Zhang Hanzhi used to be Mao's English teacher.

Liu Siqi was one of Mao's daughters-in-law.

Wang Guangmei is Liu Shaoqi's wife and Wang Guangying is Liu's brother-in-law. Liu Pingping and Li Yuan are Liu Shaoqi's children.

7. Zhu Min includes Zeng Zhi, wife of Tao Zhu, Tao Siliang, daughter of Tao Zhu, Liu Pingping, Liu Yuan and Liu Tingting (another child of Liu Shaoqi), Deng Maomao (daughter of Deng Xiaoping), Peng Meikui (niece of Peng Dehuai), Xue Ming (wife of He Long who was one of the ten marshals), Dian Dian, and Tao Xiaoyong (son of Tao Yong who was the Commander of the Chinese South Sea Fleet before the Cultural Revolution, but died in suspicious circumstances during the Cultural Revolution).

8. Zhang Hanzhi was said to be a friend of Jiang Qing, who was said to have influenced the marriage between her and Qiao Guanhua.

9. Only some figures were allowed to be interviewed. They include Yao Dengshan (who was blamed for the burning of the British Embassy in 1967), Wang Li, Guan Feng (two radicals during the Cultural Revolution who were blamed for advocating struggle against the military establishment), Lin Liheng (Lin Biao's daughter) and Ji Dengkui (personally promoted by Mao and one of the Vice-Premiers during the Cultural Revolution) and Chen Boda. One can well imagine that these people would have been very careful of what they were allowed to say during the interviews. One member of the so-called Gang of Four Yao Wenyuan wrote his memoirs but was not allowed to publish them (Boxun.com 2007).

10. Wang Dongxing was allowed to publish a book in the form of diaries. However, the diaries were limited to certain 'safe dates and safe contents'. The diaries only cover the dates from March 1947 to March 1948, from December 1949 to March 1950 and Mao's visit to the old guerrilla base Jinggangshan from 21 May to 30 May 1965. The latest book by Wang Dongxing (2004) is equally without contents.

    A book about Chen by Qin Huailu had to be smuggled out of China to be published.

11. Yu Huiyong was arrested in 1976 and committed suicide in 1977 (Dao 1994).

    Shangshan xiaxiang refers to a campaign of sending millions of urban educated youth to the rural and mountainous areas in China. For an analysis of the events surrounding Li Qinglin see Gao (1999b).

12. It is also a way to make money. Both Deng Xiaoping and Jiang Zemin had collected works published by the government in tens of millions of copies. Every CCP and government organ was then ordered to purchase them to study. The so-called *gao fei* (author's remuneration) in millions went to their families. This, of course, was following a precedent. Mao had his collected works published by the government and everyone was obliged to study, if not to purchase them. Mao also collected *gai fei*. In recent years the anti-Maoists have been having a field day on this issue. While choosing to ignore the fact that the Deng and Jiang families manage to enrich themselves from these collected works, they vilify Mao as a hypocrite who advocated serving the people while collecting *gao fei* of tens of millions. However one wants to interpret the issue, two points are clear. First, Mao's family did not enrich themselves from Mao's *gao fei* then and his descendents have not enriched themselves by possessing the *gao fei* now. Second, Mao really had something interesting and original to say in his collected works, whereas Deng and Jiang do not.

13. Authors such as Li Rui, Wang Nianyi and Jin Chunming are, however, more theoretically orientated.

14. When I visited Wang at his home in Beijing in 1992, the first thing he said to me with great indignation was that Mao slept with many women and sexual hormones were used to stimulate his sexual drive.

15. As early as the later 1970s, there was a rumour running around in China that Zhang Yufeng claimed that Mao was her son's father and that she wanted her son to receive part of Mao's inheritance. Li Zhisui, however, claims that by the time Mao met Zhang Yufeng he was sterile.

16. Positive evidence and arguments about the Red Guards, and especially the Rebels, such as Zhou Ziren (2006), can be published only in areas outside the political control of China.

17. Wu Zetian (AD 627–705) has become symbolic of an evil woman in Chinese history written by Confucian scholars.

18. Views and evidence that argue positively for Lin Biao, such as Wu

Faxian (2006), appear occasionally on the e-media and in writings that appear in areas outside the political control of China.

19. Though the Women's Federation leadership was under attack during the Cultural Revolution, as all bureaucratic institutions were, genuine efforts were made to promote women's status. Those efforts and the success they produced can be confirmed by numerous documents and statistics. One of the examples cited in this chapter is the partial list of ordinary women who were promoted to positions in the central leadership.

20. For a reappraisal of China's economic performance during the Mao period and the Cultural Revolution see Bramall (1993), Endicott (1989) and Law (2003).

Chapter 5

1. One mu is about 0.0667 hectare and one jin is half a kilogramme.

2. Marc Gellman and Tom Hartman (2002), in their piece published in the widely circulated *Reader's Digest*, are more inventive. They not only place Mao alongside Hitler, Stalin and Pol Pot, but with Osama bin Laden as well.

Chapter 6

1. By Chinese I mean those who were born and brought up in China before and during the Cultural Revolution but now may live either in China or abroad. Writers residing in Hong Kong and Taiwan may also be included in this category.

2. The questionable claims and discrepancies that have been raised by Teiwes are not discussed in this chapter.

3. One mu of land equals 0.0667 hectare.

4. For those who are not familiar with Chinese history it should be noted that the 460 so-called scholars who were reportedly executed were not killed because they were Confucian scholars but because they were considered to have cheated Qin Shihuang in the matter of finding the elixir of life and then have spread rumours against him.

Chapter 7

1. According to Latham (2007), SMS is the most widely used e-medium in China and has created an unprecedented 'public sphere'. In the 2007 Xiamen demonstration against the government approval a massive new paraxylene chemical plant, for instance, MSNs and QQs played an important role. On 1 June 2007, residents were invited though MSN and QQ by friends and family members to go for a 'walk' with a yellow band on one arm to a particular place at some particular time. That was how the demonstration was organized (Xie 2007, Cody 2007).

2. For instance on 6 August 1956 the Ministry of Health issued guidelines for contraception; on 5 March 1957 the *People's Daily* published an editorial advocating population control; on 18 December 1962 the CCP Central Committee and the State Council jointly issued instructions for the relevant authorities to take serious measures to control population. In 1964 the State Council set up what was called the Population Control Commission. From 1962 to 1964 all the provincial and municipality governments established their own population control offices (http://www.wyzxsx.com/Article/Class14/200708/23342.html, accessed on 31 August 2007).
3. The poetic beauty of the punchy headline is more obvious for those who can read Chinese: 错批一人, 误增三亿.
4. According to Huang Yunsheng (2007), Li's claim was eagerly received both in and outside China. Li Rui made this claim in his paper 'Ruhe kandai Mao Zedong' (How to regard Mao Zedong), which was read at Harvard University in November 2003, and appears as the first chapter of a book published in 2005 in Hong Kong titled *Li Rui on Mao Zedong*. In 2006 Li Rui made the same claim to a German journalist.
5. Zhang Qian was Chen Yi's wife.
6. Zhang Wentian was one of the important CCP leaders accused of being a member of the so-called Peng Dehuai anti-party clique.
7. Thanks to Wang Shaoguang who posted this source to me.
8. Wei Yan is a character in the historical novel *Romance of Three Kingdoms*. He is often cited as an example of people who are not loyal to their superiors.
9. Feng was first a warlord and then a Nationalist army general who often changed sides in alliances.
10. Wang Li was Mao's theoretical secretary during the Cultural Revolution and drafted many influential theoretical articles and CCP policy documents. It was Wang who articulated Mao's idea of 'continuous revolution'. From 1964 until 1967 Wang was allowed to attend all the important meetings held by the Standing Committee of the Politburo of the CCP, where many of the important decisions were made. He was a leading member of the Cultural Revolution Group and during late 1966 and early 1967 had almost daily contacts with Mao.
11. Ji Xianlin is a prominent professor at Beijing University and Ba Jin was a prominent novelist.
12. Liu Yuan is a son of Liu Shaoqi and Bo Xicheng is a son of Bo Yibo.

Chapter 8

1. For instance in *Wanwei tianxia luntan*, http://www4.bbsland.com/forums/ politics/ messages/5137.html.
2. During the cold war, most Western countries refused to recognize the existence of the PRC and imposed economic sanctions against China. Though China received technical support from the Soviet Union

(which was very helpful) during the 1950s, China fell out with the Soviet Union toward the end of that decade and the Soviet Union withdrew its support. In contrast, economies in the East Asian region belonging to the capitalist camp got a lifeline of support from the United States during the cold war. For instance, in return for allowing the deployment of US forces in Vietnam, South Korea received approximately $1 billion dollars from the United States from 1965–70. The Vietnam War absorbed 94 per cent of Korea's total steel exports and 52 per cent of its exports of transportation equipment (Hanley and Mendoza 2007). Japan received similar treatment. American 'special procurements' of war materials from Japan accounted for 60 per cent of Japan's steel exports during the Korean War, and for 10–20 per cent during the Vietnam War (Eiji 2007).

3. By presenting the figures laid out here by Jiang I do not mean to say that I agree with them. Jiang, like most e-media debate participants, does not cite sources of the data and does not make references. Therefore it is difficult to check or even to engage with this kind of argument in the normal sense of scholarship. However, this does not diminish the significance of this kind of debate. One reason is that this kind of narrative is likely to be read more widely than a well-researched academic paper and therefore has a greater impact. Second, as argued throughout this book, human behaviour is guided by perceptions and beliefs more than 'the truth'. Just as many a Westerner will be persuaded by the claims made by Chang and Halliday in *The Unknown Story*, many Chinese will be persuaded by Jiang.

4. For the importance of the different arrangements in terms of production organization see Chapter 5.

5. Qi was one of the Cultural Revolution radicals and a close associate of Jiang Qing.

6. Mao was a friend of Zhu Zhongli's father. When Zhu arrived in Yan'an it was Mao who introduced her to Wang Jiaxiang, who subsequently married Zhu.

7. Hao is an author of two revolutionary novels about rural China *Yan yang tian* (The Bright Sunny Sky) and *Jin guang dadao* (Golden Bright Path).

8. Yang Guang quotes a doggerel: 上学把家长逼疯，卖房把家底掏空，治病不如提前送终 (the cost of sending children to school makes parents crazy, buying a house costs a family everything, and it is better to prepare a funeral than to be treated for an illness).

9. In July 2007, following the revelation of slave labour in brick kilns in Shanxi province and shortly before the important 17th CCP national congress was to take place, 17 veteran CCP party members who used to hold official positions at ministerial level or above published an open letter calling for a change of course in China along the lines of genuine Marxism and ideas of Mao. The letter explicitly warns that there is a danger of 'Yeltin-like leaders' appearing within the CCP (Ma

Bing et al 2007). The letter was quickly circulated on many websites, but the Mao Flag website www.maoflag.net, which first published the letter, was quickly closed down by the Chinese authorities (Magnier 2007). Some other websites that published the letter were also blocked from access.

Chapter 9

1. According to another estimate, the average urban manufacturing worker's pay in 2005 in China was 60 US cents an hour, which was considerably higher than the average migrant worker's earnings. But compare that with $2.46 an hour in Mexico (McClenahen 2006).
2. Another interesting development is that many e-media chatroom contributors call for the establishment of Chinese farmers' associations to protect farmers' interests, and one even suggested that Chen should be the chairman of such an association. See 'Zhongguo nongmin diaocha zuozhe jishu zhong renwu xinlang lia tian shilu' (A chat show with the authors at sina), http://finance.sina.come.cn/roll/20040211/1632626835.shtml, accessed on 4 February 2004.

Chapter 10

1. According to Guo (2007) the poverty line in China was 206 RMB per person in 1985, 530 in 1995, and 668 in 2004 in Henan.
2. For a more detailed summary of which foreign companies have taken over which local Chinese companies in all industries see a document written by Gao Liang, a research fellow at the Research Centre of Chinese National Assets of the Institute of Structure Reform of the Chinese National Development and Reform Commission. The document was circulated through e-mails in July 2007.
3. According to Chung, among the top ten countries or regions investing in China in 2005, one was Hong Kong and another was the British Virgin Islands, a group of islands in the Caribbean with a population of only 22,000 but at least 400,000 registered companies (Chung 2007).
4. The new labour contract law was eventually passed by the Standing Committee of the National People's Congress in 2007. The law requires employers to provide written contracts to their workers, restricts the use of temporary labourers and makes it harder to lay off employees, but some provisions that foreign companies said would hurt China's competitiveness were softened. It remains to be seen how effectively the law can be enforced, especially for migrant workers from rural areas. The media exposure of the widespread slave labour in brick kilns and coal mines may have helped the passage of the law.
5. The Chinese title of the document is *Guanyu baohu senlin fazhan linye luogan wenti de jueding* (A resolution on several issues on the protection of forests and forestry development).

6.   The other essential elements of Mao Zedong Thought are supposedly to include the mass line and the strategy of the united front. During the early years of the Chinese communist revolution, Mao and his followers were branded as empiricists who had no understanding of Marxist theory. Mao's tactic to fight these so-called *jiaotiao zhuyizhe* (dogmatists) was to argue that what was right and wrong was decided not by what was said in the canon but by revolutionary practice.

Glossary of Chinese terms and names

Pinyin	Chinese Character	English
Ai Siqi	艾思奇	A leading Chinese Marxist philosopher
baogan zhi	包干制	Household responsibility system
baojian yisheng	保健医生	Health maintenance doctor
Bo Yibo	薄一波	A well-known CCP official who held important economic and financial positions
Boyang	波阳	Name of a county
caizi jiaren	才子佳人	The brainy and the beautiful
Cao Jingqing	曹景清	A leading Chinese writer on rural China
Chai Ling	柴玲	One of the 1989 Tiananmen protest student leaders
Chen Ada	陈阿大	A person of humble family background promoted to prominent official position during the Cultural Revolution
Chen Boda	陈伯达	An important CCP leader during the Cultural Revolution
Chen Guidi	陈桂棣	Author of a well-known book on rural China
Chen Yi	陈毅	Chinese Minister of Foreign Affairs before the Cultural Revolution
Chen Yonggui	陈永贵	A well-known CCP official of farming background promoted by Mao
Chen Yun	陈云	One of the very few ideologically consistent top CCP leaders

Chun Tao	春桃	Co-author of a major book on rural China
chun wan	春晚	Annual Spring Festival evening performance
cu shengchan	促生产	To promote production
cuo pi yi ren wu zeng san yi	错批一人误增三亿	Wrong criticism of one person led to the mistaken increase of 300 million people
daotai	道台	Official title in traditional China
Deng Maomao	邓毛毛	Deng Xiaoping's daughter
Deng Pufang	邓朴方	Deng Xiaoping's son
Deng Xiaoping	邓小平	Considered to be the architect of the post-Mao reform
Deng Zihui	邓子恢	A noted CCP leader in charge of agriculture during the early Mao era
Dian Dian	点点	Daughter of Luo Ruiqing
Diaoyutai	钓鱼台	Part of the CCP leadership headquarters in Beijing
diwang jiangxiang	帝王将相	Emperors/kings, prime ministers and generals
Dong Bian	董边	Wife of Tian Jiaying
Dongguan	东莞	Name of a city
duowei	多维	A website
er xian	二线	Second-line leadership
Fenghua yuan	枫华园	An e-journal
Fu Lianzhang	傅连璋	A well-known doctor who became a high ranking CCP official
Gao Changxian	高常献	A Gao villager
Gao Gang	高岗	A noted CCP leader in the 1950s who committed suicide after a failed attempt to reshuffle the CCP leadership hierarchy

gao zhuang	告状	To appeal to officialdom for justice
Gong Chu	龚楚	A well-known Red Army general
goutou junshi	狗头军师	One who pulls the string for evil action
Guan Feng	关峰	A well-known Cultural Revolution radical
Guan Weixun	官伟勋	A noted CCP official and writer
guizu	贵族	Noble or aristocratic class
Gu Atao	顾阿桃	A person of humble family background promoted to prominent official position during the Cultural Revolution
Han Deqiang	韩德强	A well-known Chinese academic
Hao Ran	浩然	A well-known writer of revolutionary literature
haojie *see* shi nian haojie		
He Kaiyin	何开荫	A think tank CCP official in Anhui
He Shang	河殇	*River Elegy*, name of the controversial TV programme
He Zhizhen	贺之珍	Mao's third wife
Hu Jintao	胡锦涛	CCP party leader since 2002
Hu Qiaomu	胡乔木	A CCP official noted for drafting important documents
Hu Yaobang	胡耀邦	A CCP party leader in the post-Mao period
Hu Zongnan	胡宗南	A well-known KMT general
Hua Guofeng	华国锋	CCP leader who was appointed by Mao as his successor
Huaxia Wenzhai	华夏文摘	*Chinese Digest* (an e-journal)
hushi zhang	护士长	Chief nurse
Ji Xianlin	季羡林	A well-known Chinese scholar
Jian Bozan	翦伯赞	A well-known Chinese historian

Jiang Qing	江青	Mao's fourth wife
Jiang Zemin	江泽民	Former General Secretary of the CCP
jianzhi mishu	兼职秘书	Part-time secretary
jiao xuefei	交学费	Pay tuition fees
jiaoyu chanyehua	教育产业化	To entrepreneurize education
jin	斤	A weight unit (0.5 kg)
Jin Xiaoding	金小丁	A critic of Jung Chang's biography of Mao
jishi wenxue	纪实文学	Factual literature, a genre of writing
kang	炕	Bed with a stove underneath
Kang Sheng	康生	A leading CCP official demonized in the official historiography
Ke Qingshi	柯庆施	An important CCP official who used to be the Mayor of Shanghai
Kong Qingdong	孔庆东	A professor of Beijing University
Kuai Dafu	蒯大富	A leading Cultural Revolution rebel
Lao Gui	老鬼	A well-known Chinese writer
Lao Tian	老田	A well-known e-media debater
Li Changping	李昌平	A well-known advocate of change in rural China
Li Jingquan	李井泉	An important CCP provincial leader who caused Sichuan to be one of the provinces worst hit by famine during Great Leap Forward
Li Min	李敏	Daughter of Mao
Li Na	李纳	Daughter of Mao
Li Rui	李锐	An influential anti-Maoist CCP official
Li Shenzhi	李慎之	A noted liberal dissident with the CCP establishment

Li Xuanyuan	李选源	An active e-media participant
Li Xuefeng	李雪峰	A noted CCP provincial leader
Li Yining	历以宁	A noted economist
Li Yinqiao	李银桥	One of Mao's bodyguards
Li Zehou	李泽厚	A noted neo-enlightenment writer
Li Zhisui	李志绥	A medical doctor who looked after Mao's health fro some years
Lian dong	联动	An organization formed by students to defend their high ranking party officials and army officers at the beginning of the Cultural Revolution
liang ge fanshi	两个凡是	Two whatevers
lianghuan hua	连环画	Story book illustrated by pictures
Lin Biao	林彪	a CCP leader second to Mao during the Cultural Revolution
Lin Ke	林克	One of Mao's secretaries
Liu Guoguang	刘国光	A CCP scholar official
Liu Pingping	刘平平	Daughter of Liu Shaoqi
Liu Shaoqi	刘少奇	An important CCP leader who was one of the main targets of the Cultural Revolution
Liu Siqi	刘思齐	Mao's daughter-in-law
Liu Xiaobo	刘晓波	A leading dissident in Beijing who advocates Western colonialism in China
Liu Yuan	刘源	Son of Liu Shaoqi
Lu Xun	鲁迅	Arguably the greatest modern Chinese writer
Luding	卢定	Name of a bridge
Luoyang ribao	洛阳日报	A daily paper in Luoyang
Lushan	庐山	A mountain

Ma Yinchu	马寅初	A well-known scholar of demography
maiban	买办	Comprador
Mao Zedong	毛泽东	The foremost leader of the Chinese 1949 revolution, who died in 1976
Maojiawan	毛家湾	A residential compound where Lin Biao and his family used to live
Mawangdui	马王堆	An archaeological site
mu	亩	A Chinese measurement (0.0667 hectare)
nian hua	年画	Traditional Spring Festival painting
Nien Cheng	念成	An autobiographical writer
Nie Yuanzi	聂元子	A leading Cultural Revolution rebel
niu gui she shen	牛鬼蛇神	Cow ghost and snake demon in folk stories
niu peng	牛棚	'Cowshed'
nongmin xiehui	农民协会	Peasant association
Peng Dehuai	彭德怀	An important CCP official and army commander who fell from political power during the Lushan Conference in 1959
Peng Zhen	彭真	A powerful CCP leader
po si jiu	破四旧	Destroy the four olds
Qi Benyu	戚本禹	A leading Cultural Revolution radical
Qiao Guanhua	乔冠华	A well-known diplomat
Qin Shihuang	秦始皇	The first emperor of China
qimeng	启蒙	Enlightenment
qinghaosu	青蒿素	The drug artemisinin
qingli jieji duiwu	清理阶级队伍	Clear the ranks of political classes

Quan Yanchi	权延赤	A well-known writer on Mao
Rao Shushi	饶漱石	A noted CCP leader in the 1950s and a close colleague of Gao Gang
Ruijin	瑞金	A town where the Red Army was active
san xian	三线	Third-line industry, referring a strategy to set up important industries in central and north-west China in preparation for foreign invasion
sannong Zhongguo	三农中国	A website
shangfang	上访	Appeal to higher authorities for justice
shangshan xiaxiang	上山下乡	A campaign by which educated youth from urban China were sent into the mountains and the countryside
Shao Li-tzu (Lizi)	邵力子	An important KMT official
Shen Tu	沈图	Head of the Chinese civil aviation authority
shi liu tiao	十六条	The 16 articles of the Cultural Revolution document issued as guidelines for the movement
shi nian haojie	十年浩劫	Ten-year catastrophe, a term frequently used to refer to the Cultural Revolution in China
Shi Zhe	师哲	A well-known interpreter who worked with Mao
shouzu yuan	收租院	Rent collection courtyard
si da ziyou	四大自由	Four big freedoms
Sima Qian	司马迁	Ancient historian
Su Yu	粟裕	A well-known PLA general
Sun Zhigang	孙志刚	A migrant from rural China who was beaten to death by the Guangdong police for not having an identity card

suzhi	素质	Quality
Suzhou	苏州	A city
Tao Zhu	陶铸	a noted CCP leader during the Cultural Revolution
Tian Jiaying	田家英	One of Mao's most important secretaries
tongtian renwu	通天人物	Those who have the ear of the people at the very top
tongxun yuan	通讯员	Correspondent
Wang Dongxing	汪东兴	CCP official who was the boss of Mao's Central Office
Wang Guangmei	王光美	One of Liu Shaoqi wives
Wang Guangying	王光英	Liu Shaoqi's brother-in-law
Wang Hui	汪晖	An influential Chinese writer and scholar
Wang Jiaxiang	王稼祥	An important CCP leader whose support of Mao was crucial for the latter's rise during the Long March
Wang Jinhong	王金红	Head of Long Bow Village
Wang Li	王力	One of the Cultural Revolution radicals
Wang Lixiong	王力雄	A well-known Chinese scholar of Tibet
Wang Nianyi	王年一	A leading Chinese historian of the Cultural Revolution
Wang Shaoguang	王绍光	A political science professor
Wang Shiwei	王实味	A writer who was executed
Wang Xizhe	王希哲	A leading critic and dissident
Wang Youqin	王友琴	A US-based writer on student violence
Wei Se	维色	Woesser, a writer of Tibetan ethnicity
Wen Jiabao	温家宝	Premier of the PRC since 2002

Wen Tiejun	温铁军	A well-known scholar of rural China
Wenzhou	温州	A city
Wu De	吴德	Mayor of Beijing during the last years of the Mao era
Wu Lengxi	吴冷西	Former head of the People's Daily
wu qi gan xiao	五七干校	May Seventh Cadre School
Wu Xujun	吴旭君	Mao's chief nurse
Wu Zetian	武则天	The only female emperor in Chinese history
Wu Zhipu	吴芝圃	Another provincial leader who was responsible for the Great Leap Forward disaster
Wuhan	武汉	A city
wuyou zhixiang	乌有之乡	A website
xi panzi	洗盘子	Wash dishes
xiangsheng	相声	Stand-up comic of cross talk
xianzhuang shu	线装书	Thread-bound traditional books
xiaoggang cun	小岗村	Xiaogang Village
Xu Guangping	许广平	Widow of Lu Xun
Yan Jiaqi	严家其	A Chinese political scientist in exile
Yan'an	延安	A town
Yang Changji	扬昌济	Mao's teacher and father in-law
Yang Kaihui	杨开慧	Mao's second wife
Yang Shangkun	杨尚昆	An important CCP official
yanhuang chunqiu	炎黄春秋	A Chinese official magazine
Yao Wenyuan	姚文元	A leading Cultural Revolution radical, one of the so-called Gang of Four
Ye Jianying	叶剑英	One of ten PLA marshals
Ye Yonglie	叶永烈	A well-known Chinese writer

yi ku si tian	忆苦思甜	To recall the bitter past and to tell of the sweet present
yi yue fengbao	一月风暴	The February Storm, referring to February 1967 when political power in Shanghai was taken over by the rebels
yiliao shichanghua	医疗市场化	To marketize health care
Yinhe	银河	Name of a Chinese ship that was searched by the US navy
Yu Huiyong	于会咏	A well-known composer and musician who committed suicide after his arrest by the post-Mao authorities
Yu Jianrong	于建荣	A major writer on contemporary China
Yu Jie	余杰	A Christian dissident
Yuan Longping	袁隆平	A scientist and expert on hybrid rice
Yun Shi	运十	A successful Chinese civil aircraft project that was shelved by the post-Mao authorities
Zhang Chunqiao	张春桥	One of the four Cultural Revolutionary radical leaders
Zhang Guotao	张国焘	A well-known CCP leader who defected to the KMT
Zhang Hanzhi	章含之	Wife of Qiao Guanhua
Zhang Naiqi	章乃器	A leading member of the non-CCP intelligentsia and one of the most famous of those who were classified as Rightists
Zhang Qian	张茜	Wife of Chen Yi
Zhang Rong	张戎	Jung Chang
Zhang Wentian	张闻天	A noted CCP leader
Zhang Xianliang	张贤亮	A noted contemporary Chinese writer
Zhang Xueliang	张学良	A well-known KMT general

Zhao Ziyang	赵紫阳	A CCP leader who was put under house arrest after the Tiananmen events in 1989
Zhengzhou	郑州	A city
zhiqing	知青	educated youth
Zhongguo gongren wang	中国工人网	A website
Zhongnanhai	中南海	The CCP leadership compound in Beijing
Zhou Enlai	周恩来	The first Premier of the PRC
Zhu De	朱德	The legendry Chinese army commander
Zhu Min	朱敏	Daughter of Zhu De
Zhu Rongj	朱镕基	A former Premier of the PRC
Zhu Zhongli	朱仲丽	Wife of Wang Jiaxiang, a doctor who became a well-known writer by publishing biographies of Jiang Qing
Zhua geming	抓革命	Grasp the revolution
zhurengong	主人公	A website
zizhi tongjian	资治通鉴	A classical history book
Zunyi	遵义	A town

Bibliography

Ai Ming (2007), 'Shi shei jiejue le Zhongguo ren chifan de wenti – Mao Zedong' (Who is it that has solved the problem of feeding the Chinese people – Mao Zedong), *Tian xia luntan*, http://bbs4.creaders.net/forums/politics/messages/1547142.html, accessed on 7 March 2007.

Amin, Samir (2005), 'Theory and practice of the Chinese "market socialism" project: is 'market socialism' an alternative to liberal globalization?', in Tian Yu Cao, ed., *The Chinese Model of Modern Development*, London and New York: Routledge, pp.128–47.

— (2006), 'What Maoism contributed', June 9–10, 2006 Hong Kong Conference: 'The Fortieth Anniversary: Rethinking the Genealogy and Legacy of the Cultural Revolution' sponsored by the China Study Group, *Monthly Review*, and the Contemporary China Research Center of City University of Hong Kong.

An Qi (1998), 'Bu pa guli cai you duli: zhuan fang ziyou zhuangaoren Cao Changqing' (Independence can only come from non-fear of isolation: exclusive interview with freelance writer Cao Changqing), *Qiansao*, No. 5, www.caochanbgqing. com, accessed on 13 May 2004.

Anagnost, Ann (1997), *National Past-Times: Narrative, Representation, and Power in Modern China*, Durham, N.C.: Duke University Press.

Anderson, Perry (1974), *Lineages of the Absolutist State*, London: N.L.B.

Apter, David E. and Saich, Tony (1994), *Revolutionary Discourse in Mao's Republic,* Cambridge Mass.: Harvard University Press.

Armitage, Catherine (2005) 'The dark side of the boom's bottomless pit', *The Weekend Australian*, 25–26 July, pp. 33, 38.

Badiou, Allan (2005), 'The Cultural Revolution: the last revolution?' *Positions: East Asia Cultures Critique*, Vol. 13, No. 3 (Winter), pp. 481–514.

— (2006), 'Comments', at the 'Is a History of the Cultural Revolution Possible?' workshop with Professor Allan Badiou, Washington University, Seattle, 22–26 January 2006.

Ball, Joseph (2007), 'Did Mao really kill in the Great Leap Forward?' http://www.monthly review.org/0906ball.htm, accessed on 23 May.

Banister, Judith (1987), *China's Changing Population*, Stanford, Calif.: Stanford University Press.

Bao Zunxin (1990), *Pipan yu qimeng* (Criticism and enlightenment), Taipei: Lianji chuban shiye gongsi.

Barmé, Geremie and Lee, Bennett, eds (1979), *The Wounded: New Stories from the Cultural Revolution*, Hong Kong: Joint Publishing Co.

— (2005), 'I am So Ronree', in the *The China Journal* Special Issue, *The Portrayal of Opportunitism, Betrayal, and Manipulation in Mao's Rise to Power*, No. 55 (January), pp. 128–39.

— (2007), 'New Years past: other spring festivals' in Danwei, http://www. danwei.org/guest.contributor/new_years_past_other, accessed 27 February 2007.

Barnouin, Barbara and Yu Changgen (1993), *Ten Years of Turbulence: The Chinese Cultural Revolution*, London and New York: Kegan Paul International.

Bartlett, Sir Frederick C. (1932), *Remembering: A Study in Experimental and Social Psychology*, London: Cambridge University Press.

Batson, Andrew (2006), 'In China, growth at whose cost?' *The Washington Street Journal online*, WSJ.com, http://online.wsj.com/public/article/ SB116415600306230140–vSeb8J3vgnI1cUuWn2Tgbpth1II_20071121. html, accessed on 27 November 2006.

Batson, A. and Oster, S. (2006), 'China: growth at whose cost?' *Wall Street Journal*, 22 November. See also *New Economist*, http://neweconomist. blogs.com/new_economist/2006/11/chinas_poor.html, accessed on 11 December 2007.

Benton, Gregor and Tsang, Steve (2005), '*Mao: The Unknown Story:* an assessment', in *China Journal* Special Issue, *The Portrayal of Opportunitism, Betrayal, and Manipulation in Mao's Rise to Power*, No. 55 (January), pp. 95–109.

Berenson, Edward (1995), 'A permanent revolution: the historiography of 1789', *Modern China*, Vol. 21, No. 1, pp. 77–104.

Bergaglio, Maristella (2006), 'Population growth in China: the basic characteristics of China's demographic transition', accessed on 6 February 2006.

Bernstein, Richard (1994), 'The tyrant Mao, as told by his doctor', *The New York Times*, 2 October.

Bernstein, Richard and Munro, Ross H. (1997), *The Coming Conflict with China*, New York: Alfred A. Knopf.

Berstein, Thomas (2005), 'Throwing the book at Mao', www.theage.com. au, accessed on 10 June 2005.

Bian, Banjie (1994), *Work and Inequality in Urban China*, Albany: State University of New York Press.

Black, Antony C. (2000), 'Black propaganda', *Guardian Weekly*, 24 February.

Blecher, Marc (2006), 'The puzzle', http://www.oberlin.edu/news-info/ observation/ observatrionsmblecher1.html, accessed on 18 November 2006.

Blinders (an e-media blogger) (2006), 'Deng Pufang de hua chufa le duo Mao Zedong huainian de kaiguan' (Remarks by Deng Pufang triggered the opening of cherishing the memory of Mao Zedong), *Tian xian luntan,* www.creaders.org, http://www4.bbsland.com/forums/ politics/messages/1537410.html, accessed on 18 December 2006.

Bo Xilai (2006), 'Zhongguo chanpin jiang di Meiguo shenghuo chengben' (Chinese products reduce the cost of living in America), www.xinhuanet.com, accessed on 14 May 2006.

Bo Yibo (1989), *Linxiu, yuanshuai, zhanyou* (Leaders, marshals and comrades-in-arms), Beijing: Zhonggong zhongyang dangxiao chubanshe.

— (1991, 1993, 1997), *Luogen zhongda zhengce yu shijian de huiguo* (Reflections on several important policies and events), Beijing: Zhonggong zhongyang dangxiao chubanshe, Vol. I, 1991, Vol. II, 1993, Vol. III.

Bosteels, Bruno (2005), 'Post-Maoism: Badiou and politics', *Positions: East Asia Cultures Critique,* Vol. 13, No. 3 (Winter), pp. 575–634.

Boxun (2006a), 'Guang fang pilu: dalu yiwan fuhao jiucheng yishang shi gaogan zi nü' (According to official sources, 90 per cent of the billionaires on the mainland are sons and daughters of high ranking party officials), http://www.peacehall.com/news/gb/china/2006/ 10/200610192021.shtml, accessed on 20 October 2006.

— (2006b), 'Hu Yaobang huajie 1975 huashi fengbo, jie ji wei Chen Jingren pingfan' (Hu Yaobang resolves the Fossils Incident and takes the opportunity to rehabilitate Chen Jingren), http://www.peacehall. com/news/gb/zspecial/2006/ 12/200612072344.shtml, accessed on 16 December 2006.

Boxun.com (2007), 'Yao Wenyuan xin zhuan huigu yu fansi bao lishi zhenxiang' (Yao Wenyuan's new memoirs expose historical truth), http://news.boxun.com/news/gb/zspecial/2007/01/200701260504. shtml, accessed on 23 February 2007.

Brady, Anne-Marie (2002), 'Red and expert: China's "foreign friends" in the Great Proletarian Cultural Revolution 1966–1969', in Woei Lien Chong, ed., *China's Great Proletarian Cultural Revolution: Master Narratives and Post-Mao Conternarratives,* Lanham, Boulder, New York and Oxford: Rowman & Littlefield, pp. 93–137.

Bramall, Chris (1993), *In Praise of Maoist Economic Planning: Living Standards and Economic Development in Sichuan since 1931.* Oxford: Clarendon Press.

Branstetter, Lee and Lague, David (2006), 'China's embrace of globalization', National Bureau of Economic Research, *Working Paper Series* Number 12373, July.

Brosius H.B. and Kepplinger, H.M. (1990), 'The agenda setting function of television news', *Communication Research,* Vol. 17, No. 2 (April), pp. 183–211.

Brown, Kerry (2007), http://www.opendemocracy.net/home/china power/china.jsp, accessed on 13 April 2007, and BBC Chinese language website http://news.bbc.co.uk/go/pr/fr/-/chinese/simp/hi/newsid_6530000/newsid_6538600/6538621.stm, accessed on 4 April 2007.

Bu Luo (2007), '上千孩子被卖山西黑砖窑最小8岁 400父亲网上呼救' (A thousand children, the smallest 8 years old, were sold to black brick kilns in Shanxi and 4,000 fathers make their appeal on the web), *Renmin wang*, www.people.com.cn, http://society.people.com.cn/GB/8217/5857901.html, accessed on 17 June 2007.

Buckley, Chris (2006),'Beijing', Reuters, May 10.

Burkett, Paul and Hart-Landsberg, Martin (2005), 'Thinking about China: capitalism, socialism, and class struggle', in China and Socialism Roundtable, *Critical Asian Studies*, Vol. 37, No. 3 (September), pp. 433–40,

Buruma, Ian (1995), 'Chinese whispers', *New Yorker*, 13 February.

— (2003), 'Tiananmen, INC', *New Yorker*, May.

Byron, John (1992), *The Claws of the Dragon: Kang Sheng, the Evil Genius behind Mao and His Legacy of Terror in People's China*, New York: Simon & Schuster.

Cai Shihua (2006), 'Lishi shi yimian jingzi: Hao Ran jiqi zuopin pingjia (History is a mirror: Hao Ran and the evaluation of his work), *Wan wei tian xia luntan*, http://www4.bbsland.com/forums/politics/messages/4538.html, accessed on 9 May 2006.

Cai Yingshen (2002), 'Kaifang shehui de diren: Mao Zedong yu Qin Shihuang, nacui faxisi zhuyi yu wenhua da geming bijiao' (Open society and its enemies: Mao Zedong and Qi Shihuang, Nazi fascism compared with the Cultural Revolution), in *Xin Shiji*, http://www.ncn.org/, accessed on 31 March 2002.

Cai Yongmei (1992), 'Zhang Yangfu chi Qian Xuesen' (Zhang Yangfu Denounces Qian Xuesen), *Kaifang zazhi* (The open journal), No. 11, pp. 68–70.

Cai Yongmei (2000), 'Liu Yuan tan Mao Liu zhizheng neimo: Liu Shaoqi zhi zi gongkai pi Mao' (Liu Yuan Talks about the inside struggle between Mao and Liu: Liu Shaoqi's son publicly criticizes Mao), *Hengguan* (Macroview) (Autumn), pp. 81–4;

Calhoun, Craig and Wasserstrom, Jeffrey N. (2003), 'The Cultural Revolution and the Democracy Movement of 1989: complexity in historical connections', in Law Kam-Yee, ed., *The Chinese Cultural Revolution Reconsidered: Beyond Purge and Holocaust*, New York: Palgrave Macmillan, pp. 241–61.

Cao Changqing (1999), 'Yihetuan jiu bu liao Zhongguo' (Boxers cannot save China), *Zhengming*, No. 6, www.caochanbgqing.com, accessed on13 May 2004.

Cao Jingqing (2004), *China along the Yellow River: Reflections on Rural Society*, introduced by Rachael Murphy and translated by Nick Harman and Huang Ruhua, London: RoutledgeCurzon.

Cao Tian Yu, ed. (2005), *The Chinese Model of Modern Development*, London and New York: Routledge.

Caoyan Jushi (2005), 'Zhongguo fangdichan yu Zhongguo jingji lameihua' (Chinese real estate and the Latin-Americanization of the Chinese economy), *Zhongguo baodao zhoukan*, http://www.mlcool.com/html/02544.htm, accessed on 22 July 2005.

CCP (1981), *Resolution on the History of the Communist Party of China*, Beijing.

Chan, Alfred (2001), *Mao's Crusade: Politics and Policy Implementation in China's Great Leap Forward*, Oxford: Oxford University Press.

— (2006), 'Mao a super monster?' *Pacific Affairs*, Vol. 79, No. 1 (Spring), pp. 97–103

Chan, Anita (2001), *China's Workers Under Assault: The Exploitation of Labor in a Globalizing Economy*, Armonk, N.Y., and London: M.E. Sharpe.

— (2003), 'A Race to the Bottom', *China Perspective*, No. 46 (March–April).

Chan, John (2004), 'Analysts warn China on verge of economic crisis', *World Socialist Website*, 18 February.

Chang, Gordon (2001), *The Coming Collapse of China*, New York: Random House.

Chang, Jung (1991), *The Wild Swans: Three Daughters of China*, London: HarperCollins.

— (2006a), *Duowei boke*, http://blog.chinesenewsnet.com/?p=16278, accessed on 3 October.

— (2006b), *Duowei boke*, http://blog.chinesenewsnet.com/?p=13117, accessed on 25 November.

— (2006c),《毛泽东-鲜为人知的故事》中文版自序, http://www.peacehall.com/cgibin/news/gb_display/print_version.cgi?art=/gb/lianzai/2006/11&link=200611220010.shtml, accessed on 15 December.

Chang, Jung and Halliday, Jon (2005), *Mao: The Untold Story*, London: Cape.

Chang, Jung (Zhang Rong) and Halidai, Qiao-en (1988), *Sun Yixian furen: Song Qingling zhuan*, Beijing: Zhongguop heping chubanshe.

Chase, Michael and Mulvenon, James (2002), *You've got Dissent? Chinese Dissident Use of the Internet and Beijing's Counter Strategies*, Santa Monica, Calif.: Rand Corporation.

Chattopadhyay, Paresh (1994), *The Marxist Concept of Capital and Soviet Experience: Essay in the Critique of Economy*, Westport, Conn.: Praeger.

Cheek, Timothy (2005), 'The new number one counter-revolutionary inside the party: academic biography of Mao', in the *The China Journal* Special

Issue, *The Portrayal of Opportunitism, Betrayal, and Manipulation in Mao's Rise to Power*, No. 55 (January), pp. 109–18.

Cheek, Timothy and Saich, Tony (1997), *New Perspective on State Socialism in China*, London and New York: M.E. Sharpe.

Chen Bisheng (2001), 'Wenge qunzhong zuzhi baokan yanjiu' (A study of newspapers and magazines of the mass organizations during the Cultural Revolution), *Xin shiji* (New Century Net), http://ncn.org, accessed on 11 June 2001.

— (2005),'2004: Zhongguo renwen' (2004: Chinese humanity), in *Shiji Zhongguo*, http://www.cc.org.cn/newcc/index.php, accessed on 8 May 2005.

Chen Donglin and Du Pu, eds (1994), *Zhonghua renmin gongheguo shilu, dian san zhuan, xia, 1972–1976* (Actual record of the PRC, Part 3, Vol. 2, 1972–76), Changchun: Jinlin renmin chubanshe.

Chen Guidi and Chun Tao (2004), 'Zhongguo nongmin diaocha' (An investigative report of the chinese peasantry), *Dangdai* (The contemporary), No. 6, 2003, and Beijing: Renmin wenxue chubanshe, 2004.

Chen Meixia (2004), 'The great reversal: transformation of healthcare in the People's Republic of China', in William C. Cockerham, ed., *Blackwell Companion to Medical Sociology*, 2nd edn, Oxford: Blackwell.

Chen Shengge (2006), '两个美国——调查中国大学生的美国观' (Two Americans: research the way Chinese university students view the USA), *Fenghua yuan* http://www.fhy.nethttp://www2.fhy.net/cgi-bin/anyboard.cgi/collections?cmd=get&cG=1313432373& zu=3131343237&v=2&gV=0&p=, accessed on 15 August 2006.

Chen Shengyong (1994) (陈剩勇), '中国传统史学的批评模式' (A model of critique in traditional Chinese historiography), 新华文摘 (Xinhua wenzhai), p. 65.

Chen Xiaonong (2006), *Chen Boda gouhou koushu huiyi* (Final oral memoirs of Chen Boda), Hong Kong: Thinkers Publishing.

Cheng, Allen T. (2004), 'Rich–poor gap among the worst, study finds: with city earnings triple rural income, mainland is on a par with Zimbabwe', *South China Morning Post*, 26 February.

Cheng Yinghong and Manning, Patrick (2003), 'Revolution in education: China and Cuba in global context, 1957–76', in *Journal of World History*, Vol. 14, No. 3, pp. 359–91.

Chengdan Jiuge (2003), 'Liu Xiaobo shuo: Meiguo zhimin di 200 nian shi Zhongguo de weiyi xiwang' (Lix Xiaobo says: China's only hope is US colonization for 200 years), *Wan wei luntan*, www.creaders.org/forums/politics/messages/466937. html, accessed on 24 February 2003.

Chin, Gregory Thomas (2003), *Building 'Capitalism with China's Characteristics': The Political Economy of Model Joint Ventures in the Automotive Industry*, PhD thesis, York University, Canada.

China Labor Watch (2004),'Puma's workers in China facing an Olympian struggle', http://www.chinalaborwatch.org/en/web/article.php?article_id=50026, accessed on 1 November 2005.

Chinese debate on the web (2003), *Wanwei luntan*, www.creaders.org/forums/politics/messages/467501.html, accessed on 25 February 2003.

Chomsky, Noam (2000), 'Millennial visions and selective vision, part one', *Z Magazine*, 10 (January).

Chou Niu (2006), '我们曾经拥有的辉煌 – – 纪念长阳'合作医疗、赤脚医生'运动四十周年' (The brilliant years we used to have: commemorate the 40th anniversary of the coop medicine and the barefoot doctor movement in Changyang), http://www.maoflag.net/Forum NoteList.asp?Board_ ID=1–3, accessed on 3 July 2006.

Chow, Gregory (1985), *The Chinese Economy*, New York: Harper and Row.

Chu Su (2006), '"Wenge" shiqi de jingji' (The economy during the Cultural Revolution), *San nong Zhongguo*, http:www.snzg.net/shonews.asp?newsid=14966, accessed on 22 June 2006.

— (2007), '"Wenge" shiqi de jingji bangkui le ma?' (Did the economy collapse during the Cultural Revolution?), *Wuyou zhi xiang*, http://www.wyzxwyzx.com/Articie/Classl4/200701/14315.html, accessed on 19 January 2007.

Chung, Olivia (2007), 'How foreign firms dodge taxes in China', *Asia Times*, 11 April.

Chuntian de Jinglei (2007), '毛泽东的大跃进，大跃进中的毛泽东' (Mao's Great Leap Forward and Mao in the Great Leap Forward), *Wuyou zhixiang*, http://www. wyzxwyzx.com/Article/Class14/200706/19605.html, accessed on 15 June 2007.

Coale, Ansley J. (1984), *Rapid Population Change in China, 1952–1982*, Report No.27, Committee on Population and Demography, Washington D.C.: National Academy Press.

Cody, Edward (2007), 'Text messages giving voice to Chinese', Washingtonpost.com, http://www.washingtonpost.com/wp-dyn/content/article/2007/06/27/AR2007062702962.html?hpid=topnews, accessed on 29 June 2007.

Cohen, Paul (1988), 'The post-Mao reforms in historical perspective', *Journal of Asian Studies*, Vol. 43, No. 3, pp. 519–41.

Cui Zhiyuan (1996), 'Mao Zedong wenge lilun de deshi yu xiandaixing' (The loss and gains of the Cultural Revolution theory and its modernity), *Hong Kong Journal of Social Sciences*, No. 7 (Spring), pp. 8–17.

Cumings, Bruce, 'Fear and loathing on the Pyongyang Trail: North Korea and the United States' (expanded and annotated version of a review essay that appeared in the *London Review of Books*), *Japan Focus*, 12 December 2005.

Dai Huang (2002), 'Lushan huiyi dao wenhua da geming (yi)' (From the Lushan Conference to the Cultural Revolution, part one), in *Huaxia wenzhai* (Chinese Digest), http://www.cnd.org/HXWZ/ZK02, accessed on 3 March 2002.

Dai Yugong (2006) (戴愚公), in *Zhongguo gongren wang*, http://www.zggr.org/index.php?entry=entry060516–143452, accessed on 4 July 2006.

Dan Shilian (2000), '*Chuangwai yese zheng cangmang: Luo Ruiqing zhi nü Luo Diandian dui Mao Zedong wangguo de zhiyi*' (The dusk of the night outside the window: Luo Ruiqing's daughter Luo Diandian questions Mao's kingdom), *Hengguan* (Macroview), (Autumn), pp. 90–3.

Dao Jiafang (1994), *Zouxiang huimie* (Towards destruction), Beijing: Guangming ribao chubanshe.

Davies, David (2002), Remembering Red: Memory and Nostalgia for the Cultural Revolution in 1990's China, Ph.D. Dissertation. Seattle, Washington: University of Washington.

Davin, Delia (2005), *The Times Higher Education Supplement*, No. 1704, 12 August.

De Certeau, Michel (1997), *The Capture of Speech and Other Political Writings*, Minneapolis and London: University of Minnesota Press.

Dearing J.W. and Rogers, E.M. (1996), *Agenda Setting* London: Sage.

DeBorja, Q.M. and Xu L. Dong, eds (1996), *Manufacturing History: Sex, Lies and Random House's Memoirs of Mao's Physician*, New York: China Study Group.

Deng Liqun, Ma Hong and Wu Heng, eds (1991), *Dangdai Zhongguo renwu zhuanji* (biographies of contemporary Chinese personalities), Beijing: Dangdai Zhongguo chubanshe.

Deng Maomao (1993), *Wode fuqing Deng Xiaoping* (My father Deng Xiaoping*), Hong Kong: Sanlian shudian.

— (2000), *Wode fuqing Deng Xiaoping: wenge suiyue* (My father Deng Xiaoping: the Cultural Revolution years), Beijing: Zhongyang wenxian chubanshe.

Deng Xiaoping (1972), 'Deng Xiaoping gei Mao Zedong de xin' (Deng Xiaoping's letter to Mao Zedong), 1972, *Shiji xuetang*, http://www.ccforum.org.cn/viewthread. php?tid=16401&extra=page%3D3, accessed 21 July 2005.

— (2007), '思想更解放一些，改革的步子更快一些' (Be more liberated in thinking and make more rapid progress in reform), in *Selected Works of*

Deng Xiaoping, Vol. 3, published by the *People's Daily*, electronic version, http://web.peopledaily.com. cn/deng/, accessed on 11 May 2007.

Dian Dian, *Feifan de niandai* (Extraordinary years), Shanghai: Shanghai wenyi chubanshe, 1987.

Ding Dong (2006), 'Zhuisui Mao Zedong de "fangeming": chong fang yuan shudu gaoxiao "hongweibing' lingxiu"' (The 'reactionaries' who followed Mao Zedong: a revisit of the former university "Red Guard" leaders), *Chunlai chaguan of guofeng luntan*, http://www.guofengnet. org/bbs/forum.php?f=4, accessed on 4 August.

Dirlik, Arif (1996), 'Reversals, ironies, hegemonies: notes on the contemporary historiography of modern China', *Modern China*, Vol. 22, No. 3 (July), pp. 243–84.

— (2006), 'The Cultural Revolution after "the Cultural Turn"', June 9–10 2006 Hong Kong Conference on The Fortieth Anniversary: Rethinking the Genealogy and Legacy of the Cultural Revolution, sponsored by the China Study Group, *Monthly Review*, and the Contemporary China Research Center of City University of Hong Kong.

Dittmer, Lowell (2005), 'Pitfalls of charisma', in the *The China Journal* Speical Issue, *The Portrayal of Opportunitism, Betrayal, and Manipulation in Mao's Rise to Power*, No. 55 (January), pp. 118–28.

Dong Bian, Tan Deshan and Zeng Bai (1992), *Mao Zedong he ta de mishu Tian Jianying* (Mao Zedong and his secretary Tian Jiaying*)*, Beijing: Zhongyang wenxian chubanshe.

Dong Qinyuan (2004), '一个尊毛者的几点看法' (Some views of someone who admires Mao), personal communication, 15 March.

Dong, Madeline Yu (2006), 'Comments', at the 'Is a History of the Cultural Revolution Possible' workshop with Professor Allan Badiou, Washington University, Seattle, 22–26 January 2006.

Donnet, Pierre-Antoine (1994), *Tibet: Survival in Question*, Delhi and London: Oxford University Press.

Dou Edong (2007), '人民公社的解体' (The dismantling of the People's Commune), in *Wanwei tian xia luntan* (www.creaders.org), htlp://bbs4.creaders.nel/forums/poli tics/messages/l549029.html, accessed on 18 April 2007.

Dower, John W. (2006), 'Throwing off Asia: woodblock prints of the Sino-Japanese War (1994–95) & Russio-Japanese war (1904–5)' MIT Visualizing Cultures website, accessed on 15 May 2006.

Dreze, Jean and Sen, Amartya (1989), *Hunger and Public Action*, Oxford: Clarendon Press, and New York: Oxford University Press.

Du Guang (2005), 'Qingcha zhengdun xuehan gongchang' (Clean up the sweatshops), *Shiji Zhongguo xilie luntan*, http://www.ccforum.

org.cn/viewthread.php?tid= 18091&extra=page%3D2, accessed on 9 August 2005.

Dutton, Michael (1992), *Policing and Punishment in China: From Patriarchy to 'the People'*, Cambridge: Cambridge University Press.

— (2005), *Policing Chinese Politics: A History*, Durham: Duke University Press.

Eiji, Oguma (2007), 'Postwar Japanese intellectuals: changing perspectives on "asia" and "modernity"', translated by Roger Brown, *Japan Focus*, http://japanfocus.org/products/details/2350, accessed on 13 February 2007.

Einhorn, Bruce (2004a), 'China drawing world's best architects', *Wall Street Journal*, 11 January.

— (2004b),'If China cools, will Asia freeze?' *Business Week*, 12 January.

Eldridge J., Kitzinger J. and Williams, K. (1997), *The Mass Media and Power in Britain*, Oxford: Oxford University Press.

Elegant, Robert (1994), 'Mao the monster', *Far Eastern Economic Review*, 22 December.

Emerson, Tony (2000), 'A letter to Jiang Zemin: the quixotic tale of three American CEOs and their ill-fated mission to change China from inside', *Newsweek International*, 29 May.

Endicott, Stephen (1989), *Red Earth: Revolution in a Sichuan Village*, Toronto: NC Press (supported by the University of Toronto/York University, Joint Centre for Asia Pacific Studies).

Esherick, Joseph W., Paul G. Pickowicz and Andrew Walder (2006), 'The Chinese Cultural Revolution as history: an introduction', in Joseph W. Esherick, Paul G. Pickowicz and Andrew Walder, eds, *The Chinese Cultural Revolution as History*, Stanford, Calif.: California University Press, pp. 1–28.

Fan Daren (1999), *Wenge yubi chenfulu: Liangxiao wangshi* (Rise and fall of the loyal pen of the Cultural Revolution: recollections of Liangxiao), Hong Kong: Mingjing chubanshe youxian gongsi.

Fei Xiaotong (1987), *Jiang cun jingji: Zhongguo nongmin de shenghuo* (Peasant life in China), Xianggang jiulong: Zhonghua shu ju.

— (1992), *From the Soil: The Foundations of Chinese Society*, a translation of Fei Xiaotong's *Xiangtu Zhongguo* (Earthbound China), Berkeley, Calif.: University of California Press.

Fenby, Jonathan (2005), 'Storm rages over bestselling book on monster Mao: China experts attack biography's "misleading" sources', *Observer*, http://www.observer.co.uk, accessed on 15 October 2005.

Feng Chongyi (1989), *Nongmin yishi yu Zhongguo* (Peasant consciousness and China), Hong Kong: Zhonghua shuju.

— (2003), 'Huainian Li Shenzhi xiansheng' (Remembering Mr Li Shenzhi), *Huaren Ribao* (Chinese Daily), 21–22 June.

Feng Xianzhi (1996), '毛泽东和他的秘书田家英' (Mao Zedong and his secretary Tian Jiaying), Beijing: Zhongyang wenxian chubanshe.

Feng Yuqing (1994), *Yi fuqin, yi zhuxi, yi Guanhua* (Memories of father, the Chairman and Guanhua), Shanghai: Shanghai wenyi chubanshe.

Fenghua yuan (2007) (枫华园), '春节又一个节目深深打动了中国人的心' (Another Spring Festival performance moves the Chinese), http://www2.fhy.net//cgi-bin/anyboard.cgi/collections?cmd=get& cG-13, accessed on 21 February 2007.

Fernandez, Nei (1997), *Capitalism and Class Struggle in the USSR: A Marxist Theory*, Aldershot, Sydney: Ashgate.

Field, Robert (1986), 'The performance of industry during the Cultural Revolution', *China Quarterly*, 108 (December), pp. 625–42.

Fitzgerald, John (1999), 'In the scale of history: politics and culture in twentieth-century China', *Twentieth-Century China*, Vol. 24, No. 2 (April), pp. 1–28.

Fogel, Joshua A. (1997), 'Mendacity and veracity in the recent Chinese communist memoir literature', in Timothy Cheek and Tony Saich, eds, *New Perspective on State Socialism in China*, London and New York: M.E. Sharpe, pp. 354–58.

Forster, Keith (2003), 'The Cultural Revolution in Zhejiang revisited: the paradox of rebellion and factionalism, and violence and social conflict amidst economic growth', in Law Kam-Yee, ed., *The Chinese Cultural Revolution Reconsidered: Beyond Purge and Holocaust*, New York, Palgrave Macmillan, pp. 123–15.

French, Howard, W. (2005), 'Putting a knife into heart of the Chairman's legend', *San Francisco Chronicle*, Sunday, 23 October.

— (2007), 'The Saturday profile: carving coal miners, he churns China', *New York Times*, 14 July 2007.

Friedman, Edward, Pickowicz, Paul G. and Selden, Mark with Johnson, Kay Ann (1991), *Chinese Village, Socialist State*, New Haven: Yale University Press.

Funkhouser, G.R. (1973),'The issues of the sixties: an exploratory study in the dynamics of public opinion', *Public Opinion Quarterly*, 37, pp. 62–75.

Furet, François (1981), *Interpreting the French Revolution*, Cambridge: Cambridge: University Press.

Furet, F. and Ozouf, M. (1989) *A Critical Dictionary of the French Revolution* (trans. A. Goldhammer), Harvard University Press.

Fuxi (2007), *Renmin wang qiangguo luntan* (The people net, strong nation forum), http://bbs.people.com.cn/postDetail.do?view=1&id=2121 777&boardId=2, accessed on 27 April 2007.

Gan Yang (1989), 'Ziyou de linian: wusi chuantong zhi queshimian' (The idea of freedom: some faults of the May Fourth Tradition), in Lin Yusheng, ed., *Wusi de duoyuan fansi* (Multireflections on the May Fourth movement), Hong Kong: Sanlian chubanshe, pp. 62–81.

Gao Changquan (2006), '深化改革是中国的唯一出路' (Further deepening reform is the only way out for China), *Yanhuang chunqiu*, No. 9 (September).

Gao Gao and Yan Jiaqi (1988), *Shi nian wenhua da geming shi* (Ten-year history of the Cultural Revolution), Tianjin: Tianjin renmin chubanshe.

Gao Liang (2007), '外资对我国企业兼并控制情况的资料' (Data on takeover and control of Chinese enterprises by foreign capital), email message from Wang Shaoguang [b887706@mailserv.cuhk.edu.hk], accessed on 1 July 2007.

Gao, Mobo (1995), 'Memoirs and interpretation of the Cultural Revolution', *Bulletin of Concerned Asian Scholars*, Vol. 27, No. 1 (January–March), pp. 49–58.

— (1998), 'Chinese reality and writings by Chinese expatriates', *Bulletin of Concerned Asian Scholars*, Vol. 30, No. 3 (July–September), pp. 61–8.

— (1999a), *Gao Village: Rural Life in Modern China*, London: C. Hurst; Hawaii: Hawaii University Press; Hong Kong: Hong Kong University Press; Bathurst: Crawford House Publishers.

— (1999b), 'Manufacturing of truth and culture of the elite', *Journal of Contemporary Asia*, Vol. 29: No. 3 (mid-August), pp. 309–27.

— (2003), 'The Great Wall that divides two Chinas and the rural/urban disparity challenge', in Joseph Cheng, ed., *China's Challenges in the Twenty-First Century*, Hong Kong: City University of Hong Kong Press, pp. 533–57.

— (2004), 'The rise of neo-nationalism and the new left: a post-colonial and postmodernism perspective', in Leong Liew and Shaoguang Wang, eds, *Nationalism, Democracy and National Integration in China*, London: RoutledgeCurzon, pp. 44–62.

— (2004–2006), 'Media ownership: one case study and two perspectives', *The International Journal of Humanities*, Vol. 2, No. 3, pp. 2103–12.

— (2005), field research, Gao Village, February.

Garnault, Ross and Song Ligang (2000), 'Private business eclipses state sector in China, study shows', AP October, http://www.hartford-hwp.com/archives/55/213.html, accessed on 2 November 2007.

Gellman, Marc and Hartman, Tom (2002), *Reader's Digest*, April, p. 98.

Giad, Luce (1997), 'Introduction: how tomorrow is already being born', in Michel de Certeaqu, *The Capture of Speech and Other Political Writings*, Minneapolis and London: University of Minnesota Press, pp. vii–xix.

Gilboy, George (2004), 'The myth behind China's miracle', *Foreign Affairs* online (July/August), http://www.foreignaffairs.org/20040701

faessay83405/george-j-gilboy/the-myth-behind-china-s-miracle.html, accessed on 7 December 2006,

Gilley, Bruce (1998), *Tiger on the Brink: Jiang Zemin and China's New Elite*, Berkeley, Calif.: University of California Press.

— (2001a),'They're back', *Far Eastern Economic Review*, October 18, p. 34.

— (2001b), 'Tiger on the brink', 159–61; *Far Eastern Economic Review*, Vol. 200, No. 8 (June 29), pp. 8–9.

Gong Chu (1978), *Gong Chu jiangjun huiyi lu* (Memoirs of General Gong Chu), Vols 1 and 2, Hong Kong: Ming Pao chubanshe.

Guan Weixun (1993), *Wo suo zhidao de Ye Chun* (The Ye Chun that I knew), Beijing: Zhongguo wenxuechubanshe.

Guardian (2005), 'This book will shake the world', Inside story, 26 May.

Guo Hailiang (2007), Zhongguo lüliang shan qu pinkun wenti yanjiu, PhD thesis, University of Sydney Technology.

Guo Jingrui (2002), The Features and Significance of Jingju (Peking Opera) Plays (1780–1911), PhD dissertation, University of Tasmania.

Guo Jinrong (1990), *Mao Zedong de huanghun suiyue* (The last days of Mao Zedong), Hong Kong: Tiandi tushu youxian gongsi.

Guo Yingqiu, with Wang Junyi (2002), 'Guo Yingqiu linzhong koushu "wenge qin li ji"' (Guo Yingqiu's death bed oral account of personal experience of the Cultural Revolution), *Yanhuang chunqiu*, 128 (November), pp. 44–53.

Guo, Yingjie (2004), *Cultural Nationalism in Contemporary China: The Search for National Identity under Reform*, London: RoutledgeCurzon.

Haar, Barend J. ter (2002), 'China's inner demons: the political impact of the demonological paradigm', in Woei Lien Chong, ed., *China's Great Proletarian Cultural Revolution: Master Narratives and Post-Mao Conternarratives*, Lanham, Boulder, New York and Oxford: Rowman & Littlefield, pp. 27–68.

Hacking, I. (1995), *Rewriting the Soul: Multiple Personality and the Sciences of Memory*, Princeton, NJ: Princeton University Press.

Halliday, Jon (1973), *Japanese Imperialism Today*, Association for Radical East Asian Studies.

Halliday, Jon (1974), *Jinri Xianggang* (Hong Kong today), trans. Yi Qun, Hong Kong: Qishi niandai zazhi.

Halliday, Jon (1988), *Korea: The Unknown War*, Pantheon Press.

Han Deqiang (2006), 'Wushi nian, sanshi nian he ershi nian' (50 years, 30 years and 20 years), *Wuyou zhixiang*, http://www.wyzxsx.com/book/012.doc, accessed on 12 August 2006.

Han Yanming (2004), 'Zhiyi Suzhou GDP shenhua' (Question the Suzhou GDP miracle), *Zhongguo baodao zhoukan-dianzi zazhi* (China report weekly – electronic journal), No. 373, ChinaNewsletter@163.net, accessed on 26 October 2004.

Hanley, Charles J and Mendoza, Martha (2007), 'The massacre at Non gun ri: army letter reveals U.S. intent' *Japan Focus*, http://japanfocus.org/products/detaisl/2408, accessed on 11 April 2007.

Hao, Yen-p'ing (1970), *The Comprador in Nineteenth Century China: Bridge between East and West*, Cambridge, Mass.: Harvard University Press.

Harrison, Ann (2003), 'Nobel Prize-nominated dissident wants to build Web site of student interest', in *Computerworld* http://www.chinasite.com/content/Interviews/cailing/computerworld19990506.html, accessed on 19 June 2003.

Hart-Landsberg, Martin and Burkett, Paul (2004), 'China & socialism: market reforms and class struggle', *Monthly Review*, Vol. 56, No. 3 (July–August).

— (2005a), *China and Socialism: Market Reform and Class Struggle*, New York: Monthly Review Press.

— (2005b), 'Thinking about China', *Monthly Review*, http://mrzine.org/, accessed on 30 July.

— (2007), 'China, capitalist accumulation, and labor', *Monthly Review*, Vol. 59 No. 1 (May), pp. 17–39.

Haynes, Mike (2002), 'Marxism and the Russian question in the wake of the Soviet collapse', *Historical Materialism*, Vol. 10, No. 4, 317–62.

He Fang (2005) '何方',《党史笔记：从遵义会议到延安整风》上、下' (notes on the CCP history: from the Zunyi conference to Yan'an rectification movement), 香港:利文出版社.

He Qinglian (2005), 'Zhonggong zhengfu guanli xia de Zhongguo jingji' (The Chinese economy under the control of the CCP government), *Da ji yuan*, http://www.dajiyuan.com/gb/4/12/15/n78244.htm, accessed on 4 January 2005.

He Xuefeng (2007), 'Zhongguo nongcun shehui zhuanxing jiqi kunjing', *Wuyou zhixiang* (The transformation of rural China and its difficulties), http://www.wyzxwyzx.com/Article/Classl9/200702/15342.html, accessed on 22 February 2007.

He Yuan (2007), '对《李锐郑州受窘……》一文的几点补充' (Some more points to support the report of how Li Rui was embarrassed), *Wuyou zhixiang*, http://www.wyzxwyzx.com/Article/Search.asp?Field=Author&ClassID=&keyword=%BA%CE%D4%B6&Submit=+%CB%D1%CB%F7+, accessed on 23 August 2007.

He Zhiguang (2007) (何之光),'《土地改革法》的夭折' (The death of the land reform law) (originally appeared *in Yanhuang chunqiu* No. 8, 2006), http://cn.qikan.com/gbqikan/view_article.asp?titleid=yhcq20060803, accessed on 27 April 2007.

Hearst, Nancy and Saich, Tony (1997),'Newly available sources on the CCP history from the People's Republic of China', in Timothy Cheek and

Tony Saich, eds, *New Perspective on State Socialism in China*, London and New York: M.E. Sharpe, pp. 323–38.

Heartfield, James (2004), 'China's comprador capitalism is coming home', *Review of Radical Political Economy*, Vol. 37, No. 2, pp, 96–214.

— (2005), 'Mao: The end of the affair', http://www.spiked-online.com/Articles/0000000 CAC41.htm, accessed on 4 July 2005.

Hensher, Phillip (2005), www.seattlepi.com, accessed on 6 August 2005.

Hinton, William (1983), *Shenfan*, New York: Random House.

— (1990), *The Great Reversal: The Privatization of China, 1978–1989*, New York: Monthly Review Press.

— (1993), 'Can the Chinese dragon match pearls with the Dragon God of the Sea? A response to Zongli Tang', *Monthly Review*, Vol. 45 No. 3, pp. 87–104.

Ho, Dahpon David (2006), 'Quotes from Zhou Enlai's talk in "To protect the preserve: resisting the destruction of the four olds campaign, 1966–1967"', in Joseph W. Esherick, Paul G. Pickowicz and Andrew Walder, eds, *The Chinese Cultural Revolution as History*, Stanford, Calif.: California University Press, pp. 64–96.

Holmstrom, Nancy and Smith, Richard (2000) 'The necessity of gangster capitalism: primitive accumulation in Russia and China', *Monthly Review*, 52, 2: 1–15.

http://www2.fhy.net/cgi.bin/anyboard.cgi/collections?cmd=get&cG =93735383&zu= 39373538&v=2&gV=0&p=, accessed on 30 January 2006.

Hu Qiaomu (1994), *Hu Qiaomu huiyi Mao Zedong* (Hu Qiaomu remembers Mao Zedong), Beijing: Renmin chubanshe.

Hu Xingdou (2005), 'Zai Zhongguo nongcun luntan de fayan' (A talk at the Zhongguancun forum), *Shiji Zhongguo xilie luntan*, http://www.ccforum.org.cn/index.php, accessed on 27 February 2005.

Huang Any Yinan (2004), Swimming against the Tide: Tracing and Locating Chinese Leftist Online, MA dissertation, B.A. Simon Fraser University.

Huang Ping (2004), 'Cuo wei: nongmin xuqiu yu zhidu gongji zhijian de maodun (Wrong position: the contradiction between rural demand and institutional supply), seminar speech, *shi ji Zhongguo* http://www.cc.org.cn/newcc/browwenzhang. php?articleid=350, accessed on 24 February 2004.

Huang Yunsheng (2007), '戳穿李锐谎言，还毛主席清白' (Lay bare Li Rui's lie and clear Chairman Mao's name), *Wuyouzhixiang*, http://www.wyzxwyzx.com/Article/ Class14/200708/22985.html, accessed on 18 August 2007.

Hughes, Christopher R. (2003), 'Review essay: China and the Internet: a question of politics or management?' *China Quarterly*, No. 157 (September), pp. 818–24.

Hughes, Christopher R. and Wacker, Gudrun, eds (2003), *China and the Internet: Politics of the Digital Leap Forward*, London: RoutledgeCurzon.

Hutton, William (2005), 'Complex legacy of Chairman Mao', *Observer*, Sunday 29 May.

— (2007), *The Writing on the Wall: China and the West in the 21st Century*, U.K.: Little, Brown.

Ji Xianlin (1998), *Niu peng zayi* (Random memories of the cowshed), Beijing: Zhonggong zhongyang dangxiao chubanshe.

Jiang Bo and Li Qing (1993), *Lin Biao 1959 nian yihou* (Lin Biao after 1959), Chengdu: Sichuan renmin chubanshe.

Jiang Chuangang (2006), 'Mao Zedong shidai shi ruhe jiejue renmin de chifan wenti de' (How the problem of feeding the Chinese was solved during the era of Mao), *San nong Zhongguo*, http:www.snzg.net/shonews.asp?newsid=14978, accessed on 22 June 2006.

Jiang Zhenghua and Li Nan (1985),'中国人口动态参数的校正' (Corrections on the dynamic parameter of the Chinese population), 西安交通大学学报,, No. 3, pp. 46 and 64.

— (1989) (蒋正华), '中国人口动态估计的方法和结果' (Approach and outcome of estimating the dynamics of the Chinese population), 中国人口年鉴, 1987年 , (Chinese population yearbook 1987), Beijing: 经济管理出版社, 1989, pp. 94–106.

Jiao Ye (1993), *Ye Chun zhi mi, yi ge mishu yanzhong de Ye Chun yu Lin Biao* (The riddle of Ye Chun, Ye Chun and Lin Biao in the eyes of a secretary), Beijing: Zhongguo wenlian chuban gongsi.

Jin Hui (1993), '灾害'备忘录' (Memorandum of 'natural disasters') , 社会 (Society), Nos 4–5, pp. 13–22.

Jin Xiaoding (2005) 'A critique of J. Chang and J. Halliday's book, *Mao the Untold Story*', http://www.geocities.com/jinxiaoding, accessed on 12 December 2005.

Jin Xinyi (2005), 'Suzhou "Dongguan hua" de youlü' (The worry about the Dongguan model in Suzhou), *Zhongguo baodao zhoukan-dianzi zazhi* (China report weekly – electronic journal), No. 395, ChinaNewsletter @163.net, accessed on 16 April 2005.

Jingan Jushi (2007), (静庵居士), '中国应当客观历史地评价毛泽东功过 (1)' (China should objectively and historically asessess the merits and demerits of Mao Zedong), *Tian xian luntan*, www.creaders.org, http://bbs4.creaders.net/forums/politics/messages/1550987.html, accessed on 22 May 2007.

Joint Economic Committee, Congress of the United States (1978), *Chinese Economy Post-Mao*, Washington, D.C.: US Government Printing Office, p. x.

Kahn, Joseph (2007), 'Murdoch's dealings with China: it's business, and it's Personal', *New York Times*, http://www.nytimes.com/2007/06/26/world/asia/26murdoch.html?pagewanted=1&ei=5070&en=84d72527 f60f5ad1&ex=1183521600&emc=eta1, accessed on 26 June 2007.

Kakutani, Michiko (2005), 'China's monster, second to none', *New York Times*, 21 October.

Kalathil, Shanthi and Boas, Taylor C. (2003), *The Impact of the Internet on Authoritarian Rule*, Washington, D.C.: Carnegie Endowment for International Peace.

Kane, Penny (1988), *Famine in China, 1959–61: Demographic and Social Implications*, Basingstoke: Macmillan.

Kao Yan, 'Yi ge lixiu gan bu de xinsheng', *Wuyou zhi xiang, zhongyao cankao ziliao* (Important reference materials on the Utopia website), http://www.wyzxsx.com/book/013.doc, accessed on 2 October 2005.

Kipnis, Andrew (1995), 'Within and against peasantness: backwardness and filiality in rural China', *Comparative Studies in Society and History*, Vol. 37, No. 1 (January), pp. 110–35.

— (2003), 'Neo-leftists versus Neo-Liberals: PRC Intellectual Debates in the 1990s', *Journal of Intercultural Studies*, Vol. 24, No. 3, pp. 239–51.

Kitzinger J. (1993)'Understanding AIDS: media messages and what people know about AIDS', in J.J. Eldridge, ed., *Getting the Message, News Truth and Power*, London: Routledge.

— (1999), 'A sociology of media power: key issues in audiences reception research', in G. Philo, ed., *Message Received*, Harlow: Longman.

Kolo, Vincent (2007), 'China's "McScandal" shows the need for real trade unions', *Chinaworker*, http://www.chinaworker.org/en/content/news/169/, accessed on 27 May 2007.

Kong Dongmei (2006), 'Qing yi tebie nong: Mao Zedong Liu Shaoqi liang jia houren jihui ji' (Feeling especially deep: meeting of the descendants of Mao and Liu), http://www.popyard.org, accessed on 1 March 2006.

Kong Qingdong (2006), 'Gen fuqin zun niu peng' (At the cowshed with father), *Wan wei tian xia luntan*, http://www4.bbsland.com/forums/politics/messages/5452.html, accessed on 20 May 2006.

Kong Shuyu (1999), 'Swan and spider eater in problematic memoirs of cultural revolution', *Position*, Vol. 7, No. 1 (Spring), pp. 241–52.

Kristof, Nickolas D., 'Mao: the Real Mao', *Times Book Review*, 23 October 2005, pp. 1 and 10.

Ku Duo (2005), 江青评传 (A biography of Jiang Qing), http://www.atgig.com/ezln/jiangqingBio.htm, *Wuyou zhi xiang, renmin chunqiu* http://www.chinese-leftists.org/ziliao/index.php?dirpath=./左派文集&order=0, accessed on 15 November 2005.

Kwong, Peter (2006), 'China's neoliberal dynasty', *The Nation*, http://www.thenation.com/doc/20061002/kwong, accessed on 17 November 2006.

Kynge, James (2004), 'China's urban workforce fuels rural economy', *Financial Times*, 25 February.

La Jiaocheng (2007), '中国评选出'新四大发明', 杂交水稻入选' (Of the four voted new great inventions in China, hybrid rice is one), *Feng hua yan*, http://www2.fhy.net/cgi-bin/anyboard.cgi/collections?cmd=get&cG=13, accessed on 11 February 2007.

Lan Yezi (2006) (兰叶子), '从思闻论江青的贴子来看，女人从政坏处多多' (from Si Wen's blog on Jiang Qing, women in politics is bad), *Zhongguo wenge yan jiu wang*, http://www.wengewang.org/bencandy.php?id=2402, accessed on 15 May 2006.

Lange, David (2002), 'Revolutionary discovery', *Far Eastern Economic Review*, 14 March, pp. 34–37.

— (2005), 'China Overtakes U.S. as Tech Supplier', *International Herald Tribune*, 12 December.

Landsberger, Stefan R. (2002), 'The deification of Mao: religious imagery and practices during the Cultural Revolution and beyond', in Woei Lien Chong, ed., *China's Great Proletarian Cultural Revolution: Master Narratives and Post-Mao Counternarratives*, Lanham, Boulder, New York and Oxford: Rowman & Littlefield, pp. 139–85.

Lao Gui (1987), *Xuese huanghun* (Blood red sunset), Beijing: Gongren Chubanshe.

Lao Tian (2004), 'Lao Tian vs Duo Yuan: Wenge yanjiu ji qita' (Lao Tian versus Duo Yuan: Cultural Revolution studies and others), June 2004, http://laotianlaotian.yeah.net, accessed on 14 September 2005.

— (2006a), '科学'的经济学理论只能是对应着'技术力'的成长条件——读钟庆新书《刷盘子还是读书》' (Scientific theory promotes growth only in corresponding technological conditions on Zhong Qing's new book *Wash dishes or study*), http://www.wyzxsx.com/xuezhe/laotian/ShowArticle.asp?ArticleID=208 accessed on 24 May 2006.

— (2006b), 'Wenge hou 'jiyi gaizao gongcheng de chengjiu' (The achievement of manufacturing memories after the Cultural Revolution), *Wan wei tian xia luntan* http://www4.bbsland.com/forums/politics/messages/1501536.html, accessed on 26 May 2006.

— (2006c), '党史国史研究中'李杜范式'的困境——兼评张素华新著《变局——七千人大会始末》' (The dilmma of the Li Du model in Chinese historiography and on Zhang Suhua's new book *Changing chessboard: what happened during the 7,000 participant conference*), http://bbs1.people.com.cn/postDetail.do?bid=2&treeView=1&view=2&id=971630 ren min wang jiang guo luntan, accessed on 28 November 2006.

— (2007a), '质疑小岗村'分田密约'并展望中国农业的未来' (On questioning 'the secret contract of dividing the land' by Xiaogang village and the future of China's agriculture), http://www.wyzxsx.com/xuezhe/laotian/ShowArticle. asp?ArticleID=88, accessed on 21 May 2007.

— (2007b),安徽的官老爷把小岗村的故事越编越传奇'(Anhui officialdom fabricated the Xiaogang village story to a legend), http://www.wyzxsx.com/xuezhe/laotian/ShowArticle.asp?ArticleID=143, accessed on 21 May 2007.

— (2007c), 重庆文革口述史-黄廉访谈录 (Oral history of the Cultural Revolution in Chongqing: interviews with Huang Qian), http://www.recordhistory.org/mediawiki/index.php/Category:%E9%87%8D%E5%BA%86%E5%8F%A3%E8%BF%B0%E6%96%87%E9%9D%A9%E5%8F%B2, accessed on 23 November 2007.

Lardy, Nicholas (1978), *Economic Growth and Distribution in China*, Cambridge and New York: Cambridge University Press.

— (2006), 'China's economy: problems and prospects', a presentation at at Carthage College, Kenosha, Winsconsin, 21–22 October.

Latham, Kevin (2007), 'SMS, communication and citizenship in China's Information Society', *Crtical Asian Studies*, Vol. 39, No. 2, pp. 295–314.

Lau, Kin Chin (2004), 'What kind of knowledge do we need'; an interview with Kin Chi Lau by Tani E Barlow, *Positions East Asia Cultures Critique*, Vol. 12, No. 1, pp. 203–36.

Law, Kam-Yee, ed. (2003), *The Chinese Cultural Revolution Reconsidered: Beyond Purge and Holocaust*, New York, Palgrave Macmillan.

Lee Hong Yong (2003), 'Historical reflections on the Cultural Revolution as a political movement', in Law, Kam-Yee, ed., *The Chinese Cultural Revolution Reconsidered: Beyond Purge and Holocaust*, New York, Palgrave Macmillan, pp. 92–112.

Lee Ching Kwan, ed. (2007), *Working in China: Ethnographies of Labor and Workplace Transformation*, London and New York: Routledge.

Lesson (2006), '往事并不如烟, 毛主席为中国科研基础和体系建立做了些什么?' (The past is not like smoke: what the Chairman did for the establishment of China's scientifice research base and system), *Tian xia luntan* http://www4.bbsland. com/forums/politics/messages/1511804.html, accessed on 17 July 2006.

Leung Laifong (1994), *Morning Sun: Interviews with Chinese Writers of the Lost Generation*, Armonk, N.Y., and London: M.E. Sharpe.

Leys, Simon (1988), *The Burning Forest: Essays on Culture and Politics in Contemporary China*. London: Paladin Grafton Books.

Li Changping (2002), *Wo xiang zongli shuo shihua* (I told the truth to the premier), Beijing: Guangming ribao chubanshe.

— (2004), 'Sannong wenti hui bu hui daozhi Zhongguo bengkui' (Would the rural problems lead to the collapse of China?), *New Century Net*, http://www.ncn.org/asp/ zwginfo, accessed on 9 March 2004.

— (2005), 'Wo de tongzhi weishenme zai guowai?' (Why are my comrades overseas?), *Shiji xuetang*, http://www.cc.org.cn/newcc/browwen zhang.php?articelid_ =3827, accessed on 6 June 2005.

Li Chengrui (1987), 《中国人口普查及结果分析》(Analysis of the oucome of China's population census), Beijing: 中国财政经济出版社, 1987 .

Li Ming (2004), 'Da chuguo he da chuxue' (Big overseas trips and big bleeding), in *Meiri wenzhai* (Daily Digest), http://www.clibrary. com.digest/pool/13Z196836.html, accessed on 15 March 2004.

Li Qiang (2005), 'Zhongguo kuanggong shi shijie shang zui weixian de gongzuo' (Mining in China is the most dangerous job in the whole world), chinalaborwatch@yahoogroups.com on behalf of clwvolunteer (clwvolunteer@yahoo.com), accessed on 8 August 2005.

Li Rui (1994), *庐山会议实录：毛泽东秘书手记* (Actual record of the Lushan Conference: notes by the secretary of Mao Zedong), Zhengzhou: Henan renmin chubanshe.

Li Weihan (1986), *Huiyi yu yanjiu, shang, xia* (Memoirs and studies Vol. I and II), Beijing: Zhongyang dangshi zilian chubanshe.

Li Xiguang (2005), 'Live coverage of lies or truth?', http://www. tbsjournal.com/Archives/Spring04/paper.htm, accessed on 24 May 2005.

Li Xuanyuan (2006), '用邓朴方的残疾人数据观照邓公子的人权控诉' (Match Prince Deng's human rights condemnation with Mr Deng Pufang's number of the disabled), *duowe boke*, http://blog. chinesenewsnet.com/?p=18679, accessed on 12 December 2006.

— (2007), '我对廖伯康说的'四川饿死1000多万人'的评说' (My comment on Liao Bokang's assertion that more than 10 million died of starvation in Sichuan), http://blog.chinesenewsnet.com/?p=26031, accessed on 24 May 2007.

Li Xuefeng, Wu De and Wang Dongxing et al (2004), (李雪峰、吴德、汪东兴), 《回首'文革'》(Look back to the Cultural Revolution), Beijing: 中共党史出版社.

Li Yang (2006), 'Daibiao renmin yu daibaio wenming' (To represent the people and to represent civilization), *Tian xian luntan, ww.creaders.org*, http://www4.bbsland.com/forums/politics/messages/1537269.htm l, accessed on 16 December 2006.

Li Yong, ed. (1993), *Zuo ye xingchen* (Stars of last night), Beijing: Zhongyang minzu xueyuan chubanshe.

Li Zehou, ed. (1989), *Zhishi fenzi ping wannian Mao Zedong* (Intellectuals on the late Mao), Hong Kong: Zhongyuan chuban shiye gongsi.

Li Zhimin (1993), *Li Zhimin huiyi lu* (Memoirs of Li Zhimin), Beijing: Jiefangjun chubanshe,

Li Zhisui (1994), *The Private Life of Chairman Mao: The Memoirs of Mao's Personal Physician*, London: Chatto & Windus.

— (1996), 'A reply to questions about my memoirs', *Kaifang*, 1995 quoted in DeBorja and Dong 1996, p. 34.

Liang Heng and Judith Shapiro (1984), *Son of the Revolution*, New York: Knopf, distributed by Random House.

Liang Xiaosheng (1988), *Yi ge hongweibing de zibai* (Confession of a Red Guard), Chengdu: Sichuan wenyi chubanshe.

Lin Ke, Xu Tao and Wu Xujun (1995), *Lishi de zhenshi: Mao Zedong shenbian gongzuo renyuan de zhengyan* (The truth of history: testimony of the personnel who had worked with Mao), Hong Kong: Liwen chubanshe.

Lin Qingshan (1988), *Kang Sheng waizhuan* (An unofficial biography of Kang Sheng), Hong Kong: Xinchen chubanshe.

Lin Yu-sheng (1979), *The Crisis of Chinese Consciousness: Radical Anti-traditionalism in the May Fourth Era*, Madison, WI: University of Wisconsin Press.

Link, Perry (1983a), *People or Monsters? And Other Stories and Reportage from China after Mao*, Bloomington: Indiana University Press.

—ed. (1983b), *Stubborn Weeds: Popular and Controversial Chinese Literature after the Cultural Revolution* Bloomington: Indiana University Press.

— ed. (1984), *Roses and Thorns: The Second Blooming of the Hundred Flowers in Chinese Fiction, 1979–1980*, Berkeley, Calif.: University of California Press.

— (1994), 'Something else', *TLS* (Times Literary Supplement), 28 October.

— (2005a), *The Times Literary Supplement*, No. 5338, 22 July.

— (2005b), 'Throwing the book at Mao', www.theage.com.au, accessed on 10 June 2005.

Liu Guoguang (2005) (刘国光), 'Dui jingjixue jiaoxue he yanjiu zhong yixie wenti de kanfa' (My view on some problems in teaching and research in the field of economics), 《高校理论战线》 (The theoretical front of tertiary education), August 2005.

Liu Jian (2005), 'Qu nian wei jiejue wenbao de pinkun renkou zengjia le 80 wan ren' (去年未解决温饱的贫困人口增加了80万人, The number of people below the poverty line increased by 800,000 last year), *Renminwang*, www.people.com.cn, accessed on 5 May 2005.

Liu Pingping et al (1992), 'Zhongguo renmin de hao erzi' (Good son of the Chinese people), in Guo Simin and Tianyu, eds, *Wo yanzhong de Liu Shaoqi* (Liu Shaoqi as I see him), She Jia Zhuang: Hebei renmin chubanshe.

Liu Siqi and Wang Hebing (1993), *Gandong 'shangdi' de ren: mianhuai Mao Zedong, renmin linxiu Mao Zedong congshu* (The man who had moved

'God': cherish the memory of Mao Zedong, a Series on the People's Leader Mao Zedong), Beijing: Renshi chubanshe.

Liu Xiaobo (1989), 'Qimeng de zaihuo: wusi de piping' (The tragedy of the Enlightenment: a critique of the May Fourth), *Mingpao*, No. 5, pp. 37–44.

— (2003), 'Meiguo gong Yi zhuguan wei zi yi keguan wei renlei' (American attack on Iraq: subjectively for self-interest but objectively for the good of human kind), *Shiji shalong luntan*, http://forum/cc.org.cn/luntan/china/showcontent1.phb3?eb=I&id=107705&id1–35816, accessed on 3 March 2003.

Liu Yuan and Wang Guangmei (2000), *Ni suo bu zhidao de Liu Shaoqi* (The Liu Shaoqi that you don't know), Zhengzhou: Henan renmin chubanshe.

Long Pan (2007), 'Mao zhuxi zhuicha "gongchan feng"' (Chairman Mao investigated the Commnist wind), *Renmin wang, jiangguo luntan*, http://bbs1.people.com.cn/ postDetail.do?id=3420706&boardId=2, accessed on 14 September 2007.

Lu Hong (2002), '1972 nian zhi 1975 nian de si ci quan guo mei zhan' (The four national fine arts exhibits from 1972 to 1975), *Shiji Zhongguo* (Century China), http://www.cc.org.cn, accessed on 4 April 2002.

Ma Beiming (2003), 'Cong gu Luoma dahuo kan Ren Bumei zhi bu kexin' (From the arson of ancient Rome to see the incredibility of Ren Bumei), *Wanweiwang tianxia luntan, www.*creaders.org, accessed on 8 July 2003.

— (2006), '卞仲耘老师死亡事件与王友琴报导的失实' (The death of Teacher Bian Zhongyun and the inaccuracy of Wang Youqin's report), *Wanwei tianxia luntan* http://www4.bbsland.com/forums/politics/messages/1502208.html, accessed on 31 May 2006.

– (2007a), 'Song Bingbing bisai sharen zhimi' (The myth of Song Bingbing participating in the race of murdering people), *Wanwei tianxia luntan, www.*creader.org http://bbs4.creaders.net/forums/politics/messages/1558422.html, accessed on 17 September 2007.

— (2007b), '姑妄言之（一）' (Tell you what it is worth), *Wanwei tianxia luntan,* http://bbs4.creaders.net/forums/politics/messages/1550685.html, accessed on 15 May, 2007.

Ma Bing (马宾) et al (2007), '关于对山西黑砖窑事件等问题的认识和关于十七大的建议' (On the problem related to the Shanxi black brick kilns incidents and suggestions for the 17th CCP party congress), *Fenghua yuan* http://www2.fhy.net/cgi-bin/anyboard.cgi/collections?cmd=get&cG=1373034303&zu=3137303430&v=2&gV=0&p=, accessed on 20 July 2007.

Ma Licheng and Lin Zhijun (1998), 当代中国三次思想解放实录 (Actual

record of the three liberations in thinking in contemporary China), Beijing: Jinri Zhongguo chubanshe.

Ma Ming (2006), 'You yangshi "Jinguang dadao" er xiang qi de' (Thoughts on hearing the musical theme of *Jinguang dadao*' from central TV), *Tianxia luntan*, http://www 4bbsland.com/forums/politics/messages/1506423.hml, accessed on 21 June 2006.

MacFarquhar, Roderick (1974–1997), *The Origins of the Cultural Revolution*, Volume 2, *The Great Leap Forward*, New York, published for the Royal Institute of International Affairs, the East Asian Institute of Columbia University, and the Research Institute on Communist Affairs of Columbia University by Columbia University Press.

MacFarquhar, Roderick and Schoenhals, Michael (2006), *Mao's Last Revolution*, Cambridge, Mass., and London: The Belknap Press of Harvard University Press.

Magnier, Mark (2007), 'The 17 signatories, ex-officials and academics, say policies make a mockery of Marxism', *Los Angeles Times*, Latimes.com, http://www.latimes.com/news/nationworld/world/la-fg-china18 jul18,0,6811467.story?coll=la-home-center, accessed 21 July 2007.

Mang Bisheng (2004), '"Zhongguo nongmin diaocha" rang women liangxin yongyuan bu de anning' (*Zhongguo nongmin diaocha* (An investigative report of the Chinese peasantry makes us feel guilty forever), *xinlang caijing zongheng*, http://finance. sina.come.cn, accessed on 21 January 2004.

Manning, Paul (2001), *News and News Sources: A Critical Introduction*, London, Thousand Oaks and New Delhi: Sage.

Mao Zedong (1953), 'Guanyu guojia ziben zhuyi jingji' (On state capitalist economy), in *Selected Works* Vol. 6, p. 282.

— (1958), 'Dui weishengbu dangzu "guanyu zuzhi xiyi lizhi xuexi zhongyiban zongjie baogao" de pishi' (Approving comment on 'The summary report of organizing Western medicine doctors seconded to study Chinese medicine' by the CCP of the Ministry of Health), 11 October, in *Mao Zedong sixiang wansui* (Long live Mao Zedong thought), unpublished.

— (1959), 'Dong nei tongxin' (Correspondence with the party), 29 April 1959, in *Mao Zedong Wenji 1 – 8* (Collected works of Mao Vols. 1 to 8), http://www.maostudy.org/archive/zhuzuo/books.php3?book= mwj, accessed on 13 November 2007.

— (1967a), 'He Kabo, Baluku tongzhi de tanhua' (Talks with Comrades Kabo and Baluku [Chinese pinyin for two Albanian names], 8 February 1967), *Huaxia wenzhai, zengkan wenge bowuguan tongxun*, No. 373 (Chinese news digest, Chinese magazine, Cultural Revolution

Supplement No. 373), http://www.cnd.org/HXWZ/ZK06/zk539. gb.html, accessed on 24 December 2006.

— (1967b), 'Jiejian arbaniya junshi daibiaotun de tanhua jiexuan' (Extracts from the talk with an Albanian Military Delegation), 1 May 1967, *Huaxia wenzhai, zengkan wenge bowuguan tongxun*, No. 373 (Chinese news digest, Chinese magazine, Cultural Revolution supplement No. 373), http://www.cnd.org/HXWZ/ZK06/zk539.gb.html, accessed on 24 December 2006.

— (1968), 'Dui zhonggong zhongyang, zhongyang wenge guanyu dui di douzheng zhong yinggai zhangwu zhengce de tongzhi gao de piyu he xiugai' (Comment and revision on a circular concerning policies on struggle against enemies drafted by the CCP Central Committee and Central Cultural Revolution Leading Group), 17 December 1968, *Jian guo yilai Mao Zedong wengao* (Mao Zedong writings since 1949) Vol. 12, online version, http://maostudy.org/archive/zhuzuo/books.php3? book=mwg, accessed 27 November 2006.

— (1983), ' 中国医药学是一个伟大的宝库' (Chinese medicine is a great treasure house), 11 October 1958, 毛泽东书信选集 *(Selected works of Mao Zedong writings and letters)*, Beijing: Renmin chubanshe.

— (1986), 'Dang nei tongxin' (Correspondence within the party 29 April 1959),《毛泽东著作选读》Vol. II *(Collected works of Mao Zedong)*, Beijing: Renmin chubanshe.

— (2006), 'The first speech of speeches on the Second Sesson of the Eight Party Congress, 8 May 1958', http://www.marxists.org/reference/ archive/mao/selected-works/volume -8/mswv8_10.htm, accessed on 3 January 2006.

McClenahen, John (2006), 'Outsourcing', *Industry Week.com*, July 1.

McCombs, M.E. and Shaw, D.L. (1972), 'The agenda setting function of the mass media', *Public Opinion Quarterly*, No. 36, pp. 176–87.

McCool, Grant (2004), 'Wal-Mart accused over Chinese factory', Reuters, 8 February.

McDonald, Hamish (2005), 'Throwing the book at Mao', www.theage. com.au, accessed on 10 June 2005.

McGregor, Richard (2006), 'China's poorest worse off after boom', *Financial Times FT.com*, http://www.ft.com/cms/s/e28495ce-7988–11db-b257–0000779e2340,dwp_uuid=9c33700c-4c86–11da-89df-0000779 e2340.html, accessed on 27 November 2006.

McLynn, Frank (2005), 'Too much hate, too little understanding,' *Independent*, 6 June.

Meisner, Maurice (1986), *Mao's China and After: A History of the People's Republic*, rev. and expanded edition, New York and London: Collier Macmillan.

Miller, D. (1994), *Don't Mention the War*, London: Pluto.

Miller D., Kitzinger, J., Williams, K. and Beharrel, P. (1998) *The Circuit of Mass Communication: Media Strategies, Representation and Audience Reception in the AIDs Crisis*, London: Sage.

Miller, Tom (2006), 'Manufacturing that doesn't compute' *Asian Times online, http://www.atimes.com/atimes/China_Business/HK23Cb01.html*, accessed on 1 December 2006.

Ming Mu (2007), '1964–65 年毛主席对《驳第三次左倾路线》四次批示期间党内两个司令部围绕社教运动的激烈斗争' (Two-line struggle between the two headquarters during 1964 to 1965 when Mao gave four directives in the document *Refutation of the third ultra leftist line*, Zhurengong, https://host378.ipowreb.com/`gongnong/bbs/read.php?f=7&i=2344&t=2341, accessed on 19 May 2007.

Mirsky, Johnathan (1994), 'Unmasking the monster', *The New York Times Review of Books*, 17 November.

— (2005a), 'Maintaining the Mao myth', *International Herald Tribune*, 6 July.

— (2005b), 'The truth about Mao, mass murderer, womaniser, liar, drug baron: book paints horrific portrait', *Independent*, 29 May, pp. 5–29.

Montefiore, Simon Sebag (2005), *Sunday Times – Books*, 29 May 2005.

Mu Xin (1997), 'Jiehou changyi: shinian dongluan jishi (Memoirs after the turmoil: an account of ten years of chaos), Hong Kong: Xintian chubanshe.

Mu, Aiping (2000), *Vermilion Gate: A Family History of Communist China*, London: Little, Brown.

Muzi.com, '厉以宁被北大光华学院撤职' (Li Yining was dismissed by the Guanghua Institute in Beida), http://news.muzi.com/news/ll/chinese/1442246.shtml?cc= 29182&ccr acessed on 18 December 2006.

Nathan, Andrew (2005), *London Review of Books*, Vol. 27, No. 22, 17 November.

Nie Yuanzi (2005a), <聂元梓口述自传》(Nie Yuanzi's oral autobiography), *Zhurengong luntan*, https://host378.ipowerweb.com/~gongnong/bbs/list.php?f=3, accessed on 30 October 2005.

— (2005b), *Nie Yuanzi hui yi lu*, Hong Kong: shidai guoji youxian gongsi.

Nien Cheng (1987), *Life and Death in Shangai*, New York: Grove Press.

Niu Aimin and Li Jinghua (2004), 'Cehua zuzhi taren feifa jiji youxing si ming shangfang renyuan bei Beijing jingfang xingju he daipu' (For planning and organizing other *shangfang* people, four *shangfang* people were arrested and detained by the Beijing police), Xinhua News Agency, 6 January.

Nolan, Peter (2004), *Transforming China: Globalization, Transition and Development*, London: Anthem Press.

Nong Nuji (2006a),'毛主席关于'大跃进 '的重要指示'(Chairman Mao's

important directives on the Great Leap Forward), *Wuyou zhixiang* http://www.wyzxwyzx.com/Article/Class14/200611/11833.html, accessed on 8 January 2007.

— (2006b), '毛泽东改变了中华民族' (Mao Zedong changed the Chinese nation), *Wuyou zhixiang*, http://www.wyzxwyzx.com/Article/Class18/200612/13343.html, accessed on 9 January 2007.

O'Brien, Kevin J. (2002), 'Collective action in the Chinese countryside', *China Journal*, No. 48 (July), pp. 38–154.

Oi, Jean (1989), *State and Peasants in Contemporary China: The Political Economy of Village Government*, Berkeley, Calif.: University of California Press.

Ortner, S. (1984), 'Theory in anthropology in the sixties', *Comparative Studies in Society and History* 26, p. 143.

Pan Yue (2006), 'China's Green Debt', *Project Syndicate*, http://www.project-syndicate.org/commentary/pan1, accessed on 6 December 2006.

Patnaik, Utsa (2004), 'Republic Hunger', http://networkideas.org/featart/apr2004/ RepublicHunger.pdf, accessed on 29 December 2006.

— (2006), 'The economic ideas of Mao Zedong: agricultural transformation', in Tan Chung, ed., *Across the Himalayan Gap: An Indian Quest for Understanding China*, http://ignca.nic.in/ks_41032.htm, accessed on 29 December 2006.

Pei Minxin (2006), *China's Trapped Transition: The Limits of Developmental Autocracy*, Cambridge, Mass. and London: Harvard University Press.

People's Daily (2004a), 'Commentary: making farmers permanent urban residents', *People's Daily*, 25 February.

People's Daily (2004b), 'Income gaps have to be closed', *People's Daily*, 25 February.

Pepper, Susanne (1996), *Radicalism and Educational Reform in 2oth Century China: The Search for an Ideal Development Model*, Cambridge (UK) and New York: Cambridge University Press.

Perkins, Dwight (1985), *Asia's Next Economic Giant?* Seattle and London: University of Washington Press.

Perry, Elizabeth (1980), *Rebels and Revolutionaries in North China 1945–1950*, Stanford, Calif.: Stanford University Press.

— (2001), *Challenging the Mandate of Heaven: Social Protest and State Power in China*, Armonk, N.Y.: M.E. Sharpe.

— (2003), '"To rebel is justified": Cultural Revolution influences on contemporary Chinese protest', in Law Kam-Yee, ed., *The Chinese Cultural Revolution Reconsidered: Beyond Purge and Holocaust*, New York: Palgrave Macmillan, pp. 262–81.

Philo, G. ed. (1999), *Message Received*, Harlow: Longman.

Ping Gu (2006), ' Zhonguo yi xie rang ren chentong de shijie pai ming' (Some of China's world records make you feel painful), *Shiji xuetang*, http://www.ccforum.org.cnviewthread.php?tid=44848 &extra=page%3D4, accessed on 28 April 2006.

Pomfret, John (2000), 'China lifts obstacles for private industry', *Washington Post*, 5 January, p. A1.

Popkin, Jeremy D. (2005), *History, Historians and Autobiography*, Chicago and London: University of Chicago Press.

Pye, Lucian (1986), 'Reassessing the Cultural Revolution' *China Quarterly*, No. 108 (December), pp. 597–612.

Qi Benyu (1996), 'Interview with Lu Yuan', in DeBorja and Dong 1996, pp. 179–230.

— (2004), 'Interview with Yu Erxin', *Xin Shiji, New Century Net*, http://www.ncn.org/asp/zwginfo/da-KAY.asp?ID=27683 &ad=1/9/2004, accessed on 14 January 2004.

Qin Chu, 'Chen Yonggui fangtan' (Interview with Chen Yonggui), *Wuyou zhixiang, zhongyao cankao ziliao* (Important reference materials on the Utopia website), http://www.wyzxsx.com/book /013.doc, acceessed on 12 October 2006.

Qin Huailu (1995), *Ninth Heaven to Ninth Hell: The History of a Noble Chinese Experiment*, ed. William Hinton, translated by Dusanka Miscevic, New York: Barricade Books.

Qiong Xiangqin, '人民公社何错有之' (What is wrong with the the people's commune?), *Tianxia luntan, www.*creaders.org, http://bbs4.creaders. net/forums/politics/messages/1550021.html, accessed on 4 May 2007.

Qiu Desheng et al (1993), *Zhonghua renmin gongheguo shilu* (Factual records of the People's Republic of China), Vol. 5, *Wenxian yu yanjiu* (documentation and research), Changchun: Jilin renmin chubanshe, pp. 290–93, Tables 12.5, 12.6, 12.7.

Quan Yanchi (1989), *Mao Zedong wei shi zhang za ji: Li Yinqiao shu* (Memories of Mao's head of bodyguards: told by Li Yinqiao), Hong Kong: Wenhua jiaoyu chubanshe.

— (1991), *Zhongguo zuida de baohuangpai Tao Zhu chenfu lu* (The rise and fall of China's greatest royalist, Tao Zhu), Hong Kong: Tiandi tushu youxian gongsi.

— (1992), *Zouxia shengtan de Zhou Enlai* (The de-canonized Zhou Enlai), Hong Kong: Tiandi tushu youxian gongsi.

— (1997), *Wei xing, Yang Chengwu zai 1967* (Inspection Tour, Yang Chengwu in 1967), Guangdong, Guangzhou luyou chubanshe.

Rawski, Thomas (1980), *China's Transition to Industrialization: Producer Goods and Economic Development*, Ann Arbor: University of Michigan Press.

— (1993), *How Fast Has the Chinese Industry Grown?*, Washington, D.C.: The World Bank.

Redmon, David (2006), *Mardi Gras Made in China, Beads, Breasts and Business: A Story of Globalization Gone Wild* (film).

Resnick, Stephen and Wolff, Richard (2002), *Class Theory and History: Capitalism and Communism in the U.S.S.R.*, New York and London: Routledge.

Reuters (2005), 'Protests by laid-off workers rumble on at China oilfield', *Nanfang dushi bao*, 26 June.

Ricoeur, Paul (2000), *la Mémoire, l'Hisotire, l'Oubli*, Paris: Seuil.

— (2004), *Memory, History and forgetting*, English translation, Kathleen Blamey and David Pellauer, Chicago: University of Chicago Press.

Rothwell, Nicolas (2005), 'Books of the year', *The Australian*, 3–4 December, p. R5.

Ruan Ming (1994), *Deng Xiaoping: Chronicle of an Empire*, Boulder, San Francisco and Oxford: Westview Press.

Sahlins, Marshal (1985), *Islands of History*, Chicago: University of Chicago Press.

Samuelson, Robert J. (2004), 'The China riddle', *Washington Post*, 30 January.

San nong Zhongguo (2006), http://www.snzg.net/shownews.asp?newsid =7096, accessed on 5 July 2006.

Santoli, Al (2002), *Unrestricted Warfare: China's Master Plan to Destroy America*, Panama City, Panama: Pan American Publishing Company.

Sarabia-Panol, Zenaida M., 'The 9/11 terrorist attacks on America: the media frames of the Far East', in Tomasz Pludowski, ed., *How the World's News Media Reacted to 9/11: Essays from Around the Globe*, Spokane, Wash.: Marquette Books, 2006, pp. 169–185.

Sato, Hiroshi and Li Shi, eds (2005), *Unemployment, Inequality and Poverty in Urban China*, New York: Routledge.

Sausmikat, Nora (2002), 'Resisting current stereotypes: private narrative strategies in the autobiographies of former rusticated women', in Woei Lien Chong, ed., *China's Great Proletarian Cultural Revolution: Master Narratives and Post-Mao Counternarratives*, Lanham, Boulder: New York and Oxford: Rowman & Littlefield, pp. 255–84.

Sautman, Barry (2001), 'Tibet: myths and realities.' *Current History*, Vol. 100, No. 647, pp. 278–84.

— (2006), 'Tibet and the (mis-)representation of cultural genocide', in Barry Sautman, ed., *Cultural Genocide and Asia State Peripheries*, New York: Palgrave Macmillan, pp. 165–272.

Schama, Simon (1989), *Citizens: A Chronicle of the French Revolution*, New York: Knopf, distributed by Random House.

Schmalzer, Sigrid (2006), 'Labor created humanity: Cultural Revolution science on its own terms', in Joseph W. Esherick, Paul G. Pickowicz and Andrew Walder, eds, *The Chinese Cultural Revolution as History*, Stanford Calif.: California University Press, pp. 185–201.

Schumann, Franz (1968), *Ideology and Organization in Communist China*, Berkeley, Calif.: University of California Press.

Schwarcz, Vera (1986), *The Chinese Enlightenment: Intellectuals and the Legacy of the May Fourth Movement of 1919*, Berkeley and Los Angeles, Calif., and London: University of California Press.

— (1996), 'The burden of memory: the Cultural Revolution and the Holocaust', *China Information 11*, No. 1 (Summer), pp. 1–13.

— (1998), *Bridge across Broken Time: Chinese and Jewish Cultural Memories*, New Haven: Yale University Press.

Schweickart, David (2005), 'Ten theses on Marxism and transition to socialism', in Cao Tian Yu, ed., *The Chinese Model of Modern Development*, London and New York: Routledge, pp. 1988–216.

Seagrave, Sterling (1986), *The Soong Dynasty*, New York: Harper Perennial.

Seidman, Michael (2004), *The Imaginary Revolution: Paris Students and Workers in 1968*, New York and Oxford: Berghahn Books.

Selden, Mark (1971), *The Yenan Way in Revolutionary China*, Cambridge, Mass.: Harvard University Press.

Selden, Mark (1988), *The Political Economy of Chinese Socialism*, Armonk, N.Y.: M.E. Sharpe.

Selden, Mark and Eggleston, Patti, eds (1979), *The People's Republic of China: A Documentary History of Revolutionary Change*, New York: Monthly Review Press.

Selden, Mark, Friedman, Edqaed and Pickowicz, Paul (1991), *Chinese Village, Socialist State*, New Haven: Yale University Press.

Sen, Amartya (2000), quoted in Antony C. Black, 'Black propaganda', *Guardian Weekly*, 24 February 2000.

Seybolt, Peter, J. (1996), *Throwing the Emperor from His Horse: Portrait of a Village Leader in China, 1923–1995*, Boulder, Colo.: Westview Press.

Shafer, Sarah (2007), 'Now they speak out,' *Newsweek International*, 28 May.

Shakya, Tsering (2002), 'Blood in the snow: reply to Wang Lixiong', *New Left Review*, No. 15 (May–June), pp. 29–60.

She Ruhui (2004), *Qinghua daxue wenge jishi: yi ge hongweibing lingdao de zishu* (The Cultural Revolution at Qinghua: a story of a Red Guard leader told by himself), Hong Kong: Shida yishu chubanshe.

Shen Zhihua (2007), '中苏蜜月的最后时刻–毛泽东，赫鲁晓夫与1957莫斯科会议的召开' (The last moment of the Sino-Soviet honeymoon:

Mao Zedong, Khrushov and the convening of the Moscow Conference in 1957), in 二十一世纪月刊 (The twenty-first century monthly) (June), pp. 77–84.

Shi Dongbing (2007) (师东兵), '王稼祥朱仲丽夫妇：完全如实地写江青能出版吗？' (Husband and wife Wang Jiaxiang and Zhu Zhongli: can a description of a real Jiang Qing be published?), in *Ba que*, http//www.popyard.com/cgi-mod/post.cgi?foruum=7&page =1&num=57702&r=0, accessed on 22 October 2007.

Shi Zhe (1991), *Zai lishi juren shenbian* (Being with historical giants), Beijing: Zhongyang wenxian chubanshe.

Shirk, Susan (1993), *The Political Logic of Economic Reform in China*, Berkeley, Calif.: University of California Press.

Shotter, John (1990), 'The social construction of remembering and forgetting', in David Middleton and Derek Edwards, eds, *Collective Remembering*, London: Newbury Park and New Delhi: Sage, pp. 120–138.

Shue, Vivienne (1988), *The Reach of the State*, Stanford: Stanford University Press.

Shui Han (2007), '历史表明马寅初人口论是错误的' (History shows that Ma Yichu's idea of population is wrong), http://www.shengyu.org/modules/article/view.article.php?14, accessed on 21 May 2007.

Shui Luzhou (2006), 'Mao Zedong sixiang hong weibing: wu yi liu tongzhi ji wenge sishi zhounian zuotan hui jiyao' (Red Guards of Mao Zedong thought: workshop notes on the 40th anniversary of the Cultual Revolution and the May 16 circular), *Wanwei duzhe tianxia luntan*, http://www4.bbsland.com/forums/politics/messages/1501374.htm l, accessed on 23 May 2006.

Siu, Helen F. (1989), *Agents and Victims in South China: Accomplices in Rural Revolution*, New Haven: Yale University Press.

Solinger, Dorothy J. (1999), *Contesting Citizenship in Urban China: Peasant Migrants, the State, and the Logic of the Market*, Berkeley, Los Angeles and London: University of California Press.

Song Bingwen, Xiong Yuhong and Zhang Qiang (2003), 'Dang qian nongmin yiliao baozhang de xianzhuang fenxi' (An analysis of the current situation of rural health insurance), *Modern China Studies*, No. 4. file://C:\Documents%20, accessed on 5 January 2004.

Song Yongyi (2002), *Zhongguo wenhua da geming wenku* (Chinese Cultural Revolution database), Hong Kong: Xianggang zhongwen daxue Zhongguo yanjiu fuwu zhongxin.

— (2007), '别忘了王光美作为迫害者的一面' (Don't forget the victimizer Wang Guangmei), *Huaxia wenzhai*, http:www.cnd.org/HXWZ/ZK07/zk550.gb.html, accessed on 1 February 2007.

Spence, Jonathan (2005), *New York Review of Books*, Vol. 52, No. 17 (3 November).

Stoler, Ann Laura (1995), *Race and Education of Desire: Foucault's History of Sexuality and the Colonial Order of Things*, Durham, N.C., and London: Duke University Press.

Stucke, John (2004), 'China wheat buy boom for farmers', *Knight Ridder*, 24 February.

Sumo3, 'Haiwai minyun rumen ABC' (The ABC for being overseas democracy activists), *Wanwei duzhe wangluo* http://www.readers.org/forums/politics/ messages/652046.html, accessed on 15 April 2004.

Sun Ge (2007) (孙歌), 'Sixiang shi miandui de Zhongguo wenti (The China question in the history of ideas), 第三届开放时代论坛 : 作为学术视角的社会主义新传统, in 学术中国, xschina.org, http://www.xschina.org/show.php?id=9190, accessed on 24 April 2007.

Sweezy, Paul and Bettelheim, Charles (1972), *On the Transition to Socialism*, New York: Monthly Review Press.

Tai Hung-chao (2000), *Shijie ribao* (World Daily), 22 July.

Tang Jinxin (2007), 'Wo canjia le feiduo Luding qiao' (I participated in the battle of taking over the Luding Bridge), *Tian xian luntan*, http://bbs4.creaders.net/forums/politics/ messages/1547536.html, accessed on 15 March 2007.

Tang Zongli (1993), 'Is China returning to semi-colonial status?' *Monthly Review*, Vol. 45, No. 3, pp. 77–86.

Tao Lujia (2003), (陶鲁笳), 《毛主席教我们当省委书记》 (Chairman Mao taught us to be provincial CCP party secretaries), Beijing: 中央文献出版社.

Taussig, Michael T. (1989), 'History as commodity', *Critique of Anthropology*, 9, pp. 2–27.

Teiwes, Frederick (1967), *Provincial Party Personnel in Mainland China, 1956–1966*, New York, East Asian Institute: Columbia University.

— (1974), *Provincial Leadership in China: the Cultural Revolution and Its Aftermath*, Ithaca, New York: China–Japan Program, Cornell University.

— (1978), *Elite Discipline in China: Coercive and Persuasive Approaches to Rectification, 1950–1953*, Canberra: Contemporary China Centre, Research School of Pacific Studies, Australian National University.

— (1979), *Politics & Purges in China: Rectification and the Decline of Party Norms, 1950–1965*, New York: M.E. Sharpe.

— (1983), *Major Dilemmas in Chinese Politics since 1949*, Sydney: Centre for Asian Studies, University of Sydney.

— (1984), *Leadership, Legitimacy, and Conflict in China: From a Charismatic Mao to the Politics of Succession*, Armonk, N.Y.: M.E. Sharpe.

— (1988), 'Mao and his lieutenants', *Australian Journal of Chinese Affairs*, No. 19–20, pp. 56–63.

— (1990), *Politics at Mao's Court: Gao Gang and Party Factionalism in the Early 1950s*, Armonk, N.Y.: M.E. Sharpe.

— (1996), 'Seeking the historical Mao', *China Quarterly*, No. 145 (March), pp. 176–88.

— (1997), 'Interviews on party history', in Timothy Cheek and Tony Saich, *New Perspective on State Socialism in China*, London and New York: M.E. Sharpe, pp. 339–353.

Teiwes, Frederick and Warren Sun, eds (1993), *The Politics of Agricultural Cooperativization in China: Mao, Deng Zihui, and the 'High Tide' of 1955*, Armonk, NY : M.E. Sharpe.

— (1994), *The Formation of the Maoist Leadership: from the Return of Wang Ming to the Seventh Party Congress*, London: Contemporary China Institute, School of Oriental and African Studies, University of London.

— (1996), *The Tragedy of Lin Biao: Riding the Tiger during the Cultural Revolution 1966–1971*, Honolulu: University of Hawaii Press.

— (1999), *China's Road to Disaster: Mao, Central Politicians, and Provincial Leaders in the Unfolding of the Great Leap Forward*, 1955–1959, Armonk, N.Y.: M.E. Sharpe.

Thomas, Gordon (2001), *Seeds of Fire: China and the Story behind the Attack on America*, Tempe, Ariz.: Dandelion Books.

Thornton, Philip (2004), 'The new China Syndrome: commodity price boom sets alarm bells ringing – mining firms cash in but policymakes increasingly worried over inflation threat', *Independent*, 25 February.

Thorpe, Vanessa (1985–86),'Victims of China's Cultural Revolution: the invisible wounds' part II, *Pacific Affairs*, Vol. 57, No. 4 (Winter), pp. 605–6.

— (2005), 'From swan to hawk', *Observer*, 1 May.

Thurston, Anne, F. (1996), 'The politics of survival: Li Zhisui and the inner court', *China Journal*, No. 35 (January), pp. 97–105.

Tian Bingxin (2006), '文革学生领袖蒯大富：不同意说 '上了毛泽东的当'' (Cultural Revolution student leader Kuai Dafu: not agreeing to 'cheated by Mao Zedong'), *Zhongguo wenge yanjiu wang*, http://www.wengewang.org/bencandy.php?id=2141, accessed on 22 February 2006.

Tian Fu (2007) (天父), '现代中国的'新四大发明'全都诞生在毛泽东时代' (The four great inventions in modern China were all invented during the Mao era), *woyou zhixiang*, http://www.wyzxwyzx.com/Article/Class22/200705/18955.html, accessed on 30 May 2007.

Ting Guang (2006), '样板戏'是中国文艺史上新的里程碑' ('Model operas'

are the milestones of Chinese literature and art), *Zhongguo wenge yanjiu wang* http://www.wengewang.org/bbs/bencandy.php?id=2342&lpage=1, accessed on 15 May 2006.

Trotsky, Leon (1997), *Stalin*, 2nd edn, New York: Stein and Day.

Unger, Jon (2002), *The Transformation of Rural China*, Armonk, N.Y. and London: M.E. Sharpe.

Vukovich, Daniel Frederick (2005), Sinological-Orientalism: The Production of the West's Post-Mao China, PhD Thesis, Rubanan-Champaign: University of Illinois.

Walder, Andrew (2000), 'When the states unravel: how China's cadres shaped Cultural Revolution politics', in Kjeld Erik Brødsgaard and Susan Yong, eds, *State Capacity in East Asia*, Oxford: Oxford University Press, pp. 157–84.

Wang Dongxing (1993), *Wang Dongxing riji* (Diaries of Wang Dongxing), Beijing: Zhongguo shehui kexue chubanshe.

— (2004), *Mao Zedong yu Lin Biao fan geming jituan de douzheng* (The struggle between Mao Zedong and the Lin Biao anti-revolutionary clique), Beijing: Dangdai Zhongguo chubanshe.

Wang Guangmei (1992), 'Furen de huiyi' (Wife remembers), in Guo Simin and Tianyu, eds, *Wo yanzhong de Liu Shaoqi* (Liu Shaoqi as I see him), Shejiazhuang: Hebei renmin chubanshe.

Wang Hui (2000), *Si huo chong wen* (Re-warm the dead fire), Beijing: Renmin wenxue chubanshe.

— (2004), 'The year 1989 and historical roots of neoliberalism in China', *Positions East Asia Cultures Critique*, Vol. 12, No. 1 (Spring), pp. 7–70.

— (2005), 'Global viewpoint, China's new left', *New Perspective Quarterly*, Vol. 22, No. 3 (Summer), http://www.digitalnpq.org/global services/Global%20viewpoint /03–07, accessed on 19 July 2005.

— (2006), 'Comments', at the 'Is a History of the Cultural Revolution Possible?' workshop with Professor Allan Badiou, Washington University, Seattle, 22–26 January.

Wang Jianzhao (2002), 'Wenge zhong de dixia shige' (Underground poetry during the Cultural Revolution), *Shiji Zhongguo* (Century China), http://www.cc.org.cn, 4 April.

Wang Li (2001), *Wang Li fansi lu, xia* (Reflections by Wang Li), Vol. 2, Hong Kong: Xianggang beixing chubanshe.

— (2006), 'Wang Li fansi lu' (Wang Li Reflections), extracts circulated on *Shijie Zhongguo*, http://www.coforum.org.cn/viewthread.php?itd=49123&extra=page%3D1, accessed on 19 June 2006.

Wang Lixiong (2002), 'Reflections on Tibet', *New Left Review*, No. 14 (March–April), pp. 79–111.

— (2003), '中国的宗教政策正在毁灭藏传佛教' (China's religious policy is

destroying Buddhism in Tibet), *xin shiji wang*, http://www.
ncn.org/asp/zwginfo/da.asp?ID=51869&ad=4/23/2003, accessed on
30 August 2006.

— (2004), 《与达赖喇嘛对话》(A dialogue with the Dalai Lama), USA:
Green Valley Publishing, http://www.ncn.org/asp/zwginfo/da.asp?
ID=60694&ad=11/16/2004, accessed on 24 July 2006.

— (2006), 'Mao Zedong zhuyi yu renjian tiantang' (Maoism and paradise
on earth), Wuyou zhixiang zhongdian yanjiu wenzhang (Key
reference materials on the Utopia website), http://www.wyzxsx.com/
book/012.doc, accessed on 13 October 2006.

Wang Mingxian and Yan Shenchun (2002), 'Wenge zhong de daxing
diaosu' (Large-scale group sculpture during the Cultural Revolution),
Shiji Zhongguo (Century China), http://www.cc.org.cn, accessed on 4
April 2002.

Wang Mingxian and Yan Shenchun (2001), *Xin Zhongguo meishu shi
1966–1976* (A history of fine arts in the new China, 1966–1976), Beijing:
Zhongguo qingnian chubanshe.

Wang Nianyi (1988), *Dadonglun de shinian* (The turbulent ten years),
Zhengzhou: Henan renmin chubanshe.

Wang Nianyi and He Shou (2000), 'She guojia zhuxi wenti lunxi' (An
examination of the issue of the Chairman of the State), in *Huaxia
wenzhai* (CND Chinese Magazine HXWZ), *zengkan* 224
(Supplementary Issue No. 224), accessed on 14 July 2000, p. 6.

Wang Ping (1992), *Wang Ping huiyi lu* (Memoirs of Wang Ping), Beijing:
Jiefangjun chubanshe.

Wang Shaoguang (1995), *Failure of Charisma: The Cultural Revolution in
Wuhan*, Hong Kong: Oxford University Press.

— (2003), 'Openness and inequality: the case of China', *Issues & Studies* 39,
no. 4 (December).

— (2006), 'Comments' at the 'Is a History of the Cultural Revolution
Possible?' workshop with Professor Allan Badiou, Washington
University, Seattle, 22–26 January.

Wang Xiaolu (2007), '灰色收入与居民收入差距' (Income disparity when
grey income is taken into account),香港传真 , *Citic Pacific Research
Advance*, No. 2 (July).

Wang Xiaotao (2004), 'Cong nongmin fudan wenti kan Zhongguo nongcun
zhengzhi guanxi de bianhua' (An examination of the change of
political relations in rural China from the perspective of the problems
of peasantry burdens), *Zhurengong luntan* http://www.gongnong.
org/bbs/read.php?f=39201&t=39008, accessed on 14 January 2004.

Wang Xizhe (2006a), 'Chedi fouding liang zhong wenge ye jiu chedi fan
mian hua le renmin de zaofan' (Thorough negation of the two kinds of

Cultural Revolution is to thoroughly demonize the people's rebellion), *Wanwei tianxia lu tan*, http://www4.bbsland.com/forums/politics/messages/ 5471.html, accessed on 20 May 2006.

— (2006b), 'Wenge women de fenqi jiujing shi shenme: yu Han Zhu xiansheng taolun' (What are our differences on the Cultural Revolution: a dabate with Han Zhu), *Wanwei tianxia lu tan*, http://www4.bbsland.com/forums/politics/messages/ 1500190.html, accessed on 18 May 2006.

Wang Yuanhua (1990), *Chuantong yu fan chuantong* (Tradition and anti-tradition), Shanghai: Shanghai wenyi chubanshe.

Wang, Fei-Ling (2005), 'Lots of wealth, lots of people, lots of flaws', *International Herald Tribune*, 22 July.

Watts, Jonathan (2007), 'Migrants suffering from China boom, says study', *Guardian*, March 2, http://www.guadian.co.uk/china/story/ O,,2024886,00.html, accessed on 6 March 2007.

Wei Cheng (2003), 'Zhongwen wang shang xiao yan nong' (The smoke is thick on the Chinese debate on the web), *Wanwei luntan*, www.creaders.org/forums/ politics/messages/467501.html, accessed on 25 February 2003.

Wei Se (Woeser) (2006), *Xizang jiyi: ershisan wei qilao koushu Xizang wenge* (Tibetan memories: 23 venerated old people talk about the Cultural Revolution in Tibet), Taipei: dakui wenhua.

Weil, Robert (2006), 'Conditions of the working class in China', *Monthly Review*, Vol. 58, No. 2 (June), pp. 24–49.

Wen Feng (1993), *Shentan xia de Lin Biao* (Lin Biao under the altar), Beijing: Zhongguo huaqiao chubanshe.

Wen Tiejun (2005), 'Zai Anhui mo xian de yanjiang' (A talk given at a certain county in Anhui Province), *Shiji Zhongguo xilie luntan*, http://www.ccforum.org.cn/viewthread.php?tid=14070&extra= page%3D73, accessed 27 June 2005.

Williems, Frank, 'Mao, the untold story', SF.Indymedia.org, http:// sf.indymedia.org/news///.phpandfrank.willems69@yucom.be, accessed on 20 November 2005.

Wills, John, E. (1994), 'The emperor has no clothes: Mao's doctor reveals the naked truth', *Foreign Affairs*, November–December.

Wittfogel, Karl (1957), *Oriental Despotism*, New Haven: Yale University Press.

Woei Lien Chong, ed. (2002), *China's Great Proletarian Cultural Revolution: Master Narratives and Post-Mao Counternarratives*, Lanham, Boulder, New York and Oxford: Rowman & Littlefield.

Wong, Christine P. (2003), 'Legacies of the Moaist development strategy: rural industrialization in China from the 1970s to the 1990s', in Law

Kam-Yee, ed., *The Chinese Cultural Revolution Reconsidered: Beyond Purge and Holocaust*, New York: Palgrave Macmillan, pp. 203–217.

Wu De with Zhu Yuanshi (2004), *Wu De koushu: shi nian feng yu jishi – wo zai Beijing gongzuo de yixie jingli* (Oral account by Wu De: weathering the ten years – my experience of working in Beijing), Beijing: Dangdai Zhonggong chubanshe.

Wu Faxian (2006), (吴法宪),《岁月艰难：吴法宪回忆录》下 , (Difficult years: Wu Faxian memoirs, volume 2), Hong Kong: 北星出版社, 2006.

Wu Guoguang (2003), 'Xianmo Yilake ren' (I envy the Iraqis), www. creaders.org/forums/politics/messages/494794.html, accessed on 3 April 2003.

Wu Lengxi (1995), *Yi Mao zhuxi: wo qinshen jingli de luogan zhongda lishi shijian pianduan* (Remember Chairman Mao: several important historical events and episodes that I was personally involved in*)*, Beijing: Xinhua chubanshe.

— (2000), '国民经济调整的领导者' (Those who led the adjustment of the national economy), in 话说刘少奇 – 知情者访谈录 (On Liu Shaoqi – interviews with the insiders), compiled by the second editorial office of Central Documentary Research Office, Beijing: 中央文献出版社.

— (2007),《同家英共事的日子》之五《庐山风云》(Being a colleague of Tain Jiaying, part five: the Lushan storm), *Wuyou zhixiang*, http://www.wyzxwyzx.com/Article/Class14/200702/15188.html, accessed on 14 February 2007.

Wu Pei-yu (1990), *The Confucian's Progress: Autobiographical Writings in Traditional China*, Princeton, N.J.: Princeton University Press.

Wu Yiching (2006), 哈佛大学张戎作品讨论会 (A seminar on Jung Chang's book at Harvard), personal communication from Yan Hairong [hairongy@gmail.com], accessed on 11 November 2006.

Wu Zhenrong and Deng Wenbi (2004), 'Yiyi renshi yu minyun renshi yitong bian' (On the differences and similarities between dissidents and democrats), *da cankao* http://www.bignews.org/3 April 2004, accessed on 7 April 2004.

Wuyou zhixiang (2005), 'Wuyou zhixiang huiguo 2006: Zhongguo gaoxiao shi da youzhengyi shijian (Looking back 2006: ten most controversial events in Chinese higher education), http://www.wyzxwyzx.com/ Article/Class4/200612/12883.html, accessed on 16 December 2006.

— (2006), '毛主席关于当前重大问题的语录(与时俱进版)' (Chairman Mao's quotations on the important issues in current China: move with the tide edition), http://www.wyzxsx.com/Article/index.asp, accessed on 8 May 2006.

Xiang Nanzi (2006), '中国历年公路和铁路的总里程' (Annual railway

mileage statistics in China), *Jiang guo luntan*, www.people.com.cn, accessed on 12 July 2006.

Xiang Wenbo (2006), 'Zai Tianze jingji suo de yanjiang' (Speech at the Tianze Economics Institute), *Renmin wang jiangguo lu tan bbs.people. com.cn*, http://bbs.people.com. cn/postDetail.do?view=1&id=892921, accessed on 15 November 2006.

Xiao Er (2007), '回乡偶遇' (Chance meeting at my hometown), *San nong Zhongguo*, http://www.snzg.cn/article/show.php?itemid-5465/ page-1.html, accessed on 18 May 2007.

Xiao Ke (1997), *Xiao Ke huiyi lu* (Xiao Ke's memoirs), Beijing: Jiefangjun chubanshe, 1997.

Xiao Ling (2005), 'Wangguo lunzhe: cong Jiao Guobiao dao Hu Shi' (These who want China to be finished: from Jiao Guobiao to Hu Shi), *Fenghua yuan*, http://www.fhy.net/11 December 2005, accessed on 27 January 2006.

Xiao Xidong (2002), *Chunzhong de wenhua da geming shi* (A history of the Cultural Revolution of the masses), unpublished manuscript, personal communication.

Xiao Yu (2000), '*Liangxiao he pi zaixiang*' (Liangxiao and the criticism of the premier), *Renmin chunqiu Monthly*, No. 3, http://maostudy.org/ july.html, accessed on 15 July 2000.

Xie Liangbing (2007), 'Expression of public opinion in the new media', *China Newsweek*, translated by Joel Martinsen, http://www. d a n w e i . o r g / s t a t e _ m e d i a / x i a m e n _ p x _ s m s _ c h i n a _ newsweek.php, accessed on 20 June 2007.

Xie Weixiong (2004), 'Shuishen huore zhong de shangfang zhe' (The *shangfang* people in deep water and scorching fire: an abyss of suffering), *Da ji yuan, www*.dajiyuan. com/ gb/4/2/12/n465210.htm, accessed on 12 February 2004.

Xin Ma (2006),'必须为文革造反派平反' (The reputation of the rebels must be restored), *Wuyou zhixiang zhongdian yanjiu wenzhang*, http://www. wyzxsx.com/book/012.doc, accessed on 14 October 2006.

Xing Xiaoqun (2006), '口述史与'文革'研究' (Oral history and the study of the Cultural Revolution), in *Modern China Studies*, file://C: \Documents%20and%20Settings\mobo\Local%20Settings/Temp\ _ZC.., accessed on 5 July 2006.

Xinhua News (2004a), 'Article recounts drafting of document on increasing peasants' income', 8 February 2004,

Xinhua News (2004b), *People's Daily Overseas Edition*, 10 February 2004.

Xu Hailiang (2005), *Donghu fengyun lu: Wuhan wenge de chunzhong jiyi* (The windy days by the East Lake: memoirs of the Cultural Revolution in Wuhan by the masses), Hong Kong: Yinhe chubanshe.

— (2006), 'Wode wenge jianwen: ling yi lei xuesheng yu wengen' (My witness of the Cultural Revolution: another kind of student and Cultural Revolution), *Huaxia wenzhai*, http://www.cnd.org/HXWZ/ZK06/zk522.gb.html, accessed 14 September 2006.

Xu Jiatun (1992), *Xinggang huiyi lu* (The Hong Kong memoirs), Hong Kong: Mingjing chubanshe.

Xu Ming (1998), 'Wu Zhipu yu Henan da yuejin yundong'(Wu Zhipu and the Great Leap Forward in Henan), *Er shi yi shi ji* (Twenty-first century), No. 48 (August), pp. 37–47.

Xu Zidong (2006), (许子东)，当代小说与集体记忆 – 叙述文革 (Contemporary novels and collective memories – narrating the Cultural Revolution), Taipie: .

Yahuda, Michael (2005), 'Bad Element', *Guardian* 4 June 4.

Yang Bo (2006), '新中国经济战线的奠基人 –   – 缅怀陈云同志对我国经济建设的巨大贡献' (Founding fathers of the new China: remember the great contribution made by Chen Yun to the construction of China's economy), *Renmin wang*, www.people. com.cn,http://finance.people.com.cn/GB/8215/48809/48959/3439501.html, accessed on 7 January 2006.

Yang Chunxia (2006), (杨春霞)，'样板戏'仍然是京剧历史上的里程碑' (Model operas are still the milestones in the history of the Peking Opera), interview with *Beijing Evening News*, 5 May, Guo wenge yan jiu wang http://www.wengewang.org/bbs/bencandy.php?id=2502&l_page=1, accessed on 15 May 2006.

Yang Fan (2005), 杨帆, '对港报记者谈文革' (Talk on the Cultural Revolution to the reporters from Hong Kong), *Zhongguo wenge yanjiu wang*, http://www.wengewang.org/bencandy. php?id=2504, 5 May 2005, accessed on 15 May 2005.

Yang Guang (2007), '改革造成的'新三座大山'：教育，医疗。住房问题的现状与成因分析' (The new three big mountains formed by the reforms: an analysis of the current state of affairs and causes of the problems of education, health care and housing), *Modern China Studies*, file://C:Documents and Settings\mobo\Local Settings\Temp_ZCTmp.D, accessed on 13 April 2007.

Yang Jian (2002), *Zhongguo zhiqing wenxue shi* (A history of literature by the educated Chinese youth), Beijing: Zhongguo gong ren chubanshe, pp. 167–8.

Yang Jiang (2003), *Women sa* (The three of us), Beijing: Shenghuo, dushuo xinzhi sanlian shu dian.

Yang Qian and Zhang Zuoguang (1987), *Wang shi* (Memories of the past), Jinan: Mingtian chubanshe.

Yang Shangkun (2001), *Yang Shangkun riji, xia* (Yang Shangkun diaries, Vol. 2), Beijing: zhongyang wenxian chubanshe.

Yang Tao (2007) (杨涛), '私企主出身于权力精英增多的趋势值得警惕' (The alarming development of more and more party and government power elite having become private owners of enterprises), *Wuyou zhixiang*, http://www.wyzxwyzx.com/Artice/Class4/200702/15480. html, accessed on 22 February 2007.

Yang Xiaokai (2006), 'Tudi siyouzhi yu xuanzheng gonghe de guanxi' (Privatization of land and its relation to a constitutional republic state), http://www.cc.org. cn/newcc/browwenzhang.php?articleid=1231, accessed on 20 May 2006.

Yang Xiguang and Susan McFadden (1997), *Captive Spirits: Prisoners of the Cultural Revolution* Hong Kong and New York: Oxford University Press.

Ye Fu (2004), 'Zhongguo yue lai yue rang "you gun" men shiwang le' (China is more and more disappointing to the fundamental rightists), *Tianxie luntan*, www.creaders.org, accessed on 14 January 2004.

Ye Lang (2005), 'Zai sixiang shang jiaru Meiguo guoji' (Become a US citizen in thinking), *Wanwei duzhe tianxia lu tan*, http://www4bbsland.com/forum/politics/ messages/1395835.html, accesed on 24 January 2005.

Ye Yonglie (1988), *Ma Sicong zhuan* (A biography of Ma Sicong), Hong Kong: Nanyue chubanshe.

— (1990), *Wang Hongwen* (A biography of Wang Hongwen), Hong Kong: Xianggang wenhua jiaoyu chuban youxian gongsi.

— (1991), *Hongse de qidian* (The red start), Shanghai: Shanghai renmin chubanshe.

— (1992a), *Lishi xuanze le Mao Zedong* (History has chosen Mao Zedong), Shanghai: Shanghai renmin chubanshe.

— (1992b), *Chenzhong de yi jiu wu qi* (The heavy 1957), Nanchang: Beihua wenyi chubanshe.

— (1993a), *Zhonggong shenmi zhangquanzhe* (Mysterious power-holders in CCP China), Taipei: Fengyun shidai chuban youxian gongsi.

— (1993b), *Zhang Chunqiao zhuan* (A biography of Zhang Chunqiao), Beijing: Zuojia chubanshe.

— (1993c), *Chen Boda zhuan* (A biography of Chen Boda), Beijing, Zuojia chubanshe.

— (1993d), *Jiang Qing zhuan* (A biography of Jiang Qing), Beijing: Zuojia chubanshe.

— (1993e), *Mao Zedong he ta de zhangquanshu* (Mao Zedong and his power-holding tactics), Taipei: Fengyun shidao chuban youxian gongsi.

— (1994a), *Zhongyang yizhi bi: Hu Qiaomu yu Mao Zedong* (The pen of the CCP: Hu Qiaomu and Mao Zedong), Hong Kong: Tiandi tushu youxian gongsi.

— (1994b), *Mao Zedong de mishumen* (Mao Zedong's secretaries), Shanghai: Shanghai renmin chubanshe.

— (1995), *Fu Lei yu Fu Cong* (Fu Lei and Fu Cong), Beijing: Zuojia chubanshe.

— (2002), *Mao Zedong he Jiang Jieshi* (Mao Zedong and Chiang Kai-shek), Taipei: Fengyun shidai chuban gufen youxian gongsi.

Yep, Ray (2004), 'Can "tax-Fee" reform reduce rural tension in China? The process, progress and limitations', *China Quarterly*, No. 177 (March), pp.41–70.

Yi Fuxian (2007), 易富贤)',历史表明马演初人口认识错误的' (History shows that Ma Yinchu's idea on population is wrong), personal communication, familyyi@yahoo.com, accessed on 13 April 2007.

Yiming (anonymous person) (2003)《怀念李慎之》, 上、下册, (Remember Li Shenzhi) no publication details, May 2003.

Yoder, Edwin M (1997), *The Historical Present: Uses and Abuses of the Past*, Jackson: University Press of Mississippi.

Young, Marilyn B. (1994),'Review', *New York Times Review of Books*, 27 November.

Yu Erxin (2006a) (余汝信), '与戚本禹面对面' (Face to face with Qi Benyu), *Zhongguo wenge yanjiu wang*, http://www.wengewang.org/bencandy.php?id=748, accessed on 10 August 2006.

— (2006b), '《红卫兵兴衰录》出版说明' (Publisher's note on the rise and fall of the Red Guard), *Huaxia wenzhai*, accessed on 10 June 2006.

Yu Gong (1988), *Lin Biao shijian zhenxiang* (The truth about the Lin Biao incident), Beijing: Zhongguo guangbodianshi chubanshe.

Yu Jianrong (2001), *Yue cun zhengzhi: zhuanxing qi Zhongguo xiangcun zhengzhi jiegou de bianqian* (The politics of Yue Village: the structural change of rural politics in transitional China), Beijing: Shang wu ying shu guan.

— (2003), *Nongmin you zuzhi kangzheng jiqi zhenzhi fengxian, Hunan H xian diaocha baogao* (Organized resistances in rural China and their political risks: an investigative report of H County in Hunan), *Zhanlüe yu guanli* (Strategy and Managemen), No. 3, republished in *Da ji yuan* http://www.dajiyuan.com/gb/4/1/6/n443600.htm, accessed on 3 September 2004.

— (2005), 'Fenghuang shiji da jiangtang yanjiang: dangqian Zhongguo de shehui chongtu' (A talk at the Fenghuang shiji auditorium: the social conflicts in current China), http://www.ccforum.org.cn/viewthread.php?tid=1357&extra=page%3D2, accessed on 31 May 2005.

Yu Jie (2003a), 'Women jian zhu hei'an zhamen de shiming' (We carry the mission of stopping the sluice gate of darkeness), *Wanweiwang tianxia luntan*, *www*.creaders.org, accessed on 8 July 2003.

— (2003b), 'Zhongguo zhishifenzi yu Yilake wei ji' (Chinese intellectuals and the Iraqi crisis), interview with Yu Jie by Ren Bumei, *Sh ji shalong luntan*, http://forum/cc.org.cn/luntan/china/showcontent1.phb3? eb=I&id=107705&id1 -35901, accessed on 3 March 2003.

Yu Jie and Xu Jinru (2003), '*Zhongguo zhishi fenzi guanyu shengyuan Meiguo cuihui sa damu duca cuihui Sadamu ducai zhengquan Yizhengquan*' (Declaration by Chinese intellectuals in support of the US destruction of the Sadam dictatorial regime), *Shiji shalong luntan*, http://forum/cc.org.cn/luntan/china/showcontent1.phb3?eb=I&id =100856&id1—3469, accessed on 21 February 2003.

Yu Qing, ed. (1994), *Wenhua mingren yiwen juanyu congshu* (Anecdotes of and meaningful remarks by well-known cultural figures: a series), Beijing: Zhongguo Qingnian chubanshe.

Yuan Ming (1994), *Deng Xiaoping, Chronicle of an Empire*, Boulder, Colo.: Westview Press.

Yuan Wenbiao (2006) (阮文彪), '小岗村的'土地集并'说明了什么' (What does the re-collectivization of land in Xiaogang Village mean?), *San nong Zhongguo*, http://www.snzg.net/shownews.asp?newsid=16036, accessed on 10 August 2006.

Yue Qingshan (2006), 'Ping jihui zhuyi zhe Li Rui fei Mao' (A critique of anti-Maoism by the opportunist Li Rui), *China and the World,* No.109, http://www.zgysj.com, accessed on 24 December 2006.

Yun Lunxiang (恽仁祥), '还庐山会议真面貌' (Restore the real face of Lushan), *Wuyou zhixiang* http://www.wyzxwyzx.com/Article/ Class14/200702/15272.html, accessed on 14 February 2007.

Zarrow, Peter (1999), 'Meanings of China's Cultural Revolution: memoirs of exile', *Position*, No. 1 (Spring), pp. 167–91.

Zhai Yuzhong (2006), 'Zhonghua minzu zaici dao le zui weixian de shihou' (The Chinese nation is again at its moment of greatest crisis), MSN: zggjzyz2002@hotmail.com: QQ: 56080975, accessed on 3 December 2006.

Zhang Chengxian, *Zhang Chengxian hui yi lu: wo qinli de dang de xuanchuan he jiaoyu gongzuo* (Memoirs of Zhang Chengxian: my participation in the party's propaganda and eduction work), Beijing: Renmin jiaoyu chubanshe, 2002.

Zhang Deqin, '催人警醒的改革大教训' (Wake up to the lesson of reform), *Tianxia luntan*, http://www4.bbsland. com/forums/politics/ messages/1523163.html, accessed on 5 September 2006

Zhang Deyuan (2005), 'Yunnan nongcun kaocha you gan: shi zai shi qiong de "jing tian di xi gui shen"' (Reflections on visiting rural Yunnan: the poverty really moves heaven and earth and makes even ghosts cry), *Shiji Zhongguo xilie luntan*, http://www.ccforum.org.cn/viewthread. php?tid=13676&extra=page%D7, accessed on 24 June 2005.

Zhang Fan (2006), '中国出现第三次毛泽东热' (A third wave of Mao Fever

in China), *Zhongguo wenge yanjiu wang* http://www.wengewang.org/bbs/bencandy.php?id=2506&l_page=1, accessed on 15 May 2006.

Zhang Guangtian (2002), 'Jiangshan ru hua heng tu zhan: cong jingju geming kan xin Zhongguo de wenhua baofu' (Landscape like a painting, the large picture: the cultural ambition of New China from the point of view of the Peking Opera revolution), *Shiji Zhongguo* (Century China), http://www.cc.or.cn. accessed on 4 April 2002.

Zhang Hanzhi, *Wo yu Qiao Guanhua* (Qiao Guanhua and Me), Beijing: Zhongguo qingnian chubanshe, 1994.

Zhang Hengzhi (2006), '还清白于毛泽东 – 把真实的历史告诉人民' (Clear Mao Zedong's name: tell people the truth), *Mao Zedong qizhi wang*http://www.maoflag.net/FilesStorage/UpFile/2005121691431.jpeg, accessed on 7 December 2006.

— (2007), '庐山会议历史真相 – – 兼评凤凰电视台马鼎盛演说' (The truth of the Lushan Conference and also on the speech by Ma Dingshen on Phenix TV), *Wuyou zhixiang*, http://www.wyzxwyzx.com/Article/Class14/200610/11295.html, accessed on 14 February 2007.

Zhang Jie (2007), '对普京的几点看法' (My opinion of Putin), b887706@mailserv.cuhk. edu.hk, accessed on 16 April 2007.

Zhang Peiyuan (2006), '城市像欧洲、农村像非洲'是最大的不和谐' (Cities are like Europe while the country is like Africa: this is the most unharmonious), *Fenghua Yuan* http://www2.fhy.net/cgi bin/anyboard.cgi/collections?cmd=get&cG=93735383&zu=39373538&v=2&gV=0&p=, accessed on 30 January 2006.

Zhang Suhua (2006) (张素华), *变局：七千人大会始末-1962年1月11日 – 2月7日* (The changing chessboard: what happened at the the 7,000 delegates meeting – 11 January to 7 February 1962), Beijing: 中国青年出版社.

Zhang Yunsheng (1988), *Maojiawan jishi* (A factual record of Maojiawan), Beijing: Chunqiu chubanshe.

Zhang Zhenglong (1989), *Xue bai xue hong* (white snow and red blood), Beijing: Jiefangjun chubanshe.

Zhang Xudong, ed. (2001), *Whither China? Intellectual Politics in Contemporary China*, Durham and London: Duke University Press.

Zhao Sishi (1984), 'Yifen wei'er, cedi fouding wenhua da geming' (One divides into two and thorough negation of the Cultural Revolution), *Hong qi*, No. 17, p. 20.

Zhao Ziyang (1982), '关于我国的对策和国内形势' (On our policy and domestic situations), in 三中全会以来重要文献选编 (Selected collection of important documents since 1978).

Zhao Ziyang (2007), '赵紫阳软禁中的谈话' (Zhao Ziyang's remarks during the years of his house arrest), edited by Zong Fengming, Hong Kong: Kaifang zazhi.

Zheng Yi (2004), 'Ning wei waiguo chou bu zuo Zhongguo ren' (Rather be a foreign animal than a China person), www.readers.org/forums/politics/messages/710505.html, accessed on 13 May 2004.

Zhong Dajun (2005), 'Zhongguo gongren jieji xianzhuang diaocha baogao: jianyi guanzhu laozi fangmian de zui xin dongdai (A investigative report on the current conditions of the Chinese working class: pay attention to new development in labour–capital relations), Business. sohu.com, http://www.ccforum.org.cn/viewhread.Php?tid=1 6777& extra=page%3D1, accessed on 22 July 2005.

Zhong hua gongshang shibao, 28 March, 2007.

Zhong Lantai (2006), '简评秦晖教授借比较中印经济抹黑新中国' (a brief comment on how Professsor Qin Hui uses a comparison between China and India to blacken the new China), *Huayue luntan*, http://washeng.net/cgi-bin/hbbs-follow.cgi?action=form &lang=gb&forum=shishi &article =145758, accessed on 24 April 2006.

Zhong Xueping, Wang Zheng and Bai Di, eds (2001), *Some of Us: Chinese Women Growing Up in the Mao Era*, New Brunswick, New Jersey and London: Rutgers University Press.

Zhong Yanlin (2006) (钟延麟), '三面红旗'执旗手 – 邓小平在'大跃进'运动中之态度，角色与作为' (The banner holder of the three flags: Deng Xiaoping's attitudes, role and performance during the Great Leap Forward), *Modern China Studies*, file://C:\Documents% 20and%20Settings\mobo\Local%20Settings/Temp_ZC..., accessed on 5 July 2006.

Zhongguo gong ren wang (2007), '河南部分国企老工人访谈录' (Interviews with some old workers from Henan), http://www.zggr.org, http://www.zggr.org/index.php?entry=entry070411–175500 accessed on 13 April 2007.

Zhou Changming (1993), *Xuelei zhencheng, yi ge hongweibing toutou de shouji* (Blood, tears and sincerity: the diaries of a Red Guard leader), Nanchang: Beihuazhou wenyi chubanshe,

Zhou Enlai (2002), 'Collected Talks', in Song Yongyi, ed., *Zhongguo wenhua da geming wenku* (Chinese Cultural Revolution database), Hong Kong: Xianggang zhongwen daxue Zhongguo yanjiu fuwu zhongxin.

Zhou Min, ed. (1987), *Lishi zai zheli chensi* (History stops here to reflect) Vols I, II and III, Beijing: Huaxia chubanshe.

Zhou Quanying (1999), '我心中的文革' (Wo xinzhong de wenge) (The Cultural Revolution in my mind), *Ershiyi shiji* (Twenty-first century), No. 52, pp. 139–143.

Zhou Ziren (2006) (周孜仁), 红卫兵小报主编自述 (An autobiographical account of the Red Guard newspapers by an editor), USA: 溪流出版社.

Zhu Di (1995), *1957: da zhuanwan zhi mi, zhengfeng fanyou shilu* (1957: the riddle of the big turning around, the actual record of the party rectification and anti-rightist movement), Taiyuan: Shanxi renmin chubanshe and Shuhai chubanshe.

Zhu Min (1996), *Wode fuqin Zhu De* (Zhu De my father), Shengyang: Liaoning renmin chubanshe.

Zhu Xueqin, 'Chuantong wenhua sichao jiqi bolan' (Waves and trends of traditional culture), *Shiji zhonguo xilie luntan*, http://www.cc. org.cn/newcc/browwenzhang.php? articleid=4450, accessed on 6 August 2005.

Zhuo Yi (2003), 'Wenjuan diaocha xianshi: nongmin dui nongcun wenti de kanfa yu zhuliu xuanchuan da xiang jing ting' (Questionnaire survey shows that views of rural China among the rural people are very different from the mainstream propaganda), *Shiji shalong luntan*, http://forum/cc.org.cn/luntan/china/showcontent1.[hp3?db+1&id =96960&id1 =33635, accessed on 12 February 2003.

Zuo Ke (2006) (左克), '辉煌的毛泽东时代 – – 中国计算机事业回顾 - - 谨以此文缅怀离开我们30周年的毛泽东主席' (The brilliant era of Mao Zedong: looking back at the computer industry to commemorate the 30th anniversary of the death of Chairman Mao), *Renmin wang qiangguo luntan*, http://bbs.people.com.cn/bbs/ReadFile?whichfile= 1531840&typeid=17, accessed on 8 September 2006.

Index